Dana Facaros and
Michael Pauls

BILBAO &
THE BASQUE LANDS

'There is no element of its landscapes,
no chapter of its history and legend,
that is not suffused with the
otherworldly and the divine.'

CADOGANguides

Contents

Introducing

The Guide

About the authors

Dana Facaros and Michael Pauls have written over 30 books for Cadogan Guides, including all of the Spain series. They have lived all over Europe but have recently hung up their castanets in a farmhouse surrounded by vineyards in the Lot valley.

About the updater

Mary-Ann Gallagher is a travel writer and editor. She has lived in New York, Japan, Spain and London, and has written and updated six titles for Cadogan Guides, as well as writing for other travel publications.

Cadogan Guides
Network House, 1 Ariel Way, London W12 7SL
cadoganguides@morrispub.co.uk
www.cadoganguides.com

The Globe Pequot Press
246 Goose Lane, PO Box 480, Guilford,
Connecticut 06437–0480

Copyright © Dana Facaros and
  Michael Pauls 2001

Cover and photo essay design by Kicca Tommasi
Book design by Andrew Barker
Cover photographs by Kicca Tommasi
Maps © Cadogan Guides,
  drawn by Map Creation Ltd
Editorial Director: Vicki Ingle
Series Editor: Linda McQueen
Editor: Christine Stroyan
Proofreading: Susannah Wight
Indexing: Isobel McLean
Production: Book Production Services

Printed in the UK by the Cromwell Press
A catalogue record for this book is available
  from the British Library
ISBN 1-86011-835-6

The author and publishers have made every effort to ensure the accuracy of the information in this book at the time of going to press. However, they cannot accept any responsibility for any loss, injury or inconvenience resulting from the use of information contained in this guide.

Please help us to keep this guide up to date. We have done our best to ensure that the information in this guide is correct at the time of going to press, but places and facilities are constantly changing, and standards and prices in hotels and restaurants fluctuate. We would be delighted to receive any comments concerning existing entries or omissions. Authors of the best letters will receive a copy of the Cadogan Guide of their choice.

01

ApiriLaren
20an
izar
berri bat
piztutzera goaz
EuskaL herriKo
zeru gainean

Kanbo

6 EiBarko Asteleñan   7 BiLbom:"La Casilla"
LLuis Jabier
LLach + Muguruza

Zea Mays +   Zea Mays +
20:00 Split 77   20:00 Split 77

Costa Vasca,
Bay of Biscay,
Euskadi

Plaza de la Virgen Blanca,
Vitoria

Guggenheim Museum,
Bilbao

Bárdenas Reales, Navarra

Dolmen, Sorginetxe

Parque Natural Urkiola

Tudela

Airport, Bilbao

Metro, Bilbao

Zubi Zuri bridge, Bilbao

Playa de la Concha,
San Sebastián

Teatro Arriaga, Bilbao

Casco Viejo, Bilbao

Café Iruña, Bilbao

Casco Viejo, Bilbao

Guggenheim Museum,
Bilbao

Forest of Oma

Logs

Legs – Bilbao shop

Dusk in the Basque lands

About the photographer

Kicca Tommasi left sunny Rome for London to pursue photography and design. She spends much of her time travelling, trying to forget the long English winters. Her pictures are regularly published in travel guides and magazines.

Introduction

While we were writing this book, the news broke that scientists, much to their wonder, had discovered traces of tobacco and cocaine in the mummy of an ancient pharaoh, and our first thought was that it was probably the Basques who supplied the Egyptians with the stuff from America. Well, on second thoughts, perhaps not, but the Basques *were* around at the time, and an air of mystery and improbability hangs about them. Above all, they are full of surprises. They cook like angels and eat red-hot peppers; they play the world's fastest ball game, run in front of bulls and dance on goblets; they have bards who improvise poetry at the drop of a hat; they founded one of the world's first multinationals, the Real Compañia Guipúzcona de Caracas, in the 18th century. Conjuring up the Guggenheim Museum in old Bilbao is only their most recent feat, and surely not the last.

There is something almost magical about their very existence. The 2.9 million Basques, a taciturn though likeable lot, are Europe's great survivors, as old as the hills they inhabit, speaking the same language for thousands of years – maybe 10 thousand, maybe more; no one knows. Since Roman times they've been squeezed into a 20,864 sq km elbow of rugged land between France and Spain on the Bay of Biscay, and in spite of their bossy neighbours they have held on tight to their identity. After long decades of suppression, their culture, festivals, music, sports, cuisine, literature and so on – among the great attractions of the Basque country – are thriving, thanks in part to the work of ardent nationalists. Nationalism isn't that popular a concept in Europe these days (although if you read a bit of Basque history, you may understand their point of view); don't confuse it with terrorism and ETA, which started out as the only armed resistance to Franco's regime, but which has been carried on and on by a handful of diehards, even though the vast majority of Basques are in favour of negotiated solutions. There is, in general, a much higher political awareness here than in most places, and certainly a lot more volunteers ready to go out and paint every highway underpass with their message.

The Basques may be nationalistic, but their global outlook predates most European nation states, and the role they've played in Spanish and French affairs is far out of proportion to their numbers. They were great sailors and explorers, shipbuilders and whalers, conquistadores and pirates, early capitalists and industrialists, and nowadays they run most of Spain's banks, insurance agencies and Mondragón, one of the world's most successful co-operative ventures. Basque sailors helped the English conquer Wales, built the Spanish Armada, and founded a number of colonies, including the Philippines, as well as cities like Buenos Aires. The conquistadores Lope de Aguirre and Pedro de Ursúa were Basques, and so was Sebastián Elcano, the first man to sail around the world. So were two of Spain's most important saints, Ignatius of Loyola and Francis Xavier, and, in more recent times, the great philosopher Miguel de Unamuno, politician Dolores Ibarruri ('La Pasionara' of the Spanish Republic), and Eduardo Chillida, Spain's best known living sculptor.

Although the Guggenheim may well be the shiny lure that brings you to the Basque country in the first place, it would be a shame to stop there. The rest of Bilbao is in the throes of one of the most dramatic makeovers of any city in Europe; and the smaller cities of Pamplona, Bayonne and Vitoria are vibrant and full of surprises.

The dramatic coast is dotted with glittering Belle Epoque beach resorts – San Sebastián, Zarautz, Fuenterrabía, Biarritz and St-Jean-de-Luz – once famous for collecting the crowned heads of Europe, now renowned for their surfing. Neat-as-a-pin villages and sloping-roofed farmhouses dot emerald landscapes that have been tended by the same people for millennia (and well they should be emerald – the Basque country gets as much rain as the west of Ireland), and are filled with quiet wonders – deep primordial forests, caves (some with Palaeolithic art), megalithic monuments, and strange and beautiful Romanesque churches, especially in Navarra along the pilgrims' road to Santiago. The Pyrenean and the Cantabrian mountain ranges keep the rain from the plain of southern Navarra and Alava, the fief of Rioja wine and perhaps the last thing you'd expect: a desert, the Bárdenas Reales.

The Basques' own integrity has made their home one of those rare places where the word 'authentic' has no meaning, because it's never been anything but. As Victor Hugo wrote, 'Everyone who has visited the Basque country longs to return; it is a blessed land.'

A Guide to the Guide

The first part of this book provides essential background information on the Basques – their remarkable history, language and civilization. As beautiful as it is, the Basque country has relatively few 'famous' sights, and is rather the sort of destination that *surrounds* visitors and begs for a little understanding. One of the most important elements of Basqueness is sport, but the games they play are radically different, right down to the national card game. We've included the rules as a possible insight into the Basque psyche, but also to give you a clue as to what the excitement in the tavernas is all about.

Even if you're just in Bilbao on a weekend break, you may want to peruse the next section on food and drink, if only to make out what's on the menu. Following this are the nuts-and-bolts **Travel** and **Practical A–Z** sections. In the latter, do skim the bit on festivals to see if any coincide with your visit; the Basques are a serious people, but they also know how to seriously put on a party.

Next comes **Bilbao**, the industrial dynamo of the Basque country, and now a role model for other cities for how to recreate themselves in a new image. The Guggenheim Museum is the showpiece, of course, and merits a trip to Bilbao on its own. But it's worth taking a look at the rest of Bilbao, a city of no little character, with a dazzling new infrastructure, excellent older museums, the largest covered market in Spain, and the Siete Calles, a great neighbourhood for exploring the city's vibrant bar culture. You may even like to spend an afternoon by the sea at Bilbao's beach resort, Getxo.

After Bilbao comes the rest of **Euskadi**, the Spanish Basque country. Vitoria (Gasteiz), south of Bilbao, is the regional capital and a fine city in its own right, although relatively little known outside of Spain. Don't miss its 'new cathedral' of María Inmaculada, begun in 1907 using only medieval building methods; the art and archaeology museums; and a museum dedicated to playing cards. To the east lie Gaceo and Alaiza, with stunning Gothic frescoes in the former and bizarre primitive and belligerent 14th-century frescoes in the latter. South of Vitoria, towards the Ebro, are the vineyards of La Rioja Alavesa and fascinating wine villages, especially Laguardia. The next section heads east of Bilbao, first taking an inland route through typical Basque villages: Markina and Elorrio are good ones to aim for. The coast is probably the biggest attraction, though: the islet of San Juan de Gaztelugatxa, the sacred town of Gernika and Upper Palaeolithic painted cave of Santimamiñe; and the beach resorts of Lekeitio, Deba, Zumaya, Getaria, and the biggest of them all, lovely San Sebastián, with a nearby museum dedicated to sculptor Eduardo Chillida. Inland from San Sebastián, the province of Guipúzcoa is home to the attractive and scholarly towns of Oñati and Bergara, as well as the striking modern Sanctuary of Aránzazu and Loyola, birthplace of St Ignatius, the founder of the Jesuits. Just before the French border, Fuenterrabía is one of the most beautiful towns, and has a long sandy beach.

Navarra, the next chapter, begins with Pamplona, once the capital of the Basque kingdom and now the capital of Los Sanfermines, the bull-running in July. But there's plenty to see at other times, and Pamplona makes a convenient base for excursions into the countryside. To the northwest is Aralar, Navarra's magic mountain; southwest lie Estella and other sites along the pilgrims' road to Santiago; while directly south, where the landscapes are distinctly more arid, are the pretty towns of Tafalla and Olite, Tudela, more Rioja vineyards and the spectacular desert of the Bárdenas Reales. To the east of Pamplona, Sangüesa, Yesa, Javier and Leyre offer a great day out for fans of funny old churches, while the nearby Hoz de Arbayún is Navarra's version of the grand canyon. To the east wait the beautiful Basque valleys of the Pyrenees, Roncal and Salazar, with their timeless villages and deep forests, and northeast of Pamplona is the famous pass of Roncesvalles, where Charlemagne's rear guard got its come-uppance from the Basques and where a famous monastery still caters to the needs of pilgrims. Northwest of Roncesvalles are the startlingly lush valleys of Baztán and Bidasoa, where you'll find Zugarramurdi, scene of a great 17th-century witch hunt.

From here it's over the border into France's **Pays Basque**, beginning along the coast and its resorts, which, like San Sebastián, first enjoyed a vogue among the aristocracy in the mid-19th century and now find themselves invaded by surfers as well as your more genteel holiday makers. The picturesque fishing town of St-Jean-de-Luz is a seductive place to stay and eat, or there are smaller resorts such as Bidart and Guéthary, and Urrugne with its castle and gardens. Biarritz, of course, is the star of the Côte Basque, a stylish old resort with a huge beach, full of memories of the Empress Eugénie, who first made it popular. Bayonne, adjacent, was an old whaling port and remains a city that works for its living, with unspoiled old neighbourhoods along the

Chapter Divisions (*see* map opposite)

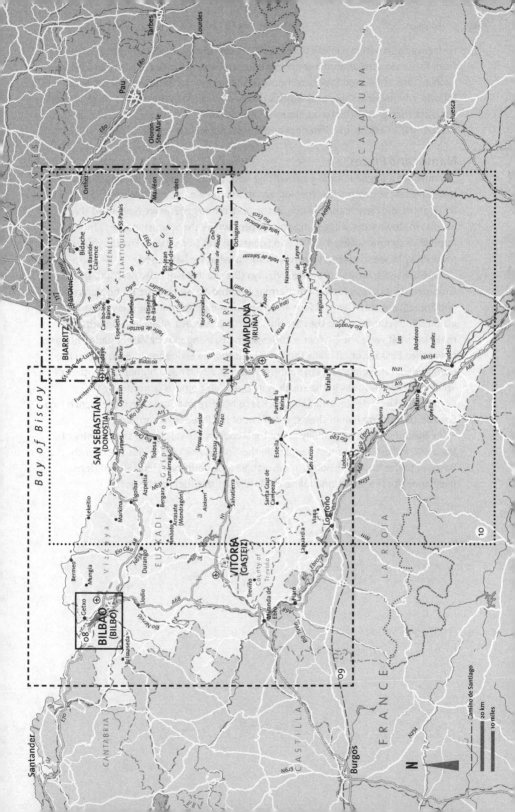

river Nive to go with a pair of El Grecos, a Botticelli and its chocolate-makers. Just in from the coast, the Labourd interior contains archetypal Basque scenery and villages such as Sare, St-Pée and Espelette, home of the famous red peppers. The valley of Nive follows, where remarkable prehistoric art was discovered in the Istaritz caves and delicious cherries grow in Itxassou. Here, too, is handsome St-Jean-Pied-de-Port, centre for exploring the lush Basque Pyrenees and the secretive little region of Soule.

Names and Places

Names are a bugbear for anyone writing about the Basque country. Many places have at least two, with a few spelling variations thrown in for fun. We've tried to list all, Spanish and French and Basque, in the text, but in general we have used the Basque for towns and villages in Spain, except where the Spanish name is more familiar or commonly used – thus San Sebastián, not Donostia. In France, you are far more likely to see the French name, and this is what we have used.

There are seven Basque provinces: Vizcaya (Bizkaia in Basque), Alava (Araba), Guipúzcoa (Gipuzkoa), Navarra (Nafarroa), Labourd, Basse-Navarre (Behe Nafarroa) and Soule (Zuberoa). The first four are in Spain, and yet even in the New Spain of autonomous communities they are divided in two. Vizcaya, Alava and Guipúzcoa make up what were known for centuries as the Bascongadas or Vascongadas, but are now called Euskadi, or officially the Euskal Autonomia Erkidegoa in Basque and the Comunidad Autonoma Vasca in Spanish. Navarra, which has a higher percentage of Spaniards than Basques in the south, is its own autonomous community, the Comunidad Floral de Navarra. Labourd, Basse-Navarre and Soule form the French Pays Basque, comprising half of the *département* of the Pyrénées Atlantic.

The Basques have traditionally called their country Euskal Herria, 'the Country of Basque Speakers'. What most people call the 'Spanish' or 'French' Basque country, the Basques prefer to call the South and North Basque Country – Hego Euskal Herria (Hegoalde) for the south, and Ipar Euskal Herria (Iparralde) for the north.

History

100,000–218 BC
European aborigines

'The Basques are like good women; they have no history.' So runs the old Basque saying. Another of their jokes is that when God created the first man, he got the bones from a Basque graveyard. No one knows for sure just how far back the Basque people go – only that someone, incredibly, was around even before them. For the area around the Pyrenees is one of the oldest inhabited places on earth, one of the cradles of human culture. The first European discovered so far, 'Tautavel Man', parked his carcass in a cave at the western end of the chain some 450,000 years ago. Traces of habitation in the Basque lands go back at least 100,000 years, and somebody was painting pictures on cave walls as early as 35,000 BC. The Cro-Magnons living in what is now the Basque country formed an integral part of the Franco-Cantabrian civilization of reindeer hunters, who painted the famous caves of Lascaux and Altamira and elsewhere. The prize examples in the Basque provinces are the rupestrian art in the caves at Santimamiñe (near Gernika), Istaritz (near Bayonne), and others usually not open to the public: Camou-Cihige in the Soule; Venta de Laperra, Arenaza and Berriatua in Vizcaya; Deba and Aya in Guipúzcoa; and Urdax in Navarre.

When did the inhabitants of Basqueland become Basques? They are rare, if not unique, in the annals of western Europe for having no migration stories and no ancestral memory of ever having been anywhere else, and recent scholarship seems to confirm that the Basques are direct descendants of Cro-Magnon hunter-gatherers and painters, having survived in their secluded valleys during the great Indo-European migrations of peoples from the east thousands of years ago. This theory has had a big boost from studies showing that the Basques have the highest proportion of type O blood in the world, along with other ancient peoples shoved long ago into Europe's nooks and crannies – the Irish, the Scots and the Cretans. Even more peculiarly, the Basques also have the world's highest incidence of Rh negative blood anywhere, a factor characteristic of the indigenous prehistoric Europeans. Another clue may be in their physique. Basques have slight but telling physical differences from their neighbours. Not only are they bigger and stronger, but they have long noses and long ear lobes, and the distinct shape of their skulls is matched by the shape of the oldest skulls found on the territory, in the Upper Palaeolithic deposit at Urtiaga, as well as in Bronze Age finds.

In the 1990s, genetic research confirmed a unique persistence of European Palaeolithic DNA markers in the ethnic Basque population (the only other people who come close are the Irish of Connaught). The French and Spanish have similar DNA markers, although they are fainter, having become more mixed over time. In the meagre 0.1 per cent of genetic differences between every human on the planet, the Basque and Lapps have the greatest distance between Europeans; Basques and New Guineans have the greatest distance on earth. Being unusual also has its drawbacks: Basques have the highest incidence in the world of the mutant gene associated with cystic fibrosis.

The Basques may be as old as their steep green hills, but their constant companions there, the sheep, only arrived in the Pyrenees around 5000 BC, followed by horses and cattle, part of the Neolithic agricultural and cultural revolution that spread across Europe. One theory has it that those with the farming know-how migrated west from the Middle East, and hunter-gatherer traditions slowly disappeared through inter-marriage. This is when the Basques remained aloof. Still, if they didn't mingle, they did learn agriculture, the domestication of animals, and building – their lasting monuments include dolmens (especially on the Alava plain by the Ebro), cromlechs (most famously at Aralar) and menhirs. They began to travel, herding their flocks up into the mountains in summer and into the lowlands between the Garonne and the Ebro in the winter – the extent of so-called 'Pyrenean culture'. Neolithic peoples were great traders and liked to live near the sea or important rivers; one of Europe's oldest known roads, the 'Salt Road', linked their lands with the Mediterranean. Most of the outlandish place names in the Pyrenees as far eastwards as the Mediterranean can be traced to these proto-Basques. Still, if the *gaztelulaks* are any evidence, the various Aquitanian tribes didn't always get along; the remains of these hilltop earthen forts are still a feature of the Basque country, which counts 242 of them,

Around 800 BC, Celtic tribes started moving through the region, probably intermar-rying with the original people as often as conquering them. Again the ancestors of the Basques, for whatever reason, remained unassimilated, while learning new skills from the newcomers, in this case metalworking and cultivating wheat.

218 BC–AD 407
Carthaginians and Romans

Modern Basques find grave fault with their ancestors for letting others write their history; the first to put stylus to tablet were the Romans. Their influence was first felt in the the Basque country in 218 BC, during the Second Punic War with the Carthaginians. The latter were probably already a familiar fixture in Biarritz and other Atlantic harbours, where they would call along the sea trading route to Cornwall and its tin mines, and Basque mercenaries were listed in Hannibal's army. But the first mention of Romans we have in the present-day Basque country is not until 71 BC, when Pompey campaigned against rebels in Spain and founded the city that still bears his name, *Pompaelo* (Pamplona), near the Basque village of Iruña.

When Caesar finally conquered Gaul in 51 BC, he wrote that it was occupied by three different peoples. Two were Celtic, but the third, occupying southwestern Gaul from the Pyrenees to the Garonne, were a people who were entirely distinct from their neighbours. The Romans called them *Aquitani* (or Aquitanians), and they spoke a language linguists call Aquitanian, an ancestral form of Basque and the only pre-Indo-European language surviving in Gaul. The conquest north of the Pyrenees was made by Caesar's partner Crassus without much fuss in 56. Many of the Aquitanians escaped over the Pyrenees into the rugged country of northern Spain, where they joined up with their cousins already there, the *Vascones*, and took their name. There was little the Romans could do about them, or even wanted to: the Romans coveted Aquitaine and the fertile Ebro valley; the aborigines could have the hills.

While the Aquitanians who stayed put in Aquitaine adopted Gallo-Roman ways, the Vascones carried on in the Pyrenees, preserving their language, culture and religion. Yet their live-and-let-live relations with the Romans were so cordial that the Basques still hold them up as a model for the larger powers that surround them today. The Romans' primary interest was transport over the mountains, and they built some useful roads which the *Vascones* were glad to have. They also learned to cultivate olives and grapes, and traded them with the Romans in Pamplona and Bayonne. Pliny wrote that the *Vascones* of Vizcaya possessed a mountain 'made entirely of iron', but a lack of fertile land led many to hire themselves out as Roman mercenaries, and they were valued warriors. By the 4th century AD, the Romanized Gauls and Iberians had converted to Christianity. However, with the exception of a few communities by the Ebro, this new religion was one foreign novelty the Basques didn't care to emulate.

407–1000
In the Dark Ages, the Basques defend their homeland

The fatal invasions came after 407. Both Vandals and Visigoths passed through the Basque country, and after 420 Aquitania found itself part of the new Visigothic kingdom, with its capital at Toulouse. But this was not to last. The Franks whipped the Visigoths at the Battle of Vouillé in 507, and gained, if not control of Aquitania, at least the right to try to collect a little tribute from it. The Visigoths retreated into Spain, where their kingdom was to last two centuries until the Arab conquest.

As Teutonic barbarians go, the Visigoths were a cut above the rest. They were Christian, and did not drink out of skulls like the Lombards, or smear bear fat all over their bodies like the Franks. However, they weren't as cordial as the Romans. The Visigoth kings launched campaign after campaign against the pagan *Vascones*, and they managed to extend Christianity as far as Pamplona. But, on the whole, the Visigoth agenda backfired; rather than subdue the *Vascones*, their persistent attacks united formerly disparate tribes (whose names and dialects survive today as the various Basque provinces) into a nation dedicated to resisting the Visigoths.

Many of the *Vascones* who had fled the Romans generations before and settled in Spain were either pushed by the Visigoths back over the Pyrenees, or decided on their own to retake their old homeland in Aquitaine, by then largely a wasteland. Whatever the case, they reappeared in the 580s, and people began calling the area as far north as the Garonne *Wasconia*, which somehow later got turned into Gascony. Those *Vascones* who remained in the western Pyrenees, fierce enough to put up a good fight whenever it was necessary to defend their homes, became specialists in guerrilla warfare and mountain ambush, and lapsed into de facto independence. They have been there ever since, and are the people we call the Basques.

As if the Visigoths were not enough, in 602, the king of the Franks appointed a 'duke of Aquitaine' and 'duke of Wasconia', military overlords charged with bringing the entire area under closer control. The chronicles of the next two centuries tell a tale of continuous and spirited resistance on the part of the Basques. A big surprise for all parties concerned came when the Moors roared through the Pyrenees in the early 8th century after their rapid conquest of Spain, only to be defeated and driven back by the Franks at Poitiers in 732. What kept them from consolidating their hold over northern Spain was a short but intense revolt by the Muslim Berber troops in 740 against their Arab leaders. Pamplona took advantage of the revolt to free itself from its Arab governor and the Basques were independent once again.

Once again, however, they had to fight to stay that way. After beating the Moors at Poitiers, the self-confident Franks came over the Pyrenees looking for new lands to conquer. One of their raids on Pamplona gave birth to the legend of Roland and Oliver, the famous knights of Charlemagne who perished at the hands of the furious Basques in an ambush at the pass of Roncesvalles in 778 (*see* pp.230–1).

The troubles of the Franks gave the Basques south of the Pyrenees a chance to assert themselves. At the beginning of the 9th century, the kingdom of Pamplona was founded under King Iñigo de Aritza, a unique Basque experiment with monarchy that would grow into the kingdom of Navarra (Nafarroa). At first this embraced the three provinces known as the Vascongadas (Gipuzkoa, Bizkaia and Araba), the French Basque country and neighbouring areas in Spain. It would remain a major actor in the region's history for centuries to come.

North of the mountains, the Basques weren't so lucky. Aquitaine and Gascony suffered the visitations of the most destructive barbarians of them all, the Vikings, or Normans. From the 840s onwards they came raiding nearly every year, completely wrecking Bayonne in 862. Not until 982 did Duke Guilhem of Gascony finally convince them they weren't wanted, but not before the Basques, who were already messing about in boats in the Bay of Biscay, had had a chance to study and imitate the well-built ocean-going hulls of the Viking ships. By this time, the Basques had mostly converted to Christianity, thanks, according to legend, to the efforts of Léon, the bishop of Rouen, who resigned his post to preach to the Basques before he was killed by Norman pirates in Bayonne.

It was also around this time that the feudal pattern was set. The king of the Franks was just a bad dream somewhere up north, and the lesser vassals the Carolingians had created drifted into near-total independence. The arrangement makes history messy and complex, but it gave the region stability and some breathing space. After almost six centuries of terror, towns were growing again and churches began to spring up everywhere. By the magic year 1000, which many expected to bring the end of the world, medieval civilization was in fact well on its way.

1000–1492
Medieval prosperity, and the founding of a Basque kingdom

The new millennium got off to an auspicious start for Christian Spain, and for a while it looked as if the big victor among the Christian states would be little Navarra.

Still Basque, but becoming increasingly Hispanicized in its southern half, Navarra reached its zenith under Sancho III 'the Great' (1004–35), capturing all of La Rioja and even much of Castile. But, like so many of the transient empires formed in the free-for-all of the Reconquista, Sancho's proved to be only a house of cards, and Alfonso VI of Castile cut Navarra down to size in the 1070s.

With prosperity came increasing power for the growing towns, and nearly all of them in this period were able to organize themselves into *comunes* and gain a high degree of independence from the kings, bishops or nobles who had formerly bossed them around. Some were new creations altogether, such as Vitoria (Gasteiz), founded by Alfonso VI in 1181, soon after he had captured the territory. Alfonso wanted a loyal town to consolidate his hold, and to keep the new settlers' loyalty he granted Vitoria a charter of liberties, or *fueros* (*see* below). *Fueros* such as these would give medieval Spain a less oppressive government than most countries, and they were made possible by the good example of the Basques.

The Middle Ages were a prosperous time for the industrious Basques, as they began to turn their talents to the sea. In winter, the Bay of Biscay was full of whales, where they had long been hunted from shore. Copying the Viking ships and their methods of provisioning for long journeys (basically living off wind-dried cod) enabled Basque sailors to follow the whales north to their summer quarters in the North Atlantic, and they had reached the Faroe islands by 875.

At home, Basque shipbuilders, using oak from the Pyrenees and iron from the Vizcayan mother lode, gained a reputation as the best in the world. In 1296 a kind of

The Fueros

... after studying the customary laws of Europe, I place the Basque Foral Laws above the Swiss laws, also endorsed by their centuries'-long existence. For their virtues, their union and above all the local freedoms they enjoy, the Basques provide us with an example that one scarcely knows how to praise enough, maintaining their allegiance to the best social constitution in Europe.
L'Organization de la Famille, Frédéric Le Play (1806–82)

Fueros (*fors* in French, *foruak* in Basque) are municipal charters or privileges, whether you derive the word from the Latin *forum*, the public square where municipal business was conducted, or from *fuera* (outside), as exceptions to royal authority. During the early Middle Ages, cities and towns, and sometimes entire provinces, were granted fueros by the kings of France and Spain.

As any Basque nationalist will hasten to remind you, however, the word *fueros* has over time been distorted in an important way. Basque *fueros* were not privileges and favours conceded or taken away by the will of a king, but were the Basques' own ancestral laws. It was the Basques of the three Vascongada provinces who consented to be ruled by a king (of Castile after 1200, when they broke away from Navarra), but only if the king swore to abide by their *fueros*, not the other way around. This was done under the sacred tree in Gernika, where the main Basque council, or *junta*

Hanseatic League of Basque ports was founded, the *Hermandad de las Marismas*; shipping whale oil and Castile's wool northwards, the *Hermandad* grew to control a disproportionate share of the Atlantic trade. In 1351 an innovative peace treaty was signed between Vizcaya, Guipúzcoa and Edward III of England, guaranteeing the freedom of the seas. In 1482 another one signed with Edward IV guaranteed that even if England and Castile went to war, it would not effect relations between England and Guipúzcoa.

The Basques remained feistily independent, but as the medieval states surrounding Basque property – Asturias-Castile, Catalunya-Aragón, England (through its duchy of Aquitaine), Béarn and France – grew in wealth and power, there was increasingly little chance that an event like Roncesvalles could ever be repeated. This was a world dominated by a feudal aristocracy, and with such bossy neighbours it is not surprising that the Basques never coalesced into a nation state. All through the Middle Ages, Basque boundaries shrank gradually but inexorably, as the natives were either pushed out, diluted or assimilated by Spaniards, Gascons and Catalans. By the 14th century the Basque lands had contracted roughly to the boundaries they retain today. Navarra, condemned by geography to lose out in the Reconquista land grab, was in full decline.

French involvement in the kingdom dated from the blazing of the main pilgrimage route to Compostela through its confines (*see* pp.57–9) and became official after 1284, when an heiress to the kingdom, Juana I, married King Philip the Fair of France. Afterwards, members of the Capetian dynasty would rule Navarra as a quaint Pyrenean Ruritania.

general, met for two or three weeks to legislate on *foral* matters. There were obviously proper *fueros*, too, granted by the king when he wanted to curry favour with the Basques, but in general, when Basques wax nostalgic about their old *fueros*, they mean their ancient laws.

And in many ways these ancient laws were remarkable. Thanks to their *fueros*, the Basques remained free of the depredations of a nobility that ravaged the rest of Spain and France; the Basques with their egalitarian ethos had no nobles, and the only Basques with titles, besides the king of Navarre, were those like the Loyolas, who were ennobled by the Castilians for services rendered. Tax demands (and demands for military conscripts) were negotiated through Basque authorities, who kept both far below the levels of money and men demanded elsewhere in Spain. Nor were Basque soldiers expected to serve outside their province.

Women were granted more rights than in most medieval codes; for example, the family's first born, whether male or female, inherited the family house. The *fueros* also made the Basque provinces into a duty-free zone: Spanish customs were located at the Ebro, so the Basques paid considerably less for imports than their French and Spanish neighbours. When the *fueros* were revised in Gernika in 1526, they went even further, abolishing torture and eliminating debtors' prisons – nothing less than the first human rights legislation in Europe, well in advance of any other government.

1492–1792
Reconquista to Revolution

Throughout the 14th and 15th centuries, the Spanish kingdoms occupied themselves with consolidating the gains of the Reconquista. On the whole, the experience coarsened the life of Castile, creating a pirate ethos where honest labour was scorned, and wealth and honour were things to be snatched from one's neighbours. The climax came in 1469 with the marriage of *los Reyes Católicos*, Ferdinand of Aragón and Isabella of Castile, during whose reign Spain's borders were rounded out. Not only did they finally conquer the kingdom of Granada, the last remnant of Moorish al-Andalus, but Spain was also embarking on its career as a grand imperialist, invading Italy and colonizing the Americas (often, as in the case of Columbus, taking along experienced Basque pilots to guide the way). The religious bigotry of the 'Catholic Kings', Isabella in particular, put a perverse twist on Spanish life that was to last a long time. Under their rule, the Inquisition was reintroduced, and Jews expelled from Spain. The kings of Navarra took them under their wing, at least until 1514, when Navarra itself was slyly gobbled up by Ferdinand, who got permission to march through, and stayed. He kept the peace, however, by swearing to respect its sovereignty and *fueros*, in an arrangement identical to that of the other Basque provinces of the peninsula.

North of the Pyrenees, the end of the Hundred Years' War and departure of the English in the 1450s allowed France to extend its control over all of the southwest. Only this time, the French kings were not content with being mere feudal overlords; the heavy-handed authoritarianism of Paris brought with it economic stagnation that was to last for centuries, especially in Gascony. The 1539 Decree of Villars-Cotterets, mandating the use of the French language in all matters of law and government, was a preview of coming events. French Navarre enjoyed its last 15 minutes of fame in 1589 when its king became one of the very best rulers of France, Henri IV.

Still, of all the peoples of the south, the Basques adapted best to French rule, primarily because they retained a substantial degree of self-government up until the French Revolution. In the Labourd, a kind of parliament called the *biltzar*, with elected representatives (but no nobles or clergy), met regularly to set tax rates and look after local business, and each small region or town possessed its *fors*, which the French usually respected. In return, the Basques remained stalwartly loyal to the French Crown, and performed important services for it in time of war, especially on the seas, thanks to the feared privateers of Bayonne.

In Spain, whatever wealth remained was soon sucked out by Ferdinand and Isabella's grandson, the Habsburg Charles I, better known to history as Holy Roman Emperor Charles V. As the country embarked on a remarkable and ultimately successful attempt to destroy its own economy, the Basques, safeguarded by their *fueros*, got by; a golden moment occurred when their own Juan Sebastián Elcano, lieutenant of Magellan's fleet, became the first man to sail around the world in 1522 (*see* p.173). Their aptitude for learning from outsiders made the Basques more open to innovations than most Europeans: they were among the first to appreciate tobacco, chilli peppers and especially corn, brought back by Columbus in 1492. It was one of the few crops to do well in the meagre soil of the Basque lands. Within three decades the Basques had marketed it as far as China.

Under Charles' neurotic son Philip II (1556–98), Spain reached the height of its book- and heretic-burning frenzy, while the economy stayed wrecked and military defeats piled up on every side. The heretic-free Basques made their own special contribution to the age, the Jesuits, founded by St Ignatius of Loyola with his right-hand man, the Basque Francis Xavier. A particular blow to Bilbao and other northern ports, motivated by corrupt ministers, was Philip's decision in 1573 to allow Sevilla to monopolize trade with the New World. The northern ports dwindled, and all the poor souls whose prospects had been ruined even had to find their way to the south to catch a boat just to emigrate. The majority of the crew of the Spanish Armada of 1588 were Basques, whose whaling fleet had been requisitioned for the effort and sank with the rest. But the greatest setback to the Basque whaling industry was the Basques' own willingness to teach others their secrets, in spite of (or perhaps to spite) the Spanish Crown's rule that they were to use their seafaring skills only in the service of Spain. Defiantly they taught the English and the Dutch, and as these states claimed the high seas and fishing grounds, the Basques were increasingly muscled out.

The early 17th century witnessed a series of dust-ups between France and Spain. The intermission set by the Treaty of the Pyrenees in 1660 fixed the current international border through the Basque country; peace was cemented that year by the marriage of Louis XIV and the Spanish infanta, Maria Teresa, in St-Jean-de-Luz. In the next round, the War of the Spanish Succession, the Basque provinces and Navarra were smart enough to back the right horse for the throne of Spain, Louis XIV's grandson, and as a reward got to keep their *fueros* (unlike the Catalans, who backed the Habsburg and lost theirs).

Under Spain's new Bourbon king, Philip V (1701–46), the semi-autonomous Basques regained the right to trade with the New World, and they soon found ways to wring a penny from the Americas. In 1730 the Compañía Guipuzcoana de Caracas broke the Dutch monopoly over the chocolate trade in the West Indies and brought a lot of money home to the Basque country. From cocoa it expanded into tobacco, coffee and beans, while shipping iron, sardines and wine to Venezuela. The other regions of northern Spain, as well as France, Germany and the Netherlands, soon began to deal with the Compañía Guipuzcoana, exporting their own goods to the New World. By the late 18th century, Bilbao was the busiest port in Spain.

1792–1876
Revolution, Carlism and steel mills

The French Revolution marked a turning point for the Basques, and brought with it the irony of this most democratic of peoples ranging themselves solidly on the side of reaction. It wasn't their fault. In the name of equality for all, the Jacobins up in Paris abolished the last *foral* rights, self-government and traditional liberties north of the

Pyrenees, but even more resented than the Revolution's push for centralization and Frenchification were its attacks on the Church.

In 1793 the Convention sent a large army down to the Pyrenees. Four thousand Basques from Labourd were deported for refusing to fight in the southern Basque country. On the Spanish side, however, urban Basques were fascinated by the Revolution, and the French army occupied the Basque provinces with hardly a fight; Guipúzcoa's assembly even welcomed them. In Madrid, the nervous Bourbon cousins of Louis XVI, who had counted on the Basques to defend their frontier homeland, blamed them for the humiliation and got the French to retreat in 1795, in exchange for rights over Santo Domingo.

They were soon back, however, under Napoleon. Basque guerrilla resistance this time was impressive enough to lead him to seek their support by promising to safeguard their *fueros* in the constitution he imposed on Spain, even suggesting the creation of a Basque state that would be controlled by France. The Navarrese, especially around French-occupied Pamplona, didn't believe a word of it and fought all the harder. French reprisals and executions in Pamplona further hardened positions; it took a four-month siege in 1813 by the Spanish-British allies to finally dislodge the French. If Navarra would later become the most intransigent and conservative of Basque provinces, the roots of their position are there.

In the end, the only real fruit of the Revolution and Napoleon for the three French Basque provinces was a lasting economic depression, helped along by the British blockade and Wellington's siege of Bayonne. All remnants of self-rule were stripped away, and in spite of protests from both the Basques and Béarn, they were made to share the same *département* of the Pyrénées-Atlantique. Paris-appointed prefects replaced Paris-appointed *intendants*, but few of the ephemeral governments of the 19th-century Gallic banana republic/monarchy/empire ever stirred themselves much to help the Pays Basque. Nor did the region ever show much energy of its own. The railway arrived at Bayonne in the 1850s, but this served mainly to help make it easier for young people to leave, and for imported goods to flow in and ruin the region's already hard-pressed farmers and manufacturers. The only positive thing the train brought was tourists, as 19th-century Biarritz found its vocation as a resort, promoted by Napoleon's nephew, Napoleon III.

Like 19th-century France, Spain too seemed the very image of the banana republics that had just gained their independence from it in Latin America. But unlike their French counterparts, Spanish Basques played a major role in keeping the pot boiling. The first sign of trouble came in 1812, during the war with Napoleon, when the newly formed Liberal Party in Cádiz produced a constitution for Spain, citing the Basques as the model for the freedom they intended for everybody in Spain, but without offering much hope that traditional Basque rights would be respected. Although the absolutist King Ferdinand VII snuffed Liberal yearnings in the so-called 'nefarious decade' (1823–33), and even brought back the Inquisition, his death and the succession of his infant daughter Isabella II to the throne under the regency of her mother María Cristina rekindled Liberal hopes across Spain; a weak queen would enable them to realize their secular anticlerical agenda in a modern centralized nation-state.

This suited the capitalists of Vizcaya and Guipúzcoa just fine. They were beginning to find the traditional *fueros* a hindrance: the duty-free status they gave the Basque provinces were a serious obstacle when they needed custom barriers to develop their own industry. Furthermore, the *fueros* protected Vizcaya's iron mountains as the Basques' greatest asset and forbade the sale of ore abroad, when it was precisely the money-spinner the new industrialists needed to start up their own mills.

Rural Basques, however, looked down on Bilbao and San Sebastián from their mountains in growing anger. Their priests had warned that the anticlerical Liberals meant to banish God from Spain and expropriate Church property and rights, threatening not only the religious but the poor, who depended on the Church's charity. The Liberals, they feared, meant to abolish the *fueros* which kept prices low. The abolition of common pastures, sold at auction and bought by the rich, had already forced shepherds to pay rent for what used to be free. The Bilbao bourgeoisie began to purchase farms as investments, and rents for farmers rose.

In 1833 the Liberals – the military, the bourgeoisie, capitalists and upper aristocracy – hoisted Isabella II onto the throne. The Vatican refused to recognize her. The Church's privileges were rescinded and the Inquisition abolished. The country was divided into artificial, uniform provinces; even Navarra, until then still nominally a kingdom, was reduced to provincial status. For the rural conservatives, the peasants and the priests, this meant war, and they rallied around Ferdinand's brother, the pretender Don Carlos, who promised to restore the status quo for the Church and maintain the Basques' *fueros*.

Although all Spain took sides, the brunt of the first Carlist War of 1833–9 was borne in the Basque country, where it became a civil war pitting city Basque against country

The Basque Diaspora

Leaving is hard: the peasants' name for places outside of the Basque country is 'wolf's land'. Yet the Basque country has always had a hard time supporting its population; in spite of appearances, it isn't very fertile. According to traditional Basque property laws, only one child would inherit the *exte* (house) and estate, leaving the others the choice of a career in the Church or at sea, or the option of moving elsewhere. In the 19th century rural poverty, combined with the loss of Basque *fueros* in the Carlist Wars, drove many young Basques from their mountain uplands to the Americas, especially to Argentina, Chile and the USA, where the Basque connection goes back to the 1,500 sailors, many of them veteran corsairs, who came to join Lafayette and fight for American independence. In the bayous of Louisiana and east Texas, as well as on the Argentine pampas, Basques became some of the New World's first sheepherders and cowboys in the 1840s, setting the model and contributing much to the image (*lariat*, *chaparral* and *honcho* are derived from Basque words). The centre for Basque studies today in the USA is the University of Nevada at Reno. There are scores of Basque place names in Mexico and South America; in Chile, many of the vineyards have Basque names. Some Basques opened restaurants, and often as not, in the middle of an American Nowheresville in Idaho or Utah, what will you find? A decent Basque restaurant.

Basque. Bilbao's leading families sent Isabel II 33 million *reales* for the war effort. The underdog Carlists, in their romantic costumes, long hair and red berets were led by the brilliant guerrilla tactician Zumalacárregui until he died during the siege of Bilbao in 1835. Fighting, atrocities and church burnings continued for four years until the Carlists surrendered, on the promise that their *fueros* would be maintained.

But Madrid was just fooling, and stripped away much of Basque autonomy in a law of 16 August 1841. Spanish customs were moved to Hendaye from the Ebro. The big loan to Isabel II by Bilbao's financiers was no hindrance to the founding of the Banco de Bilbao in 1857, soon to be followed by the Banco de San Sebastián and Banco de Vizcaya. Vizcaya's iron mountain turned out to have the perfect ore for making steel according to the new Bessemer process. Easily transported to the port of Bilbao, huge quantities could now be exported to England. The three banks financed new rail links, shipyards, hydroelectric plants and the first steel mills and blast furnaces, knowing they would have a monopoly in Spain thanks to the new customs arrangements.

Bilbao became a noisy boom town, but its new shipyards, factories, mills, mines, blast furnaces, chemical works and refineries required something the Basques were not prepared for: an influx of poor Spanish workers, who were willing to work in appalling conditions for abysmal wages because the alternatives in Andalucía were even worse. The Basques were not particularly kind to the *maketos*, as they called the new arrivals, regarding them as sowers of revolution, unrest and bad habits.

The second Carlist War (1872–6), spurred by new legislation on civil marriages and freedom of religion, led again to an unsuccessful siege of Bilbao, bitter defeat and the Law of Abolition of the *fueros* in July 1876. From now on, Basques would have to do compulsory service in the Spanish army and pay taxes to the State (to soften the blow in prosperous Vizcaya, this was done through the new provincial parliament, the Diputación, which soon came under the control of Bilbao's big industrialists). After all, Spain needed the Basque country more than the Basque country needed Spain.

1876–1923
The birth of Basque nationalism

Throughout history, the Basques have wanted only to be left alone to run their own affairs, and they nearly always support any sort of politics that promises to uphold their ancient rights and liberties; in modern times, this has meant adventures with both the far right and the far left. Now that the the *fueros* were dismantled and industrialization was rapidly changing almost every aspect of what had been a relatively isolated and balanced society (in the most radically changed province, Vizcaya, the population nearly doubled between 1850 and 1900), local historians began to define what had been lost, and polish it up to fit the spirit of the age.

Nationalism was hardly a recent phenomenon. In the 18th century, Enlightenment thinkers such as Manuel de Larramendi had already developed a concept of Basque nationhood based on language and tradition. The French Basque historian Augustin Chaho (1811–58) was the first to popularize the idea of the Basques as an oppressed nation, spurring a renewed interest in Basque things. Navarra's intellectuals led a minor Basque Renaissance, forming the Asociación Euskara to study and propagate Basque studies. Journalist and politician Arturo Campion (1854–1937) became a leader in the movement, linking language to independence and organizing poetry contests with traditional Basque games. By the end of the century, the Basque country reverberated with choral societies belting out arrangements of traditional songs.

Basque nationalism, however, owes nearly everything else to a one-man band named Sabino de Arana y Goiri (1865–1903). Arana's family owned a shipbuilding firm in Vizcaya, building wooden ships (which were quickly becoming obsolete), and as supporters of the Carlists, they had been forced into exile in France. The bitterness of the experience convinced Arana that what the Basques needed most was their own country. In 1890 he wrote *Bizkaya por su Independencia*, in which he inflated four historic battles between Basques and Castilians into an epic struggle for Basque independence. He invented all the national elements that were lacking: a name for the country, Euskadi (formerly, to talk about themselves, the Basques would say *Euskal Herrera*, 'the land of Euskera speakers'), and a flag, the red, green and white *ikurriña*, modelled on the Union Jack (like many Basques, he admired the feisty island nation as a role model). The day of his political conversion, Easter Sunday 1882, became the Basque national holiday, *Aberri Eguna* (the Day of the Fatherland). In 1895 Arana founded the first Basque nationalist party, Eusko Alderdi Jeltzalea, or the Partido Nacional Vasco (PNV), with the motto *Jaungoikua eta Lagizarra* ('God and the old laws'), and in prison he composed what would become the words of Euskadi's national anthem, *Gora ta Gora*. As a humourless ideologue, however, Arana was also an embarrassment. Many of his other ideas have been discarded – among them, the requirement that PNV members have at least one pure Basque grandparent and at least four Basque surnames in their ancestry, and that they be practising Catholics. The racism has been explained by sympathizers as a method of instilling a sense of separate destiny in the Basques, while the Catholicism was a sincerely held conviction of Arana, who detested the immorality of the new secular state in Bilbao: 'All of us know that today the poor are inhumanely exploited and treated like beasts by industrialists and businessmen, mine owners and property owners.' In 1890, 20,000 workers in Bilbao underlined his point by leading Spain's first general strike. Another aspect of Arana's Catholicism was a policy of seeking nationalist goals through nonviolence, which remains PNV doctrine to this day.

Arana, who suffered from Addison's disease, died in 1903 aged 38. In his lifetime the PNV's political victories had been minor (he himself had been elected to Vizcaya's provincial assembly), but his more pragmatic heirs would make it a force to be reckoned with as the PNV attracted voters from across the political spectrum: former Carlists and priests, but also former Liberals, intellectuals and professionals, disillusioned by the nepotism and corruption in Madrid. Even bankers, industrialists and shipping magnates, who would have had little voice in Spain's larger national parties, found in the PNV a ready-made power base and ideology.

Although Arana's Euskadi was to include all seven Basque provinces under the slogan *Zazpiak-bat* ('seven in one') or '4+3=1', his addition ran into a brick wall in the more repressive climate of France; the French, after all, knew better than to leave economic power in the hands of ethnic minorities, and could safely ignore the Basques, along with the Bretons and Corsicans. The seven Basque provinces would undergo dramatically different experiences in the First World War. In France, the war contributed mightily to the already existing trend towards abandonment and depopulation; many villages lost a third or even half of their young men. For Basques in neutral Spain, these were boom years as Bilbao pumped out armaments to supply the belligerents; by the end of the war, Bilbao's banks controlled a third of the investments in Spain. From 1917 on, the PNV controlled a majority of the region's parliamentary seats. Under their rule, the first Basque-language elementary schools, *ikastola*, were opened, and the Academy of Basque Studies was founded in Oñate, with the goal of distilling the very diverse Basque dialects into a Standard Euskera all could understand, a project that would take half a century to complete.

The deep depression that followed the war brought social problems to a head. Increased immigration of Castilians and others to Basque industrial centres exacerbated labour troubles, homelessness, urban crowding and pollution, and attracted many migrants to socialism, whose internationalism was anathema to the PNV. Its concern for social justice, however, attracted a fair number of Basques; one was the eloquent Dolores Ibarruri, who would become famous as 'La Pasionara', the voice of the Second Republic.

1923–75
Autonomy, civil war and Franco

Political and cultural repression under dictator Primo de Rivera (1923–30) only broadened support for the PNV and, after the creation of the Second Republic in 1931, it won a huge electoral victory under the moderate José Antonio Aguirre, who began the difficult negotiations with Madrid for autonomy, despite reservations about the new Second Republic's secularism. The Statutes of Basque Autonomy were hastily granted shortly after Franco and his fellows revolted in July 1936. The Navarrese, whose politics still revolved around Carlism and who wanted nothing to do with the 'church burners', supported Franco's right-hand man General Mola, who took Pamplona to widespread acclaim on the day of the coup.

In the other three Basque provinces, the vote for an autonomous Euskadi topped 80 per cent and was hugely supported, even by the socialists. The 32-year-old Aguirre was made president, or *lehendakari* and chose the equally young aristocrat Telesforo de Monzón to run the new Basque police, which he did with aplomb. The Basques, even the priests, sided enthusiastically with the Republic in the war against the rebels. Unlike Catalunya, where anarchists murdered priests and nuns before the communists murdered the anarchists, the Basque country under Aguirre and Monzón was well run. To break their spirit, the German Condor Legion practised the world's first saturation bombing of civilian targets at Durango and Gernika in early 1937. The Basques fought on; then Bilbao, for the third time in a century, was besieged. As food ran out, 20,000 children were sent abroad on refugee ships, including 4,000 who went to England. Unfortunately, the architect of Bilbao's defences gave the plans to the enemy, and the city surrendered. After only nine months in existence, autonomous Euskadi ceased to exist. Aguirre, who escaped by foot into France, formed the Basque government in exile in New York.

Franco's rule was a catastrophe for the Basques: over 100,000 prisoners were taken, 200,000 Basques went into exile and thousands (21,780 according to Basque nationalists) were executed after the Civil War, including the entire intelligentsia and political leadership. Franco took special pains to single out the Basques for reprisals of all kinds, suppressing even casual use of their language, and forbidding most festivals and cultural manifestations. State industrial schemes were consciously planned in a way to bring in large numbers of Spanish job-seekers to dilute the Basque population (by 1975, 40 per cent of the population had no Basque parents at all). But just as the Visigoths had long ago oppressed the Basques into uniting, so did Franco; even the thousands of Castilians who emigrated to Euskadi to work in the factories felt oppressed enough in the years of hunger, stagnation and police brutality to sympathize with Basque nationalist goals. In contrast, plenty of Navarrese Carlists found posts in Franco's army and government; the Spanish fascists even borrowed the Carlists' yoke-and-arrows symbol for their own party, and the province was allowed to keep a number of its traditional *fueros* in exchange for good behaviour.

The mass exodus of Basques and other republicans into France after the war added some new blood and new energy to many towns and villages in the southwest. No one thought Franco would last for long, especially as the Spanish Civil War turned out to be only a warm up for the atrocities of the Second World War. Although less costly and destructive for France than the First World War, it was still a miserable and dangerous time. From the beginning, the Germans seized a strip along the entire Atlantic coast as part of the occupied zone. The 'border' with Vichy-controlled territory was heavily guarded, and locals needed special papers to cross it. The Basques, including many former republican soldiers and civilians, did good work smuggling escapees over into Spain, and helping Allied agents coming the other way. The Basque Gernika Battalion fought alongside the forces of liberation, and the *ikurriña* flew proudly among the Allies' flags as De Gaulle entered Paris. At the end of the war, in Bordeaux (the last French city to be liberated), De Gaulle promised the Basques that the Allies would not stop at the Pyrenees but would carry on to rid Europe of fascists once and for all.

Only they didn't. The Basques were frustrated with the Allies, and frustrated with their beloved Church for supporting Franco. Aguirre and the PNV in exile sat on their hands, waiting for Franco to wither away, ostracized from the world community. They didn't count on the Cold War, and Franco playing the anti-Communist card. Feelings of frustration soon turned into feelings of betrayal. In 1953, Spain signed a bilateral treaty with the United States and received millions of dollars in exchange for the right to establish military bases. In 1955, in spite of heated protests from the Basque government in exile, Spain, still run by the same men who had condoned the bombing of Gernika, was admitted to the United Nations.

Disillusioned with the fossilized PNV, the first student resistance groups formed in 1952. The grim atmosphere of Francoist repression and American 'betrayal' determined the equally poisonous nature of the antidote. The ETA (Euskadi Ta Askatsuna, or Basque Homeland and Liberty) was founded by seven young intellectuals in 1959 as a study group. Its first action was painting 'Our Euskadi' and the Basque flag on walls (daring enough back then, when such things meant extended prison sentences). In 1967 radical members, inspired by Cuba, Algeria and Vietnam, took over ETA and formulated the means it would use to achieve an independent Euskadi: taking action to provoke the State into over-reacting, so that its oppression would mobilize the majority of people in the Basque country; race, religion and language, all that was so precious to Arana, no longer counted. The violence began haphazardly, in 1968, when the first Guardia Civil was killed after pulling over a car carrying ETA leader Txabi Etxeberrieta. Etxeberrieta was tracked down and killed at the next road block. The next death, of Manzanas, a notorious police torturer, was ETA's first planned assassination, and led to just the kind of reaction the group sought: the infamous Burgos trial of 16 *etarristas* in 1970, which showed Franco's regime in the worst light and lead to an international uproar that persuaded Franco, much against his will, to commute the four death sentences to life imprisonment.

As the only active resistance to the dictatorship, ETA attracted widespread sympathy within Spain and elsewhere. In 1973, ETA could take credit for changing history when they blew the car of Franco's hand-picked successor, Admiral Carrero Blanco, over the roof of a Madrid church. With Carrero Blanco gone, Spaniards for the first time began to see a light at the end of the tunnel. But the repression in Euskadi worsened, and it became a battleground between the ETA (whose new slogan was 'Actions Unite, Words Divide') and the Guardia Civil, whose State violence was enough to convince many Basques that nationalist violence was legitimate. Every ETA action defiantly confirmed that the Basques still existed, in spite of Franco's boast that he had unified the State and rid it of ethnic minorities forever. By the time Franco finally performed his long-awaited exit from the stage in 1975, the Spanish State in the eyes of many Basques had lost all right to govern their land.

1975–
Big changes, but not big enough for everyone

The Spanish have always sided with the Basques when they found themselves in opposition. But once they come to power, this sympathy always wanes. When the Left was in power, we became troglodytes, dwellers in caves, capitalists, a Vatican in miniature. When the Right was in power, we were Freemasons, Reds, Separatists, people who had sold out to Moscow.
                                          Telesforo Monzón

After 40 years of Franco, the Basques were to explode. No region had suffered more, but during the delicate transition period Madrid did little to encourage the notion that change was imminent. The king proclaimed a general amnesty of political prisoners, but it included fewer than 10 per cent of Basque prisoners, leading to the formation of the Gestoria Pro-Amnistía, a Basque human rights organization that brought their plight to the attention of the rest of Europe. Because of the need to appease the numerous Francoists and right-wingers still in power ('the bunker', as Spaniards called them), the Basques were the chosen target for a stringent law and order campaign. Demonstrations were brutally broken up, while ETA continued its campaign against Francoist politicians and the Guardia Civil.

In 1977 the first elections in the new Spain brought back exiles such as Telesforo Monzón and Dolores Ibarruri. Parties in favour of autonomy, led by the PNV, won the majority. The following year, voters were presented with a referendum on the new Spanish constitution. The mass demonstrations in Catalunya and Euskadi had pushed its authors to adopt a regional form of government, in fact regionalism for all of Spain, whether a region wanted it or not. These *Comunidades Autónomas* would have the right to their Basque, Catalan or Gallego language and culture, but the constitution insisted that Castilian was the official language of the State and that 'The Constitution is based on the indivisible unity of the Spanish Nation, common and indivisible fatherland of all the Spaniards.'

It was to this that the majority of Basques objected; in fact, they no longer considered themselves Spaniards at all. They remembered their *fueros* and wanted autonomy from Madrid as before, on their terms, as a right, not as a favour from a government they mistrusted. The PNV refused to vote for the constitution in the Spanish parliament, and called on Basques to abstain from voting in protest. Over 40 per cent followed their lead; in Guipúzcoa and Vizcaya 56 per cent of voters abstained. The majority of Basques who did actually vote, voted against it. To this day, it remains a major nationalist complaint that the constitution was imposed on them against their will. They were next asked to approve the statutes of autonomy, which PNV did support, and 53 per cent voted in favour, despite anger over the fact that the Navarra was left out and never offered the chance to vote on whether or not it wanted to remain with the other three Basque provinces (this, too, remains a very bitter bone of contention). The Basque government in exile returned after 43 years. Vitoria (Gasteiz) was chosen to be the capital of the autonomous Basque Community of Euskadi, and in 1980 a new PNV *lehendakari* was sworn in under the oak tree in Gernika.

But most Basques were not satisfied. One Basque in particular, old Telesforo Monzón, an ex-member of the government in exile, broke with the PNV in 1978 in disgust at the constitutional referendum and founded a new radical party called Herri Batasuna, or Popular Unity. He was imprisoned as an apologist for terrorism, and went on a hunger strike, then was elected to the Cortes where, as many elected Herri Batasuna members do to this day, he refused to take his seat. As the party's main stance is opposition, pure and simple, Herri Batasuna soon became one of the most unorthodox parties in Europe, attracting a heterogenous group from radical priests to gay rights activists, feminists, ecologists, students, Marxists, and so on. It also openly supported ETA, although it always denies being its political wing.

Reflecting the Basque opinion that the State had railroaded them into accepting an imposed autonomous solution, 1978–80 was ETA's most murderous period, with some 80 killings a year. Its operatives waged an intractable campaign against the Lemoiz nuclear power plant, planned by Franco only 16km from Bilbao, until it was finally shut down in 1982 (*see* pp.164–5). In the 1970s, drug addiction among young Basques was well above the national norms; sensing a conspiracy from Madrid, the ETA started knocking off drug dealers. The situation became so polarized that no Basque would talk to a Guardia Civil or the police. Ostracized with their families from normal life, the police began to be inflicted with what has been dubbed the 'northern syndrome'. They hated the Basques and pleaded to be relocated. Suicide rates among the Guardia Civil soared. They often took out their miseries on Basque demonstrators.

If in the New Spain ETA often seemed like a relic of the bad old days, its Basque sympathizers countered that the government was still rife with Francoists and torturers, not a single one of whom had ever been brought to justice. The Spanish call this the *pacto de olvido*, the pact of forgetfulness. The attempted coup in 1981 in the Cortes by the Guardia Civil Lieutenant Tejero was a bitter reminder of the nightmare that Spain wanted to forget. To keep the peace, no one would be blamed. To placate 'the bunker', each party would vie to prove it was the toughest on ETA. Spain would remain the only country in western Europe where prisoners were routinely tortured. As documented by Amnesty International, most of the victims were Basques, so they didn't care to forget.

In 1982, the country overwhelmingly voted in the Socialist Party (PSOE) of Felipe González on the promise of change. One change was a new anti-terrorist law that allowed police to detain suspects for up to 10 days incommunicado. Many detainees were bullied or tortured, then released without ever being accused or tried; nationalist journalists were a favourite target. Basque conspiracy theories about Madrid's intentions were not totally loony; the Socialist government was secretly waging a 'dirty war' through the Anti-terrorist Liberation Group (GAL), passing it off as an extreme right-wing death squad unrelated to the government. By extending its activities into the French Basque country, it finally spurred Paris to act against suspected ETA members who always used France as a safe haven and extradite them for the first time in 1984, even though the old reason for not doing so – reasonable suspicion that they would be tortured in Spain – had not changed. In 1989 slip-ups by its mercenaries traced GAL back to its mastermind, González's law enforcement chief. González himself managed to survive this scandal, but not a host of other corruption scandals that plagued his government, and in 1996 the Socialists lost the election to the rightwing Partido Popular (PP) and José María Aznar. Aznar (who had survived an ETA assasination attempt the year before) claimed that González hadn't been tough enough on the Basques, and to show that he was, he imprisoned all 23 members of the directorate of Herri Batasuna for showing an ETA film during their 15 minutes of free air time during the election. This hasn't stopped their garish posters from covering every spare bit of wall. Herri Batasuna remains the ultimate opposition party, and regularly gets about 15 per cent of the vote.

The autonomous community of Navarra, as ever, stands apart, with a PP majority. Some have called it the Basque Ulster and, similarly to Northern Ireland, its union with the rest of Euskadi is a chief ETA demand. North of Pamplona live a majority of

Basques, to the south of Pamplona the majority is Spanish. Between the two of them, Navarra remains the most reactionary part of Spain, maybe of all Europe; it still has a strong Carlist streak, even though the current pretender, Prince Hugo de Borbón, has tacitly acknowledged King Juan Carlos by paying him a social visit. Pamplona, its bright and prosperous capital, is the Mecca of the Opus Dei, the sinister, secret Catholic organization that in Franco's later years attempted to gain control of the Spanish government by insinuating its members into high positions. In a recent poll, a higher percentage of Navarrese claim to feel 'Navarrese' as opposed to Basque or Spanish. No one is really sure how they would vote in a referendum to join Euskadi, but according to the Spanish constitution, even a referendum is illegal.

In the French Pays Basque, or North Euskadi as the Basques prefer to call it, the biggest political change since the Second World War has been the creation of regional governments under the Socialists' decentralization programme in 1981. So far it isn't much, but as the first reversal in five centuries of Parisian centralism, it at least gives provinces a start in reclaiming some control over their own destinies. Mitterand actually promised a separate Basque *département*, but in spite of repeated reminders over his 14 years in office, he reneged. The French Basques constitute a mere 0.4 per cent of the national population, but, jealous of the autonomy their countrymen have won over the border in Spain (where they comprise 7.5 per cent of the population), continue to be quietly assertive in trying to push decentralization even further. An informal council of mayors, heir to the old *biltzar*, meets regularly. In the 1990s, when the French government started cracking down on ETA operatives and sympathizers, the organization responded by bombing Renault dealerships around Spain. Then suddenly they stopped, which suggests that somewhere a deal has been cut. France may be a democratic country, but in affairs like this we know as little of what goes on as we do about political factions in China.

Although most French Basques decided long ago that being French wasn't so bad, there are still plenty of nationalists. The police watch over them and manipulate them silently and skilfully. This is something at which the French have had centuries of practice – all over the Midi, as well as in Brittany, Corsica and the colonies – and they're extremely good at it, probably the best in the world.

In Spain, widespread disgust with terror tactics in recent years has made ETA fall out of favour. Three-quarters of all Spaniards regard Basque terrorism as the country's worst problem, and among the Basques themselves the percentage may even be higher, because they have to live with it from day to day. Support for an independent Euskadi remains considerable, but Basques today recognize that the political situation has changed, and would rather see independence brought about as part of a peaceful process and constitutional amendments.

Some 70 per cent of Basques vote for nationalist parties, mostly for the moderate PNV and the more nationalist but still peaceful Eusko Alkartasuna (Basque Solidarity); on the whole they lean to the left on most issues, and are strongly anti-nuclear and anti-NATO. The two Basque regions, Euskadi and Navarra, have the highest level of self-government in Spain. Taxes are collected by local governments, and local rule covers education, culture, industry, health services, police, agriculture, fishing, and so on. Many parents, even Spanish families, choose to have their children educated bilingually. The Basque government in Vitoria is held up in Spain as a model of efficiency and progressiveness, more supportive than any of new technologies and ways of doing business.

Financed by bank robberies, kidnappings and 'revolutionary taxes' imposed on Basque businesses, ETA diehards continue their murders and bombing campaigns in the name of the Basque people, although the ETA's logic of violence now seems to be its only logic. The surprise truce declared in September 1998 brought 15 months of peace, during which it was hoped that a peaceful solution could be found. Aznar's government held talks with the PNV, but refused to budge on the general Basque demand of amending the constitution. Unfortunately, the ETA found its marginalization in peace worse than the disgust it inspired when it was active, and in December 1999 the organization resumed the terror. The following summer it conducted a particularly fierce campaign of murders throughout the country, including that of a high court judge in Madrid, and some local Basque politicians who publicly opposed them. Successive raids in September 2000 in both the French and Spanish Basque territories may have whittled down the ETA, but the issue is far from settled; like the hydra, when one head is lopped off another springs up, as witnessed in the November 2000 assassination of the well-respected former health minister Earnest Lluch, who was shot in Barcelona for supporting negotiations with the Basques, but not on ETA terms. Estimates of active ETA militants place them at fewer than one hundred. Meanwhile, the voices for peace grow bolder: the Euskal Herriko Bakearen Aldeko Koordinakundea (Association for Peace in the Basque Country) organizes silent gatherings in 160 places in Euskadi after every murder or death caused by political violence. A similar group, Gesture for Peace, has a big blue A for its symbol, the A standing for Freedom in Basque. Many, looking at the beginnings of a peaceful settlement in Northern Ireland, want the government to abandon its hardline stance. The government staunchly refuses to negotiate with terrorists.

The real story in Euskadi is not this relic of a troubled past, but the surprising rebirth of Bilbao as a symbol of the Basques' future. Long known only for industrial obsolescence, under the auspices of the PNV the city has pulled itself up with such projects as Frank Gehry's Guggenheim Museum, a new metro and a huge riverfront redevelopment plan; in only a few years, Bilbao has emerged from nowhere to become one of the most exciting cities in Spain, and the showcase for a small, ancient nation that in the past has always been able to absorb new ideas, innovate and prosper. The Basques, in spite of their current troubles, seem poised to do it again.

Culture

The Language that Defeated the Devil Himself

Want to impress your hosts with a few words of Basque? Go ahead and try it! The Basques point out with great pride that their language, which they call Euskera, is not only Europe's oldest, but the most difficult: an old story tells how the Devil came to the Basque country to learn Euskera and tempt the Basques, but could only manage to learn 'yes' and 'no' (*bai* and *ez*) before he gave up and returned to hell.

As a general rule, the more declensions a language has, the older it is: Euskera shoots the moon with 20. Verbs can vary according to the gender of the person you are addressing (pluri-personal). Nouns are described in a three-number system (singular, plural and indefinite). The vast number of grammatical tenses includes not only a subjunctive, but two different potentials, an eventual and a hypothetical. Euskera is also maddeningly, spectacularly indirect, in what linguists call ergative constructions. For example, to say 'I am spinning', comes out *Iruten ari nuzu*, or literally, 'In the act of spinning doing you have me'! Or try out this proverb: *Izan gabe eman dezakegun gauza bakarra da zoriona.* 'Having without, give (*Izan gabe eman*), we can (*dezakegun*), one thing only is (*gauza bakarra da*), happiness (*zoriona*)' – 'happiness is the only thing we can give without having'. But such grammatical complexity permits beauty and economy; you can express anything in Euskera in far fewer words than in most other languages. Other advantages to learning it are its regular spelling, no grammatical gender, no irregular nouns and hardly any irregular verbs.

Pronunciation, thank goodness, is not a problem, either. Euskera is phonetic, and there are only a few letters you need to know: **e** as long 'a', **u** as 'oo', **j** as 'ee', **s** as something halfway between 's' and 'sh', **tz** or **z** as 's' and **x** as 'sh'.

Like eskimos, who know no generic word for 'ice', the Basques, at least originally, had no word for 'tree' or 'animal'. And being the democratic folk they are, there is no word for 'king' either – they had to borrow one from the French and Spanish potentates to whom they were forced to pay taxes.

Basque Basics

ongi-etorri welcome
kaixo, zer moduz? hello, how are you?
bai yes
ez no
nik ez dut ulurtzen I don't understand
agur goodbye
gero arte see you later
gizonak men's
emakumiak ladies'
turismo bulegoa tourist office
hondartza beach
tren geltokia train station
atzerapena delay
itxita closed
zuzen straight ahead
kontuz, lanak danger, roadworks

zuritoa a small beer
garagardoa a large beer
eskerrik asko thank you
sardinak, mesedez some sardines, please
zer da hau? what is this?
xipiroiak squids

Numbers
1 *bat*
2 *bi*
3 *hiru*
4 *lau*
5 *bost*
6 *sei*
7 *zazpi*
8 *zortzi*
9 *bederetzi*
10 *hamar*

Language and Identity

One is born Basque, one speaks Basque, one lives Basque, one dies Basque. The Basque
language is a country, I almost said a religion. Say a word in Basque to a mountaineer,
and although before you were scarcely a man to him, you suddenly become a brother.
Victor Hugo, *Alpes et Pyrénées*, 1843

Language remains the crux of Basque identity, and for many its survival is a major
concern. In Euskera, a Basque is an *Euskaldun*, one 'who speaks Euskera'. The Basque
country is *Euskal Herria*, 'the land of Euskera speakers'. Or at least it was until Sabino
Arana, the founder of Basque nationalism, conjured up the neologism *Euskadi* as the
name of a country. After all, 'everything with a name exists' (*Izena duen guztiak izatea*
ere badauke), according to the most famous of Basque proverbs, although another,
lesser-known bit of wisdom adds, *Izenak ez du egiten izana* ('a name doesn't make
something true'). Existing in name but not in truth sums up the current status of
Euskadi for nationalists, but it also defines many an Euskaldun: so many, in fact, don't
speak their own language that another neologism, *Euskotar*, was invented for an
ethnic Basque with the O negative blood, but without the tongue. 'To lose your
language is to lose your soul,' warn the Sards, another of Europe's linguistic minorities. The Catalans to the east have had tremendous success in revitalizing their
language in the New Spain. The Basques are having a much harder time of it.

Euskera's very strangeness weighs against it. No one has yet found another
language related to Basque, although linguists have put forth scores of candidates
over the past two centuries (the most convincing is the most recent one, Ainu, the
language of the Caucasian Ainu people of Japan, proposed by Edo Nyland; have a look
at *www.islandnet.com/~edonon*). Pre-dating the invasions that carried Indo-European
languages west, some linguists believe Euskera has been spoken in the Basque lands
since 7000 BC, and they could be right: practically every word for common tools, for
instance, comes from the ancient root *haiz*, meaning stone – even *haiztur*, scissors.
Writing, unfortunately, came late. Although the names of people and places (with
useful Latin translations) were recorded in Roman times, written Euskera hibernated
until the 9th century, when a few words and phrases were jotted down by missionaries. On the other hand, the Basque oral tradition was exceptionally strong, and
continues even today with the *bertsulari*, the bards, often scarcely literate shepherds,
who have memorized a vast repertoire of traditional pieces and are dazzlingly skilled
at improvisation. Another oral legacy in Euskera are the plays known as *pastorales*,
descended from medieval mystery plays (you can still see them produced at festival
times, especially in the villages of Soule).

The first book in Euskera, *Lingua Vasconum Primitiae*, a collection of poems, was
published in 1545 by the French Basque priest Benat Etxepare (or Detchepare, among
other spellings); one of his desires, he stated, was to show that 'this language is as
good a written language as any other'. In 1729 the Jesuit university professor Manuel
Larramendi followed with the first Euskera grammar book, *El Imposible Vencido* (The
Impossible Overcome). In the same century, Pierre de Agerre, or 'Axular', wrote *Gero*, a

literary version of his own sermons, which may not sound like something you'd curl up with for a good read, but nevertheless is considered the first masterpiece of Euskaldun literature. Most Basque authors, however, including the most famous, Miguel de Unamuno, wanted to reach the widest possible audience and wrote in Spanish or French. One deterrent was the sheer number of dialects in Euskera, one for each of the seven provinces, with variations in every valley; a Bilbaino, for instance, can only with great difficulty make out a farmer from Soule. Perhaps an even greater deterrent was the abandonment of Euskera by the 18th-century Basque bourgeoisie, who stigmatized it as lower-class hick talk and eliminated it from the schools, the government and their new university at Bergara.

Some fought back, especially Ignacio Iztueta de Zaldibia (1767–1845), a man of humble origins who wrote about Basque music, dance and folklore, fearing they were in danger of extinction. His fears spread after the loss of Basque political autonomy in the Carlist Wars, and with the industrialization that brought in a huge influx of immigrants from across Spain. As the language began to die out in the street, a 19th-century cultural flowering, a Basque Renaissance, arose to preserve it. Plays, poems, novels, grammatical works and dictionaries appeared, many designed to rally the Basques to a sense of themselves as a nation. Among the classics of the period were Augustin Chaho's creation of the myth of Aïtor, the father of all Basques, in 1848, a story that has become a part of Basque culture.

In 1914 the nationalist community founded the first *ikastola* (private Euskera-language elementary school) and they soon became widespread under the Republic. Although some *ikastolas* survived underground during the severe cultural oppression under Franco, his 38 years in power left a huge generational gap in transmitting Euskera; for a while, the fascist campaign to 'Speak Christian!' was so bad that older Basques who couldn't speak Spanish feared to even leave their homes. Combined with the French-only policies in the north, and the fact that now even the most remote Basque farmhouse is bombarded with radio and TV broadcasts in Spanish and French, the oldest spoken language in Europe is now in danger of becoming a museum piece. In Hugo's day, half the inhabitants in all the Basque country spoke fluent Euskera. Today only a quarter do, some 660,000 people altogether. The percentages (from a 1991 survey) are higher on the French side, although they add up to fewer than 80,000 souls: 64 per cent in Basse-Navarre, 54 per cent in the Soule, and 26 per cent in Labourd, as opposed to 45 per cent in Guipúzcoa, 18 per cent in Vizcaya, 10 percent in Navarra, and only 4 per cent in Alava. And half of these say they are more comfortable in French or Spanish. On the bright side, for the first time in two centuries the number of Basque speakers is not declining. One reason is the completion of Modern Standard Basque (Euskera Batua) by Bilbao's Academy of Language, a task begun in 1911 but only competed in the 1960s; now, for the first time, in theory at least, there exists an Euskera comprehensible to speakers of all dialects. Banned under Franco, Batua at first was taught on the sly in the *ikastolas* and at nationalist cultural events; Gabriel Aresti's *Harri eta Herri* (Rock and People) in 1964, boldly published in the face of government opposition, became the inspiration for a whole new generation of Basque writers.

> ### A Basque Outline
> Very few Basque words have made it into English, although one is 'silhouette', derived in a most roundabout way from the Basque word for 'many holes', *zuleta*. The surname Zulueta or Zuloeta was probably given to a family who lived among the holes, or caves. One branch of the Zulueta family in France adopted the spelling Silhouette. Their most famous member, Etienne de Silhouette (1707–67), was a writer and politician who held the powerful post of controller-general. He wasn't very good at it and didn't keep his office long, and his meagre policies cast but a shadow (according to one explanation), although others say Silhouette himself liked to draw portraits in outlines and hang them on the walls of his château.

Today, both Euskera and Spanish are the official languages of the three provinces of Euskadi and the valleys of northern Navarra. In Euskadi, parents can choose whether to educate their children just in Spanish (53 per cent do), bilingually, or just in Euskera (22 per cent). In the past decade some 100,000 adults, mostly middle-aged people denied the chance under Franco, have learned to speak it; the recently coined *Euskaldunberri* ('new speaker of Basque') embraces them, whatever their ethnic origin. Euskera-language TV and radio are broadcast on both sides of the border, encouraging interest among French Basques, where the language still has no official status and less than 2 per cent of children are in *ikastolas*.

For all that, the explosion in print inspired by the creation of Batua is nothing short of amazing. The Basque country is now served with two daily Euskera newspapers, the left-wing *Egin* (founded by thousands of small subscribers) and the more independent *Egunkaria*. Over 1,000 books of all kinds are published annually, all for a population of 660,000 potential readers; one Basque novel, *Obabakoak*, by Bernardo Atxaga (1989), was the first ever to be translated from Euskera into English. Equally encouraging is the continuing popularity of the *bertsulari*, the Basque bards, who like rappers improvize at festivals, where they compete; given a theme, each must immediately compose and sing an original song about it, sometimes singing alternate verses, each trying to get the upper hand. One is the hero of a Basque cartoon series for children – or what few children there are: the Basque birth rate is the lowest in western Europe, with only 7.7 births per 1,000.

For more, seek out Euskera on the web:
www.cogs.susx.ac.uk/users/larryt/ An excellent site by linguist Larry Trask
http://bips.bi.ehu.es/bakio/web/bakio.htm Hear the sound of spoken Basque
www.uzei.com/scripts/uzei/Euskalterm.cfm On-line English, French, Spanish and Euskera dictionary
http://ixa.si.ehu.es/tresnak/euspell.html Euspell, the Basque on-line spell-checker.

Giants, Shaggy Men and a Not-So-Virgin Mari

The Basques are not alone. In fact, their long intimacy with their land has forced them to share it with an unreasonably large number of gods, demons, spirits and fairies, creatures of one of the richest mythologies in Europe. There is no element in the Basque landscape, no chapter of Basque history and legend, that is not suffused with the otherworldly and the divine. Christianity, after all, didn't take a firm hold in this isolated region until the 10th century (the Arabs, during their lightning strike through in the 8th century, called the Basques *majus*, meaning pagans or wizards), and the old gods and spirits who lingered were still lively enough to bedevil Basque children in their catechism classes well into the 20th century. When they questioned the priests – themselves inevitably Basque, because they had to speak Euskera – what was real and what wasn't, the standard reply was: 'Everything that has a name exists in the world...but it's best to keep that a secret!'

One myth the Basques don't have is a migration myth. They were always there, and paradise, where the rivers ran with milk, was deep in the bowels of the Basque country. Ortzi or Ost, god of the heavens, and the sun, Eguzi, were the bright forces of the day and the earth, since the sun was the earth's daughter, reborn every day in the east. Solar symbols decorated the Basques' pre-Christian tombs, and old houses are nearly always orientated towards the east. The moon, Ilargi, the 'light of the dead', had to do with all that was hidden, with souls and the spirit world. The fact that old people familiarly called both the sun and moon 'Grandma' suggests that they were once two aspects of the same deity. There are vague hints – curiously, very similarly to the Ainu (*see* above, p.49) – that the Basques believed themselves to be descended from bears, as in the ancient carnival figure Artza, whose emergence from hibernation in spring is also a symbol of renewal.

One possible origin of the name Pyrenees is 'mountains of fire', after the ritual bonfires that shone from their peaks on the great holidays of the year. Every Basque mountain had its attendant deity; some of these live on in folklore, such as Jauna Gorri, the 'Red Lord', who lives atop the Pic d'Anie (*Ahunamendi* in Basque) and sends the storms down to the valleys. Jauna Gorri tends a garden on the mountain top where the flowers of immortality grow, and he keeps his treasures there, guarded by hairy black giants called *pelutlaks*. Beneath the mountains are the caves, sites of worship from the Palaeolithic era.

The dolmens were built by the *jentillaks*, the race of giants that once lived side by side with the Basques. The *jentillaks*, often a great help to their neighbours, invented metallurgy and the saw, and introduced the growing of wheat. One day, a strange storm cloud appeared from the east, and the wisest of the *jentillaks* recognized it as an omen and interpreted it as the end of their age. The giants marched off into the earth, under a dolmen (still visible in the Arratzaran valley in Navarra). One was left behind, Olentzero the charcoal burner, and he explained to the Basques: 'Kixmi [Jesus] is born and this means the end of our race.' Olentzero lives on today (after nearly vanishing after Franco, he has made a dramatic comeback in all seven Basque provinces) as the jolly, fat doll in a hundred different guises, the leader of all the processions, his ancient association with the winter solstice making him a prominent participant in celebrations of Christmas and New Year's Day; the Basque yule log is 'Olentzero's trunk'. You will find Olentzero in Basque homes and even in the churches, often bearing an uncommon resemblance to the Michelin man, puffing a pipe; he'll probably be surrounded by food and wine because, being one of the *jentillaks*,

Olentzero likes to eat all day. In many places, straw effigies of Olentzero are paraded through the streets, distributing sweets, before going up in a midnight bonfire.

Then there are the strong, shaggy lords of the wood, the *basajaunaks*, who worked the land but kept agriculture secret from the Basques, until St Martin (a Christian-ization of the original hero) won a bet with them, with their seeds as the wager. Today, when the sheep suddenly start and weird cries echo in the mountains, Basque shepherds say the *basajaunaks* are warning of a storm. Other creatures include the *laminaks*, small female fairies with webbed bird feet and fish bodies who live by the shore and rivers and comb their hair with golden combs, and have a capacity to help or harm; in modern times they have become a bit like leprechauns and get blamed for everything that goes wrong. They often have little goblin assistants, the *prakagorris*, or 'red pants' (the Devil in Basque, Galtzagorri, dresses in a similar fashion).

And where mythology fades off into nursery-lore, we have the 'man with the sack' who comes to carry off naughty children, and a large bestiary with jokes like the elusive *dahu*, a kind of lizard with legs that are shorter on one side – the better to walk the mountain slopes. Along with the myths goes a remarkable body of pre-Christian religious survivals, including rituals that lasted well into the 20th century; many old Basques in isolated villages can remember festivals with midsummer bonfires in their childhood, and in some villages the custom is coming back (any excuse for a party).

Springtime and Carnival in the Basque country are as atavistic as any ethno-grapher's heart could desire; besides the aforementioned Artza, or bear, a whole range of primordial characters are unleashed, especially in rural villages in Navarra and Alava. There's Artza's grotesque sidekick, Zirpot, who comes covered with old sacks and is attacked by the Xaldiko, a malicious man-horse, until he is caught and shod by the *Lxatxoak*, young men completely covered with hairy pelts. Mielotxin, who is 10ft tall, stuffed with straw and covered with boar skins, is burned at the end of Carnival, as is Marquitos, covered with ferns and wearing a beret and necklace of feathers and eggshells. Truly alarming *momotxorroaks*, 'cow men' in horns and bloody aprons, attack onlookers, while the shaggy but more peaceful *joaldunaks* awaken spring with pairs of giant bells, symbolic of testicles, strapped to their backs.

All the wealth of folk- and fairy tales give only teasing hints of the ancient rites and beliefs from which they are descended. Without much in the way of written records, trying to reconstruct the details is difficult indeed. A large number of inscribed votive altars from Roman times have been dug up around the Pyrenees and, just to tease (or so it seems), nearly each one bears the name of a different god: religion for the proto-Basques may have been a local affair; the same deities, more or less, might go under a different name and carry different attributes in every valley or village.

But concerning the most important deity in the Basque pantheon there is no confusion. Her name is Mari, of all things, and she is the Pyrenees' version of the transcendent Great Goddess that ruled the old religion throughout Europe before the coming of the Indo-European peoples. At once the queen of heaven and of the underworld (she dwells in caves, with direct links to the Basques' underworld para-dise), she sent thunder and storms down from the mountain tops, the places where her rites were always observed (favourite abodes were Gorbea, Anboto, Aketegi and Aralar), and she travelled from peak to peak in a blazing fire ball. All the other goddesses, spirits and fairies created by the pantheistic mind are just aspects of her, manifest in various forms. This Mari is no virgin; her consort, shocking as it must have seemed to the ears of the Christian proselytizers, was a great serpent named Sugaar or Maju – the prototype for all the Pyrenees' many dragons and, according to legend, the founding father of many of the oldest Basque families.

Like many mountain regions, the Basque country has always been fantastically conservative in terms of religion; today it's the last corner of the world that will ever keep the pope up at night worrying. Mari and Mary may bear the same name only by coincidence, but 1,200 years ago, when Christian missionaries began to expropriate the sacred sites, holidays and processions of the old Basque religion to wean people away from it, they probably didn't realize they were helping to maintain a religious continuity that goes back to the beginnings of time.

Basque Accessories

Typically for the mystery people of Europe, no one has a clue how they came by their most beloved and widespread symbol, the *lauburu*, or 'four heads' (*see* box). Fashion is a bit less mysterious. No old Basque gentleman would be complete without a *txapela*, or beret, and a walking stick, or *makila*. The Basques may have been the first to wear berets. The first recorded ones are the red Jesuit *birettas*, which went on to become the symbol of the Carlists in the 19th century and have never fallen out of fashion since; both men and women don them for festive occasions, along with a red neck scarf and sash. For everyday wear, Basques prefer berets in black or dark blue. In *bert-solari* or other competitions, the prize is nearly always a beret, hence *txapeldun*, or 'champion', is 'one with the beret'. Occasionally, even the beret itself is the object of a competition, as in Hendaye (*see* pp.238–9).

Makilas, likewise, are taken very seriously. Descended from the Basque shepherd's staff, they represent authority, justice and respect. The reliefs on the wood originate from incising the wild medlar in the forest, causing the sap to swerve around the cuts and form designs. The branch is cut in winter, peeled, stained with quicklime and heat-straightened. The bottom is then fitted in brass or silver and hand-engraved with Basque motifs. The other end is topped with a horn grip and covered with plaited leather. Traditionally, there is always a coin built into the *makila*, and each one will usually carry an inscribed motto, such as *hitza hitz* – 'one's word is one's word'. The Basques customarily offer a *makila* to anybody they wish to honour: Churchill, General De Gaulle and Pope John Paul II were all beneficiaries.

On festive occasions, at least, many Basques of all ages still wear espadrilles, their traditional black-cloth, hemp-soled shoes that lace up around the ankle. They've been around at least since the 13th century, and are still hand sewn today in Mauléon. They are worth looking out for, although the majority of the cheaper espadrilles you find in the shops these days are machine sewn, in China.

The Lauburu

Nothing except the relatively recently invented Basque flag, the *irrikiña*, better conveys the message that Here Be Basques. Known sometimes as the pre-Christian Basque cross, the *lauburu* resembles four commas joined at their points, contained in a circle. Some say it represents the four elements, while others find it a variation of the swastika, a solar symbol of ancient China, India, Egypt and America before the Nazis got their hands on it. Modern Basques consider it a sign of good luck. And that's all anyone knows.

The real monument of Euskadi is the *etxe*, a word that means much more than just 'house'. Set on its own on the velvet hillsides, the traditional Basque farmhouse, usually called a *baserri* (or *borda*, in the French Basque country), is one of the most distinctive characteristics of the whole region: pretty, simple, functional and nearly always painted white, they are usually two stories high, with a distinctive long, low gable along the façade and a built-in shelter for animals or other farm business on the ground floor. The upper section often has half-timbering and shutters – trimmed, of course, with green and *rouge basque* (really more of a maroon 'ox blood', which was, in fact, used before the invention of paint).

Most *etxes* face east, towards the rising sun; older houses have carved lintels over the main door, with the year and name of the builder, accompanied by a *lauburu* or two and a sententious inscription.

A Basque house is not only a place to live, but the symbol of the clan, its identifying tartan, its Shinto-style shrine to its ancestors. All Basque houses have names (always bestowed by neighbours, not by the residents) that still serve as the postal address in most cases. Older Basques, when meeting other Basques, will identify themselves by the name of their ancestral *etxe*, even if the house no longer physically exists. The *etxekojaun*, 'master of the house', and the *etxekoandere*, 'lady of the house', make all the decisions affecting the clan. In the old days, the *etxekojaun* also attended the communal assemblies where the Basques made their laws, while the *etxekoandere* took charge of more spiritual matters, thwarting evil spirits with a fire in the hearth, gathering laurel, ash leaves or thistle heads (*eguzki-lorea*, 'flower of the sun'), and keeping the memory of departed family members alive. One way they do this is by lighting *argizaiolaks*, thin candles wrapped around wood. After the arrival of Christianity, much of this was transferred to the church, where every family has in perpetuity its special place, the *yarleku*. When the master and mistress grow old, the titles are formally handed over to the most suitable child (son or daughter) and to that child's spouse. It is common to find Basque families that have kept their home on the same site for over a thousand years.

The cemeteries have been around even longer, and here, too, each family has its special tomb or area set aside. The Basques have their own distinctive 'discoidal' or round-headed tombstones. Archaeologists have dug up some models 4,500 years old, and the same style has been in use ever since. The earliest ones often had human figures, sun symbols or other symbols carved on them; since the coming of Christianity, the stones usually show crosses. You will see them in any churchyard, usually turned south so that the sun shines on the carved face all day.

Music, Dance and the Basque Yodel

Basques, considered rather taciturn by their French and Spanish neighbours, lose all their inhibitions when it comes to music. 'To sing like a Basque' is a nice compliment in French, and they do do it well, with passion, whether it's choral music, traditional tunes played by village bands, or Basque rock (rare, fortunately, although as one of the few things that Franco couldn't be bothered to suppress, it became a popular vehicle of national solidarity in the 1960s and 70s). Several Basques have enjoyed international success, including Maurice Ravel (who had a Basque mother), Crisóstomo de Arriaga, the great child prodigy composer from Bilbao who died at the age of 19, and the 19th-century opera tenor Julián Gayarre.

The Basques have their share of traditional musical instruments, which are played in both the traditional and classic Basque repertoire; special quartets and so on have been composed for them since the 16th century. One of the most widespread instruments is the *txistu*, a three-holed flute (the word, rather distressingly, also means 'saliva', although we've stood near one, safe and dry). One was discovered among the Upper Palaeolithic finds at Istaritz cave, making it the oldest known musical instrument in the world. The *txistu* is usually played with one hand, while the other hand beats out the rhythm on a tambour. Rhythms can also be supplied by the *txalaparta*, a long wooden plank suspended across padded barrels and struck with sticks. Other ancient instruments are the *dultzaina*, a clarinet-like flute, and the *alboka*, a pipe made of straw, wood and horn. A more recent addition is the *trikitixa*, a small diatonic accordion. In Navarra, the archetypal instrument is the *gaïta*, a trumpet that plays an essential part in any fiesta.

Dozens of traditional dances are still current, and small groups in many villages keep them up; you'll have a chance to see them at any village fête – and especially in Guipúzcoa, where you can tour the villages on a Sunday morning and usually find at least one or two with traditional dances going on in the square. When they're in the mood, the Basques perform some of the most furiously athletic dances in the world, such as the *Bolant Dantza* ('flying dance'), the *Espata Dantza* ('sword dance') and the impossible *Godalet Dantza* ('goblet dance') of Soule, performed by four men in elaborate costumes, one wearing a large paper horse around his waist so he cannot see his own feet as he leaps on and off a glass of wine without spilling a drop. Many dances are descended from ancient war dances, pitting one set of dancers against another in choreographed battles using swords or poles. There are social dances as well, where men and women hold hands or each others' handkerchiefs in a circle, while the experts, the *dantzari*, do the fancy footwork in the centre.

In a different category altogether is the *irrintizina*, the uncanny yodel of the Basques, descended from shouts made by the worshippers of Mari (*see* above, pp.53–4) as they approached her mountain shrines. Basque linguist Larry Trask describes it as 'a ululation characterized by a rising pitch and concluded with a kind of demented laugh'. The shepherds later adopted the *irrintizina* to communicate across the mountains, and they still occasionally let a joyful one rip one when they're feeling good. Perhaps the best place to hear it is at Urcuray's *irrintizina* contest, generally held the first weekend in August, when both male and female *irrintzinari* compete for the prize.

Surviving the Pilgrimage to Santiago

Although the medieval Basques, who chased whales up to the Arctic Circle back in the 10th century, were never as insular as most people think, they laboured under the bad press they received (and this is a bit embarrassing) from a travel guide. A millennium before there were pilgrims to Bilbao's Guggenheim, pilgrims to Santiago tramped through the Basque country, and a French monk, writing a guide for them, slammed the Basques so hard that it took them centuries to recover, if they ever have, from the aspersions he cast.

What made it such a rotten deal is that the pilgrimage was cooked up by the French to begin with, without ever once asking the Basques if they wanted the equivalent of an international highway going through their lands, with all the riffraff of Europe piling through. The story was far-fetched from the beginning. Santiago, or James the Greater, the fisherman was one of the first disciples chosen by Jesus, who nicknamed him Boanerges, 'the son of thunder', after his booming voice. After the Crucifixion, he seems to have been a rather ineffectual proselytizer for the faith; in the year 44 Herod Agrippa in Caesarea beheaded him and threw his body to the dogs. End of story, or so it seemed for about 800 years, until Spain found him another task: nothing less than posthumously leading a 700-year-old crusade against the infidels.

All the evidence suggests that it was really the French who put him up to it: the first mention of the Apostle's relics in Spain appear in an 830 appendix to the *Martirologio de Florus*, written in 806 in Lyon. After the fright of 732, when the Arabs invaded as far as Poitiers, the French were ready to pull out all the stops to encourage their old Christian neighbours to rally and defeat the heathen, and a new history of James emerged. First, before his martyrdom he went to Zaragoza to convert the Spaniards and failed. Second, after his martyrdom two of his disciples piously gathered his remains and sailed off with them in a stone boat. The destination was remote Galicia, where the disciples buried Boanerges. In 814 a shower of shooting stars guided a hermit shepherd to the site of James' tomb at Compostela, 'the field of stars'. Another legend identifies Charlemagne (who died in 814) with the discovery of the relics: in the emperor's tomb at Aachen you can see the *Vision of Charlemagne*, with a scene of the Milky Way, the Via Lactea, a common name for the pilgrims' road.

In 844, not long after the discovery of the tomb, James was called into active duty at the Battle of Clavijo, appearing on a white horse to help Ramiro of Asturias defeat the Moors. This new role as Santiago Matamoros, the 'Moor-Slayer', was a great morale booster for the forces of the Reconquista, who made 'Santiago!' their battle cry. Ramiro was so pleased by his divine assistance that he made a pledge, the *voto de Santiago*, that ordained an annual property tax for St James' church at Compostela.

Never mind that the bones, the battle and the *voto* were as bogus as each other; the story struck deep spiritual, poetic and political chords that fitted in perfectly with the great cultural awakening of the 10th and 11th centuries. The medieval belief that a few holy bones or teeth could serve as a hotline to heaven made the discovery essential. After all, the Moors had some powerful juju of their own: an arm of the Prophet Muhammad in the Great Mosque of Córdoba. Another factor in the early 9th century was the Church's need for a focal point to assert its doctrinal control over the newborn kingdoms of Spain, especially over the Celts in Galicia and the very recently converted Basques. A third factor must have been the desire to reintegrate Spain into Europe – and what better way to do it than to increase human, commercial and cultural traffic over the Pyrenees? Pilgrimages to Jerusalem and Rome were already in vogue; after the long centuries of the Dark Ages, the Church was keen on re-establishing contacts across the old Roman empire it had inherited for Christianity.

The French were the great promoters of the road to Santiago, so great, in fact, that the most commonly tramped route through the pass at Roncesvalles became known as the *camino francés*. The first official pilgrim was Gotescalco, bishop of Le Puy, in 950. In the next century, the French monks of the reforming Abbey of Cluny did more than anyone to popularize the pilgrimage, setting up sister houses and hospitals along the way. Nor were the early kings in Spain slow to pick up on the commercial potential of the road; the great Basque king Sancho the Great of Navarra and Alfonso VI of Castile founded a number of religious houses and institutions along the way and invited French settlers to help run them. It was at this time, too, that the French stuck another oar in with their *Chanson de Roland*, which made Charlemagne something of a proto-pilgrim, although his adventure into Pamplona happened decades before the discovery of James' relics. The 12th century witnessed a veritable boom along the *camino francés*, and the arrival of new monastic and military orders, including the Templars, the Hospitallers and the Knights of Santiago, which all vowed to defend the pilgrim from dangers en route. The final bonus came in 1189, when Pope Alexander III declared Santiago de Compostela a Holy City on equal footing with Jerusalem and Rome, offering a plenary indulgence – a full remission from Purgatory – to pilgrims on Holy Years (the next will be 2004; other years only offer half-time off).

The Tour de Saint-Jacques in Paris was a traditional rallying point for groups of pilgrims (there was more safety in numbers); from there, the return journey was 800 miles and took a minimum of four months on foot. It was not something to go into lightly, but for many it was more than an act of faith; it was a chance to get out and see the world. Many who went were ill (hence the large number of hospitals), hoping to complete the pilgrimage before they died. Not a few were thieves, murderers and delinquents condemned by the judge to make the journey as punishment. Sometimes dangerous cons had to do it in chains. To keep them from cheating or stealing someone else's indulgence (the Compostellana certificate), pilgrims had to have their documents stamped by the clergy along the route, just as they do today.

In 1130 the Abbey of Cluny commissioned Aymery Picaud, a priest from Poitou, to write the *Codex Calixtinus*, the world's first travel guide, chock-full of prejudices and practical advice for pilgrims: he describes the four main roads through France and gives tips on where not to drink the water, where to find the best lodging and where to be on guard against 'false pilgrims' who come not to atone for crimes but to commit them. Aymery was also the first to write extensively about the Basques, and they come in for a sound thrashing, 'expert in all deeds of violence, fierce and savage, dishonest and false, imperious and rude, cruel and quarrelsome'. In fact, according to Aymery, they were the biggest menace on the road. The Basques serve bad food and overcharge at the inn; they are more than likely to ambush the unwary pilgrim (shades of Charlemagne's Rear Guard) and demand his clothes, money or even his life. 'A Basque or a Navarrese would kill a Frenchman for a copper,' warns the *Codex Calixtinus*. 'The Navarrese fornicate shamelessly with animals.' No one can ever know how much, if any of it, was true; perhaps one or two bad experiences or misunderstandings (needless to say, Aymery didn't speak Euskera) were enough for the monk to condemn the whole race as barbaric. An estimated half a million pilgrims a year made the trek in the Middle Ages (out of a European population of about 60 million). Thousands read the *Codex*, and it made such an impression that not long after it was written, the Church in France petitioned to have all Basques excommunicated as heretics. Basques today feel the same way when people who don't know any better stigmatize them all as terrorists.

The Sporting Life

The real national sport, of course, is smuggling, or it was until the EU took the fun out of it. But the Basques do love to play, and over the millennia they have evolved a number of outlandish games that are unique in the world. Many of these are based on pure brute strength, the celebrated *force basque* that is a major element of the national mystique. Even today, particularly strong, tall people are said to be descendents of the *jentillaks* (*see* above, p.52). One can imagine them, back in the mists of time, impressing each other by carrying around boulders – because that's what they do today, in a number of events generally called the *harri altxatzea*, literally 'stone-lifting'. In one, contestants see how many times they can lift a 500lb stone in 5 minutes; in others, they roll round boulders around their shoulders. Related to this is the *unlziketariak*, in which we see how fast a Basque can run with 100lb weights in each hand. They're fond of the tug-of-war (*sokatira*) too; they probably invented it.

Besides these, you will see them at village festivals pulling loaded wagons (or making teams of oxen do it), or lifting them (*orgo joko*), or racing with 200lb sacks of grain on their shoulders, or chopping huge tree trunks against the clock. Shepherds indulge in sheep fighting, or *aharitalka*. Don't fool with these people.

The miracle is that at the same time they could develop a sport like *pelota* (*pelote* in France), the fastest ball game in the world. Few sports can offer an image as beautiful and memorable as the *pelotari* in his traditional loose, pure-white costume, chasing down the ball with a long, curving *chistera*. *Pelota* takes a wide variety of forms, but the basic element is always the ball: a hard core, wrapped tightly with woollen string (which was replaced with rubber after its discovery in America) and covered with hide – like a baseball, only smaller and with much more bounce. In a serious match this ball can reach speeds of 150mph. The oldest form of the game is *rebot*, played bare-handed without a wall. Other versions soon evolved, played in an outdoor *fronton* (court) with a leather glove (*pasaka* or *joko garbi*), a raquet, or the *chistera*, a basket made of leather and osier, which enables a player to scoop up the ball and fling it back in the same motion. This last game is *cesta punta*, the fastest and most furious form of *pelota*. Thanks to Basque emigrants, this has become a popular sport around the Caribbean and Florida, where it is known as *jaï-alaï* (the 'festival game'), which curiously enough is a Basque expression not used in the Basque country (don't ask us why!). Whatever the game, it usually requires teams of two players each. The ground in front of the wall is marked off in *cuadros* every 13ft from it; to be in, a ball bounced off the wall must usually hit between the 4th and 7th *cuadros*, if it is not returned on the fly. Games are usually to 35 points.

Every Basque village has a *fronton* as its principal monument, usually right in the centre. On some village churches from as far back as the 17th century you can see how the architects left one smooth blank wall to accommodate the game. Besides the *fronton*, the game may be played in a covered court (*trinquet*). If you want to get in a little action yourself, you might try to talk your way into it at any village *fronton* when they're practising (they'd be charmed), or see p.100. As for getting in on the gambling aspect of *pelota* – go ahead and throw your money away if you want to. Each tourist office has schedules of matches; they're usually played at the same time every week.

The *zezenketa* or *encierro* (bull running), requires agility similar to that required for *pelota*. The Basques make no great claims to have invented the sport, although they may well have; they painted the beasts on their caves 15,000 years ago and were probably being chased by them even back then. The goddess Mari is guarded by a fierce red bull who lives in caves. Whatever the case, the Navarrese have perfected the sport, culminating in the greatest *zezenketa* of all, the Sanfermines at Pamplona (*see* pp.206–7). The casualties are almost always tourists. The *sokamutur*, on the other hand, offers many of the thrills but fewer chills; the bull is held by ropes attached to a ring in its nose, which allows its handlers to pull it back (in theory) if it looks as if someone is about to be seriously injured.

The Basques have their own very lively and exciting card game, too, called *mus*, with rules as inscrutable as Philadelphia pinochle (*see* opposite). In most *tabernas* you'll

The Rules of Mus

Along with fish soup and structural iron, one of the great contributions of the Basques to Spanish life is the popular card game of *mus*. Like most things Basque, it is a game that outsiders might find inscrutable, perhaps unfathomable. The most endearing feature is institutionalized cheating, which will occasionally cause the player to stick his tongue out at his partner, perhaps even twice.

Mus works best with four players in two partnerships, seated as in bridge, with a deck of Spanish cards (which has 40 cards in it). The suits are swords, staffs, cups and coins (which correspond respectively to spades, clubs, hearts and diamonds), and each suit consists of *Rey* (R), *Caballo* (C), *Sota* (S), 7, 6, 5, 4, 3, 2, ace. The *Rey* (king) is numbered 12 on the card, the *Caballo* (a knight on a horse; in this macho country there are no females in the deck) is numbered 11; the *Sota* (jack) is numbered 10. Note well that a 3 is the equal of a king and a 2 is the same as an ace (1). Don't ask why. You will also need 22 pebbles or beans, in a saucer in the centre of the table.

Mus is like poker, in that you do not play the cards, but hold them and make bets on their value. But while poker is a game for the avaricious and simple-minded, *mus* is not usually played for money. What's more, it offers all the complexity you could ask for and probably more; opportunities for creative bluffing are endless. You've got to bet on your hand four times, in four different ways.

Dealing

First, the dealer hands out four cards to each player, dealing backwards (to the right). All the betting goes backwards too, and always starts with the *mano*, the player to the right of the dealer. If you don't like your cards, you may have a chance to get rid of some or all of them, for the first thing that happens is the discard. Starting with the *mano*, each player in turn says either '*mus*' (call for new cards) or '*no hay mus*' (or for Basques, '*hasi*' or '*mintza*': 'start the game'). One '*no*' vote is an absolute veto, and the game begins immediately. Otherwise, all players can discard as many as they like after the fourth '*mus*', and the dealer replaces them in turn; then the *mano* says '*mus*' or '*no hay mus*', and so on. If everyone keeps saying '*mus*', you might conceivably go through the whole deck; if so, shuffle all the discards and keep going.

Cheating

This business of the *mus* is accompanied by the start of the cheating, which consists of a series of signals (*kenuak*) to let your partner know what you've got. The signals in accepted use are:

Biting your lower lip means you have two kings (doing this twice shows four kings).

Showing the tip of your tongue means you have two aces (twice for four aces).

Raising both eyebrows means you have *duples* (two pairs).

Twisting your mouth to one side means you have *medias* (three of a kind).

A wink means you have a Juego of 31, the best Juego you can get (see below). Closing (or lowering) both eyes (*ciego*) means you have a bum hand.

No other signals are permitted; that *would* be cheating. Of course you want to try and do it when your opponents aren't looking, at the same time peeking to catch their signals while pretending to look the other way, Shifty eyes are a definite advantage; another is keeping your opponents' glasses full at all times.

The Game

Now come the four stages of the game, in each of which there may or may not be betting (*see* below).

First is **Grande**, or Haundia, where the highest hand wins – the highest card, and in case of a tie, the next highest, and so on. Thus R-3-4-4 beats R-C-C-7 (remember a 3 is as good as a king).

Next comes the **Chica**, or Txikia, which is the like the Grande only backwards: the lowest hand wins (note that in the example given above the first hand wins this too, because the 4 is lower than the 7).

In the **Pares**, or Pareak, the best hand is the one with *duples* (*dobleak* in Basque) – two pairs of anything (in case of a tie the highest pair wins). Four of a kind counts simply as two pairs. If no one has *duples*, three of a kind wins (*medias*, or *mediak*), and again, the highest threesome rules. If no one has three of a kind, the highest *par simple* (or *parea*) is tops.

It gets trickier in the last stage, the **Juego**, or Jokoa. Here you need to learn another system of values for the cards. R, 3, C and S are worth 10 each; 7, 6, 5 and 4 are worth their face value, and ace and 2 count as 1. If your hand totals exactly 31 points (R-3-7-4, for example), then you have the best Juego. The next best is 32. Then come in descending order 40, 37, 36, 35, 34 and 33. Anything with 30 or under is no Juego at all (and 38 and 39 are impossible to get). If no one has a Juego, then you compete instead for the best **Punto**, or Puntuak, which is a hand totalling 30 or fewer points. The highest Punto is a hand with 30 points, then 29, 28 and so on, down to 4 (the lowest).

Betting

In each of the four stages there is a separate round of betting, though no one shows their cards until all four are completed. The betting is where the saucer and the 22 pebbles come in. In *mus*, you do not bet your own stake of money or counters, but simply the amount of points each stage will be worth. The pebbles are used for keeping score. A round of betting starts with the *mano*, who may pass (*paso*), or bet (*envido*, or *enbido*) an amount of 2 or more. If all four players pass the chance to bet, the betting is over and the stake for that stage is one.

After a bet is made the opposing team may fold (*no quiero*, or *tira*), see (*quiero*, or *edoki*) or raise (*reenvido*, or *beste hiru*) any amount. To do this, either player may speak – the two might disagree, in which case one partner can overrule the other by saying 'we fold' or 'we see' ('*no queremos*' or '*queremos*'). Then, if the bet has been raised the other team must answer. When one side folds, the other wins the previous amount staked (not the raise that caused the fold). When one side sees, the betting is done, though settling the bet is put off until the end of the game when the cards are revealed.

In the Pares, before the betting each player in turn must say whether or not he has at least a pair (say just '*si*' or '*no*'). If neither side has a player who does, there is no betting and no score. If only one side does, they score one. If both sides do, there is a round of betting. Before the Juego, each player must say whether or not he has a Juego (31 points or more). Then, as in the Pares, if both sides have one there is a round of betting. If there is no betting in the Pares, the best Pares scores 3 points for *duples*, 2 for *medias*, and 1 for a *par simple* from both hands (if there is betting, at the end of the game these points are scored in addition to any bets). If there is no betting on the Juego, the winning side scores 3 points for a Juego of 31, 2 for any other Juego, or 1 for any Punto; as in the Pares the winning side scores these points from both hands, in addition to any betting.

There is a special bet called **Hordago** that any player may make at any time in the four stages (when it's his or her turn). *Hor dago* means 'here it is' in Basque, and it's an immediate showdown, a bet to stake the whole game on whatever stage it is in at the moment. If the opponents fold, they concede that stage at whatever level the betting has reached (1 point only if no previous bets were made). If they see it, the cards are shown and the best hand wins the game.

Note that in any of the four stages there can be ties – hands of absolutely equal value (for example, in the Pares, if both sides have pairs of the same rank). If this happens, the *mano*, or the player closest to him on the right, wins.

Scoring

A game of *mus* is 40 points, and this usually requires several hands. The deal alternates, naturally, since being the *mano* is such a big advantage. The play of *mus* is really more simple and straightforward than it looks, once you get the hang of it, but the method of keeping score is something that could only have been dreamt up by Basques. Remember the 22 pebbles? Instead of using them like poker chips, they are simply markers to keep score. One member of the partnership keeps 'ones' (*piedras*) and the other keeps 'fives' (*amarracos*, or *hammarekos* in Basque). So if a team has 4 points, the keeper of *piedras* will have four pebbles taken from the dish in front of him. If they then score 3 more, he will give one to his partner, where it becomes a *hammareko*, keep two and put one back in the dish. You'll never need more than 22 of them – if both sides are on the threshold of winning at 39 points, each will have seven *hamarrekos* (35 points) and four *piedras*.

Scoring after a hand is always done in precise order of the stages, because the first side to hit 40 wins, even if their opponents racked up big scores in later stages that would have beaten them.

find a game going, especially at weekends. There are any number of variations on the rules – with only four kings and four aces in Navarre, or with '10 kings' in Eibar (Guipúzcoa), or the Juego Real. If you want to have a go, the following rules should be enough to get started. More details are available on *www.pagat.com/vying/mus.html* and *www.Buber.net/Basque/Sports/mus.html*, and while you are getting in shape for the big national *mus* tournament held each year by the national association, NABO, you can even play *mus* over the Internet at Cybermus, *www.cybermus.com*.

Food and Drink

05

Nomansland, the territory of the Basques, in a region called Cornucopia, where the vines are tried up with sausages. And in those parts there was a mountain made entirely of grated parmesan cheese on whose slopes there were people who spent their whole times making macaroni and ravioli.

Boccaccio, *The Decameron,* VIII

Boccaccio may have got the recipes all wrong, but even in the 14th century his antennae caught culinary signals emanating from the Basques. By popular acclaim they are the champion cooks of Spain, and they come out fairly well in the gourmet stakes in France, too. It is one of their great sorrows, however, that the Basque country isn't quite the cornucopia of the Florentine's imagination. There were mountains made of iron, but not of parmesan. In the steep hill country, arable land is rare.

Basque cuisine is not elaborate but based on high-quality ingredients from the sea or small Basque farms. Much of its theory lies in the timing, in *el punto,* knowing during preparation precisely when a dish has achieved perfection. Although the ingredients are often few in number, the knack can be maddeningly elusive, as anyone who has tried to prepare *bacalao pil-pil* at home can attest. Sauces are simple, too, and come in two basic hues: gastronomes say forget all that mumbo jumbo about the green of their hills and the blood of their warriors, the colours of the Basque flag represent green sauce and red sauce.

One peculiarly Basque institution are those freemasons of food, the *txokos,* exclusively male gastronomic clubs formed in the middle of the 19th century 'to eat and sing'. San Sebastián alone has 75 of them; to join one must be sponsored by at least two members, and the waiting lists are long. They take turns cooking lavish meals for each other, although according to their wives they would never touch a saucepan at home. A few *txokos* allow women in to eat, but they are never allowed to cook.

Traditional Basque Cuisine

Not surprisingly, Basque cooks exert most of their talent on seafood, the one thing the region has always had in abundance. They have had plenty of practice – a 12,000-year-old painting of sea bream decorates the walls of one ancient cave and remains of sea urchins have been found in settlements 10,000 years old. The bounty of the sea finds expression in famous fish soups and stews, and there are any number of prized delicacies – surprising things like *cocochas,* 'cheeks' of the hake or spider crab.

Marseille has its *bouillabaisse,* among a score of other treasured fish soups of southern Europe, but the French Basques stoutly maintain that their version, called *ttoro* (pronounced 'tioro'), is the king of them all. Naturally, as in Marseille, there is a solemn confraternity of the finest *ttoro* chefs dedicated to maintaining standards, although there are as many variations of *ttoro* as there are cooks. A proper one requires a pound of mussels and a mess of crayfish and congers, as well as three different kinds of other fish. The dish was invented by fishermen of St-Jean-de-Luz and the other small ports at the mouth of the Nivelle river, and it's there that you'll find the best versions. St-Jean de-Luz holds a *ttoro* festival with a competition and *dégustation* in early September; this may be your last chance on the coast to try it as *ttoro* runs out of popularity west of here.

Tuna, bonito (a more streamlined, bullet-shaped tuna) and cod are caught on the high seas. *Thon basquaise* is fresh tuna cooked with tomatoes, garlic, aubergine and spices; bonito goes into a popular fisherman's stew called *marmitako*, cooked with potatoes, tomatoes, garlic and a red pepper. Salt cod, once a cheap staple and increasingly a rare delicacy, achieves a kind of epiphany in *bacalao pil-pil* (originally named for the sound it made while frying), where somehow olive oil, garlic and chillies magically meld with the cooking juices of salt cod to form a sauce with the consistency of a soft mayonnaise. There are at least a dozen other Basque recipes for *bacalao*, including *a la bizkaina*, with a red sauce of tomatoes, onions and roasted bell peppers, and crumbled and baked with potatoes or bread in a *zurrukutuna* (wood-oven) that gives the dish its name. You can even find it stuffed in red peppers. Another variation is *ajorriero*, a succulent dish prepared with cod, tomatoes, and green peppers.

Other favourites from the sea are scallops, big eels (served with parsley and garlic) and the unusual *chipirones* or *txipirones* (cuttlefish served stuffed or in a casserole in their own ink) – reputedly the only dish in the world that's all black, and better than it sounds. Basques also have an insatiable passion for tiny worm like elvers (known as *angulas, pibales, civelles* or *txitxardin*) that arrive in January on the Basque coast straight from the Sargasso Sea, only to be drawn by the lights of night fishermen and tossed in the hot oil of a frying pan with a garlic and chilli pepper sauce. The fact that they are increasingly rare is a cause for great dismay and quests for substitutes; if your bowl of *angulas* doesn't cost a kingly sum, you can bet they're not the real McCoy. Another Basque classic is *txangurro* – spider crab, which is flaked, seasoned, stuffed and served in its own shell; order it with a side dish of *kiskillas* (prawns), *nécoras* (small crabs) or *txirlas* (baby white clams). In summer, the ports have tempting stands of fresh roast sardines. Gourmets particularly recommend hake, a delicate white fish, in green sauce (*hake koskera*) or *kokotxas a la Donostiarra*, hake cheeks with a garlic and parsley green sauce, clams and slightly piquant red Basque peppers. Or with cider, *a la ondarresa*. The important thing is that the hake in question has to be a large (and expensive) one, weighing at least 7lbs.

In a country of shepherds, lamb grazed in mountain pastures is, not surprisingly, the favourite meat, especially lamb chops, sweetbreads and roast leg of lamb. In land-locked Navarra, look for *chuletas de cordero a la navarra* (lamb chops), *chilindron* (lamb cooked in a sauce), *truchas con jamón* (trout stuffed with ham), *estofado de toro* (beef stew, especially after a *corrida*) or, for something out of the ordinary, *liebres con chocolate* (hare with chocolate), washed down by the strong wines from Tudela and Estella. The Basques are also known for their charcuterie, such as *tripotcha*, a kind of pudding made from sheep's tripe, *pâté basque*, spicy *chorizo* sausage (try it with a *talo*, a cornmeal pancake, a mainstay in the countryside in the 17th century) and *loukinkos* (also spelled *lukenques*), little garlic sausages. The famous Bayonne ham is hung for over a year; it has a strict set of rules and an *appellation contrôlée* status like fine wines. In the north, you'll also find the archetypal delights of southwest France: duck and goose *confits*, *maigrets* and foie gras. Other meaty staples include *txistorra*, a long, thin, spicy red sausage which is normally eaten fried in small chunks, and *morcilla*, a pungent black pudding. For a special treat, tuck into a *chuleton*, a great slab of t-bone steak grilled over charcoal, at a local *asador*.

Red peppers, notably the *piments d'Espelette* (*pimientos del piquillo* in Spain) that pack a bit of heat, are another icon of the Basque kitchen; Basque housewives still hang strings of them on the walls of their houses for drying (and for decoration). The season for fresh ones is short, from September to November. They go into spicy sausages, or into *piperade*, a kind of ratatouille made from roast red peppers, green peppers, tomatoes, garlic and whipped eggs, lightly fried and served with *jambon de Bayonne*. Milder peppers turn up everywhere: in omelettes, or in *poulet basquaise*, a free-range corn-fed chicken stewed in a pot with peppers, onions and tomatoes. In Alava, chard leaves are stuffed with ham and cheese and fried in batter, and the wide variety of vegetables from the plains gets mixed up into *menestra*. Everywhere in winter you'll find *purrusalda,* a hearty leek and potato soup. In Bilbao they make a sweetish spinach pie, and the bunches of sweet, plump asparagus piled up at the markets throughout the Basque country are famous throughout Spain.

The Basques, like their Spanish and Gascon neighbours, are also partial to beans, which were a mainstay at the table for centuries. A winter favourite, *cocido*, is a thick bean stew flavoured with a ham bone and miscellaneous pork parts; in Labourd, where it's called *eltzekari*, the beans are flavoured with duck fat, making it a bit like cassoulet. One classic is *habas a la vitoriana*, the broad beans of Vitoria, although the Basques swear the best by test is a hearty mess of *alubias de Tolosa* served with cabbage and chunks of cured sausage like *chorizo* or *morcilla*, and sometimes pickled green *guindilla* peppers. And *après* beans? The Basque cure for indigestion is curded milk (*mamia* or *cuajada*).

Other treats made the old-fashioned way include pure sheep's milk cheese. On the Spanish side it's called Idiazabal, DO since 1988, a strong cheese with bite made only from the milk of *latxa* ewes, a special Basque race of sheep; it's delicious with grapes or slices of quince or a handful of plump walnuts. To the north, the best known Basque cheeses are Etorki and Kerkou, sold everywhere in France. There's also the AOC Iraty-Ossau. Some of the real mountain cheeses pack a wallop.

The Basques in the south often end things fairly simply with cheese or maybe an apple, but you may be able to finish a meal in grand style with a *pantxineta*, an almondy *gâteau basque* filled with cream or cherry jam (made from special Basque cherries, from Itxassou). In Bilbao, try the *canutillos*, rolls of flaky pastry stuffed with custard, or the sweeter version in the south of Alava, *hojaldres a la crema*. Around Pamplona, sweet-tooths shouldn't miss the *crema frita de almendras,* a quickly fried ball of almond dough. Otherwise, desserts, even in the smartest restaurants, are often quite restrained in the Spanish Basque lands: tarts piled with fresh fruits are a summer favourite, and bitter-sweet lemon tarts do the rounds in spring. Bayonne is a different story, with chocolate gateaux, mousses, ice creams and, the ultimate treat, the *pavé de chocolat*, a dense, rich truffle cake.

New Basque Cuisine

Franco's regime has been compared to stale white bread, and in 1976 it had scarcely come to an end when two Basque chefs, Juan Mari Arzac and Pedro Subijana, attended a course run by *nouvelle cuisine* pied piper Paul Bocuse. At the time Basque cooking was suffering from a certain malaise and boredom, and while the old recipes still held sway, they had begun to seem lacklustre; restaurants kept their clients with quantity rather than quality. A dose of Bocuse was enough to send the chefs off on their own path of *cocina nueva vasca* to transform the age-old Basque ingredients into new and exciting dishes such as *ensalada de angulas* (baby eel salad), *lubina a la pimienta verde* (sea bass with green pepper), *crepes de txangurro* (spider crab crêpes), and (on the French side) *petits piments rouges farcis a la morue sauce brune* (baby red peppers stuffed with cod in a brown wine sauce), and *brochette de langoustines au sesame*. New Basque cuisine also makes good use of wild mushrooms. Alava province is the best place to go for these, particularly for the exquisite and very delicate spring mushroom, *perretxiku* (*lyophylum georgii*), served lightly cooked with eggs. Truffles are found in Alava, too, around Campezo, and modern Basque chefs are not having too much trouble inventing new dishes to put them in.

Nowadays, chefs like Arzak, Irizar, Subijana and Pildain, leading figures of the revolution in Basque cuisine, are household names throughout Spain, and the mere mention of their celebrated restaurants can bring a longing gasp to the lips of admirers. A new generation – Martín Berasategui, Hilario Arbelaitz, Ramón Roteta and José Juan Castillo, as well as bright new stars like Koldo Lasa and Alberto Elorza – has sprung up under their tutelage, and Karlos Arguiñano has even got his own hugely popular TV show. Today, even the old recipes in the hands of the new Basque maestros are no longer stuck-in-the-mud reruns, but personalized culinary variations on a theme, prepared with centuries of savvy, and always *el punto*.

Washing it Down: Wine, Sidra and Other Nice Things

Biba Rioja, Biba Nafarroa Haren famaren izarra
Hemen guziak aneiak gira Hustu dezagun Pitxarra
Glugluglu glu glugluglu glu glugluglu glugluglu glugluglu
Glu glugluglu glu glugluglu gluglu glu glugluglu gluglugluglulglu glu.

popular Basque drinking song

With its gentle climate, the Basque region has been making wine at least since Roman times. On the French side, the best known are the soft AOC reds and rosés of Irouléguy from the Pyrenean foothills (*see* p.271), good with chicken dishes and grilled or roast lamb. The most distinct Basque vintage is a tangy young 'green' wine called *txakoli* (in 1994 made a DO, or *denominación de origen*, the Spanish equivalent of AOC), which is poured into the glass with bravura from a height. There are red and rosé versions, but the *gree* (white) is by far the most common. *Txakoli* was made according to old family recipes which were passed down from generation to generation, but the tradition had almost died out by the mid-19th century. Technological improvements have meant that it is once again everyone's favourite tipple, an emblematic, entirely Basque accompaniment to *pintxos* (*see* pp.72–3). It is made along the coast with just a modicum of sunlight around Getaria and Zarautz, as well as in small areas in Vizcaya and Alava provinces, and is especially good with seafood.

Navarra grows its own DO Navarra, mostly reds using traditional grapes such as tempranillo and garnache, although other varieties – merlot and cabernet sauvignon – are becoming increasingly popular. The rosés are renowned for their quality, and the rosé of Olite is especially good. An extraordinary percentage of it never gets beyond Pamplona, in the week of the Sanfermines. The Navarrese also have a grand tradition of mellow Muscatel dessert wines.

Then there's Rioja, the best-known wine region in Spain, famous for its soft, warm, mellow, full-bodied reds, with a distinct vanilla bouquet. The Cathaginians, it seems, introduced the first vines, which after the various invasions were replanted by the Church; the first law concerning wine was decreed by Bishop Abilio in the 9th century. The arrival of masses of thirsty pilgrims in the Middle Ages proved a boon to business, much as mass tourism would do in the 1960s and 70s.

Despite a long pedigree, the Rioja we drink today dates from the 1860s, when growers from Bordeaux, their own vineyards wiped out by phylloxera, brought their techniques south of the border and wrought immense improvements on the native varieties. By the time the plague reached La Rioja in 1899, the owners were prepared for it with disease-resistant stock. During the First World War, when the vineyards of the Champagne were badly damaged, the French returned to buy up *bodegas*, sticking French labels on the bottles and trucking them over the Pyrenees. Rioja finally received the respect it deserved after Franco. On the bad side, prices have skyrocketed as the *bodegas* have attracted investors from around the world.

Rioja's growing area covers 48,000 hectares, comprising three zones: Rioja Alta, in La Rioja proper, home of the best red and white wines; this is followed by the pride of the Basques, Rioja Alavesa (on the left bank of the Ebro), known for its lighter, perfumed wines. The decidedly more arid Rioja Baja, east of Logroño, is in Navarra, where the wines are coarse and mostly used for blending – a common practice in La Rioja. The varieties used for the reds are mostly the spicy, fruity tempranillo, followed by garnacha tinta (a third of the red production and a good alcohol booster), with smaller portions of graciano (for the bouquet) and high-tannin mazuelo (for acidity and tone). Traditional Rioja whites are relatively unknown but are excellent, golden and as vanilla-scented as the reds: viura is the dominant grape, with smaller doses of malvasia and garnacha blanca.

Unlike French wines, Riojas are never sold until they're ready to drink (although of course you can keep the better wines even longer). DO rules specify that La Rioja's Gran Reserva, which accounts for only 3 per cent of the production, spends a minimum of two years maturing in American oak barrels (six months for whites and rosés), then four more in the *bodega* before being sold. Reservas (6 per cent of the production) spend at least one year in oak and three in the *bodega*. Crianzas (30 per cent of the production) spend at least a year in the barrel and another in the bottle. The other 61 per cent of Rioja is *sin crianza* and labelled CVC (*conjunto de varias cosechas*, combination of various vintages): this includes the new young white wines and rosés (*claretes*) fermented at cool temperatures in stainless steel vats, skipping the oak barrels altogether and losing most of the vanilla tones.

Besides wine, Basques make good hard cider (*sidra* or *sagardo*) in an enclave in Guipúzcoa. The story goes that paradise was located in the Basque country (it's now gone underground) and that when the first Basques, Adam and Eve, were given their walking papers, Adam was so furious that he hurled the rest of the apples he had picked into a hole, and for good measure ground them up with stones so he would never have to see them again. A few days later, Eve was thirsty and found a fermented juice that resembled liquid gold. The Basques then (they say) passed the secret knowledge on to the Vikings, who went on to become the more famous cider makers of Normandy. Back in the 16th century Basque fishermen used to trade the stuff to the American Indians for furs. *Sidra*, like *txakoli*, has to be poured from a great height, and is best drunk in February.

Anís (anisette, sweet or dry) is also quite popular; mixed with cognac it becomes a *sol y sombra* (which, however, isn't as vile as a *kalimotxo*, red wine mixed with Coke, the crazy juice favoured by the bull runners in Pamplona). Look for Bayonne's famous Izarra, a potent mix of Pyrenean herbs with exotic spices, based on Armagnac, which comes in either green or the less potent yellow. For something more unusual, you can top off your meal with a *carajillo* (coffee with cognac or rum flambé), *manzana* (a liqueur made from apples), or a tipple of Basque hooch, *patxaran* or *pacharán*, made from sloes grown around Pamplona and soaked in *anís*.

Practicalities

Learning to Eat Like a Basque

Jan-edanaren gozoa! Kontu-emanaren gaiztoa!
('How sweet it is to eat and drink! How terrible to have to pay the bill!')
old Basque saying

The essential fact is that Basques like to eat *all day long* – this scheme spreads the gratification evenly throughout the waking hours. Give it some consideration (only the quantities will probably kill you). Go into a village restaurant at 9 in the morning on a market day, and just watch the boys tuck into their three-course breakfasts – soup, tons of meat, fish and potatoes, with a gallon or so of wine for each. If you're planning to spend an afternoon running around with boulders or some other Basque sport, join them. Otherwise, start out with a big coffee and a pastry, or find a progressive-looking bar (usually called a *taberna*, but you may also see *ardangehi*, 'wine place'), where you might find a more fitting breakfast – a glass of wine or brandy, and a salami sandwich or a glazed doughnut. These will be around all day, the piles of treats under the glass cases growing by the hour. They peak mid-morning, when Basques stop off for their *hamaiketako* ('elevenses', literally). Lunch at 2 or so is fairly substantial, followed at around 5pm by a late-afternoon snack, or *merienda*. Then come apéritifs on the run (*see* 'Bar Life and the *Txikiteo*', below), which help work up an appetite for dinner at 10; this is usually the main meal of the day, taking an hour or two to eat with all its courses, wine and coffee (at the end of the meal, ask for a *completo* – coffee, cognac and a cigar). And more drinks (*kopas*).

At the upmarket end of the scale you'll find plenty of new restaurants serving New Basque cuisine, but there are still plenty of old-fashioned restaurants around – along with many of the sort that travellers have been complaining about for centuries. The worst offenders are often the *cafeterías*, those flag-bedecked places that feature photographs of their *platos combinados* ('combination plates') to eliminate any language problem in the most touristy areas, and in general you'd do better to buy some bread, cheese and a bottle of Rioja red and have a picnic.

In any coastal town or village, the best seafood restaurants sit around the harbour. The fancier ones will post set menus, while at the rest a chalkboard lists the prices for grilled fish or prawns or whatever else came in that day; just choose a dish, or negotiate a full dinner with the waiter. Don't expect seafood to be a bargain, though; a plate of prawns in garlic all by itself usually goes for about 1,000–1,200 pts/€6–7.5. Places called *marisquerías* serve only fish and shellfish. Don't neglect the rapidly disappearing shacks on the beach – they often serve up baked sardines that are out of this world.

Away from the sea, you'll find *asadores* that specialize in roast or grilled meat, and *sidrerías* (or *sagardotegiak*) that specialize in cider and serve simple dishes such as cod omelettes, pork chops and fried potatoes, all accompanied by as much *sidra* as you can drink. The season is between 21 January and Easter, when the *sidra* is in wooden barrels (once it's bottled it's not as good). Expect to be splashed – rather than the *sidra* being poured from a jug, the big wooden barrel is unbunged, the cider gushes out in a stream and everyone queues up to fill their glass. Don't bother dressing up, and do wear sturdy shoes. Both *asadores* and *sidrerías* are often packed out with families at weekends, when it's a good idea to book.

If you dine where the locals do you'll be assured of a good deal, if not necessarily a good meal. Almost every restaurant offers a *menú del día/menu du jour* or a *menú turístico/menu touristique* featuring a starter, a main course, dessert, bread and drink at a set price, always lower than if you had ordered the items à la carte. These menus are always posted outside the restaurant, in the window or on the plywood chef by the door; decide what you want before going in, because these bargains are hardly ever listed on the menu the waiter gives you at the table. In Spain, unless it's explicitly written on the bill (*la cuenta*), service is *not* included in the total, so tip accordingly. In France, service is generally included on the *addition*; if not, it will say s.n.c. or *service non compris*.

The Basque country is celebrated for its *pintxos* or *pinchos* (Basque *tapas*), little morsels served on a slice of bread or with a toothpick, which have evolved into one of the world's great snack cultures. Bars that specialize in them offer platter after platter of delectable titbits, from shellfish to slices of omelette, mushrooms baked in garlic, vegetables in vinaigrette and stews. All you have to do is pick out what looks good and order a *porción* (two or three bites), or a *ración* (a big helping) if it looks really good. It's hard to generalize about prices, but on average 1,200 pts/€7.5 of *tapas* and wine or beer can fill you up. You can always save money in bars by standing up; sit at that charming table on the terrace and prices jump considerably. The hard part comes when trying to remember what you've had (if you ever knew the name in the first place) when the time comes to settle up, as drinks and *pintxos* are on the honour system and you only pay as you leave.

Another advantage of *pintxos* is that they're available at what most Americans or Britons would consider normal dining hours. If you stay for a few months, late dining makes perfect sense, but it's exasperating to the average visitor whose stomach growls at a much earlier hour. On the coasts, restaurants tend to open earlier to accommodate foreigners, but you may as well do as the Basques do – if you can find a restaurant at all. In non-touristy areas they will be inconspicuous. If you ask around, however, you should find a nice *comedor* (dining room) with home-cooked meals for around 1,200–1,500 pts/€7–9 tucked behind a bar – if you hadn't asked you never would have found it. You'll find as many good ones as real stinkers, where the food and décor are equally drab.

Vegetarians are catered for in the cities, which always manage to come up with one or two veggie restaurants, usually rather good ones too. In the countryside and away from the main resorts, proper vegetarians and vegans will find it hard going, though *tapas* make it easier to get your nutrition than in some other southern European countries.

In France, you can also find *pintxos*, although the cult isn't as engrained as it is further south, perhaps because people tend to dine earlier, getting in the door by 8.30pm. Along the Côte Basque you'll find as many, if not more, French restaurants as Basque. Don't overlook hotel restaurants, some of which are absolutely top notch, even if a certain red book refuses on some obscure principle to give them their full quota of stars. To avoid disappointment, call ahead in the morning to reserve a table, especially in the summer. In French restaurants, if you order a *rouge, blanc* or *rosé*, you'll usually get a decent *vin de pays*, by the glass (*un verre*), the quarter-litre (*un pichet*) or the bottle (*une bouteille*). Don't neglect the wines with less-exalted labels, especially those labelled VDQS (*vin de qualité supérieure*). *Vin ordinaire* (or *vin de table*), at the bottom end, may not send you to seventh heaven, but is usually drinkable and cheap. Think twice before you order champagne (or *cava* in Spain) if you have any opinion whatsoever of age-old Basque wisdom, which warns *Ez ardo bizidunik, ez andre bizardunik* ('Beware of sparkling wine and bearded women').

Bar Life and the *Txikiteo*

It has been suggested that just as geneticists study Basque DNA and linguists bruise their brains trying to find a cousin to the Basque language, anthropologists should study the basic form of Basque socializing. This is the *txikiteo*, where bands of friends (a *koadrila*) gather before dinner and lunch from bar to bar, staying just as long in each as it takes to drink a glass of wine or a *zurito* (a tiny glass of beer, or a bigger *cana* for quick chug-a-luggers) and devour a *pintxo* or two. Speed and noise are of the essence: one should never linger more than 15 minutes in a single spot; everyone should talk as loudly as possible, mostly about the fortunes of the Bilbao or San Sebastián football teams, usually while smoking as furiously as an old Bilbao chimney; and it's anathema to address the opposite sex, even members of one's *koadrila*. After a hard day at work, this is what the Basques do to relax.

At least the drink is cheap. No matter how much other costs have risen in Spain, wine has remained refreshingly inexpensive by northern European or American standards. A restaurant's *vino del lugar* or *vino de la casa* is always your least expensive option when dining out; it usually comes out of a barrel or glass jug and may be a surprise either way. In bars, the one question is *tinto* (red) or *blanco* (white)?

Many Basques prefer beer, which is generally nondescript. The most popular brand is San Miguel, but try Mahou Five Star if you see it. Imported whisky and other spirits are pretty inexpensive, although even cheaper are the versions Spain bottles itself, which may come close to your home favourites. Coffee, tea, all the international soft-drink brands and the locally-made *Kas* round off the average café fare. Spanish coffee is good and strong; if you want a lot of it order a *doble* in a *vaso*.

On the French side, you can get all the old standbys in a café or bar. Prices are listed on the Tarif des Consommations: note that they go up depending whether you're served at the bar (*comptoir*), at a table (*la salle*) or outside (*la terrasse*). If you order *un café* you'll get a small black espresso; if you want milk, order *un crème*. If you want more than a few drops of caffeine, ask them to make it *grand*. For decaffeinated, the word is *déca*. The French only order *café au lait* (a small coffee topped off with lots of hot milk) when they stop in for breakfast, and if what your hotel offers is expensive or boring, consider joining the bar crowd. *Chocolat chaud* (hot chocolate) is usually good; Bayonne is famous for it. If you order *thé* (tea), you'll get an ordinary bag. An *infusion* is a herbal tea – *camomille, menthe* (mint), *tilleul* (lime or linden blossom), or *verveine* (verbena). These are kind to the all-precious *foie*, or liver.

Mineral water (*eau minérale*) can be addictive, and comes either sparkling (*gazeuse* or *pétillante*) or still (*non-gazeuse* or *plate*). If you feel run down, Badoit has lots of peppy magnesium in it. Some bars also do fresh lemon and orange juices (*citron* or *orange pressé*). Then there are the fruit syrups – red grenadine and ghastly green diabolo *menthe*.

Beer (*bière*) in most bars and cafés is run-of-the-mill big brands from Alsace, Germany and Belgium. Draft (*à la pression*) is cheaper than bottled beer. Red and white wine round out the usual fare. Nearly all resorts have bars or pubs offering wider selections of draughts, lagers and bottles; some even do cocktails, although the prices can be a kick in the pants.

For a Spanish and French menu decoder, see pp.288–94. For general information on eating out and prices, see 'Eating Out', p.89.

Travel

06

Getting There

By Air

There is an astounding variety of flight options to Spain and France these days, especially from the UK. A high-season return costs from around £80 on a no-frills carrier to around £200 on a national airline. However, even the national carriers **Air France** and **Iberia** offer special deals. Discounts are also available for domestic flights and for children under the age of 12. No matter how you go, you can always save by travelling off-season (15 September–early June) and booking in advance (APEX).

There are international airports in Bilbao and Biarritz, and smaller airports that receive internal flights in San Sebastián, Pamplona and Fuenterrabía.

Air France flies to Biarritz from Paris Orly daily.

British Airways flies to Bilbao from London Heathrow twice daily.

Go flies to Bilbao from London Stansted daily.

Iberia flies direct to Bilbao from London Heathrow daily, and to Bilbao via Barcelona from Manchester. There are also flights via Madrid and Barcelona to San Sebastián, Pamplona and Vitoria.

Ryanair has daily no-frills cheap flights to Biarritz from London Stansted.

Charter flights, which are often much cheaper than scheduled flights (roughly £100 for a high-season return to Bilbao), can be booked through travel agents such as those shown in the grey box below.

There are no direct flights to Bilbao or other airports in the Basque region from the USA and Canada, but numerous carriers fly direct to Madrid, Barcelona and Paris, and Delta has flights to Toulouse. A high-season return will cost around US$1,100–2,000.

Alternatively, it may be cheaper to fly to London and pick up an onward flight to Spain from there, especially off-season.

Charters from New York cost around $400–800, depending on the season.

Airline Carriers

UK
Air France, t 0845 0845 111,
www.airfrance.co.uk
British Airways, t 0345 222 111,
www.britishairways.co.uk
Go, t 0845 60 54321, *www.go-fly.com*
Iberia, t (020) 7830 0011, *www.iberia.com*
Ryanair, t 08701 569 569,
www.ryanair.com

USA and Canada
Air Canada, t 888 247 2262,
www.aircanada.ca
American Airlines, t 800 433 7300,
www.im.aa.com
British Airways, t 800 247 9297,
www.britishairways.com
Continental Airlines, t 800 231 0856,
www.continental.com
Delta, t 800 241 4141, *www.delta.com*
Iberia, t 800 772 4642, *www.iberia.com*
United Airlines, t 800 538 2929,
www.ual.com

Charters, Discounts and Special Deals

UK and Ireland
Budget Travel, 134 Lower Baggot St, Dublin 2, t (01) 661 1866
Trailfinders, 194 Kensington High St, London W8 7RG, t (020) 7937 1234,
www.trailfinders.co.uk
Travel Cuts, 295A Regent St, London W1R 7YA, t (020) 7255 1944
United Travel, Stillorgan Bowl, Stillorgan, County Dublin, t (01) 288 4346/7
www.cheapflights.co.uk
www.lastminute.com

USA and Canada
Air Brokers International USA t 800 883 3273,
www.airbrokers.com
Last Minute Travel Club USA t 800 527 8646, Canada t 877 970 3500, *www.lastminute club.com*. Payment of an annual membership fee gets you cheap standby deals; there are also special rates for the major car rental companies in Europe, and for train tickets.

By Train

Travelling by high-speed train is an attractive alternative to flying from the UK. **Eurostar** trains, t 0990 186 186, depart from London Waterloo, with direct connections to Paris (Gare du Nord; 3hrs) and Lille (2hrs). Fares are cheaper if booked at least seven days in advance and you include a Saturday night away. You must check in at least 20 minutes before departure, or you will not be allowed on to the train. Prices range from around £70 (if booked more than two weeks in advance) to £300 for a standard return.

France's high-speed **TGVs** (*trains à grande vitesse*) shoot along at an average of 180mph, when they're not breaking world records. TGVs from Paris go to Bayonne (4½hrs) and Biarritz (5hrs). Fares are only minimally higher than on slower trains; some weekday departures require a supplement and all require seat reservations, which you can make when you buy your ticket or at the station before departure.

People aged under 26 are eligible for a 30% **discount** on fares (*see* the student travel agencies listed in the box below) and there are other discounts if you're aged over 65, available from major travel agents.

From London to Bilbao or San Sebastián it's a full day's trip, changing trains in Paris and usually at Bordeaux or Hendaye in the small hours of the morning. The TGV service from Paris to Bordeaux can cut some hours off the trip if the schedule works right for you. Time can also be saved by taking the Eurostar to Paris.

If you plan to take some long train journeys, it may be worth investing in a rail pass. The excellent-value **Euro Domino** pass entitles EU citizens to unlimited rail travel through France for three to eight days in a month for £99–£198, or £79–£159 for 12–25-year-olds.

There's also the **Inter-Rail** pass (for European residents of at least six months), which offers 22 days' unlimited travel in Europe (countries are grouped into zones), plus discounts on trains to cross-Channel ferry terminals and

---

New Frontiers USA t 800 677 0720; Canada, Montréal t (514) 871 3060; *www.newfrontiers.com*

Spanish Heritage Tours, 116–47 Queens Bd, Forest Hills, NY 11375, t (718) 520 1300, *www.shtours.com*

Travel Avenue USA t 800 333 3335, *www.travelavenue.com*

www.traveldiscounts.com. Members get special rates on flights, hotels and tours.

Student Discounts

Students and those aged under 26 are eligible for considerable reductions on flights, train fares, admission fees to museums, concerts and more. Agencies specializing in student and youth travel can help you apply for the correct ID cards, as well as filling you in on the best deals.

Council Travel, 205 E 42nd St, New York, NY 10017, t (212) 822 2700. Specialist in student and charter flights; branches across the USA.

Europe Student Travel, 6 Campden St, London W8, t (020) 7727 764

STA Travel, 86 Old Brompton Rd, London SW7 3LH, t (020) 7361 6145, *www.sta-travel.com*. Also many other branches in

the UK, including:117 Euston Rd, London NW1 2SX, t (020) 7581 4132; Bristol, t 0870 167 6777; Cambridge, t (01223) 366 966; Leeds, t 0870 168 6878; Manchester, t (0161) 839 7838; Oxford, t 0870 163 6373. For insurance, overland travel and hotels call t (020) 7361 6150. In the **USA**, New York, t (212) 627 3111.

Travel Cuts, 187 College St, Toronto, Ontario M5T 1P7, t (416) 979 2406, *www.travelcuts. com*. Canada's largest student travel specialists; it has branches in most provinces.

usit Campus, 52 Grosvenor Gardens, London SW1, t 0870 240 1010, *www.usitcampus. co.uk*. Also branches at most UK universities: Birmingham, t (0121) 359 5955; Bristol, t (0117) 929 2494; Cambridge, t (01223) 360 201; Edinburgh, t (0131) 225 6111; Manchester, t (0161) 274 3105; Oxford, t (01865) 242 067.

usit, Aston Quay, Dublin 2, t (01) 602 1600, *www.usitnow-ie*. Also: Belfast, t (028) 9032 4073; Cork, t (021) 270 900; Galway, t (091) 524 601; Limerick, t (061) 332 079; Waterford, t (051) 872 601.

returns on Eurostar from £59. Inter-Rail cards are not valid on trains in the UK.

Visitors from North America have a wide choice of passes, including **Eurailpass, Flexipass** and **Saver Pass**, which can all be purchased in the USA. A one-month Eurailpass costs around $623/890 for those aged under/over 26 years.

For long-distance train travel, **bicycles** need to be transported separately, and must be registered and insured. They can be delivered to your destination, though this may take several days. On Eurostar you need to check in your bike at least 24 hours before you travel, or wait 24 hours at the other end.

Rail Europe handles bookings for all services, including Eurostar and Motorail, and sells rail passes.

UK, Rail Europe, 179 Piccadilly, London W1V 0BA, **t** 08705 848 848, *www.raileurope.co.uk*. Calls cost 50p a minute.

USA, Rail Europe, 226 Westchester Ave, White Plains, NY 10064, **t** 800 438 7245, *www.raileurope.com*.

By Bus

Eurolines offers services from London to Bilbao (22hrs; £89–123 return), San Sebastián (19hrs; £89–123 return), Vitoria (23hrs; £89–123 return) and Bayonne (20hrs; £69–99); there are usually two or three services a week. There are discounts for those aged under 26, senior citizens and children under 12. In summer, the coach is the best bargain for anyone over 26; off-season you'll probably find a cheaper charter flight.

Information and booking: **t** (020) 7730 8235, **t** (01582) 404 511, *www.gobycoach.com*.

By Boat

P&O Ferries, **t** 0870 2424 999, **t** 0990 980 555, *www.ponsf.com*. Sailing from Portsmouth to Bilbao, P&O's *Pride of Bilbao* is the UK's largest ferry, with accommodation for 2,500 passengers and 600 cars. It also offers several restaurants, a cinema, sauna and swimming pool, and has cabins for all passengers. The service is year-round and usually departs from Portsmouth on Tuesday and Saturday evenings. Getting a

car to Bilbao and back can range from £160 to £525, with an additional £95–150 per person; children can pay as little as half-price, depending on time of travel. Cabins cost an additional £70–150. P&O offer a special discount rate for a one-week return trip, and 'mini-breaks' at £250–460 for a car and up to five passengers. Note that the Spanish terminal is at the port of Santurzi, 13km from the centre of Bilbao. In Bilbao, contact Ferries Golfo de Vizcaya, Cosme Echevarrieta 1, **t** 94 423 44 77.

Brittany Ferries, **t** 08705 360 360, *www. brittany-ferries.com*. Ferries from Plymouth to Santander, west of Bilbao; prices and services are comparable to the P&O ferry.

If you prefer to cross the Channel to France, **Brittany Ferries** sail from Portsmouth to Caen and St-Malo, Poole to Cherbourg and St-Malo, and Plymouth to Roscoff; **P&O** can transport you from Dover to Calais and from to Le Havre and Cherbourg; **Sally Line**, **t** (020) 7409 2240, goes from Ramsgate to Dunkirk; **P&O Stena**, **t** 0870 600 0600, sail from Dover to Calais, Southampton to Cherbourg and Newhaven to Dieppe.

Hoverspeed Fast Ferries, **t** 08705 240 241, *www.hoverspeed.com*, have a new Super Seacat that goes from Newhaven to Dieppe in 2hrs. Prices range from £58 return for a foot passenger to £418 return for a vehicle with two passengers, but cheaper APEX fares are available if you book in advance.

By Car

From the UK via France you have a choice of routes. If you get the ferry or train (*see* below) to Calais you may face going through or around Paris on the abominable *périphérique*, a task best tackled on either side of rush hour. To avoid it, you can get a ferry from Portsmouth to Cherbourg, Caen, Le Havre or St-Malo (*see* above). From any of these ports, the most direct route takes you to Bordeaux down the western coast of France, past Biarritz to the border at Irún, and on to San Sebastián and Bilbao.

For something different, opt for one of the routes the pilgrims to Santiago followed over the Pyrenees, through Somport-Canfranc (down the E7 south of Pau) or the classic route through Roncesvalles (on the D933 from St-Jean-Pied-de-Port).

In high season, and really any time of year when bored customs officers decide to act up, there can be long backups on the busy *autoroute* at the Hendaye–Irún border – a 3hr wait is not impossible.

Eurotunnel trains (information and bookings t 0990 353 535) carry cars and their passengers through the Channel Tunnel from Folkestone to Calais on a simple drive-on-drive-off system (journey time 35mins). Payment is made at toll booths (which accept cash, cheques or credit cards). Prepaid tickets and booked spaces are available, but no booking is necessary as you can just turn up and take the next available service. Eurotunnel runs 24 hours a day, all year round, with a service at least once an hour through the night. Return fares range from around £177 to £369, but special offers can bring them as low as £99.

Drivers must carry registration and insurance papers. If you're coming from the UK or Ireland, the dip of the headlights must be adjusted to the right. Carrying a warning triangle is mandatory, and it should be placed 50m (55 yards) behind the car if you have a breakdown. Seat belts are mandatory; in addition, all cars in France are required to have rear seat belts and these must be worn by rear seat passengers. Drivers with a valid licence from an EU country, Canada, the USA or Australia don't need an international licence for Spain or France.

Entry Formalities

Passports and Visas

Holders of EU, US, Canadian, Australian and New Zealand passports do not need a visa to enter Spain or France for stays of up to three months; most other nationals do.

If you intend staying longer in Spain, you must report to the Foreign Nationals Office (*Oficina de Extranjeros*) at the local police station and apply for a community resident's card (*tarjeta de residente comunitario*). In France, the equivalent is a *carte de séjour* from the *mairie* (town hall), a requirement EU citizens can easily get around as passports are rarely stamped. Non-EU citizens had best

apply for an extended visa at home, a complicated procedure requiring proof of income, etc. You can't get a *carte de séjour* without this visa.

Customs

Duty-free allowances have been abolished within the EU. For travellers coming from outside the EU, the duty-free limits are 1 litre of spirits or 2 litres of liquors (port, sherry or champagne), plus 2 litres of wine and 200 cigarettes. Much larger quantities – up to 10 litres of spirits, 90 litres of wine, 110 litres of beer and 800 cigarettes – bought locally and provided you are travelling between EU countries, can be taken through customs if you can prove that they are for private consumption only.

If you are travelling from the UK or the USA, don't bother taking any alcohol – it's cheaper to buy drink off the supermarket shelves.

Getting Around

By Train

If you're using public transport in Spain, it is almost always better to take a bus than a train; they are faster, cheaper and more direct. In the French Basque lands, however, the opposite is often true.

Trains often take a more scenic route around rural villages which can be worth the extra time and cost.

Spain

National bookings (in English): t 90 224 02 02. **International bookings:** t 93 490 11 22.

Democracy in Spain has made the trains run on time, but western Europe's most eccentric railway, **RENFE**, still has a way to go. The problem isn't the trains themselves; they're almost always clean and comfortable, and do their best to keep to the schedules, but the new efficient RENFE network remains phenomenally complex.

To start with there are no fewer than 13 varieties of train, from the luxury **TEE** (Trans-Europe Express) to the excruciating *semidirecto* and *ferrobús*. Watch out for these; they stop at every conceivable hamlet to deliver mail. The best are the **Talgo** trains, speedy, stylish beasts in gleaming stainless steel, designed and built entirely in Spain; the Spaniards are very proud of them. **TER** trains are almost as good.

Every variety of train has different services and a different price. RENFE ticket people and conductors can't always get them straight, and confusion is rampant. Prices are never consistent. There are discounts for children, large families, senior citizens and regular travellers, and 25% discounts on *Días Azules* ('blue days') for round-trip tickets ('blue days' are posted in the RENFE calendars in every station – really almost every day is 'blue'). There is a discount pass for people aged under 26, the *tarjeta joven*, and BIGE or BIJ youth fares are available from TIVE offices in the large cities. Interpretations of the rules for these discounts differ from one ticket-window to the next, and you may care to undertake protracted negotiations like the Spaniards do.

Every city has a **RENFE travel office** in the centre, and you can make good use of these for information and tickets. Always buy tickets in advance if you can; one of RENFE's little tricks is to close station ticket-windows 10 minutes before your train arrives, and if you show up at the last minute, you could be out of luck.

Fares average 1,000 pts/€6 for every 100km (63 miles) – 1,500 pts/€9 first class – but there are supplements on the faster trains that can raise the price by as much as 80%.

To add to the confusion, northern Spain has two private narrow-gauge railway lines: in Euskadi, the **Eusko Trenbideak** (Basque Railways) connects Bilbao and San Sebastián by way of Zarautz and Zumaya; and **FEVE** has tracks along the north coast of Spain connecting Bilbao to Oviedo via Santander. Both these lines show off rural Spanish life and scenery at their best, and both are fun to ride, though slow and more expensive than the bus. The Eusko Trenbideak line maintains an electric train from the 1920s with wooden carriages, and runs it in summer for excursions around San Sebastián; ask at the train station there for details.

After disappearing for many years because of terrorism, **left luggage** facilities have reappeared in Spanish stations; the word in Spanish is *consigna*.

France

SNCF general information: t 08 36 35 35 35.

The southwest of France has a decent network of trains, although many of the smaller lines have only two or three connections a day, making it rather difficult to see much of the country by rail; in some places SNCF buses have taken over former train routes.

Prices, if not a bargain, are still reasonable, and **discounts** are available, especially if you travel off-peak in a *période bleue* ('blue period') with a return ticket. Couples are eligible for a **Découverte à Deux** tariff, which gives a discount of 25% on all trains when travelling together in a blue period. Anyone aged over 60 can purchase a **Carte Sénior** (290F/€44), valid for a year and giving 25–50% off individual journeys according to availability, and 25% off train journeys from France to 25 countries in Europe. There is also a **12–25 Carte**, which offers 50% reductions in blue periods and a 25% reduction in white periods. Anyone can save money by buying a second-class ticket at least a week to a month in advance (**Découverte J8 or J30**), the only condition being that you must use it at the designated time on the designated train, with no chance for reimbursement if you miss it.

Tickets must be **stamped** in the little orange machines by the door to the tracks that say *Compostez votre billet* (this puts the date on the ticket, to stop you from using the same one over and over again). Any time you interrupt a journey until another day, you have to re-*compost* your ticket.

Nearly every station has banks of mechanical **left luggage** lockers (*consignes automatiques*) that spit out a slip with the lock combination when you use them; they take about half an hour to puzzle out the first time you use them, so plan accordingly.

By Bus

Spain

Like the trains, buses in Spain are cheap by northern European standards but no memorable bargain. Usually, whether you go by train or bus will depend on simple convenience: in some places the train station is a long way from the centre, in others the bus station is out of town.

Small towns and villages can normally be reached by bus only through their provincial capitals. Buses are usually clean and dependable, and there's plenty of room for baggage in the compartment underneath. On the more luxurious buses you even get air conditioning and a movie (Kung Fu, sappy Spanish flicks from the Franco era or locally produced rock videos). Tourist information offices are the best sources of information. They almost always know every route and schedule.

France

Do not count on seeing the rural Basque country by public transport. The bus network is barely adequate between major cities and towns (places often already well served by rail) and rotten in rural areas, where the one bus a day fits the school schedule, leaving at the crack of dawn and returning in the afternoon; more remote villages are linked to civilization only once a week or not at all.

Buses are run either by the SNCF (replacing discontinued rail routes) or private firms. Rail passes are valid on SNCF lines. Private bus firms, especially when they have a monopoly, tend to be a bit more expensive than trains.

Some towns have a *gare routière* (coach station), usually near the train station, while in others the buses stop at bars or any other place that catches their fancy. Stops are hardly ever marked, though in some areas there are conspicuous bus stops everywhere while in fact no service exists.

The posted schedules are not always to be trusted. The tourist office or shopkeepers near the bus stop may have a more accurate instinct for when a bus is likely to appear.

By City Bus and Taxi

Every city in Euskadi and Navarra has a perfectly adequate system of public transport. You won't need to make much use of it, though, for even in the big cities nearly all the attractions are within walking distance of each other.

City buses usually cost 125 pts/€0.75, and if you intend using them often there are books of tickets called *abonamientos* or *bono-Bus*, or

tarjeta cards to punch on entry, available at reduced rates from tabacconists. Bus drivers will give change if you don't have the correct amount (within reason; don't give them a large note). In many cities the entire route will be displayed on the signs at each bus stop (*parada*).

Taxis are cheap enough for the Spaniards to use them regularly on their shopping trips. The average fare for a ride within a city will be 700–1,000 pts/€4.5–6. Taxis are metered and the drivers are usually quite honest; they are entitled to certain surcharges (for luggage, night or holiday trips, to the train or airport, etc.), and if you cross the city limits they can usually charge double the fare shown. It's rarely hard to hail a cab from the street, and there will always be a few around the stations. If you get stuck where there are none, or in a small village, call information (t 003) for the number of a radio taxi.

On the French side, the only city buses you'll find are in Biarritz and Bayonne). Nearly every town, however, has at least one taxi service; the numbers are usually posted in the phone booths or bars.

By Car

Spain

Driving is probably the most pleasurable way of getting about, though the convenience is balanced by a considerably greater cost; petrol is as expensive in Spain as anywhere else in Europe. In cities, **parking** is always difficult; another problem is that only a few hotels – the more expensive ones – have garages or any sort of parking. Spaniards may still have a reputation as hotheads behind the wheel, but you will find that the Basques potter about rather serenely, and on the whole they are as careful and courteous as you could wish. Basque nationalists, however, are very keen that you learn the Basque names for towns and tend to black out the Spanish ones on the bilingual road signs, so you may want to double-check the Basque name in the text before setting out.

Spain's highway network is adequate and in good repair, and many major cities are now linked by dual carriageways. The government is currently investing trillions of pesetas on a full-scale motorway system, but until it is completed you will often have to be content with the two-lane roads that blanket the country. The good news is that a proper road is finally being built following the entire length of the northern coast. The bad news is that this difficult undertaking will not be complete for a few years yet. The Bilbao area is a motorist's nightmare; even if you're just passing through, you'll probably get good and lost among the bizarre topography and endless roadworks. Be warned that tolls on the motorways (*autopistas*) are sheer highway robbery.

The **speed limit** is 100km/62mph on national highways, unless otherwise marked, and 120km/75mph on motorways.

France

A car is, regrettably, the only way to get around the rural Pays Basque. This, too, has its drawbacks: high car rental rates and Europe's priciest petrol, and an accident rate double that of the UK (and much higher than the USA). Go slowly and be careful; never expect any French driver to be aware of the possibility of a collision.

Roads are generally excellently maintained, but anything of less status than a departmental route (D road) may be uncomfortably narrow.

Petrol stations are rare in rural areas and closed on Sunday afternoons, so consider your fuel supply when planning any forays into the back country. The scoundrels will expect a tip for oil, windscreen-cleaning or air. Petrol (*essence*) at the time of writing is 7.4F/€1.12 a litre for unleaded, 7.8F/€1.18 a litre leaded, 5.3F/€0.8 for diesel (gasoil), but varies considerably, with motorways always more expensive.

France used to have a rule of giving priority to the right at every intersection. This has largely disappeared, although there may still be intersections, usually in towns, where it applies – these will be marked. Watch out for the *Cedez le passage* (Give Way) signs and be careful. Generally, as you'd expect, give priority to the main road, and to the left on roundabouts. If you are new to France, think of every intersection as a new and perilous experience. Watch out for byzantine street parking rules, especially in village centres on market days.

Speed limits are 130km/80mph on the *autoroutes* (toll motorways), 110km/69mph on dual carriageways (divided highways), 90km/55mph on other roads, 50km/30mph in an 'urbanized area': as soon as you pass a white sign with the town's name on it and until you pass another sign with town's name barred. Fines for speeding, payable on the spot, begin at 1,300F/€198 and can be astronomical if you flunk the breathalyzer. The French have one admirably civilized custom of the road; if oncoming drivers unaccountably flash their headlights at you, it means the *gendarmes* are lurking just up the way.

If you wind up in an **accident**, the procedure is to fill out and sign a *constat aimable*. If your French isn't sufficient to deal with this, hold off until you find someone to translate for you so you don't accidentally incriminate yourself.

If you have a **breakdown** and are a member of a motoring club affiliated to the Touring Club de France, ring the latter; if not, ring the police, t 17.

Car Hire

This is moderately cheaper in Spain than elsewhere in Europe. Most of the big international companies are expensive, but budget firms like **Holiday Autos** and **ATESA**, the government-owned Spanish firm (*www.atesa.es*), offer cheaper rates. Prices for the smallest cars begin at about 24,000 pts/ €144 (£90) per week with unlimited mileage, but insurance can add considerably to the costs. Small local firms can sometimes offer a better deal, but these should be treated with some caution. Ask your travel agent about the 'Tour Spain' package that offers an inclusive price for ATESA car hire and accom-

---

Car Hire Offices

Avis France t 01 55 38 68 68, Spain t 94 486 96 48, *www.avis.com*
Budget France t 08 00 10 00 00, Spain t 94 415 08 70, *www.budget.com*
Europcar France t 01 30 43 82 82, Spain t 94 471 01 33, *www.europcar.com*
Hertz France t 01 39 38 38 38, Spain t 91 509 73 00, *www.hertz.com*
Holiday Autos France t 01 45 15 38 68, Spain t 90 244 84 49, *www.holidayautos.com*
Rent-a-Car France t 08 36 69 46 95

Self-catering and Special-interest Holidays

Companies are springing up offering information and on-line booking only. Try *www.francedirect.co.uk*, who have a large selection of cottages and villas. The Spanish tourist information site *www.tourspain.es* has accommodation listings for the Basque region. To stay in a rural farmhouse, log onto *www.encomix.es/nekazal/*, or contact the Office for Agrotourism, 48200 Garai (Bizkaia), t/f (00 34) 94 620 11 88.

Alternative Travel Group 69–71 Banbury Rd, Oxford OX2 6PE, t (01865) 315 678, *info@alternative-travel.co.uk, www. alternative-travel.co.uk*. Pilgrimage to Santiago de Compostela on foot, and walking tour around the northeast from Fuenterrabía.

Cobblestone Tours 757 St Charles Av, Suite 203, New Orleans, LA 70130, t 800 227 7889, t (504) 522 7888, f (504) 525 1273, *www.cobblestonetours.com*. Small group culture tours in the Spanish and French

Basque country, including Bilbao and a visit to the Guggenheim; also offers a wine and gastronomy tour.

French Villas 175 Selsdon Park Rd, Croydon CR2 8JJ, t (020) 8651 1231. Farmhouses and villas along the southwestern coast of France.

Martin Randall 10 Barley Mow Passage, London W4 4PH, t (020) 8742 3355, *www.martinrandall.com*. Lecturer-accompanied cultural tours.

Mundi Color Travel 276 Vauxhall Bridge Rd, London SW1V 1BE, t (020) 7828 6021, *www.mundicolor.co.uk*. Tailor-made city break and *parador* holidays.

Pata Negra 28 Parsons Green, London SW6 4UH, t (020) 7736 1959, *www.patanegra.net*. Cooking holidays in San Sebastián with award-winning Basque chefs.

Pyrenees Adventures Clifton House, Hill Head, Bradwell, Sheffield S30 22HY, t (01433) 621 498. Arranges guided walks in the Basque region of the western Pyrenees, based at a farmhouse.

Tandem Centro Intercultural Tandem, Apdo. 1075, E-20080 San-Sebastián-Donostia, t (00 34) 94 332 20 62, *tandem@tandem-*

modation in any of Spain's *paradores* for seven nights or more. The plan is for a minimum of two people or maximum of four in one car; savings are considerable. Car rental can also be booked through British Airways, Iberia and Go.

Unless sweetened in an air or holiday package deal, car hire in France is an expensive proposition (350–400F/€53–61/£33–38 a day, without mileage, for the cheapest cars). Prices vary widely from firm to firm; beware the small print about service charges and taxes.

By Bicycle

The Basques, who produced three-times Tour de France winner Miguel Indurain, are keen cyclists, and if you haven't brought your own bike, the main towns and holiday centres always seem to have at least one shop that hires out **mountain bikes** (*BTT* in Spanish, *VTT* in French) or **touring/racing bikes**; local tourist offices have lists. Be prepared to pay a fairly hefty deposit on a good bike, and you may

want to inquire about theft insurance. Do take into account how fit you are: Basqueland is a seriously steep and hilly place, although one advantage in the summer is that the (relatively) cool temperatures should keep sunstroke at bay. Roads, however, are often distressingly narrow. Wear a helmet.

Maps and information are available from the **Federación Española de Ciclismo**, C/ Ferraz 16, 28008 Madrid, Spain, t 91 542 04 21, *www.rfec.com*; the **Fédération Française de Cyclotourisme**, 8 Rue Jean-Marie Jégo, 75013 Paris, France, t 01 44 16 88 88; and the **Cyclists' Touring Club**, Cotterell House, 69 Meadrow, Godalming, Surrey GU7 3HS, UK, t (01483) 417 217.

On Foot

A network of long-distance paths, the *Grandes Randonnées*, or GRs for short (marked by distinctive red and white signs), take in some of the most beautiful scenery in France, and the Pyrenees make up some of the most gorgeous walking territory in Europe.

f.org, www.tandem-f.org. Spanish courses and cultural exchanges in San Sebastián.

Tenedor Spain t/f (00 34) 94 313 929, *www.euskalnet.net/tenedor.* Tours of the Basque coast, the pilgrimage route to Santiago de Compostela, Bilbao and Barcelona, and San Sebastián to La Rioja. Also classes in English on preparing traditional Basque food, *tapas*, New Basque cuisine and wines.

Totally Spain C/ San Prudencio 29, Edificio Ópera, Pl 3, Oficina 62-B, Vitoria 01005, Spain, t (UK) 0709 229 6272, t (Spain) 94 514 15 38, f (UK) 0870 1372049, *info@totallyspain.com*, *www.totallyspain.com.* Organises tailor-made and themed holidays in Bilbao and the Spanish Basque lands, as well as tours and city breaks.

Tour Adour *www.touradour.com/couleurs basques/fr/themes.asp.* Offers a range of specialized tours in the Basque country, including golf tours, bullfights in Bayonne and Pamplona, surfing, walking and cookery.

Unicorn Holidays Ltd 2–10 Cross Rd, Tadworth, Surrey KT20 5UJ, t (01737) 812 255 400. Tailor-made fly-drive and self-drive touring holidays featuring the *paradores* and other excellent hotels.

University Studies Abroad Consortium University of Nevada, Reno/323, Reno, NV 89557, USA, t (775) 784 6569, f (775) 784 6010, *usac@unr.edu, http://usac.unr.edu/usacweb/default.asp.* Offers Basque language courses in the Basque country.

VFB Holidays Normandy House, High St, Cheltenham GL50 3FB, t (01242) 240 339, *www.vfbholidays.co.uk.* Accommodation in France from rustic *gîtes* to luxurious farmhouses.

Voyages Linguistiques BMA Biarritz Villa Natacha, 110 Rue d'Espagne, 64200 Biarritz, France, t/f 05 59 47 14 17, *bma.biarritz@wanadoo.fr.* Intensive, all-inclusive sports holidays or French language courses for students.

Waymark Holidays 44 Windsor Rd, Slough SL1 2EJ, t (01753) 516 477. Guided walks along the Camino de Santiago.

Wilderness Travel 1102 9th St, Berkeley, CA 94710, t 800 368 2794, t (510) 558 2488, *www.wildernesstravel.com.* Hiking in the Basque country.

The most popular trail is the **GR10**, which goes straight across the Pyrenees, passing through many villages, and is accessible to any fit walker. There's also the more difficult **Haute Randonnée Pyrénéenne**, higher up and more or less following the French–Spanish frontier, and passing through fewer villages.

Each GR is described in a Topoguide, with maps and details about camp sites, *refuges*, *gîtes d'étape* and so on, available in area bookshops or from the **Centre d'Information Sentiers et Randonnée**, 64 Rue Gergovie, 75014 Paris, t 01 45 45 31 02. A good source in the UK is **Stanford's International Map Centre**, 12–14 Long Acre, London WC2E 9LP, t (020) 7730 1354.

In the Pyrenees, the best maps and trail guides and much of the mountain accommodation is administered by the **Randonnées Pyrénéennes**, 4 Rue Maye Lane, 65420 Ibos, t 05 62 90 09 90. For details, contact the **Centre d'Information sur la Montagne et les Sentiers (CIMES)**, BP 24, 65420 Ibos, t 05 62 90 09 92, f 05 62 90 67 61.

Spain has its equivalent of the Grandes Randonnées, the *Gran Recorridos*, but they are poorly marked on the ground, the guides which cover them are usually out of date or in Basque, and the paths are not marked on most maps. Contact the **Federación Vasca de Montaña**, Paseo de Anoeta 24, San Sebastián-Donostia, t 94 347 42 79, for the most up-to-date information.

Practical A–Z

07

Before You Go

A little preparation will help you get much more out of your holiday. Check the list of events (see pp.91–3) to help you decide where you want to be and when, and book accommodation early: if you plan to base yourself in one area, write ahead to the **local tourist offices** listed in the text for complete lists of self-catering accommodation, hotels and camp sites in their areas, or else contact an agency in the UK or USA (see pp.83–4). For more general information, get in touch with a French or Spanish national tourist offices.

French Government Tourist Offices

Canada: 1981 Av McGill College, No.490, Montréal, Québec H3A 2W9, **t** (514) 288 4264, **f** (514) 845 4868

UK: 178 Piccadilly, London W1V 0AL, **t** 09068 244 123, **f** (020) 7493 6594, *piccadilly@mdlf.demon.co.uk*

USA: 16th Floor, 444 Madison Av, New York, NY 10020, **t** (212) 838 7800, **f** (212) 838 7855, *www.francetourism.com*; Suite 715, 9454 Wiltshire Bd, Beverly Hills, Los Angeles, CA 90212–2967, **t** (310) 271 2693, **f** (310) 276 2835

Spanish National Tourist Offices

Canada: 2 Bloor St West, Toronto, Ontario, M4W 3E2, **t** (416) 961 3131, **f** (416) 961 1992, *www.tourspain.toronto.on.ca*

UK: 22–23 Manchester Square, London W1M 5AP, **t** (020) 7486 8077, **f** (020) 7486 8034, *www.tourspain.co.uk*

USA: Water Tower Place, Suite 915 East, 845 North Michigan Avenue, Chicago, Illinois 60611, **t** (312) 642 1992, **f** 642 9817, *www.okspain.org*; 8383 Wiltshire Bd, Suite

---

Useful Web Sites

There are several good web sites with information on the region:

www.bilbao.net
www.euskadi.net
www.cfnavarra.es/turismonavarra
www.basquecountry-tourism.com
www.tourisme64.com
www.franceguide.com
www.buber.net/Basque/ This is the most extensive Basque site on the web, with hundreds of links.

956, Beverly Hills, California 90211, **t** (323) 658 7188, **f** (323) 658 1061; 666 Fifth Av, New York, NY 10103, **t** (212) 265 8822, **f** (212) 265 8864; 1221 Brickell Av, Suite 1850, Miami, Florida 33131, **t** (305) 358 1992, **f** (305) 358 8223

Japan: Daini Toranomon Denki Building, 4F, 3-1-10 Toranomon, Minato Ku, Tokyo 105, **t** (813) 3432 6141, **f** (813) 3432 6144, *www.spaintour.com* (provides information for Australian and New Zealand nationals).

Climate and When to Go

You get just one guess to figure out what makes the Basque country so luxuriantly green. The Cordillera Cantábrica and the western Pyrenees meet all the weather fronts coming over the Atlantic and squeeze out all the precipitation. It rains on average over 200 days a year all along the Spanish–French border, including some 50 or so days of snow. The coast gets 3–4 inches of rain in August – and the real rainy season doesn't start until September. It all adds up to 7 or 8ft of the stuff a year, as much as Wales or the west of Ireland; it's no wonder the ancient Basques worshipped the sun. Southern Euskadi, especially in La Rioja Alavese, enjoys a more reasonable, drier climate, which is very good for the vines. On the bright side, the pocket around the Basque coast enjoys something of a microclimate, with winter temperatures often as warm as the Mediterranean coast. Winds can make it nippy though, so bring a warm coat as well as an umbrella.

The weather from March into May is wonderfully inconsistent: it can be hot enough for a dip in the pool or so cold that you need a coat, and it can vary from week to week. May and June are often good months to come: usually summer has set well in, and the sights are open while hotel rates are still low. The high season is intense, squeezed in between June and September, when the ocean is warm enough for water sports, the festival calendar is in full swing and everything is open; July is by far the driest month (with only an inch or two of rain). Of course, July and August also coincide with school holidays, when everything is packed, prices are high, and the Pyrenees are apt to be pummelled by sudden and very violent thunderstorms.

Average Maximum Temperatures in °C/°F

	Jan	Feb	Mar	April	May	June
Bayonne	13/55	14/57	16/61	18/64	21/70	25/77
Bilbao	9/48	10/50	11/52	13/55	16/61	19/66
	July	Aug	Sept	Oct	Nov	Dec
Bayonne	28/82	27/81	26/79	24/75	19/66	13/55
Bilbao	21/70	21/70	20/67	16/61	12/53	9/48

The region often looks its best in October, when most of the tourists have gone (although late August–October are fine months for surfing). November and December can be dismal and overcast when not spewing down buckets, but wild mushrooms, game dishes and masses of holiday oysters offer some consolation.

Crime and the Police

The Basque country on both sides of the border, because of the terrorist activities of ETA (which very rarely involve tourists), is the most densely policed corner of Europe, and the presence of several different kinds of police does keep the everyday crime rate relatively low. Pickpocketing and robbing parked cars are the specialities; and except for some quarters of the largest cities, walking around at night is no problem. Crime is increasing in the tourist areas; even there, though, you're generally safer than you would be at home: the national crime rate of Spain is roughly a quarter that of Britain.

There are several species of **police** in the Spanish Basque country, and their authority varies according to the area. The Basques have been the only community so far to take advantage of the new autonomy laws and set up their own police force, the Ertzantza. You'll see them looking dapper in their red berets, waiting by the roadsides for motorists in a barely legal hurry. The Ertzantza also has an important anti-terrorist unit, and is not notably sympathetic to the Basques, partly in an attempt to prove their trustworthiness to the national government.

Franco's old goon squad, the Policía Armada, has been reformed and relatively demilitarized into the Policía Nacional, whom the Spaniards call 'chocolate drops' because of their brown uniforms; their duties largely consist of driving around and drinking coffee.

Mostly in rural areas, you will also see the Guardia Civil, with green uniforms. They, too, are resented by the Basques for historical reasons (*see* pp.42–4), and because today they often break up demonstrations and torture the Basques they arrest; Basques are nearly unanimous in wanting them to go away. For visitors, they are probably most conspicuous as a highway patrol, assisting motorists and handing out tickets (ignoring 'no passing' zones is the easiest way to get one). Most traffic violations are payable on the spot; the traffic cops have a reputation for honesty.

The Pays Basque isn't a high crime area either. Isolated holiday homes get burgled, as anywhere else; cars are occasionally broken into or stolen. By law, Gendarmes can stop anyone anywhere and demand ID; in practice, they tend only to do it to harass minorities, the homeless and scruffy hippy types.

On either side of the border, report thefts to the nearest police station: not a pleasant task but the reward is the bit of paper you need for an insurance claim. If your passport is stolen, contact the police and your nearest consulate for emergency travel documents.

The **drug** situation is the same in France as anywhere in Europe: soft and hard drugs are widely available, and the police only make an issue of victimless crime when it suits them (your being a foreigner may just rouse them to action). Smuggling any amount of marijuana into France can mean a prison term, and there's not much your consulate can or will do about it. Note that in Spain, less than 8g of marijuana is legal; anything else may easily earn you the traditional 'six years and a day'.

Disabled Travellers

The Channel Tunnel is a good way to travel to the Basque country by car from the UK, since passengers are allowed to stay in their vehicles. By train, Eurostar gives wheelchair passengers first-class travel for second-class fares. Most ferry companies will offer special facilities if contacted beforehand. Vehicles fitted to accommodate disabled people pay reduced tolls on *autoroutes* in France. An *autoroute* guide for disabled travellers, *Guides des Autoroutes à l'Usage des Personnes à Mobilité Réduite*, is available free from the Ministère des Transports, Direction des Routes, Service du Contrôle des Autoroutes, La Défense, 92055 Cedex, Paris, t 01 40 81 21 22.

Facilities for disabled travellers are limited. Within Spain, public transport is not particularly wheelchair friendly, though RENFE usually provides wheelchairs at main city stations. The Spanish Tourist Office has compiled a two-page fact sheet and can give general information on accessible accommodation. Access and facilities in 90 towns in France are covered in *Touristes Quand Même! Promenades en France pour les Voyageurs Handicapés*, a booklet usually available in the tourist offices of large cities, or write ahead to CNRH (*see* below). Hotels with facilities for the disabled are also listed in Michelin's Red Guide to France. One sign of progress has been the creation of Handiplages, with beach facilities, easy sea access, and surfing and diving opportunities for the wheelchair bound at Anglet, t 05 59 93 12 42, and Hendaye, t 05 59 93 12 42.

The following organizations provide services for people with disabilities:

France

Association des Paralysés de France, 22 Rue du Père-Guérain, 13e, Paris, t 01 44 16 83 83. A national organization with an office in each *département*, providing in-depth local information; headquarters are in Paris. Publishes *Où Ferons-Nous Étape?* (85F/€13), listing French hotels and motels accessible to those with limited mobility.

Association Handiplage, La Barraca, 64480 Jatxou, t 05 59 93 12 42. Publishes a booklet, *Le Guide de Roullard*, on sporting activities for wheelchair users in the Pays Basque.

CNRH (Comité National Français de Liaison pour la Réadaptation des Handicapés), 236 bis Rue de Tolbiac, 13e, Paris, t 01 53 80 66 63. Provides information on access and produces useful guides to various regions in France.

Spain

ECOM, Gran Via de les Corts Catalanas 562 Principal, Barcelona, t 93 451 55 50, f 93 451 69 04. A federation of private Spanish organizations which offer services for disabled people.

ONCE (Organización Nacional de Ciegos de España), Paseo del Prado 24, Madrid, t 91 589 46 00, t 91 429 31 18. The Spanish association for blind people, offering a number of services to blind travellers (such as Braille maps).

UK

RADAR (Royal Association for Disability and Rehabilitation), Unit 12, City Forum, 250 City Rd, London EC1V 8AF, t (020) 7250 3222, f (020) 7250 0212, *radar@radar.org.uk*, *www.radar.org.uk* (*open Mon–Fri 10–4*). Information and books on travel.

RNIB (Royal National Institute for the Blind), 224 Great Portland St, London W15 5TB, t (020) 7388 1266, *www.rnib.org.uk*. The RNIB's mobility unit offers a 'Plane Easy' audio-cassette which advises blind people on travelling by air. It will also advise on accommodation.

USA

American Foundation for the Blind, 11 Penn Plaza, Suite 300, New York, NY 10001, t (212) 502 7600, t 800 232 5463. This is the best source of information in the US for visually impaired travellers.

Mobility International USA, PO Box 10767, Eugene, OR 97440, t (541) 343 1284, f (541) 343 6812, *www.miusa.org/*. Provides information on international educational exchange programmes and volunteer service overseas for the disabled.

SATH (Society for the Advancement of Travelers with Handicaps), 347 5th Av, Suite 610, New York, NY 10016, t (212) 557 0027, f (212) 725 8253, *www.sath.org*. Travel and access information; also details other access resources on the web.

Other Useful Contacts

The Able Informer, *www.sasquatch.com/ableinfo*. International on-line magazine with tips for travelling abroad.

Access Ability, *www.access-ability.co.uk*. Information on travel agents catering specifically for disabled people.

Access Tourism, *www.accesstourism.com*. Pan-European web site with information on hotels, guesthouses, travel agents and specialist tour operators, etc.

Access Travel, 6 The Hillock, Astley, Lancashire M29 7GW, **t** (01942) 888844, *info@access-travel.co.uk*, *www.access-travel.co.uk*. Travel agent for disabled people: special air fares, car hire and wheelchair accessible accommodation.

Alternative Leisure Co, 165 Middlesex Turnpike, Suite 206, Bedford, MA 01730, **t** (718) 275 0023, *www.alctrips.com*. Organises vacations abroad for disabled people.

Australian Council for Rehabilitation of the Disabled (ACRODS), PO Box 60, Curtin, ACT 2605, Australia, **t/TTY** (02) 6682 4333, *www.acrod.org.au*. Information and contact numbers for specialist travel agents.

Disabled Persons Assembly, PO Box 27-254, Wellington 6035, New Zealand, **t** (04) 472 2626, *www.dpa.org.nz*. All-round source for travel information.

Emerging Horizons, *www.emerginghorizons.com*. International on-line travel newsletter for people with disabilities.

Global Access, *www.geocities.com/Paris/1502/index.html*. On-line network for disabled travellers, with links, archives and information on travel guides for the disabled, etc.

Holiday Care Service, Imperial Buildings, Victoria Rd, Horley, Surrey RH6 7PZ, **t** (01293) 774 535, **f** (01293) 784 647, Minicom **t** (01293) 776 943, *holiday.care@virgin.net*, *www.holidaycare.org.uk*. Travel information and details of accessible accommodation and care holidays. All places recommended have been visited and assessed by Holiday Care representatives.

Eating Out

Basques in Euskadi and Navarra share the Spanish habit of dining late. In the morning it's a coffee and a roll grabbed at the bar, followed by a huge meal at around 2 or 3pm, then after work at 8pm a few *tapas* at the bar to hold them over until supper at 10pm. A wide array of snacks will help fill in the gaps in your day, wherever you are.

In non-touristy areas restaurants are inconspicuous and few. Just ask someone and you

Restaurant Price Categories

Expensive	over 5,000 pts/200F/€30
Moderate	3,000–5,000 pts/100–200F/€15–30
Cheap	under 3,000 pts/100F/€18

will find a nice *comedor* with home cooking tucked in a back room behind a bar. If you dine where the locals do you'll be assured of a good deal if not necessarily a good meal. Almost every restaurant offers a *menú del día* or a *menú turístico*, featuring an appetizer, a main course, dessert, bread and drink at a set price, always a certain percentage lower than if you had ordered the items à la carte.

French restaurants generally serve between 12 and 2pm and in the evening from 7 to 9pm, with later summer hours. In the southwest people tend to arrive early, to have a better choice of dishes and to get a crack at the specials or *plats du jour* – turn up at 1 for lunch or 8 for dinner and your choice may be very limited. All restaurants post menus outside the door so you'll know what to expect; if prices aren't listed, you can bet it's not because they're a bargain. If you have the appetite to eat the biggest meal of the day at noon, you'll spend a lot less money.

In France, there's often a choice of dishes on the set price *menu*. Some restaurants offer a gourmet *menu dégustation* – a selection of chef's specialities, which can be a great treat. At the other end of the scale, in the bars and brasseries, is the no-choice *formule*, which is more often than not steak and *frites*.

If you're a **vegetarian**, you may have a hard time, especially if you don't eat eggs or fish. But most establishments will try to accommodate you somehow.

In Spain, unless it's explicitly written on the bill (*la cuenta*), service is *not* included in the total, so tip accordingly. In France, if service is included it will say *service compris* or s.c., if not *service non compris* or s.n.c.

Prices quoted in the 'Eating Out' sections throughout this book are prices for the set menus, per person; it's safe to double the price for an à la carte meal.

For further information about eating and drinking in the Basque lands, including local specialities and wines, *see* the **Food and Drink** chapter. For a menu decoder, *see* the back of the book.

Electricity

The current is 225AC/220V, the same as most of Europe. Americans will need converters, and the British will need two-pin adapters for the different plugs.

Embassies and Consulates

Embassies are based in Madrid and Paris. Ireland, France and the UK have consulates in Bilbao. Otherwise, the nearest consulates in Spain are in Madrid (there are also consulates in Barcelona). In France, there are British and American consulates in Bordeaux.

Consulates are usually open for visa inquiries on weekday mornings only.

Spain

Australia: Plaza Descubridor Diego Ordaz 3, Madrid, t 91 441 60 25

Canada: C/ Núñez de Balboa 35, Madrid, t 91 423 32 50

France: C/ Disputacíon 7, Bilbao, t 94 420 78 03

Ireland: C/ Amann 2, Bilbao, t 94 491 25 75

New Zealand: Plaza de la Lealtad 2, Madrid, t 91 523 02 26

UK: Alameda Urquijo 2, Bilbao, t 94 415 76 00

USA: C/ Serrano 75, Madrid, t 91 587 22 00. Consulate: Paseo de la Castellana 52

France

Australia: 4 Rue Jean-Rey, 15e, Paris, t 01 40 59 33 00, Ⓜ Bir-Hakeim

Canada: 35 Av Montaigne, 8e, Paris, t 01 44 43 29 00, Ⓜ Franklin D. Roosevelt. Visas: 37 Av Montaigne, t 01 44 43 29 16

Ireland: 12 Av Foch, 16e, Paris, t 01 44 17 67 00, Ⓜ Charles de Gaulle/Etoile. Consulate: 4 Rue Rude, 16e, as above

New Zealand: 7 Rue Léonard de Vinci, 16e, Paris, t 01 45 00 24 11, Ⓜ Victor-Hugo

UK: 35 Rue du Faubourg St-Honoré, 8e, Paris, t 01 44 51 31 00, Ⓜ Concorde. Consulate: 353 Bd de President Wilson, Bordeaux, t 05 57 22 21 10

USA: 2 Av Gabriel, 8e, Paris, t 01 43 12 22 22, Ⓜ Concorde. Consulate: 10 Place de la Bourse, Bordeaux, t 05 56 48 63 80

Festivals

One of the most spiritually deadening aspects of Francoism was the banning of many local and regional fiestas in Spain. These are now celebrated with gusto, while the pronounced Spanish influence in the French Basque lands, added to the inhabitants' natural panache, tends to make its fêtes among the liveliest in France. Besides those listed in the Calendar of Events, every single village or town in this book puts on a party at least once a year, usually in honour of its patron saint, and if you can arrange your itinerary to include one or two you'll be guaranteed an unforgettable holiday.

Music, dancing, food, wine and fireworks are all necessary ingredients of a proper fiesta or fête, while the bigger ones often include bullfights, funfairs, circuses, Basque sports and sometimes poetry competitions. In Euskadi and Navarra, summer fiestas often feature a loose bull or two stampeding through the streets – an *encierro*. The music is often provided by local *bandas* (brass bands of 20–40 local musicians in dashing costumes), who play Basque or Navarrais tunes, sometimes all night long.

For a list of the major and minor festivals in the Basque lands, *see* the Calendar of Events, opposite.

Health and Emergencies

Ambulance t 112 (Spain), t 15 (France)
Fire Brigade t 080 (Spain), t 18 (France)
Police t 091 (Spain), t 17 (France)

No inoculations are required to enter Spain or France, though it never hurts to check that your tetanus jab is up to date. The tap water is safe to drink, but at the slightest twinge of queasiness, switch to the bottled stuff.

Citizens of the EU are entitled to a certain amount of free medical care in EU countries if they have an E111 form (available from post offices in the UK), although this is a fairly complex procedure in both Spain and France. On arrival in Spain you should take your E111 to the local office of the Instituto Nacional de Seguridad Social, where you'll be issued with a

Calendar of Events

Note that many of these dates are subject to change (to fit weekends, etc.); a call ahead to the tourist office is always a good idea. Or you could contact **Abentura Elkartua**, 29 Rue Sainte Catherine, 64100 Bayonne, **t** 05 59 50 25 25, **f** 05 59 50 25 26, which publishes a complete list of festivals with exact dates every year.

January

19–20 St Sebastian Day, *Tamborrada*, when scores of drum corps bang their way through the streets, followed by feasting, in San Sebastián (Guipúzcoa).

3rd Sunday *San Vicente*, bachelors' party, Los Arcos (Navarra).

Last Tues and Wed *Foire aux Pottoks*, Basque horse fair, Espelette (Pays Basque).

Last Mon and Tues *Zanpantzar*, pre-Christian dances of the *joaldunaks*, with pointed hats, sheepskins and big bells, Ituren and Zubieta (Navarra).

31 St Agatha, traditional Basque singing in the streets in many places.

February

Carnival A big affair everywhere in Spain. Some of the biggest celebrations are in Bilbao, San Sebastián, Vitoria, Tolosa (with a *pelota* championship) and Lantz, where a huge dummy representing Miel Otxin, a famous bandit, is paraded. Cavalcades on Carnival Sunday in Valcarlos, Uhart-Cize and Lasse. On Carnival Tuesday in Altsasu there's a parade of *momotxorroaks*, monsters dressed in sheep pelts stained with blood

Every Sun Horse-racing in San Sebastián.

March

Two Sundays after 4th *Javierada*, two important pilgrimages for St Francis Xavier, Javier (Navarra).

Mid-month International organ competitions, Biarritz (Pays Basque).

April

Semana Santa (Holy Week).

Good Friday *Los Picaos*, medieval-style self-flagellants, San Vicente de la Sonsierra (La Rioja); mystery play, Balmaseda (Vizcaya); processions in Fuenterrabía and Segura (Guipúzcoa).

Thurs, Fri, Sat Ham fair, Bayonne (Pays Basque).

Easter Saturday *Volatin* – Judas Iscariot gets his comeuppance in Tudela (Navarra).

Easter Sunday *Aberri Eguna*, Basque National Day, celebrated everywhere, beginning with a Mass in Euskera, followed by dancing, singing and Basque sports. 'Descent of the Angel' in Tudela (Navarra).

1st Sun after Easter Easter Fair, Tardets (Pays Basque); festivities for San Telmo, including bull running on the beach, Zumaya (Guipúzcoa).

May

First weekend *Día de las Almadías*; rafts are built and floated down river to commemorate the ancient method of log transport, followed by picnics in the Irati and and Salazar valleys (Navarra).

Mid-month Sheepdog trials at Mt Jaïzkibel (Guipúzcoa).

End of May/early June Corpus Christi (Thursday after Trinity Sunday), four days of general festivities in Spain.

Last three days *Arrain Azoka*, sea fair, Bermeo (Vizcaya).

June

First week *Fêtes locales*, Boucau and Urcuit (Pays Basque).

2nd Sun Cherry festival, Itxassou (Pays Basque).

2nd week *Fêtes locales*, Arcangues (Pays Basque).

2nd Sun after Pentecost *Processions de la Fête Dieu*, Bidarray and Iholdy (Pays Basque).

21 Midsummer's Day, 'bonfires of San Juan' in many Basque villages. On the nearest Saturday, Sorceror's Festival at Zugarramurdi (Navarra).

21–24 *Lu Magdalena*, with Basque sports, Bermeo (Vizcaya), followed by a nautical *romería* to the isle of Izaro.

24 *Fiesta de San Juan*, Laguardia (Alava).

26 *Fiesta de San Pelayo*, Zarautz (Guipúzcoa).

24–27 St John's Day festival, St-Jean-de-Luz (Pays Basque).

Last week *Fêtes locales*, St Pierre-d'Irube, Hasparren (Pays Basque).

29 *Fiesta de San Pedro*, Orio and Zumaya (Guipúzcoa).

30 *Fiesta de San Marcial*, Irún (Guipúzcoa).

End of June *San Felices de Bilibio*, pilgrimage and drunken 'wine battles', Haro (La Rioja); *La Semana Gastronomica*, San Sebastián.

July

Month-long International Jazz Festival, San Sebastián.

Early July *Fêtes locales*, St-Pée-sur-Nivelle, St-Jean-Pied-de-Port and Lahonce (Pays Basque).

5–9 Getxo Jazz Festival, both international and national bands, Getxo (Vizcaya).

7–14 Famous running of the bulls and mad party for San Fermín, Pamplona (Navarra).

2nd Sun Tuna Festival, St-Jean-de-Luz (Pays Basque).

2nd fortnight International horse-racing competition, San Sebastián.

Mid-month Jazz festival and medieval market, Bayonne; international piano recitals, St-Jean-de-Luz (Pays Basque).

13 *Fête du Chipiron*, Hendaye (Pays Basque); *Tributo de las Tres Vacas*, Piedra de San Martín, French mayors from the Baretous valley give Spanish mayors from the Roncal valley a tribute of three cows, renew their peace vows and name the keepers who will watch the common grazing land.

14 Re-enactment of a Basque wedding, St-Etienne-de-Baïgorry; medieval fair featuring bullfights in Bayonne (both Pays Basque).

3rd week Surfing championships and Basque folklore, Biarritz (Pays Basque); jazz festival, Vitoria (Alava).

22 Boat races, Basque sports and dancing, Bermeo (Vizcaya); *Fiesta de Santa María Magdalena*, Rentería (Guipúzcoa).

24 *Santa Ana*, music and dancing for a week, Tudela (Navarra).

25 Vitoria and Bilbao's saint's day, Santiago, known in Vitoria as the 'Day of the Blouse'; *fêtes locales*, Gotein-Libarrenx (Pays Basque).

29 *Fiesta de San Pedro*, Mundaka (Vizcaya).

31 *Fiesta de San Ignacio*, Getxo (Vizcaya) and Azpetia (Guipúzcoa).

End of month International festival of humorous drawing, Anglet (Pays Basque); *Fête de la Madeleine*, with a competition of the unusual, St-Palais (Pays Basque); *fêtes locales*, La Bastide-Clairence and Arbonne (Pays Basque).

August

1 Sheepdog competitions, St-Jean-Pied-de-Port (Pays Basque); *Foire de Garris*, cattle fair, St-Palais (Pays Basque).

First Wed Beginning of huge 5-day *Fêtes de Bayonne*, Bayonne (Pays Basque).

First Sat *Irrintzina* (Basque yodelling) contest, Urcuray (Pays Basque).

3–9 Ancient fiesta, with giants and the only *encierro* in Spain where women can run with the bulls, Estella (Navarra); Basque sport finals, Biarritz (Pays Basque).

4–10 Giants, music, bonfires and more for the Virgen Blanca – one of Spain's best parties, Vitoria (Alava).

6 *Fiesta de San Salvador*, Getaria (Guipúzcoa).

First weekend *Fêtes Basques*, Hendaye (Pays Basque); crafts fair, Mauléon, Soule (Pays Basque); *Pastorale*, shepherds' festival (first Sun), Gotein Libarrenx (Pays Basque).

8–15 **Basque Sports Week**, with *pelota* and *force Basque* competitions everywhere in the Basque lands.

10 *San Juan Dantzak*, procession and traditional dancing at Berástegui (Guipúzcoa).

2nd week *Fêtes locales*, St-Etienne-de-Baïgorry, Cambo-les-Bains (Pays Basque).

13 Basque shepherd hollering contest, Hasparren (Pays Basque); sardine festival, Ustaritz (Pays Basque).

13–25 Assumption Day fêtes, Bayonne and Ainhoa (Pays Basque).

14 Festival of Basque song, Garindein (Pays Basque).

15 *Nuit Féerique* and fireworks, Biarritz (Pays Basque); Espadrille festival, Mauléon, Soule (Pays Basque); regional products fair, St-Pée-sur-Nivelle (Pays Basque); also fêtes in Bidart and Bardos (Pays Basque); *Zikiro-Jatea* festival in Zugarramurdi (Navarra) with a popular picnic held in the caves on the third day.

15–16 *Fiesta de San Rocco*, Gernika (Vizcaya); on the Saturday after the 15th, Bilbao starts its *Aste Nagustia* or *Semana Grande* ('Great Week'), with Basque sports and races; a week-long international fireworks festival starts in San Sebastián (Guipúzcoa).

19 Cheese fair, Tardets (Pays Basque).

19–21 Gastronomic and crafts fair, St-Jean-Pied-de-Port (Pays Basque).

20 International professional *Cesta Punta* finals, St-Jean-de Luz (Pays Basque).

3rd Sun Fair and smugglers' cross-country race, Sare (Pays Basque); *force Busque* festival, St-Palais (Pays Basque).

Last Sun *Encierro del Pilón*, bull running in a small village.

Last week *Fêtes locales*, Bassussarry (Pays Basque).

31 St Ignacio de Loyola Day, Loyola (Guipúzcoa).

September

First half Quicksilver Surf master championships and *Musique en Côte Basque*, big name recitals, Biarritz (Pays Basque); *corridas*, Bayonne (Pays Basque); *fêtes patronales*, Urrugne (Pays Basque).

First week Basque food festival, San Sebastián (Guipúzcoa).

1–8 Festival with Basque 'goose games', a contest between boatmen to pull the head off a goose with a greased neck, Lekeitio (Vizcaya).

1st Sat *Fêtes du ttoro*, best Basque fish soup competition, St-Jean-de-Luz (Pays Basque).

First two Sundays Traditional regattas at San Sebastián.

8 Fiesta of the Virgin of Guadalupe, Fuenterrabía (Guipúzcoa); Virgin's birthday, celebrations in many places.

8–10 *Fiesta de Santa Eufemia*, Bermeo (Vizcaya).

12 International Film Festival, San Sebastián.

2nd week Basque fun and games, Zarautz (Guipúzcoa).

2nd fortnight *Quincena Musicale*, classical music fortnight in San Sebastián.

14 Festival, Altsasu (Navarra).

2nd Sun *Fêtes de Sare*, Sare (Pays Basque).

19 *Fête des Corsaires*, St-Jean-de-Luz (Pays Basque).

Mid-month World *Cesta Punta* Championship, Biarritz (Pays Basque).

3rd week Festival of stories and storytellers from around the world, Hasparren (Pays Basque).

29 *Fiesta de San Miguel*, Oñati (Guipúzcoa); traditional Basque dancing, Markina (Vizcaya).

End of month International festival of Latin American cinema and culture, Biarritz (Pays Basque); world champion fishing from boats competition, Anglet (Pays Basque).

October

13 *Fiesta de San Fausto*, Durango (Vizcaya).

Mid-month Important international theatre festival, Bayonne (Pays Basque).

Last Sun *Fête du Piment*, Espelette (Pays Basque).

November

7–11 *Fêtes du St-Martin*, Biarritz (Pays Basque).

19 *Fiesta de San Andrés*, Estella (Navarra).

24–25 *Pottok* fair, Helette (Pays Basque).

December

Throughout month *Marchés de gras* – foie gras, fattened ducks and geese markets – are held in most towns in the Pays Basque.

4–5 *Fêtes patronales*, Guéthary (Pays Basque).

6 *San Nicolás Obispillo*, Segura (Guipúzcoa).

13 *Santa Lucía* fair, Zumárraga (Guipúzcoa).

21 *Santo Tomás* fair, with processions, San Sebastián, Bilbao and Azpeitia.

Last weekend before Christmas *Olentzero* processions in many villages, honouring the Basques' jovial pre-Christian 'Santa Claus'.

Spanish medical card and some vouchers enabling you to claim free treatment from an INSS doctor. In France you pay up front for medical care and prescriptions, and 75–80% of the costs will be reimbursed later. Canadians are usually covered in France by their provincial health coverage; Americans and others should check their individual policies.

In an emergency ask to be taken to the nearest *hospital de la seguridad social/urgences*. Tourist offices can supply lists of local English-speaking doctors, but if it's not an emergency, consider consulting a pharmacist first. They are trained to administer first aid and dispense free advice for minor problems.

As an alternative, consider a travel insurance policy covering theft and losses and offering 100% medical refund; check to see if it covers extra expenses if you get bogged down in airport or train strikes. Beware that accidents resulting from sports are rarely covered by ordinary insurance. Be sure to save all doctor's receipts, pharmacy receipts and police documents (if you're reporting a theft).

Internet

Getting on-line is easy and cheap in Spain. Every city of any size has a couple of places, while heavily visited towns are likely to be infested with '*cibers*', as the Spanish call their Internet cafés. Even the most unlikely and out-of-the-way one-horse towns sometimes have Internet facilities – if you can get past the hordes of local youths indulging their aggression on digitized baddies. The average price in Bilbao is around 200–300 pts/€1–2 per hour. Outside of big towns in the French Pays Basque, however, you'll be lucky to find any; tourist offices should be able to guide you to the closest possibilities.

Maps

Rural Spain is not well mapped or signposted; rural France does a bit better, but you can still get lost. For general touring, a Michelin map or the equivalent is fine; for walking or finding dolmens and so on, the best maps are the IGN (*Instituto Geográfico*

Nacional in Spain, *Institut géographique national* in France) maps, comparable to the Ordnance Survey or US Geodetic Survey map. They come in several different scales, from the highly detailed 1:25000 on up. The maps distributed by local tourist offices are often the best for pinpointing places of interest, beaches, and so on.

Markets and Shopping

In most villages and towns, market day is the event of the week, and rightfully so. Celebrated for their fresh farm produce, markets are fun to visit on their own, and become even more interesting if you're cooking for yourself or are just gathering the ingredients for a picnic. In the larger cities they take place every day, while smaller towns and villages have markets but one day a week; these double as social occasions for the locals. Most markets finish up around noon.

With a striking, healthy inclination for combining beauty and utility, Basque artisans excel at the simple things of everyday life: furniture and woodcarving, and especially linens. *Linge basque*, whether factory-made or woven on an old wooden loom, may be your best bet for a beautiful and practical souvenir. Other archetypal Basque buys are hand-sewn espadrilles, berets, chocolates, sheep's cheese, ham, red peppers (dried whole, or in a powder or paste), bottles of wine or *patxaran* (Basque fire water), figurines (Christmas crib or characters from Basque folklore) and recordings of traditional Basque music.

For the ultimate Basque souvenir, a *makila* (walking stick), the best place is the 200-year-old family firm of Ainciart-Bergara, in the village of Larressore, or else the Fabrique de Makilas on Rue de la Vieille Boucherie in old Bayonne – but they don't come cheap.

If you can't get to the shops, you can buy Basque crafts on-line at *www.basquearts.com/marketplace*.

Money

Spanish currency comes in notes of 1,000, 2,000, 5,000 and 10,000 pesetas (pts), and coins of 1, 5, 10, 25, 50, 100, 200 and 500 pts.

The French franc (F) is divided into 100 centimes. Banknotes come in denominations of 20, 50, 100, 200 and 500F; coins in 0.5, 1, 2, 5, 10 and 20F, and 5, 10 and 20 centimes.

1 Jan 1999 saw the start of the transition to the **Euro**. On that date it became the official currency in Spain and France (and nine other nations of the European Union) and the official exchange rate with the peseta and franc was fixed (the US dollar and UK sterling exchange rates fluctuate). Shops and businesses are increasingly indicating prices in both currencies. You can open Euro bank accounts, and some places will accept payment in Euros by cheque or credit card, although Euro coins and notes will not be circulated until January 2002. It will then be possible to use both the Euro and national currencies until March 2002, when national currencies will be abolished. At the time of publication, exchange rates were:

French F	€0.152
Spanish Pta	€0.006
UK £	€1.565
US $	€1.067

Traveller's cheques are the safest way to carry money. Major international credit cards are widely used in France (although American Express is often not accepted), but not as widely in Spain. However, cash withdrawals in pesetas and francs can be made from bank and post office automatic cash machines (ATMs) using your PIN. The specific cards accepted are marked on each machine, and most give instructions in English. Credit card companies charge a fee for cash advances, but rates are often better than bank rates.

Most banks will change traveller's cheques and cash. For opening hours, see below. Exchange rates vary, and nearly all take a commission of varying proportions. Places that do nothing but exchange money (and hotels and train stations) usually have the worst rates or take the heftiest commissions, so be careful.

Natural Parks

The Basque country has several areas of outstanding natural beauty which have been designated Natural Parks or Biosphere Reservations. The **Uridaibai Reservation**, near Bermeo, covers the Gernika-Mundaka estuary and is an important migrating ground for barnacle geese, eider ducks and sawbills, among other species, which flock here on their way to the warmer African climates.

The **Pagoeta Natural Park**, inland from Orio and Zarautz, offers dense forests, river valleys and the impressive Hernio-Gaztume massif. Mountain birds such as the mountain greenfinch, pipits and peregrine falcons, and animals such as the cat-like genet, martens, badgers and foxes live here, and in autumn the leaves dramatically change colour. To the northeast, the monumental granite **Aia Rocks** (Aiako Harrio) are the oldest piece of land in the Basque country, with three main summits called the Three Crowns, the Battles or the Face of Napoleon – you may spot booted eagle, polecats and roe deer among the oak forests. There is a stunning 330ft waterfall in the Aitzondo gulley.

In the heart of Euskadi lies **Urkiola**, one of the least populated of the natural parks, which has inspired dozens of legends – Mari (see pp.53–4) was said to inhabit one of the spectacular caves scooped out of the limestone. All kinds of wildlife have made this area their home: vultures, peregrine falcons and Egyptian vultures circle lazily overhead and reptiles like the Seoane viper and the green lizard sun themselves on the rocks.

The **Aralar Sierra**, part of which is in Navarra, has the greatest density of dolmens in the region; the emblematic silhouette of Txindoki (also known as Larrunari) can be seen from afar and is a much-loved symbol of Guipúzcoa. The sierra has provided grazing grounds for millennia and tiny shepherds' huts dot the landscape. There is wonderful walking among the beech woods, and lots of waterfalls along the Amundarain river.

The **Gorbea Massif**, is the highest point in Vizcaya and was once one of the five Basque 'signal' mountains, when messages were sent by horn or fire to the surrounding villages. There are several pretty hermitages lost in the forests and valleys and the park is home to birds of prey as well as kingfishers, the aquatic blackbird and otters. **Aizkorri**, spreading into Navarra, has dolmens, cave remains and other megalithic monuments as well as the lovely

Sanctuary of the Virgin of Aránzazu. Beech groves, oak forests, peat bogs and limestone crags are home to a wide variety of birds and beasts: wild boar, martens and snow rats, as well as the Egyptian vulture, chough and mountain greenfinch.

The **Entzia Sierra**, which spreads across the Navarrese border, is a very popular spot for walking and mountaineering, partly because it is easily accessed (from the delightful village of Salvatierra, for example). There are stunning beech groves, some curious megalithic monuments and several species of fauna: jays, royal redstars, birds of prey, peat bog lizards, polecats and wild boar. The **Izki mountains**, in the southeastern corner of Alava, are covered with magnificent white oak forests and dotted with peat bogs and small springs. Abrupt limestone crags offer spectacular views across the surrounding Alavan mountains. You might spot golden eagle, eagle owl, goshawk and spotted woodpecker, or catch a glimpse of an otter or the flash of a kingfisher upriver.

Over in Navarra, the **Parque Natural del Señoro de Bértiz**, in the Bidasoa valley, is dense oak, beech and chestnut forest, attached to a park of exotic trees. Up in the Salazar valley, in the Pyrenees of Navarra, the **Forest of Irati** is not only the largest primeval beech and yew forest in Spain, but has more animal species than most places in the mountains, including the extremely rare white-backed woodpecker and the Pyrenean aquatic shrew. To the south, near Lumbier, the **Hoz de Arbayún** is one of the country's most spectacular gorges with soaring, sheer-sided limestone walls, and is home to Spain's largest colonies of mighty griffon vultures and eagles.

In southern Navarra, near Tudela, you'll find the most exotic natural park of them all, the **Bárdenas Reales**, a slice of Arizona's Monument Valley.

Although the Pays Basque doesn't have any natural parks, it does have places that are beautiful, quiet and unspoiled. The holy mountain of **La Rhune**, reached by a tramway and covered with megalithic monuments, is one; the so-called '**Route des Contrabandiers**' over the Pyrenees between Sare and Zugarramurdi, and the valleys around St-Jean-Pied-de-Port are others, especially if you aim for the primeval beech **Forêt d'Orion**.

Opening Hours

Shops

Spain Shops usually open at 9.30am. Spaniards take their main meal at 2pm and, except in the larger cities, most shops close for 2–3 hours in the afternoon, usually from 1pm or 2pm. In the evening, most establishments stay open until 7 or 8pm.

France Most shops close on Sunday afternoons and some on Mondays, though some grocers and *supermarchés* open on Monday afternoons. In many towns, Sunday morning is a big shopping period. Markets (daily in cities, weekly in villages) are usually mornings only, although clothes, flea and antiques markets run into the afternoon.

Banks

Spain Mon–Thurs 8.30–4.30, Fri 8.30–2, and in some places Sat 8.30–1.

France 8.30–12.30 and 1.30–4; they close on Sunday, and most close either on Saturday or Monday as well.

Post Offices

Spain Officially, post office opening hours are Mon–Fri 8.30am–8.30pm, Sat 9–1. This isn't necessarily the case, particularly outside the big cities. Also, many post offices close early in summer.

France In the cities, opening hours are Mon–Fri 8am–7pm, Sat 8–12. In villages, offices may not open until 9am and close at 4.30 or 5; they also close for lunch.

Museums

We've done our best to include opening hours in the text, but don't be surprised if they're not exactly right. Most close on national holidays and give discounts if you have a student ID card, or are an EU citizen under 18 or over 65 years old; most charge admission.

Spain Museums and historical sites tend to follow shop opening hours, though abbreviated in the winter months. Nearly all close on Mondays. Seldom-visited sites have a raffish disregard for their official hours, or open only when the mood strikes them. Don't be discouraged: bang on doors and ask around.

France With a few exceptions, museums close on Mondays or Tuesdays, and for lunch, and sometimes for all of November or the entire winter. Hours change with the season: longer summer hours begin in May or June and last until September – usually. Some change their hours every month.

Churches

Spain Most of the less important churches are always closed. If you're determined to see one, it will never be hard to find the *sacristán*, or caretaker. Usually they live close by and will be glad to show you around for a tip. Don't be surprised when cathedrals and famous churches charge for admission – just consider the cost of upkeep.

France Churches are usually either open all day, or closed all day and only open for Mass. Sometimes notes on the door direct you to the *mairie* or priest (*presbytère*), where you can pick up the key. If not, ask at the nearest house – they may well have it. There are often admission fees for cloisters, crypts and special chapels.

National Holidays

On national holidays, banks, shops and businesses close. In France, some museums and most restaurants stay open, while in Spain you are likely to find much more shut.

1 January New Year's Day
6 January Epiphany (Spain)
Holy Thursday (Spain)
Good Friday (Spain)
Easter Sunday
Easter Monday (France)
1 May Labour Day
8 May Victory Day (France)
Ascension Day (France)
Pentecost (Whitsun) and Monday (France)
Corpus Christi May/June (Spain)
14 July Bastille Day (France)
25 July St James' Day (Spain)
15 August Assumption
12 October Columbus Day (Spain)
1 November All Saints' Day
11 November First World War Armistice (France)
6 December Constitution Day (Spain)
8 December Immaculate Conception (Spain)
25 December Christmas Day

Post Offices

Every city in Spain, regardless of size, seems to have one post office (*correos*) and no more. Post everything air mail (*por avión*) and don't send postcards unless you don't care when they arrive. Don't confuse post offices with the Caja Postal, the postal savings banks, which look just like them. In France, post offices are known as PTT or Bureau de Poste and are marked by a blue bird on a yellow background. For opening hours, *see* above.

Post offices will often be crowded, but unless you have packages to send you may not need ever to visit one. Most tobacconists sell stamps and they'll usually know the correct postage for whatever you're sending. Mail boxes are bright yellow.

You can receive mail *poste restante* (in Spanish, *lista de correos*) at any post office; the postal codes in this book should help your mail get there in a timely fashion. To collect it, bring some ID.

Sports and Activities

The Basque country's rare combination of ocean, rivers and mountains offer plenty of opportunities to play in the great outdoors. The Basques themselves are crazy about sport, from football to running in front of bulls, and have even invented a few games of their own (*see* pp.59–64) that you can attempt, or at least lose some money on.

Individual tourist offices in the regions have literally reams of information on local activities. If you speak some Spanish, a wide range of adventure sports from paragliding to white-water rafting in the Basque country are offered by dozens of 'Active Tourism' companies including Troka Abentura, *www.troka.com*.

The Basque government publishes several very helpful leaflets with comprehensive lists of local tour operators and guides to which sports are on offer where, including *Everything Worth Seeing Visiting and Knowing in Euskadi*, *The Active Basque Country* and, for Spanish-speakers, *Espacios Naturales y Turismo Activo*. These are well worth ordering in advance if you are interested in adventure sports.

Bull Running

The biggest and most famous bull-running festival is the Sanfermines in Pamplona (*see* pp.206–7), but bull running (called *encierros* in Spanish) is also a highlight of plenty of local festivals in the smaller villages of central Navarra. The custom dates back to the times when herds of cattle were chased down from their summer pastures in the mountains, a hair-raising journey which now takes place in

Bullfighting

The *corrida* is big in the Basque country. Sometimes, as at the Sanfermines, you'll also see the bloodless *course landaise*, where the humans in the ring are the ones in danger.

Corridas tend to coincide with big holidays:

6–14 July Pamplona, the Sanfermines

14 July Bayonne, which also has fights most weekends, and on **14–15 Aug**

25 July and 4–9 Aug Vitoria

8–15 Aug San Sebastián

3rd week in Aug Bilbao

In Spanish newspapers, you will not find accounts of the bullfights (*corridas*) on the sports pages; look in the 'arts and culture' section, for that is how Spain has always thought of this singular spectacle. Bullfighting combines elements of ballet with the primal finality of Greek tragedy. To Spaniards it is a ritual sacrifice without a religion, and it divides the nation irreconcilably between those who find it brutal and demeaning and those who couldn't live without it. Its origins are obscure. Some claim it derives from Roman circus games, others that it started with the Moors, or in the Middle Ages, when the bull faced a mounted knight with a lance.

The present form had its beginnings around the year 1800 in Ronda in Andalucia, when Francisco Romero developed the basic pattern of the modern *corrida*; some of his moves and passes are still in use today. Fernando VII, the reactionary post-Napoleonic monarch who also brought back the Inquisition, founded the Royal School of Bullfighting in Sevilla, and promoted the spectacle across the land.

In keeping with its ritualistic aura, the *corrida* is one of the few things in Spain that begins strictly on time. The show commences with the colourful entry of the *cuadrillas* (teams of bullfighters or *toreros*) and the *alguaciles*, officials dressed in 17th-century costume, who salute the 'president' of the fight. Usually three teams fight two bulls each, the whole taking only about two hours. Each of the six fights, however, is a self-contained drama performed in four acts. First, upon the entry of the bull, the members of the *cuadrilla* tease him a bit, and the *matador*, the team leader, plays him with the cape to test his qualities. Next come the *picadores*, on padded horses, whose task is to slightly wound the bull in the neck with a short lance or *pica*, and the *banderilleros*, who agilely plant sharp darts in the bull's back while avoiding the sweep of its horns. The effect of these wounds is to weaken the bull physically without diminishing any of its fighting spirit, and to force it to keep its head lower for the third and most artistic stage of the fight, when the lone *matador* conducts his *pas de deux* with the deadly, if doomed, animal. Ideally, this is the transcendent moment, the *matador* leading the bull in deft passes and finally crushing its spirit with a tiny cape called a *muleta*. Now the defeated bull is ready for 'the moment of truth'. The kill must be clean and quick, a sword thrust to the heart. The corpse is dragged out to the waiting butchers.

More often than not the job is botched. Most bullfights, in fact, are a disappointment, especially if the *matadores* are beginners, or *novios*, but to the aficionado the chance to see one or all of the stages performed to perfection makes it all worthwhile. When a *matador* is good, the band plays and the hats and handkerchiefs fly; a truly excellent performance earns as a reward from the president one of the bull's ears, or both; or rarely, for an exceptionally brilliant performance, both ears and the tail. You'll be lucky to see a bullfight at all; there are only about 500 each year in Spain, mostly coinciding with holidays or a town's fiesta. Tickets can be astronomically expensive and hard to come by, especially for a well-known *matador*; sometimes touts buy the lot. Buy in advance, if you can, and directly from the *plaza de toros* to avoid the hefty commission charges. Prices vary according to the sun – the most expensive seats are entirely in the shade.

the village streets. The most popular *encierros* outside Pamplona take place in Tudela (last week of July), Pilón (last week of August), Tafalla (20 January) and Sangüesa (mid-September) during their local festivals.

Caves

Speleology, potholing, spelunking – whatever you want to call it, it's very popular. In the Pays Basque, expeditions are operated by **Tendance Sud Loisirs**, Oloron Ste-Marie, t 05 59 34 39 00. Alternatively, contact the **Fédération Française de Spéléologie**, 130 Rue St-Maur, 75011 Paris, t 01 43 57 56 54.

Several adventure tourism companies in Euskadi offer potholing trips, including **Uraik Aventura**, Heuertas de la Villa 5, 4th floor, 48007 Bilbao, t 94 445 19 73, f 94 423 82 35; **Naturlan**, Villamonte B-13, 48990 Algorta-Getxo, t 94 430 46 57, mobile t 609 24 56 78; and **Troka Abentura**, C/ Zabalide 26 bajo (ground floor), 48006 Bilbao, t 94 432 04 45, mobile t 689 39 40 88.

Cycling

See 'Getting Around', p.83.

Fishing and Hunting

Both are popular pastimes in the Basque region. Contact local tourist offices for details of the necessary licences.

Football (Soccer)

In Bilbao, football is a passion (*see* p.111), and in San Sebastián it ranks not far behind food.

Goiti Behera

In Basque this means 'from up to down', and it is just that: an unmotorized soap-box derby for home-made three-wheeled vehicles, many of which bear more than a passing resemblance to wheelbarrows.

Naturally, only the steepest, windiest mountain roads are chosen for the course, although in an attempt to spare life and limb, the most dangerous sections are lined with tyres and hay bales. It's a very popular summer sport throughout the Basque country; in the north, the *Goiti Behera* championship takes place over a month in three stages, at Ustaritz, Ascain and Hasparren.

Golf

In the 19th century, English tourists introduced golf to Biarritz (which has some of the oldest courses in France), while employees built Spain's first golf course at the Rio Tinto mines. Most golf courses hire out clubs. Green fees have taken a leap in recent years, however, and even the humblest clubs charge 3,000 pts/€18. On the French side, you'll find some of the oldest and most beautiful fairways. Summer green fees for 18 holes are 300–350F/€45.5–53.5.

Euskadi and Navarra:

Bilbao Real Sociedad Golf Neguri, t 94 491 02 00

Fontarabie Golf de Ondarribia, t 94 361 68 45

Pamplona Valle de Egües, t 94 833 70 73; Valle de la Ulzama, t 94 830 51 62

San Sebastián Golf de Basozabal, t 94 830 51 62

Urturi Hotel Borja y Yon Golf (designed by Severiano Ballesteros), t 94 537 82 32

Vitoria Complejo Izki Golf, t 94 537 82 62

Zarautz Real Club de Golf, t 94 383 01 45.

Pays Basque:

Anglet Golf de Chiberta, t 05 59 52 51 10

Arcangues t 05 59 43 10 56

Bassussarry Makila Golf, t 05 59 58 42 42

Biarritz Le Phare, t 05 59 03 71 80

Ciboure Golf de la Nivelle, t 05 59 47 18 99

St-Jean-de-Luz Chantaco, t 05 59 26 14 22

Souraïde Golf Epherra, t 05 59 93 84 06

Association Golf Côte Basque–Sud Landes t 05 58 48 54 65. Provides information on golfing in southwest France.

Harri Alzatzea (Force Basque)

Don't pass up a chance to watch the Basques flex their mighty muscles (*see* pp.59–60). *Force basque* competitions are usually held in July and August. Many villages put something on for Basque Sports Week, the second week in August; the biggest festivals are at St-Palais (in August) and St-Etienne-de-Baïgorry (mid-July and early August).

Horse-riding

Tourist offices have lists of riding centres that hire out horses. Most offer group excursions, although if you prove yourself an experienced rider you can usually head off down the trails on your own. The Basque government publications listed on p.97 have a comprehensive list of horse-riding centres.

Microlites

For microlite clubs (ULM in French) in the Pays Basque, try **Escary Espace Découvertes**, Aramits, **t** 05 59 34 11 34.

Pelota/Jaï-Alaï/Pelote

The Basques invented the fastest game in the world (*see* p.60) and show no sign of slowing down. In summer, matches take place at least once a week, and there are games indoors year-round in the *trinquets*, which are let out by the hour if you feel like playing. Serious summer training courses can be arranged on either side of the border through the **International Pelota Federation**, Poblado Vasco de Urbanibia, Palacio de Urbanibia 20300 Irun, **t** 94 361 00 06, **f** 94 361 00 44, *Fipv@Facilnet.es*; and the **Fédération de Pelote Basque**, Trinquet Moderne, 60 Av Dubrocq, 64100 Bayonne, **t** 05 59 59 05 22; **f** 05 59 25 49 82, *ffpb@wanadoo.fr*.

Most of the championships are held in the summer. One of the biggest events is the August International Cesta Punta au Jaï-Alaï tournament in St-Jean-de-Luz .

Rowing Regattas

The Basques have been fishing in small boats (*traineras*) in the open sea for over a thousand years, and some say they may have even invented the regatta. The biggest events are in July, at St-Jean-de-Luz, and in September, in Bilbao and San Sebastián.

Rugby

The sturdy Basque physique makes for natural rugby players, and there are usually one or two Basques on the French national team (the most famous player in recent years, Serge Blanco, is from Biarritz). Bayonne always fields a good team, and in the summer rugby tournaments (*le rugbeach*) are organized on the sands. The **Côte Basque rugby committee**, **t** 05 59 63 36 57, has schedules.

Skiing

The Pyrenees don't get as much of the white stuff as the Alps and anyway, snow has been fiendishly unpredictable of late. The Basque region is at the westernmost end of the French Pyrenees, where rains and mists can be troublesome. Resorts include Iraty (cross-country, 3,940–4,920ft), **t** 05 59 28 51 29, and St-Jean-Pied-de-Port (cross-country and snow shoes, 3,280–4,760ft), **t** 05 59 28 51 29. For further information, contact the **Fédération Française de Ski**, 50 Av des Marquisats, 74000 Annecy, **t** 04 50 51 40 34, *www.ffs.fr.*

Surfing and Water Sports

Most resorts on the coast have places which hire out equipment for water sports such as water-skiing, sailing and Jet-ski. The Côte Basque has a number of diving schools that hire out equipment: try the **Union Sportive de Biarritz**, Allée des Passereaux, **t** 05 59 03 29 29.

Surf bums from all across Europe flock in late summer to ride the big rollers that hit the Bay of Biscay. Hendaye, St-Jean-de-Luz, Anglet, Guéthary and Biarritz are the major spots on the French side (for wave conditions, contact Ocean Surf Report, **t** 05 36 68 13 60). In Euskadi, San Sebastián, Zarautz, Mundaka, Bakio, and Punta Galea and Sopelana near Bilbao are the main centres; there are schools to learn and world championships to watch, but you'll also find plenty of small clubs that hire out both surfboards and body boards.

Walking

See 'Getting Around', pp.83–4. An unusual mountain trek of 3–7 days is run by **Gaves du Sud**, 64390 Laas, **t** 05 59 67 08 69, in the Pays Basque, with little Basque *pottok* horses carrying the luggage and/or children (from Easter to mid-Nov).

Telephones

For emergency numbers, see 'Health and Emergencies', above.

Calls within Spain are comparatively cheap (15–25 pts/€0.1–0.15 for a short local call), although overseas calls from Spain are among the most expensive in Europe: calls to the UK cost about 250–350 pts a minute, to the USA substantially more. Most tobacconists sell PIN number phonecards that make international phone calls much cheaper.

Public phone booths have instructions in English and accept phonecards, available from newsstands, tobacconists and post offices.

In some Spanish phone booths, there will also be a little slide on top that holds coins.

In every big city in Spain there are central telephone offices (*telefónicas*), where you call from metered booths (and pay a fair percentage more for the comfort). *Telefónicas* are generally open 9–1 and 5–10pm and closed on Sundays. Expect to pay a big surcharge if you do any telephoning from your hotel.

Calling internationally from France is a bit cheaper. French phone cards (*télécartes*) are available from *tabacs*, newsstands, post offices and bars for either 50 or 98F/€7.6 or 14.9. The only coin phones that you'll find are in bars; they don't give change and are a bit of a ripoff.

In both countries, telephone codes have now been incorporated into the telephone numbers. All numbers in this guide are listed as they must be dialled. If you're ringing from abroad, the code for Spain is 34 followed by the number; for France the code is 33, but drop the first '0' of the 10 digit number.

For **international calls** from Spain, dial 07, wait for the higher tone and then dial the country code and the rest of the number (omitting the 0 in any area code). To make an international call from France, dial 00, then the country code and the number. Country codes include: Australia 61, Canada 1, Republic of Ireland 353, UK 44, and USA 1.

Toilets

Apart from bus and train stations, public facilities are rare on both sides of the border. On the other hand, every bar on every corner has a toilet. Just ask for *los servicios* in Spain, *les toilettes* in France, and take your own toilet paper to be on the safe side.

Tourist Information

Every city and town, and most villages, have a tourist information office, called a *turismo* in Spanish and *syndicat d'initiative* or *office du tourisme* in French. In smaller French villages this service is provided by the town hall (*mairie*). They distribute free maps and town plans, and hotel, camping and self-catering accommodation lists for their area, and can inform you about sporting events, leisure activities, festivals and wine estates open for visits. Addresses and telephone numbers are listed in the text and if you write to them they'll post you their booklets to help you plan your holiday before you leave.

In Spain, opening hours for most offices are Mon–Fri 9.30–1.30 and 4–7, and Sat morning (closed Sun). In France, hours are generally Mon–Sat 9–12.30 and 3–7, closed Sun.

Where to Stay

For specialist companies offering self-catering accommodation, see **Travel**, pp.83–4.

Spain

The Spanish government regulates hotels more intelligently, and more closely, than any other Mediterranean country. Room prices must be posted in the hotel lobbies and in the rooms, and if there's any problem you can ask for the complaints book, or *Libro de Reclamaciones*. No one ever writes anything in these; any written complaint must be passed on to the authorities immediately, and hotel keepers would always rather correct the problem for you.

The prices given in this guide do not include VAT (IVA), charged at 15% on five-star *hoteles*, and 7% on other *hoteles*. No VAT is charged on other categories of accommodation. Prices for single rooms will average about 60% of a double, while triples or an extra bed are around 35% more. Within the price ranges shown, the most expensive are likely to be in the big cities, while the cheapest places are always in provincial towns. On the whole, prices are surprisingly consistent. Look for the little **blue plaques** next to the doors of all *hoteles*, *hostales*, etc., which identify the classification and number of stars. Local tourist

Accommodation Price Ranges

Note: Prices listed here and elsewhere in the book are for a double room with bathroom.

luxury	over 22,000 pts/1,500F/€132
expensive	13–22,000 pts/600–1,500F/ €78–228
moderate	8–13,000 pts/400–600 F/ €48–91.2
inexpensive	5–8,000 pts/200–400F/ €30–60.8
cheap	under 5,000 pts/200F/€30

offices have complete accommodation lists for their province, and some can be very helpful with finding a room when things are tight.

Paradores

The government, in its plan to develop tourism in the 1950s, started this nationwide chain of classy hotels to draw some attention to little-visited areas. They restored old palaces, castles and monasteries for the purpose, furnished them with antiques and installed fine restaurants featuring local specialities. *Paradores* for many people are one of the best reasons for visiting Spain. Not all are historic landmarks; in resort areas, they are as likely to be cleanly designed modern buildings, usually in a good location with a pool and some sports facilities. As their popularity has increased, so have their prices; in most cases both the rooms and the restaurant will be the most expensive in town, though most offer substantial off-season discounts.

Hoteles

Hoteles (H) are rated from one to five stars, according to the services they offer. These are the most expensive places, and even a one-star hotel will be a comfortable, middle-range establishment. *Hotel residencias* (HR) are the same, only without a restaurant. Many of the more expensive hotels have some rooms available at prices lower than those listed. They won't tell you, though; you'll have to ask.

You can often get discounts in the off season but will be charged higher rates during important festivals. These are supposedly regulated, but in practice hotel keepers charge whatever they can get. If you want to attend any of these big events, be sure to book your hotel as far in advance as possible.

Hostales and Pensiones

Hostales (Hs) and *pensiones* (P) are rated with from one to three stars. These are usually more modest places, often a floor in an apartment block; a two-star *hostal* is roughly equivalent to a one-star hotel, but not always. The vast majority are clean, welcoming places run by nice families that go out of their way to keep up the place.

Pensiones may require full- or half-board; there aren't many of these establishments, only a few in resort areas. *Hostal residencias*

(HsR), like *hotel residencias*, do not offer meals except breakfast, and not always that. Of course, *hostales* and *pensiones* with one or two stars will often have cheaper rooms without private baths.

Fondas, Casas de Huéspedes and Camas

The bottom of the scale is occupied by the *fonda* (F) and *casa de huéspedes* (CH), little different from a one-star *hostal*, though generally cheaper. Off the scale completely are hundreds of unclassified cheap places, usually rooms in an apartment or over a bar and identified only by a little sign reading *camas* (beds) or *habitaciones* (rooms). You can also ask in bars or at the tourist office for unidentified *casas particulares*, private houses with a room or two. Almost all of these will be pleasant enough. Prices are usually negotiable (before you are taken to the place, of course). Always make sure the location suits you – '5 minutes away' can mean 5 minutes on foot or 10 minutes in a car.

In many villages these rooms will be the only accommodation on offer, but they're usually clean – Spanish women are manic housekeepers. The best will be in small towns and villages, and around universities. Occasionally you'll find a room over a bar, run by somebody's grandmother, that is nicer than a four-star hotel – complete with frilly pillows, lovely old furnishings and a shrine to the Virgin Mary. The worst are inevitably found in industrial cities or dull modern ones. It always helps to see the room first.

In cities, the best places to look are right in the centre, not around the bus and train stations. Many inexpensive establishments will ask you to pay a day in advance.

Youth Hostels

Youth hostels exist in Spain, but they're rarely worth the trouble. Most are open only in summer, there are the usual inconveniences and silly rules, and often hostels are in out-of-the-way locations. You'll be better off with the inexpensive *hostales* and *fondas* – sometimes these are even cheaper than hostels.

Camping

Camp sites are rated from one to three stars, depending on their facilities and, in addition to the ones listed in the official government handbook, there are always others, rather primitive, that are unlisted. On the whole camping is a good deal, and facilities in most first-class sites include shops, restaurants, bars, laundries, hot showers, first aid, swimming pools, telephones and, occasionally, a tennis court. Caravans (campers) converge on all the more developed sites, but if you just want to pitch your little tent or sleep out in some quiet field, ask around in the bars or at likely farms.

Camping is forbidden in many forest areas because of fears of fire, as well as on the beaches (though you can often get close to quieter shores if you're discreet). If you're doing some hiking, bring a sleeping bag and stay in the free *refugios* along the major trails.

The government handbook *Guía de Campings* can be found in most bookstores and at Spanish Tourist Offices. Further details can be obtained from the **Federación Española de Empresarios de Campings**, San Bernardo 97–99, Edificio Colomina, 28015 Madrid, t 91 448 12 34, where reservations for sites can also be made.

Private Homes and Self-catering Accommodation

With the rise in hotel prices, this has become an increasingly popular way of vacationing in Spain. Write ahead to any provincial tourist office (addresses in the various sections of this book) for the area you're interested in; most will send you complete listings, with detailed information and often photos. Self-catering is usually lumped together with what the Spanish call *Agriturismo*, or *Turismo Rural*, or in Basque (wait for it) *Nekazalturismoa*, because almost all the places are in rural areas.

Accommodation can be anything from modern bungalows to the bottom floor of a traditional half-timbered cottage; some places are simply large, purpose-built houses with a number of rooms. Kitchen facilities may or may not be available, and prices generally fall in the range of 3,000–5,000 pts/€18–30 per day for a double room. Contact **Asociacion Nekazalturismoa**, Edificio Kursaal, Zurriola, 20002 San Sebastián-Donostia, t 90 213 00 31, t 94 332 70 90, f 94 332 67 00, *agroturismo@nekatur.net*; or **Agroturismo de Navarra**, C/ Estafeta 85, 31007 Pamplona, t 94 820 65 41, f 94 820 70 32. *See* also **Travel**, pp.83–4.

France

Hotels

As in Spain, French tourist authorities grade hotels by their facilities (not by charm or location) with stars from four (or four with an L for luxury – a bit confusing, so in the text luxury places are given five stars) to one. There are even some cheap but adequate places undignified by any stars at all, simply because the hotel owners have not applied to be graded. Almost every establishment has a wide range of rooms and prices; a large room with a view and a complete bathroom can cost much more than a poky back room in the same hotel, with a window overlooking a car park and the WC down the hall. Most two-star hotel rooms have their own showers and WCs; most one-stars offer rooms with or without.

Single rooms are relatively rare and usually cost two-thirds the price of a double; rarely will a hotelier give you a discount if only doubles are available (because each room has its own price). On the other hand, if there are three or four of you, triples or quads or adding extra beds to a double room is usually cheaper than staying in two rooms. **Prices** are posted at the reception desk and in the rooms to keep the management honest. Flowered wallpaper, usually beige, comes in all rooms at no extra charge. **Breakfast** (coffee, a croissant, bread and jam for 30–40F/€4.5–6) is nearly always optional: you'll do as well for less in a bar. As usual, rates rise in the busy season, when many hotels with restaurants will require that you take **half board** (*demi-pension* – breakfast and lunch or dinner). Many hotel restaurants are superb and described in the text; non-guests are welcome.

Your holiday will be much sweeter if you **book ahead**, especially from May to October. July and August are the only really impossible months; otherwise it usually isn't too difficult to find something. Many tourist offices will call around and book a room for you on the spot for free or a nominal fee.

There are various umbrella organizations like Logis et Auberges de France, Relais de Silence, and the prestigious Relais et Châteaux, which promote and guarantee the quality of independently owned hotels and their restaurants. Many are recommended in the text. Larger tourist offices usually stock their booklets, or you can pick them up before you leave from the French Tourist Office.

Bed and breakfast: in rural areas, there are plenty of opportunities for a stay in a private home or farm. *Chambres d'hôte*, in the tourist office brochures, are listed separately from hotels with the various *gîtes* (*see* below). Some are connected to *ferme-auberge* restaurants, others to wine estates or a château; prices tend to be moderate to inexpensive. Local tourist offices will usually provide you with a list if you ask them.

Youth Hostels, *Gîtes d'Etape* and *Refuges*

Most cities have youth hostels (*Auberges de Jeunesse*) which offer simple dormitory accommodation and breakfast to people of any age for around 40–70F/€6–10.5 a night. Most also offer kitchen facilities or inexpensive meals. They are the best deal for people travelling alone; for people travelling together a one-star hotel can be just as cheap. Another down side is that most are either in the suburbs, where the last bus goes by at 7pm, or miles from any transport at all in the country. In summer, the only way to be sure of a room is to arrive early. To stay in most hostels you need to be a member of Hostelling International, which you join by becoming a member of your national YHA organization.

A *gîte d'étape* is a simple shelter with bunk beds (but no bedding) and a rudimentary self-catering kitchen set up by a village along GR walking paths or scenic bike routes. In the mountains, similar rough shelters along the GR paths are called *refuges*; most of them are open in summer only. Both charge around 50F/€7.5 a night.

Camping

Camping is a very popular way to travel, especially among the French themselves, and there's at least one camp site in every town, often an inexpensive, no-frills site run by the town (*Camping Municipal*). Other camp sites are graded with stars like hotels from four to one: at the top of the line you can expect lots of trees and grass, hot showers, a pool or beach, sports facilities, and a grocer's, bar and/or restaurant, for prices rather similar to one-star hotels. Camping on a farm is especially big in the southwest, and is usually less

expensive than organized sites. If you want to camp wild, ask permission from the landowner first, or you risk a furious farmer, his dog and perhaps even the police.

Tourist offices have complete lists of camp sites in their regions. If you plan to move around a lot, the *Guide Officiel Camping/Caravaning* is available in most French bookshops. A number of UK holiday firms book camping holidays and offer discounts on Channel ferries: try **Canvas Holidays, t** (01383) 644 000; **Eurocamp Travel, t** (01565) 625 544; and **Keycamp Holidays, t** (020) 8395 4000. The French National Tourist Office has complete lists. The Michelin Green Guide *Camping/Caravanning France* is very informative and also lists sites with facilities suitable for disabled visitors. In the UK, a couple of useful organizations are: **Camping and Caravanning Club**, 11 Lower Grosvenor Place, London SW1; and **Caravan Club**, East Grinstead House, East Grinstead, Sussex RH19 1UA.

Gîtes de France and Other Self-catering Accommodation

The Pays Basque offers a vast range of self-catering accommodation, from inexpensive farm cottages to fancy villas. The Fédération Nationale des Gîtes de France is a French government service offering inexpensive accommodation by the week in rural areas. Lists with photos for the Pays Basque are available from **Gîtes de France**, 12 Place Pasteur, 64100 Bayonne, **t** 05 59 46 37 00, **f** 05 59 46 37 07, or in the UK from the official rep **The Brittany Centre**, Wharf Rd, Portsmouth PO2 8RU, **t** 08705 360 360. Prices are 1,000–3,000F/€152–456 a week, depending very much on the time of year as well as facilities; you'll nearly always be expected to begin your stay on a Saturday.

Many *départements* also have a second (and usually less expensive) listing of *gîtes* in a guide called *Clé-confort*.

The Sunday papers are full of options, or contact one of the firms listed on pp.83–4. The accommodation they offer will nearly always be more comfortable and costly than a *gîte*, but the discounts holiday firms offer on ferries, plane tickets or car rentals can make up for the price difference.

Bilbao

08

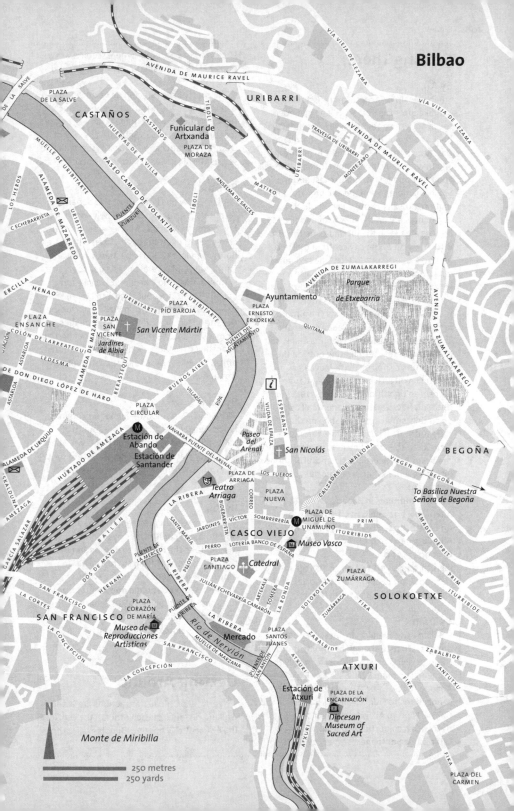

Bilbao

AVENIDA DE MAURICE RAVEL

DE LA SALVE

PLAZA
DE LA SALVE

URIBARRI

VÍA VIEJA DE LEZAMA

VÍA VIEJA DE LEZAMA

CASTAÑOS

HUERTAS DE LA VILLA

CASTAÑOS

Funicular de
Artxanda

PLAZA DE
MORAZA

TIBOLI

TRAVESÍA DE URIBARRI

AVENIDA DE MAURICE RAVEL

MUELLE DE URIBITARTE

ALAMEDA DE MAZARREDO

URIBITARTE

PUENTE
ZUBIZURI

PASEO CAMPO DE VOLANTÍN

TIBOLI

ANSELMA DE SALCES

MATIKO

URIBARRI

MONTE ZANO

LOS HEROS

C ECHEBARRIETA

PASEO CAMPO DE VOLANTÍN

MUELLE DE URIBITARTE

AVENIDA DE ZUMALAKARREGI

Parque
de Etxebarria

AVENIDA DE ZUMALAKARREGI

ERCILLA

HENAO

URIBITARTE

PLAZA
PÍO BAROJA

Ayuntamiento

PLAZA
ERNESTO
ERKOREKA

QUITANA

BEGOÑA

PLAZA
ENSANCHE

ALAMEDA DE MAZARREDO

PLAZA
SAN
VICENTE

San Vicente Mártir

Jardines
de Albia

BUENOS AIRES

VILLARÍAS

RÍA

PUENTE DEL
AYUNTAMIENTO

VIUDA DE EPALZA

ESPERANZA

i

CALZADAS DE MALLONA

VIRGEN DE BEGOÑA

ASOCIACIÓN COLÓN DE LARREATEGUI

ASTARLOA

LEDESMA

BERÁSTEGUI

DE DON DIEGO LÓPEZ DE HARO

ASTARLOA

PLAZA
CIRCULAR

NAVARRA

PUENTE DEL ARENAL

Paseo
del
Arenal

San Nicolás

LOS FUEROS

To Basílica Nuestra
Señora de Begoña

ALAMEDA DE URQUIJO

 M

Estación de
Abando

Estación de
Santander

HURTADO DE AMEZAGA

PLAZA DE
ARRIAGA

PLAZA
NUEVA

PLAZA DE
MIGUEL DE
UNAMUNO

PRIM

ITURRIBIDE

AMADEO DEPRIT

SKALDUNA

AMÉZAGA

GARCÍA SALAZAR

BAILÉN

LA RIBERA

SANTA MARÍA

Teatro
Arriaga

JARDINES

BIDEBARRIETA

CORREO

VÍCTOR

SOMBRERERÍA

CASCO VIEJO

Museo Vasco

M

PRIM

ITURRIBIDE

DOS DE MAYO

HERNANI

PUENTE DE
LA MERCED

PERRO

LOTERÍA BANCO DE ESPAÑA

PLAZA
SANTIAGO

Catedral

PLAZA
ZUMÁRRAGA

SOLOKOETXE

SOLOKOETXE

ZUMÁRRAGA

FIKA

PLAZA
ZUMÁRRAGA

ITURRIBIDE

SAN FRANCISCO

LA CORTES

LA CONCEPCIÓN

PLAZA
CORAZÓN
DE MARÍA

Museo de
Reproducciones
Artísticas

LA RIBERA

PUENTE DE
LA RIBERA

JULIÁN ECHEVARRÍA

CAMARÓN

ARTEKALE

SOMERA

LA RONDA

ZUMÁRRAGA

ZABALBIDE

ZABALBIDE

SAN FRANCISCO

LA CONCEPCIÓN

SAN FRANCISCO

Río de Nervión

Mercado

MUELLE DE MARZANA

LA RIBERA

PLAZA
SANTOS
JUANES

PUENTE DE
SAN ANTÓN

ATXURI

ATXURI

SANTUTXU

ATXURI

Estación de
Atxuri

PLAZA DE LA
ENCARNACIÓN

Diocesan
Museum of
Sacred Art

ATXURI

FIKA

N

Monte de Miribilla

250 metres
250 yards

PLAZA DEL
CARMEN

FIKA

Getting There

By Air

Bilbao's airport (confusingly first named Sondika after the nearest village and now called **Loiu** since the shiny new terminal was built and it was edged closer to the village of the same name) is the busiest in northern Spain, with daily flights from London, Brussels, Frankfurt and Milan, and to most airports in Spain, including Santiago and Vigo (for information, t 94 453 23 06). Check-in desks for departures are on the first floor and the arrivals area is on the ground floor. The airport is 10km north of the city centre; a taxi in costs around 3–4,000 pts/€18–24 (the taxi rank is outside the arrivals hall). There is also a bus service (number A-3247, t 94 475 82 00), which runs roughly every 30 minutes from 6am to 10.45pm from directly outside the airport arrivals hall. It costs a mere 145 pts/€1 and stops near the Basilica de Beguña and Paseo del Arenal before terminating outside the Vellido music shop on Plaza Moyúa.

Note: If you arrive early for your departing flight, don't go through the departure gates until you have to. There is one small café and an equally small duty-free shop on the other side, and you will have to stare through glass walls at all the lucky lunchers munching out in the ticket hall, which has a handful of shops, including a bookshop, a bigger café and a restaurant.

Airline numbers in Bilbao:
AirEuropa: t 94 486 97 95, f 90 240 15 01
Air France: t 94 486 97 50, f 90 111 22 66
Alitalia: t 94 486 97 66, f 90 210 03 23
Go: t 90 133 35 00
Iberia: t 94 486 98 42, f 90 240 05 00
Lufthansa: t 94 486 97 84/85, f 90 222 01 01
Spanair: t 94 486 98 77, f 90 213 14 15.

By Train

Bilbao has several train lines and about a dozen stations, although as a non-suburban commuter you have to be aware of only three of them. The main RENFE station, **Estación de Abando** (t 90 224 02 02), on Pza Circular, has connections to France, Madrid, Barcelona and Galicia. Next to Abando, at Bailén 2, facing the river with a colourful tiled front, is the **Estación de Santander** (t 94 423 22 66), also known as La Concordia, where scenic, narrow-gauge FEVE trains set off for Santander and Oviedo.

The pretty little **Estación de Atxuri**, at Atxuri 6 in the Casco Viejo, is used by the Basque regional line, Eusko Trenbideak, t 94 433 95 00, for connections to San Sebastián by way of Durango, Zarautz and Zumaya. A separate line serves Gernika, Mundaka and Bermeo.

By Bus

All intercity bus lines arrive and depart from **Termibus** (t 94 439 52 05), a newly constructed bus terminal near San Mamés stadium. It has coin-operated left-luggage lockers. There are hourly services to San Sebastián, Vitoria and Santander, and several buses a day to Pamplona, Madrid, Barcelona, Galicia and Castilla-León. BizkaiBus (t 94 448 40 80) serves destinations within Vizcaya, including Durango, Gernika and the coastal villages, from a separate terminal on Paseo del Arenal, near the Casco Viejo, next to the main tourist office. Its yellow buses also serve the airport (*see* above).

By Boat

The P&O Portsmouth–Bilbao ferry operates twice weekly and arrives in the suburb of Santurzi, 13km from the centre of town. There is an information and bookings office (t 94 423 44 77) on C/ Cosme Echebarrieta 1, in the centre of town.

By Car

Bilbao is well connected to France and other major Spanish cities by road. From Madrid take the *autovía* to Burgos and then the A68 motorway from there. The A2 motorway also connects Bilbao with Barcelona. Closer at hand, the A8 motorway runs between Bilbao and San Sebastián, from where it soon becomes the A63 and crosses into France. Note that motorway tolls in Spain are fairly high.

Getting Around

Nearly all of Bilbao's attractions are within walking distance of each other in the centre; the efficient city bus line (Bilbobus) and the metro will take you there if you're elsewhere. To continue around the coast from Plentzia you'll need your own transport (*see* below), or take a taxi to Mungia (2,000 pts/€12) from where buses go to Bermeo.

By Metro

The city is very proud of its metro, designed by Sir Norman Foster and opened in 1995 – so proud, in fact, that the glass and chrome tubes resembling transparent larvae which lead down to it have been affectionately dubbed '*Fosteritos*'. The metro at present consists of a single line, and offers the easiest way to the beaches at Getxo and Plentzia; there are stations at the Casco Viejo, Abando (for long-distance trains), Plaza Moyúa (closest to the Guggenheim), Indautxu and San Mamés (for Termibus). A single ride costs 140–200 pts/€0.85–1.5 depending on the distance travelled; tickets valid for 10 rides offer a small saving. There is also a 500 pts/€3 ticket which offers unlimited metro travel for one day. Services run about every 5 minutes within the centre, and every 20 minutes to Plentzia. For information call **t** 94 425 40 25, or visit the web site *www.bilbaometro.net*. A second line which will head up the left bank of the river is under construction.

By Bus

It is unlikely you will need the local bus service in this pocket-sized city with such an efficient metro. The local buses have red and white stripes and each stop has a route map. For more information call **t** 94 475 82 00.

For buses to the airport, *see* 'Getting There', above.

By Tram

The first line of a new tram system is expected to be complete by the end of 2001, filling the last gap in inner Bilbao's public transport network. The line runs alongside the Nervión, connecting Estación Atxuri with San Mamés via Abando, the Guggenheim and Abandoibarra.

By Car

Bilbao's excruciatingly complex topography of hills and valleys makes it a beast to negotiate by car; miss one turn and you may have to circle 40km (no exaggeration) back and around, only to end up in a field of orange barrels called Asua Crossroads, from which few have ever returned. If you ever make it to the centre, parking will prove equally frustrating; you'll find municipal garages at Plaza Nueva, Plaza del Ensanche, Plaza de Indautxu and near the Termibus. If the car you parked in the street vanishes, call the Grúa Municipal (towing), **t** 94 420 50 98.

Car hire companies include:
A-Rental, t 94 427 07 81
Budget Car Rental, t 94 471 01 33
RentCar Europcar, t 94 471 01 33, **t** 94 442 22 26.

There are several car hire booths at the airport in the arrivals hall next to the luggage carousels. As with the airport tourist information office, you can't get back to them once you have passed through customs.

By Taxi

Taxis in Bilbao are white with a red stripe. A green light on the roof indicates that they are free. For a radio taxi, call **t** 94 426 90 26, **t** 94 444 88 88, **t** 94 410 2121.

Tours

Walking tours: Bilbao Paso a Paso, **t** 94 473 00 78, **f** 94 412 26 33, *bilbao.pap@euskalnet.es*, organize walking tours around the city, including the Casco Viejo, as well as guided visits of the Guggenheim, gastronomic tastings and special trips into the surrounding hills. Phone in advance for prices and timetable information.

Bus tours: Bilbao BusVision, **t** 94 415 36 06, make a circuit of everything from the Guggenheim to the Funicular de Artxanda. The bus departs daily from the Plaza del Sagrado Corazón at 10am, midday, 3pm and 5pm (1,000 pts/€6).

Funicular railway: The Funicula de Artxanda departs every 15 minutes from Plaza Funicular, off C/ Castaños, and heads up to the summit of Artxanda (*Mon–Sat 7.15am–10pm, Sun 8.15am–10pm, until 11pm in summer on Sat, Sun and hols*).

River tours: El Barco Pil-Pil, **t** 94 424 59 21, offers hour-long sightseeing tours (1,800 pts/€11) and dinner cruises at weekends. Tickets are sold at their stand in the car park of the Guggenheim.

Tourist Information

Tourist offices: The main offices are at Paseo del Arenal 1, t 94 479 57 60 (*open Mon–Fri 9–2 and 4–7.30, Sat 9–2, Sun 10–2*), and in front of the Guggenheim at Abandoibarra 2. There is also an airport office, t 94 453 23 06, near the luggage carousel; visit it before you leave the luggage hall as it isn't accessible once you have passed through customs.

Post offices: The main post office is at Alameda de Urquijo 19, t 94 422 05 48 (for telegrams call t 94 424 20 00). There is another branch at Alameda de Mazarredo 13. You can also buy stamps at *estancos* (tobacconists), recognizable by their maroon and yellow sign marked *tabacos*.

Telephones: There are public telephones on many street corners, in stations and in most museums (in the basement of the Guggenheim, for example), which usually take cards (*tarjeta telefónica*, bought at newsagents and tobacconists for 1,000 or 2,000 pts/€6 or 12) and coins.

Banks: The section of the Gran Vía between Plaza Moyúa and Plaza Circular has dozens of banks. The department store El Corté Ingles, also on this section of the Gran Vía (Nos.7–9), offers a money-changing service.

Internet and email: Net House, C/ Villarias 6, t 94 424 63 78, with an automatic coffee machine and some basic snacks; Web Press, C/ Barraincue, near the Guggenheim; Cybercafé Antxi, C/ Luis Briñas 13, t 94 441 04 48, a friendly café-bar serving snacks which has just got some new computers (*only available Mon–Fri 11.30–13.30 and 4–10*); and Cyber Tec, C/ Euskaldena 8, t 94 422 23 76 (*open Mon–Fri 10am–10pm, weekends 5pm–10pm*), which does coffee and snacks.

Magazines and newspapers: There are local versions of Spain's two major publications, *El Pais* and *El Mundo*, but everyone reads *El Correo*, Bilbao's local newspaper. It contains listings for music, exhibitions, cultural events and cinemas in Spanish. The *Bilbao Guide*, available from tourist information offices and some hotels, has plenty of listings, some in English.

Useful web sites: *www.bilbao.net* (official site run by the tourist information office), *www.guggenheim-bilbao.es* (the official Guggenheim site) and *www.tourspain.es* (official Spanish tourist office site). Best of all is *www.euskadi.net*, a Basque government web site with excellent links to other sites and a wide range of useful information.

Tours: *see* 'Getting Around', above.

Festivals

2 February The Pilgrimage to St Nicholas culminates at the church of the same name just off El Arenal.

16 July A marine procession navigates the Río de Nervión in honour of the Virgin Mary.

Semana Grande This begins on the Saturday after 15 August and is a huge city-wide party with balls, parades of huge papier-mâché giants, and bullfights. The tourist office has information on the different events.

Shopping

There's no shortage of opportunities to spend your money in Bilbao. The Siete Calles of the Casco Viejo are a good place to start, particularly C/ Bidebarrieta and C/ Correo, with plenty of upmarket clothing and shoe shops, and tacky souvenir places knocking out ceramic Puppys. For something slightly funkier, try C/ Somera, where youthful fashions dominate and subversive 'grow shops' line the street. The trendiest boutiques are concentrated in the Ensanche, mostly south of the Gran Vía around Plaza Indautxu; C/ Ercilla is a good place to start hunting. Best buys in Spain are leather goods, clothes and food.

Department Store

El Corte Inglés, Gran Vía Diego López de Haro 7–9. Everything you would expect from Spain's largest department store chain – fashion, leather goods, books (some in English), music, cosmetics, sports goods, household goods, electronic equipment and more. There is also a bureau de change. Another branch at C/ Ercilla 24 has a wider selection of books and music.

Fashion and Leather Goods

Bolsos Ferrara, Gran Vía 39 (just off the Plaza Moyúa). Well-made handbags, shoes, leather garments and travel goods.

Javier de Juana, Gran Vía 18. A long-established and very prestigious tailor's and fashion shop with beautiful evening clothes and classic fashions.

Lilibet, C/ Ercilla 33. A wonderful range of children's clothes.

Loewe, Gran Vía 39 (next door to Bolsos Ferrara). Expensive, elegant leather clothes, bags, shoes and other goods.

Tisdana, C/ Rodríguez de Arias 21. The best of Spanish and international designer fashions for men and women.

Zara, Gran Vía 16. Very popular Spanish chain with well-priced fashion for men, women and children (several branches).

Books

Borda, C/ Somera 45. Maps and books on outdoor activities and mountain-climbing and hiking.

La Casa del Libro, Colón de Larreategui 41. Has a wide range of maps and books, including a good selection in English.

Urretxindorra, C/ Iparraguirre 26. More of the same (including Basque cook books in English), and one of the best selections of Basque music.

Food and Wine

Almacen Coloniales y Bacalao Gregorio Martin, C/ Artekale 22. A wonderful old shop in the Casco Viejo, still with its old fittings, almost overtaken by the sheets of *bacalao* (salted cod) hanging from the ceiling. All kinds of regional fishy specialities are sold, some easily transportable in jars or tins.

Arrese, Gran Vía 24. An old and very famous confectioners which is renowned for its chocolate truffles and the best pastries in Bilbao, especially the rice cakes, apple cakes, *canutillos* and *milhojas*.

Casa Rufo, C/ Hurtado de Amézaga 5. All imaginable kinds of cured meats and sausages, and plenty of other Spanish delectables.

Mercado de la Ribera (*see* p.128). One of the biggest covered markets in the world, with a wealth of fresh produce.

Pescaderias Vascos, C/ Astarloa 1. This miniature fishmongers has become known as 'the Jewellers' for the excellent quality of its products and the artistry with which they are are displayed.

El Rincón del Vino, C/ General Concha 5. Stocks an excellent range of Spanish and Basque wines.

Gifts and Souvenirs

Basandere, C/ Iparraguirre 4. Just a skip away from the Guggenheim, this attractive Basque boutique has ceramics, glassware, hand-crafted jewellery, tasteful household linens and other goods. There are also Basque music CDs, T-shirts and mugs.

Kukuxumusu, C/ Rodríguez Arias 27. All kinds of souvenirs from T-shirts, postcards and mugs, to posters and hand-made ceramics.

Regalos Rui-Wamba, Plaza Nueva 10. All kinds of kitsch, from religious ornaments to souvenirs.

Sports and Activities

Football

Football is a highly charged national passion and something of a war without bullets throughout Spain, but in Bilbao it becomes almost a religion. Even the stadium (at San Mamés, near the Plaza del Sagrado Corazón) is known as 'the Cathedral'.

Atlético was founded in 1898 by Englishmen working in the city, and unlike most European teams staunchly fields only Basque players, yet manages to remain in the top ranks of the Spanish leagues. One of its first great stars in the 1920s was José Antonio Aguirre, who became the president of Euskadi during the Republic. If you want to see a game, call t 94 424 08 77 for information.

Pelota

There's a *fronton* on Calle Esperanza in the Casco Viejo behind the church of San Nicolás if you want to watch the players practise. To see a game with one of the local teams, call t 94 423 11 09 – and don't forget to place a bet, all part of the *pelota* ritual.

Bullfighting

The bullfighting season runs from April to October, although the highlight is the Semana Grande (*see* 'Festivals', above) in August. For ticket information, call t 94 444 86 98.

Where to Stay

Bilbao ✉ 48000

The 'Guggenheim Effect' has filled Bilbao's hotels to the brim with the kind of educated, culture-seeking tourist other cities dream of, so book in advance. Most of the inexpensive rooms are in the Casco Viejo.

Luxury

Bilbao has quite a few luxury hotels catering for the businesspeople who pass through; some of these offer discounts of up to 50 per cent at weekends. The following are centrally located and popular:

12 *****Lopez de Haro**, Obispo Orueta 2, t 94 423 55 00, f 94 423 45 00, *www.hotel lopezdeharo.com*. This is currently the most fashionable option, with one of the city's finest restaurants Club Náutico (*see* below). It doesn't look much from the outside, but the interior is opulent. Close to the pretty Jardines de Albia, it is also only a 5-minute walk to the Guggenheim.

11 *****Carlton**, Pza de Federico Moyúa 2, t 94 416 22 00, f 94 416 48 28. In the city's heart, this was once the headquarters of the Republican Basque government. A plush, romantic 19th-century hotel, it has lodged most of the famous bullfighters, along with Hemmingway, Ava Gardner and Lauren Bacall, and is perfectly placed for shopping and the Guggenheim.

5 ****NH Villa de Bilbao**, Gran Vía 87, t 94 441 60 00, f 94 441 62 59, *www.nh-hoteles.es*. On the city's grandest street, near Plaza del Sagrado Corazón, this sleek, modern hotel with its striking marble and iron façade offers all the amenities. It is particularly geared towards business people, but that means its weekend prices offer excellent value.

10 ****Ercilla**, C/ Ercilla 37–39, t 94 410 20 00, f 94 443 93 35, *www.hotelercilla.es*. A concrete monster, this grand, business-oriented hotel has a fine restaurant, Bermeo (*see* below). Thanks to its proximity to the Plaza de Toros, this is the place to come during the bullfighting season, when you may catch a glimpse of Spain's best *toreros*. It's also very handily placed for designer boutiques.

9 ****Hotel Indautxu**, Plaza del Bombero Etxaniz, t 94 421 11 98. This giant glass cube has all the necessary comforts in a good quiet location; the house restaurant, Etxaniz (*see* below), is one of the best in the city. It catches some spill-over bull-fighting fever during the summer season.

Expensive

1 ***NH Deusto**, C/ Francisco Macia, t 94 476 00 06, f 94 476 21 99. Very much a business hotel, it is nonetheless well located near the University of Duesta and not too far from the Guggenheim. Check out the weekend deals.

17 ***Meliá Confort Arenal**, C/ Los Fueros 2, t 94 415 31 00, f 94 415 63 95. A bland, if well-equipped, option on the edge of the Casco Viejo. The building has been sympathetically restored and it also offers excellent weekend prices.

14 ***Barcelo Hotel Nervión**, C/ Campo Volantin 11, t 94 445 55 66. One of the newest hotels in the city, this presents a sleek glass façade overlooking the river not far from the town hall. Geared towards businesspeople, it is frighteningly efficient.

13 ***Conde Duque**, Campo de Volantin 22, t 94 445 60 00, f 94 445 60 66, *www.hotel condeduque.com*. Across the river from the Guggenheim, at the lower end of this price category, this slightly shabby establishment offers all the amenities despite being slightly impersonal.

Moderate

21 **Hotel Iturrienea Ostatua**, C/ Santa María 14, t 94 416 15 00, f 94 415 89 29. Definitely the best choice in the Casco Viejo; great care has gone into equipping the rooms with a mix of antique and new furniture, while flowering plants trail from the balconies. You can't miss its bright blue-and-yellow façade.

8 **Hotel Zabalburu**, C/ P. M. Artola 8, t 94 443 71 00, f 94 410 00 73. Pleasant rooms in a modern setting, with parking facilities. It is family run, friendly and in a quiet neighbourhood just down from the Plaza de Zabálburu. It's also handy for the bus and train stations.

25 ****Sirimiri**, Pza de la Encarnación 3, t 94 433 07 59, f 94 433 08 75. A peachy little hotel offering a simple, reasonably priced option on a pretty square near the old church of San Anton and the Ribera market.

6 ****Estadio**, Avda J. Antonio Zunzunegui 10, t 94 442 42 41. On the other side of town, handy for the Termibus. A little pricey for what it offers (it's at the top end of this price category).

7 ****Vista Alegre**, C/ Pablo Picasso 13, t 94 443 14 50, f 94 443 14 54. This offers good facilities at a reasonable price, although it is a bit of a trot (comparatively) to the city's main sights.

20 ****Hostal Mardones**, C/ Jardines 4, t 94 415 31 05. An engaging, spotless little *hostal* overlooking one of the old quarter's most animated streets. It's at the bottom end of this price category.

15 ***Hotel Ripa**, C/ Ripa 3, t 94 423 96 77. On the riverfront just opposite the Casco Viejo; nice, recently renovated rooms with balconies overlooking the old opera house and the town hall.

18 ***Arriaga**, C/ Ribera 3, t 94 479 00 01, f 94 479 05 16. On the edge of the Casco Viejo, very close to the Teatro, this offers modern, comfortable rooms and parking, an important consideration in this crowded town. It is run by a slightly eccentric family, who are more than happy to give advice on the neighbourhood.

Inexpensive

2 ****Plaza San Pedro**, C/ Luzarra 7, t 94 476 31 26, f 94 476 38 95. Across the river from the Guggenheim in the Duesta district, this small hotel is set in a rather unprepossessing area, but it has pretty good facilities for the price, which is at the top end of this category.

19 ****Hs Arana**, C/ Bidebarrieta 2, t 94 415 64 11. An old-fashioned hotel in a 19th-century building very near the Teatro Arriaga, with comfortable rooms.

3 ****HR Ria de Bilbao**, C/ Ribera de Deusto 32, t 94 476 15 57, *www.riobilbao.arrakis.es*. A 10-minute walk from the Palacio Euskalduna, this quiet riverside *hostal* is mainly used as a student residence and has a garden and cooking facilities. Several

rooms are reserved for visitors, if you don't mind being away from the centre.

Cheap

22 ****Hs Gurea**, C/ Bidebarrieta 14, t 94 416 32 99. From the outside this looks pretty shabby and tumbledown, but inside you'll find clean simple rooms (with bath) and friendly owners.

4 ****Don Claudio**, C/ Hermógenes Rojo 10, t 94 490 50 17. A good bet, although away from the centre.

24 ***Hs Roquefer**, Lotería 2, t 94 415 07 55. By the cathedral, in a dimly lit old building with high ceilings and very friendly owners. Some rooms have sunny little balconies overlooking the Plaza Santiago and the cathedral – pretty during the day but bring ear plugs if you want to lie in.

16 **Pensión Martinez**, C/ Villarias 8, t 94 423 91 78. A good, clean cheapie in the centre of town.

23 **Pensión Ladero**, C/ Lotería 1, t 94 415 09 32. A pretty, sympathetically run place on the 4th floor of an old Casco Viejo building. It fills up quickly in summer (no bath).

Getxo ✉ 48990

***Hotel Igcretxe, Playa Areaga, t 94 491 00 09, f 94 460 85 99 (*moderate*). This Belle Epoque hotel is slap on the beach front and pampers guests with salt-water therapy and algae baths.

**Artaza, Avda Los Chopos 12, t 94 491 28 52, f 94 491 29 34, *hotelartaza@euskalnet.net* (*expensive*). Offers comfort with elegance in a distinctly refined mansion surrounded by tranquil parkland, a short walk from Neguri metro station.

Pensión Areeta, C/ Mayor 13, t 94 463 81 36 (*cheap*). Clean, comfortable rooms with bath.

Plentzia ✉ 48630

*Hotel Uribe, C/ Erribea 13, t 94 677 44 78, f 94 677 44 61 (*moderate*). The choice place to stay, set in a restored mansion overlooking the *ría*; some of the rooms boast luxurious glassed-in balconies.

*Hostal Palas, C/ Ribera 42, t 94 677 08 36 (*inexpensive*). Has pleasant rooms with shared bath and a funky café.

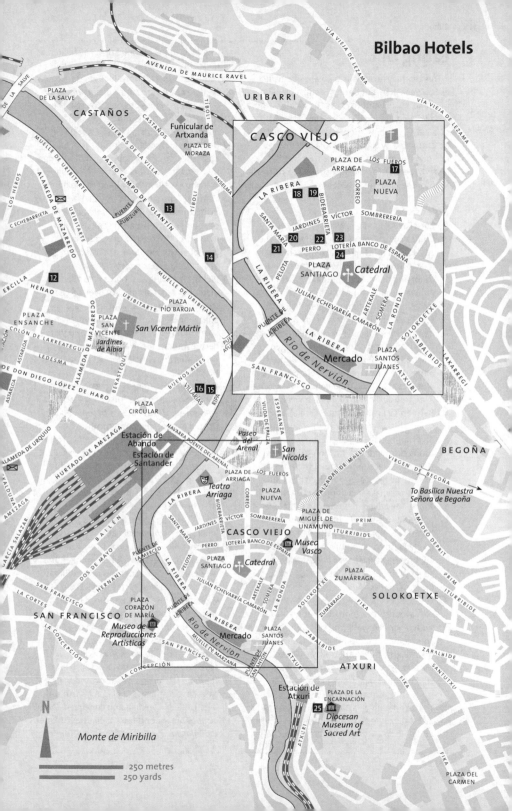

Bilbao Hotels

VÍA VIEJA DE LEZAMA

AVENIDA DE MAURICE RAVEL

VÍA VIEJA DE LEZAMA

URIBARRI

PLAZA DE LA SALVE

CASTAÑOS

DE LA SALVE

CASTAÑOS

Funicular de Artxanda

PLAZA DE MORAZA

CASCO VIEJO

PLAZA DE ARRIAGA

LOS FUEROS

17

CORREO

PLAZA NUEVA

HUERTAS DE LA VILLA

PLAZA DE LA VILLA

MUELLE DE URIBITARTE

PASEO CAMPO DE VOLANTÍN

TÍBOLI

ANSELMA

LA RIBERA

SANTA MARÍA

18 **19**

BIDEBARRIETA

VÍCTOR

SOMBRERERÍA

LOS HEROS

ALAMEDA DE MAZARREDO

PUENTE ZUBIZURI

13

JARDINES

20

22

23

LOTERÍA BANCO DE ESPAÑA

C ECHEBARRIETA

URIBITARTE

MUELLE DE URIBITARTE

14

PELOTA

21

PERRO

24

ERCILLA

HENAO

12

URIBITARTE

PÍO BAROJA

PLAZA PÍO BAROJA

PLAZA SANTIAGO

✝ **Catedral**

PLAZA ENSANCHE

ALAMEDA DE MAZARREDO

BETASTEGUI

PLAZA SAN VICENTE

✝ **San Vicente Mártir**

JULIÁN ECHEVARRÍA CAMARÓN

ARTEKALE

SOMERA

LA RONDA

SOLOKOETXE

ZABALBIDE

LAKARREGI

COLÓN DE LARREATEGUI

Jardines de Albia

LA RIBERA

LA RIBERA

PLAZA SANTOS JUANES

ASTARLOA

LEDESMA

BILBAO AIRES

PUENTE DE LA RIBERA

Mercado

Río de Nervión

DE DON DIEGO LÓPEZ DE HARO

VILLARÍAS

RIPA

SAN FRANCISCO

ASTARLA

PLAZA CIRCULAR

16 **15**

NAVARRA

PUENTE DEL ARENAL

VIUDA DE EPALZA

ESPERANZA

Paseo del Arenal

San Nicolás

CALZADAS DE MALLONA

VIRGEN DE BEGOÑA

BEGOÑA

ALAMEDA DE URQUIJO

HURTADO DE AMEZAGA

Estación de Abando

Estación de Santander

LA RIBERA

SANTA MARÍA

PLAZA DE ARRIAGA

LOS FUEROS

✝ Teatro Arriaga

CORREO

PLAZA NUEVA

PLAZA DE MIGUEL DE UNAMUNO

PRIM

ITURRIBIDE

To Basílica Nuestra Señora de Begoña

AMADEO DEPRIT

AMEZAGA

GARCÍA SALAZAR

BAILÉN

DOS DE MAYO

BIDEBARRIETA

VÍCTOR

SOMBRERERÍA

CASCO VIEJO

LOTERÍA BANCO DE ESPAÑA

🏛 **Museo Vasco**

PLAZA ZUMÁRRAGA

PRIM

ITURRIBIDE

VALDUNA

SAN FRANCISCO

HERNANI

PERRO

PLAZA SANTIAGO

PELOTA

✝ **Catedral**

ZUMÁRRAGA

FIKA

SOLOKOETXE

LA CORTES

LA CONCEPCIÓN

PLAZA CORAZÓN DE MARÍA

JULIÁN ECHEVARRÍA CAMARÓN

ARTEKALE

SOMERA

LA RONDA

SOLOKOETXE

ZABALBIDE

ZARALBIDE

SANTUTXU

SAN FRANCISCO

LA CONCEPCIÓN

🏛 Museo de Reproducciones Artísticas

PUENTE DE LA RIBERA

SAN FRANCISCO

MUELLES MARZANA

Río de Nervión

LA RIBERA

PLAZA SANTOS JUANES

Mercado

PUENTE DE SAN ANTON

ATXURI

ATXURI

FIKA

ZARALBIDE

Estación de Atxuri

PLAZA DE LA ENCARNACIÓN

25 🏛 Diocesan Museum of Sacred Art

ATXURI

FIKA

N

Monte de Miribilla

PLAZA DEL CARMEN

250 metres
250 yards

Eating Out

This city may not get as wild about cuisine as San Sebastián, but eating is still a pleasure in Bilbao. If you want to do as the locals do, go for a *txikiteo*, the local civilized version of a pub-crawl, stopping for *pintxos* and *tapas* accompanied by a glass of Rioja or a beer at lots of different bars (*see 'Tapas/Pinchos/ Pintxos'*, below). For the purest Basque cuisine, look for the strangest names.

Expensive

6 **Zortziko**, Alameda de Mazarredo 17, t 94 423 97 43. You can splurge at this, the city's finest (Michelin-starred) restaurant, in an historic building, where the quirky décor and fine service prepare you for innovative and immaculately presented treats from the kitchen: green almond soup, *pichón* (pigeon) *a la moda Zortziko*, *lomo de merluza con almejas* (fillet of hake with clams) and *estofado* of wild pigeon, washed down with the finest of Rioja wines. The lunch menu is a relative bargain at 6,500 pts/€39. *Closed all day Sun, Mon eve, last week in Aug and first 2 weeks Sept.*

15 **Bermeo**, C/ Ercilla 37 (Hotel Ercilla), t 94 470 57 00. This offers a delicate blend of new and traditional Basque cuisine in sumptuous surroundings. If it's on the menu, this is the place to try one of the ultimate Basque treats, *cocochas* – the 'cheek and throat' of a hake in a garlic and parsley sauce. The *lubina al horno con salsa* (oven-baked sea bass) and *salpicón de pulpo con hongos* (octopus salad with wild mushrooms) also come highly recommended. Try the lunchtime *menú degustación* at 5,650 pts/€40. *Closed Sat lunch, Sun eve and first 2 weeks Aug.*

7 **Guría**, Gran Vía 66, t 94 441 57 80. Another old favourite, this is an elegant restaurant with blood-red walls and soft lighting to complement the traditional Basque fare on offer. The house speciality is salted cod (*bacalao*); try the *surtidos de bacalaos de chef*. Menus range from 3,500 to 9,000 pts/€21–54. *Closed Sun eve.*

8 **Goizeko-Kabi**, C/ Particular de Estraunza 4–6, t 94 442 11 29. The name sounds right, and it offers excellent, innovative cooking

to match. It has scooped up a Michelin star under the auspices of its vibrant young chef; recommendations include *tronco de bacalao de las Feroe* and *conejo relleno de cigalas*. Don't miss out on dessert, either – the bitter chocolate and banana tart is a marvel. *Closed Sun and first 2 weeks Aug.*

17 **Gorrotxa**, Alameda de Urquijo 30, t 94 443 49 37. In spite of its shopping mall setting, this restaurant offers another Michelin star and excellent New Basque cooking by Carmelo Gorrotzategui, served in a sophisticated ambience. Try the *lubina al horno con gambas* (oven-baked sea bass with prawns) or the *rodaballo encebellado* (turbot with onion sauce). *Closed Sun, the first 2 weeks Sept and Holy Week.*

26 **Victor**, Plaza Nueva 2, t 94 415 16 78. Victor has been around for over 40 years, overcoming the disadvantage of a pronounceable name to build up its enviable reputation as one of the Casco Viejo's best restaurants; the *bodega* boasts over 1,500 different wines. *Closed Sun, Aug and Holy Week.*

2 **Guggenheim**, Guggenheim Museum Bilbao, t 94 423 93 33. Full of light, organic lines formed with pale-coloured wood and frosted glass panels, and furniture designed by Frank Gehry; the food, created by chef Martín Berasategui, is an excellent snapshot of some of the best of Basque cooking. It's extremely popular so book in advance. There are three *menú degustacións* on offer between 5,300 and 7,200 pts/€32 and 43.5, and a very good-value lunchtime *menu del día* at 1,500 pts/€9.

23 **El Perro Chico (Perrotxico)**, C/ Arechaga 2, t 94 415 05 19. Close to Ribera market and overlooking the river, this is one of Bilbao's most talked-about restaurants. Deep blue walls, tiles and lots of paintings give it a chic, Bohemian atmosphere in which to dine on *bonito en milhojas*, or a delicious *pato asado* (roasted duck) in a piquant orange sauce. *Closed Mon eve and Sun.*

5 **Club Náutico**, C/ Obispo Orueta 2 (Hotel López de Haro), t 94 423 55 00. Innovative New Basque cuisine in elegant surroundings. Grilled monkfish and *canelón de rabo de guey* are among the specialities on offer. *Closed 15 June–Aug, Sat lunch and Sun.*

18 Etxaniz, C/ Gordóniz 15 (Hotel Indautxu), t 94 421 11 98. In a traditional white annexe to the modern hotel, this renowned establishment serves excellent New Basque cuisine. Crisply elegant surroundings complement the beautifully presented dishes: *lomos de merluza con jugo de hongos y almejas* (fillet of hake with mushroom and clam sauce) and *milhojas de rabo de buey* (pastries with oxtail) are recommended. *Closed Sun and first 2 weeks Aug.*

11 Matxinbenta, C/ Ledesma 26, t 94 424 84 95. In a street full of old-fashioned bars and eating places, this is one of Bilbao's most established restaurants. Formal and popular with businessmen, it offers robust, traditional Basque dishes using seasonal specialities. Try *lubina al hinojo* (sea bass with fennel) and finish with *canutillos de Bilbao con natillas*, a creamy custard dessert with biscuits. *Closed Sun eve.*

4 Baita, Alameda Mazarredo 20, t 94 424 22 67. A chic, elegant restaurant favoured by local bankers and industrialists. Enjoy fine views over the river and sample the house speciality, *bacalao*, prepared in a dozen different ways – *al pil-pil*, invented during the first Carlist siege of Bilbao in 1835, is especially good. The chef is also proud of his *solomillo*, a hefty portion of succulent steak from locally reared cattle.

Moderate

12 Nicolás, C/ Ledesma 10, t 94 424 07 37. Another of the old-fashioned gems on Calle Ledesma, this restaurant is particularly, although not exclusively, acclaimed for its fish dishes. Definitely a good place to try local *bacalao* (cod) and *merluza* (hake) in traditional sauces. Come just for the *pintxos* at the bar if you don't want to sit down to a full meal. *Restaurant closed Sun eve.*

24 Begoña, C/ Virgen de Begoña s/n, t 94 412 72 57. At the foot of the Basilica de Begoña, high above the rest of the city in a quiet residential area, this is an old-fashioned establishment offering fine, traditional Basque cuisine. Among the dishes on offer are *alcachofas con almejas* (artichokes with clams) and *solomillo Bordelesa* (a thick slab of steak). *Closed Sun, Aug and Holy Week.*

9 Asador Jauna, Avda Juan Antonio Zunzunegui 7, t 94 441 73 81. A classy, old-fashioned grill house with a big reputation for its meats and fish roasted over charcoal. *Closed Aug and Holy Week.*

14 Serantes, C/ Licenciado Poza 16, t 94 421 21 **16** 29, and Serantes II, C/ Alameda de Urquijo 51, t 94 421 10 45. Famous local favourites, these classic restaurants are always busy. Specializing in fish, but with a good selection of options for carnivores too, the secret of their success is very fresh, simply prepared dishes; try the *medallones de merluza a la romana*, or go for the fish of the day. The *menú del día* is attractively priced at 1,500 pts/€9, but be warned that à la carte can be up to 7,000 pts/€42.

28 Arriaga Asador, C/ Santa María 13, t 94 416 56 70. Another grill house, a little less expensive than the Jauna; this long, long, brick-walled restaurant is packed with tables and can get very busy.

10 Metro-Moyúa, C/ Gran Via 40, t 94 424 92 73. Set on the corner of the Plaza Moyúa, this family-run restaurant serves good Basque home cooking with flair. There is a cafetería offering a very reasonable *menú del día* and a huge terrace from where you can watch the world go by as you tuck into *mero al txakoli* (halibut with tart white wine) followed by a piquant *tarta de limón*.

1 Casa Vasca, C/ Avda Lehendakari 13–15, t 94 475 47 78. Over in Deusto, this stalwart offers traditional regional dishes (and good breakfasts), in pleasant surroundings.

20 Euskalduna, C/ Euskalduna 4, t 94 421 31 25. A perennial local favourite, offering tasty home cooking such as *anchoas rebozadas* (anchovies) or *caracoles a la vizcaína* (snails). The *menú del día* and a *menú Bilbao* make it very good value. *Closed Sun.*

22 Bola Biga, C/ Enrique Eguren 4, t 94 443 50 26. This friendly little place, famous all over the city, specializes in the three things the Basques do best: *merluza* (hake), *bacalao* (cod) and *rabo de toro* (oxtail).

Inexpensive

27 Amboto, C/ Jardines 2, t 94 415 61 48. A bustling seafood place off Plaza de Arriaga that specializes in *merluza* (hake) in a delicious sauce made from crabs. Lots of locals chattering above the TV in the bar and a friendly atmosphere.

29 Aitxar, C/ María Muñoz. You can eat very well here at this place in the Casco Viejo, which has good seafood and typical dishes for about 1,000 pts/€6.

13 La Granja, Plaza Circular 3. One of Bilbao's oldest cafés, this Belle Epoque establishment with its engaging air of genteel shabbiness is a very popular meeting point right on the *plaza*. Snack on plentiful *pintxos* and *raciones*.

3 Guggen, Alameda de Recalde 5. Perhaps the best of those restaurants cashing in on their proximity to the Guggenheim, with a solid 1,000 pts/€6 *menú*.

25 Café Boulevard, C/ Arenal 3, t 94 415 31 28. First opened in 1871, giving opera-goers a meeting place, and revamped 50 years later, the café retains its elegant Art Deco interior; pop in for an afternoon iced coffee or for an early evening *copa*.

Vegetarian

19 Vegetariano, Alameda de Urquijo 33, t 94 444 55 98 (*cheap*). Has great-value *menús* full of innovative vegetable-based dishes. *Open Mon–Fri lunch only.*

21 Garibolo, C/ Fernández del Campo 7, t 94 422 32 55. Another pleasant little cheapie with a daily *menú* at a mere 1,000 pts/€6.

By the Sea (Getxo and Plentzia)

Jolastoki, Avda Leioa, Getxo, t 94 491 20 31 (*expensive*). Has an enviable reputation for its elaborate fish and fowl dishes; choose between the posh dining room and the sunny patio, and feast on delicately grilled turbot with saffron oil or chicken stuffed with truffles.

El Puerto, Aretxandra 20, Getxo, t 94 491 21 66 (*moderate*). This old-time portside restaurant keeps things simple and unadorned, serving mighty portions of fresh fish.

Gaminiz, Areatza 38, Plentzia, t 94 677 30 93 (*expensive*). Overlooking the port, this restaurant offers an intriguing mix of cuisines, from traditional *kokotxas* to the most innovative of creations; try the seaweed *tempura* with fresh oysters.

Bar Urizarra, C/ Artekale 12, Plentzia. Looks a bit dingy but comes up with the goods for cheap Basque soul food; all the beans, fish and wine you could want for 1,100 pts/€6.5.

Tapas/Pinchos/Pintxos

One of the city's greatest pleasures is the *txikiteo*, the ritual bar crawl, selecting a titbit from the groaning bar tops (*see* pp.73–4). There are three main areas to enjoy this: in the Casco Viejo, in the streets around Calle Ledesma in the Ensanche, and the central area around Calle Licenciado Poza and the Plaza Indautxu. Among the local specialities are *tigres de Yurre*, mussels served in a piquant tomato and anchovy sauce; endless varieties of *bacalao* (cod) with different sauces, such as the mild, green *pil-pil* sauce; *champis*, mushrooms cooked in a garlic, parsley and lemon sauce; *pimientos*, slivers of fried or roasted pepper; fresh squid cooked in its own ink; and the ubiquitous little slices of bread with a breathtaking variety of toppings, from *tortilla* with ham, seafood or cheese, or a pungent slab of sheep's cheese topped with a strip of roasted pepper, to marinated anchovies and creamy salads with vegetables or meat. Wash it all down with a glass of Rioja or *txakoli*. Many of the city's finest restaurants also serve *pintxos* at the bar and it's a great way to get a taste of some of the best cuisine in the city if you can't quite manage a big blowout.

Casco Viejo

The pretty arcaded Plaza Nueva is a good place to start.

1 Víctor Montes, Plaza Nueva 8. One of the city's most celebrated eating places, a Belle Epoque classic with a florid ebony and gilt façade. A vast array of *pintxos* wait inside, such as crisp *croquetas de bacalao* (cod croquettes), with plenty of wine to wash them down. Sunday lunchtime is the best time to come – local families turn up to eat and chat with their neighbours, followed by a stroll around the Sunday market.

26 Víctor, Plaza Nueva 2. With a terrace overlooking the animated square, a lively bar downstairs and elegant dining rooms upstairs (*see* above), this is one of the city's finest and most traditional establishments. The *caldo* (a clear broth) is delicious, and for something more substantial, there is a very good *menú* at 1,500 pts/€9.

S **Fernando**, Plaza Nueva 12. This tiny bar doesn't have quite the same reputation as the Víctor or the Víctor Montes, but it's a bustling little place all the same. On offer is old-fashioned home cooking – tripe (*callos*) *a la vizcaina* and *bonito con tomate* (tuna with tomato) – at reasonable prices.

R **Los Fueros**, C/ Los Fueros 6. This bar's reputation rests on one thing: *gambas a la plancha* – fresh, simply cooked prawns. Try them with a glass of chilled *amontillado* sherry.

25 **Café Boulevard**, C/ Arenal 3. Near the Arriaga theatre, the city's oldest café has a wide range of *pintxos* on offer, but come for the ambience rather than the food. It is always packed with locals relaxing in the sumptuous Art Nouveau grandeur.

X **Saibigain**, C/ Barrencalle Barrena 16. Curing hams dangle from the rafters above a lovely tiled wooden bar. It's a lively bar, packed with locals; the picture behind the bar is of the Atlético Bilbao stadium.

U **Río Oja**, C/ El Perro 6. Another old-fashioned establishment with plenty of charm. It's a great place to try regional specialities like *bacalao al pil-pil* or *u la vizkaína*, or *rabo de toro* (oxtail).

V **Egiluz**, C/ El Perro 4. One of the excellent, almost unchanged little bars in this busy street full of drinking and eating places. The house speciality is *cazuela*, a local stew cooked in an earthenware pot. The snails (*caracoles*) here are also very tasty.

W **Xukela**, C/ El Perro 2. Another good bar on this narrow street, though this one is a mere child compared to its venerable neighbours. There is an enormous variety of *pintxos*, many with toppings of local cheeses, including a strong soft goat's cheese from Asturias (*queso de Cabrales*) topped with anchovies that is delicious.

28 **Txiriboga**, C/ Santa María 13. A minute bar hidden under piled-up platters of tiny slices of bread with dozens of different toppings. The *croquetas* are good too.

The Ensanche

Across in the Ensanche, the streets around Calle Ledesma keep going until a bit later.

C **Café Iruña**, Berastegui 5, **t** 94 424 90 59. A lot of the action is centred around this legendary, beautiful Mudéjar-style café that comes alive with the evening crowd.

B **Jardines**, Avda de Mazarredo 8. Across the Jardines de Albia from the Iruña, this is a pleasant little spot with a popular terrace in summer. You'll find all the usual *pintxos* here, from good *tortilla* to very tasty fried anchovies.

A **María Mani**, C/ Henao 3. Across the road from the Jardines de Albia, this bar serves an imaginative range of *pintxos*: *morros* (pig's cheeks) *a la vinagreta*, *salpicón* (a kind of salad with meat or fish) and a very refreshing *gazpacho* soup in summer.

13 **La Granja**, Plaza Circular 3. Another of the city's stalwarts, a lively, lovely Art Nouveau-style bar with wooden tables, little alcoves and a good selection of traditional *pintxos* on one of the city's main *plazas*.

12 **Nicolás**, C/ Ledesma 10. A neighbourhood institution with a fine dining room (*see above*) and a lively bar with a smart clientele of businesspeople. Famous for *bacalao* and *merluza*, it's also good for stuffed anchovies (*anchoas rellenos*) and a wide selection of *embutidos* (cured sausage).

F **Artajo**, C/ Ledesma 7. There's never any room in this little bar; everyone is here for the *tigres*, mussels in a spicy tomato and anchovy sauce – the best in Bilbao.

D **La Museo del Vino**, C/ Ledesma 10 (next to Nicolás). Fine hams, cheeses and cured meats accompany the wonderful selection of wines here. The Antomar bar, at No.14, is run by the same people and offers a similar range, all of excellent quality.

E **La Taberna Taurina**, C/ Ledesma 5. One of the oldest, most traditional bars around, this gets packed during the summer bull-fighting season. The *tortillas*, with dozens of different fillings, are the highlight here.

H **El Globo**, C/ Diputación 8. A genial, modern bar which has recently won awards for its elaborate *pintxos*; it's also a good place to find imaginative vegetarian toppings.

G **Lekeitio**, C/ Diputación 1. This attractive bar has a reputation for serving some of the best *pintxos* in Bilbao. Try the famous three-tiered *tortilla*, stuffed with tuna and ham, or the stuffed artichokes in season.

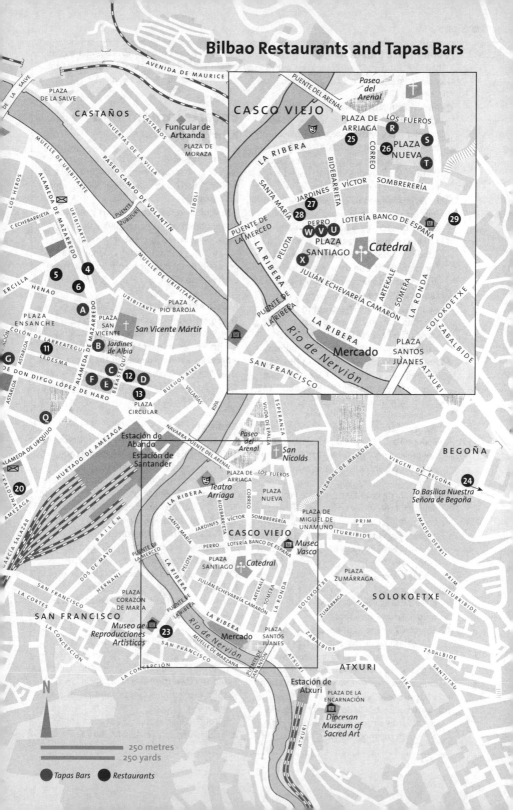

Bilbao Restaurants and Tapas Bars

AVENIDA DE MAURICE

PLAZA DE LA SALVE

CASTAÑOS

Funicular de Artxanda

PLAZA DE MORAZA

CASCO VIEJO

Paseo del Arenal

PUENTE DEL ARENAL

LA RIBERA

PLAZA DE ARRIAGA

LOS FUEROS

R

25

CORREO

26 PLAZA NUEVA

S

T

BIDEBARRIETA

VÍCTOR

SOMBRERERÍA

SANTA MARÍA

JARDINES

27

28

PUENTE DE LA MERCED

PERRO

LOTERÍA BANCO DE ESPAÑA

29

W **V** **U**

PELOTA

PLAZA SANTIAGO

Catedral

X

JULIÁN ECHEVARRÍA CAMARÓN

ARTEKALE

SOMERA

LA RONDA

SOLOKOETXE

ZABALBIDE

LA RIBERA

Mercado

PLAZA SANTOS JUANES

ATXURI

SAN FRANCISCO

Río de Nervión

MUELLE DE URIBITARTE

ALAMEDA DE MAZARREDO

PASEO CAMPO DE VOLANTÍN

HUERTAS DE LA VILLA

CASTAÑOS

PLAZA DE LA VILLA

TÍBOLI

PUENTE ZUBIZURI

LOS HEROS

C ECHEBARRIETA

URIBITARTE

5 **4**

6

ERCILLA

HENAO

A

PLAZA PIO BAROJA

URIBITARTE

PLAZA ENSANCHE

COLÓN DE LARREATEGUI

PLAZA SAN VICENTE

San Vicente Mártir

11

LEDESMA

B

Jardines de Albia

ASTARLOA

G

F **C** **12** **D**

E

13

PLAZA CIRCULAR

Q

ALAMEDA DE URQUIJO

BUENOS AIRES

VILLARÍAS

RIPA

NAVARRA

PUENTE DEL ARENAL

VIUDA DE EPALZA

ESPERANZA

20

KALDUNA

AMEZAGA

Estación de Abando

Estación de Santander

HURTADO DE AMEZAGA

BAILÉN

DOS DE MAYO

HERNANI

Paseo del Arenal

San Nicolás

PLAZA DE ARRIAGA

LOS FUEROS

Teatro Arriaga

CORREO

PLAZA NUEVA

BIDEBARRIETA

VÍCTOR

SOMBRERERÍA

CASCO VIEJO

SANTA MARÍA

JARDINES

PLAZA DE MIGUEL DE UNAMUNO

ITURRIBIDE

PRIM

CALZADAS DE MALLONA

VIRGEN DE BEGOÑA

BEGOÑA

24

To Basílica Nuestra Señora de Begoña

AMADEO DEPRIT

PERRO

LOTERÍA BANCO DE ESPAÑA

Museo Vasco

PLAZA SANTIAGO

Catedral

JULIÁN ECHEVARRÍA CAMARÓN

ARTEKALE

SOMERA

LA RONDA

PLAZA ZUMÁRRAGA

SOLOKOETXE

ZUMÁRRAGA

FIKA

SOLOKOETXE

PRIM

ITURRIBIDE

SAN FRANCISCO

LA CORTES

PLAZA CORAZÓN DE MARÍA

LA CONCEPCIÓN

Museo de Reproducciones Artísticas

23

SAN FRANCISCO

LA CONCEPCIÓN

PUENTE DE LA MERCED

LA RIBERA

MUELLE DE MARZANA

Río de Nervión

Mercado

LA RIBERA

PLAZA SANTOS JUANES

ATXURI

ZABALBIDE

ATXURI

Estación de Atxuri

PLAZA DE LA ENCARNACIÓN

Diocesan Museum of Sacred Art

FIKA

SANTUTXU

ZADALBIDE

N

250 metres
250 yards

● Tapas Bars   ● Restaurants

Around Plaza Indautxu

There are dozens of bars lining the Calle Licenciado Poza, and plenty of good ones just off the main *plaza* itself.

(N) Anduriña Indautxu, Alameda de San Mamés 46. Just off Plaza Indautxu, this is a popular place with a mixed clientele of businessmen and tourists. It's justly renowned for its house specialities, among them *pulpo a la gallega* (spicy boiled octopus) and fresh wild mushrooms.

(M) Urdazpi, Alameda de Urquijo 48. With bull-fighting memorabilia and a busy local crowd, this bar has a good restaurant serving traditional Basque favourites. The *jamón de Jabugo*, served as a *racione* at the bar, is excellent, and there is a decent wine list with a good range of *txakoli* wines.

(Q) Gernika, Alameda de Urquijo 6. At the Abando end of the street, not too far from the train station, this is the place to come for stuffed peppers (*pimientos rellenos*) packed with a dizzying variety of fillings.

(K) Joserra, Particular de Indautxu 4 (just off C/ Gregorio de la Revilla). A pleasant, trim establishment specializing in seafood, and particularly in squid cooked in its own ink (*chiperones*) and octopus served in a variety of different ways.

(P) Bodeguilla, C/ Licenciado Poza 1. A traditional bar with a good range of *pintxos* to wash down with *mistela*, a refreshing drink made with aniseed, water and cinnamon.

(O) Tabernilla de Poza, C/ Licenciado Poza 3. A delightful throw-back, this old-fashioned tavern still serves its wines in a *porrón*, a ceramic jug with a long spout. Accompany the wine with *anchoas con pimientos rojos* (anchovies with red peppers) or a freshly made sandwich.

(L) Or Konpon, C/ Licenciado Poza 33. A young place, serving sandwiches and *raciones* of fried hake (*merluza frita*).

(I) Ziripot, C/ Licenciado Poza 40. All manner of beers on tap and sturdy *pintxos* to mop them up. There's a young, lively crowd enjoying the *croquetas de jamón* (ham croquettes) and *tortilla* served with a hunk of fresh bread.

(J) Busterri, C/ Licenciado Poza 43. This café-bar also has a very decent restaurant if you are not in the mood to face the crowds at the bar. The *pintxos* and *raciones* are good – stuffed anchovies, spicy octopus and tuna – and the wine list is excellent.

Entertainment and Nightlife

For listings information, check the back pages of the local newspaper, *El Correo,* or pick up the *Bilbao Guide* available at tourist information offices.

Fans of Bertolt Brecht and Kurt Weill will be disappointed to learn that 'Bill's Ballhaus in Bilbao' was only a figment of their imagination. In this serious working city, nightlife is generally limited to weekends, in the streets of the Casco Viejo.

Music and Theatre

Teatro Arriaga, Plaza de Arriaga 1, t 94 416 33 33. Regular performances of opera, along with a programme of theatre and comedy.

Palacio Euskalduna de Congresos y de la Música, Abandoibarra 4, t 94 403 50 00. Also puts on plays and musicals, and sometimes big-name foreign acts.

Clubs and Bars

C/ Barrenkale is a busy place with a number of clubs, while C/ Somera has friendly and funky bars, very popular with the Basque nationalist community. In the Ensanche there are more on C/ Pérez Galdós and C/ Licenciado Poza. The **Cotton Club,** C/ Gregorio de la Revilla 25, has occasional live jazz and blues, as does the **Palladium,** C/ Iparraguire 11.

Karaoke is big in Bilbao: if you want to display your singing talents (you'd better be pretty good) head for **Cocos,** C/ Uhagón 9, or **Dakar,** C/ Heros 13, which specializes in Spanish music. The big techno-disco in town is called **Distrito 9,** on C/ Ajuriagerra.

Cinemas

Check listings in the newspaper *El Correo* (*see* above) for undubbed films, which will be listed as v.o. (*version originale*).

Astoria, Plaza Emilio Campuzano 4, t 94 441 69 58

Capitol, C/ Villarias 10, t 94 423 27 52

Mikeldis, Alameda Urquijo 66, t 94 441 17 28

If you were to say only a decade ago that Bilbao was destined to become an international art Mecca, the select few who had ever visited the place would have laughed in your face. Bilbao meant rusty old steel mills and shipping. Travellers who weren't there on business didn't linger, unless they got lost in the maddening traffic system. Getting lost, however, would have allowed more people to better appreciate Bilbao's uncommon setting, tucked in the lush green folds of Euskadi's coastal mountains, the grimy city filling up every possible pocket for miles along the Nervión, a notorious industrial by-product of a river the colour of chocolate milk or robin's-egg blue, depending on the day. The name is Bilbo in Basque, just like the hobbit, but its inhabitants lovingly call it the *Botxo*, the Basque word for hole or orifice.

The orifice was originally a scattering of fishing hamlets huddled on the left bank of a deep *ría*, where the hills offered some protection from the Normans and other pirates. In 1300, when the coast was clear of such dangers, the lord of Vizcaya, Diego López de Haro, founded a new town on the right bank of the Ría de Bilbao. It quickly developed into the Basques' leading port and Spain's main link to northern Europe, exporting Castile's wool to Flanders and the swords Shakespeare called 'bilbos'. In 1511 the merchants formed a council to govern their affairs, the Consulado de Bilbao, an institution that survived and thrived until 1829.

The 19th century had various tricks in store: the indignity of a French sacking in 1808 and sieges by the Carlists in both of their wars; Bilbao was the 'martyr city' of the Liberal cause. But the 19th century also made Bilbao into a great industrial dynamo. Blessed with its fabled iron mountain, nearby forests, cheap hydraulic power and excellent port, Bilbao got a double dose of the Industrial Revolution. Steel mills, shipbuilding and other industries sprang up, quickly followed by banks and insurance companies and all the other accoutrements of capitalism. Workers from across the country poured into gritty tenements, and smoke clogged the air. It became the fourth city of Spain, and still is; it was Spain's Pittsburgh, and still looks like it, and back at the turn of the century it was just as full of worker misery and exploitation. Social activism combined with Basque nationalism made a sturdy antifascist cocktail; during the Civil War, Bilbao was besieged again and Franco punished it crushingly. Then, in the late 1950s, Bilbao was whipped forward to become once more the industrial powerhouse of Spain, but on an artificial life-support system that was unplugged in the new Spain of the EU. The iron mines gave out. In the 1980s, unemployment soared from 6 per cent to 20 per cent.

Something had to be done to save the *Botxo* from becoming a real hole, and the Basques found the political will to do it. Thanks to banking, insurance and such less obviously dirty business, the economy was doing pretty well in spite of all the layoffs, and this has allowed the city to embark on an ambitious redevelopment programme, reclaiming vast areas of the centre formerly devoted to heavy industry. The rusting machinery has been removed and the once-seedy dock area gentrified. The hugely popular Guggenheim Museum, which opened in October 1997, has by itself significantly boosted the city's prestige, attracting almost 4 million visitors so far. Other new projects include cleaning up the Nervíon (it even has a few fish now), a concert hall and convention centre (completed in 1998), and a library, a park, a hotel, offices and residential buildings all to be built on the site of the old shipyards. A 'passenger interchange', which will put local and international bus and train services under one enormous roof, is planned, and the metro, with sleek modern stations designed by Sir Norman Foster, was completed in 1995. The airport got an elegant new terminal designed by Santiago Calatrava in December 2000, and the port is being given a boost as part of a vast harbour expansion project. New industries are being enticed here, too: the European Software Institute has based its headquarters in the 370-acre technology park in nearby Zamudio. Bilbao is shaping up to become one of the cities of Europe's future; come back in a few years and see.

The Casco Viejo

The Casco Viejo, the centre of the city from the 15th to the 19th centuries, is a snug little quarter on the east bank of the Nervión. Tucked out of the way across the Puente del Arenal from the bustling centre, it remains the city's heart. The bridge takes you to **Plaza de Arriaga**, known familiarly as *El Arenal* from the sand flats that stood here long ago.

Fittingly for a Basque city, El Arenal's monuments are both musical: a small Art Nouveau pavilion in steel and glass (concerts every Sunday afternoon) and the opera house, the **Teatro Arriaga**, with its frilly neo-Baroque façade. This is really the third opera house to stand on the site; the first was demolished after only a decade, and the second was built in 1890 when business was booming and the newly rich entrepreneurs decided to bring a little culture to city life. It opened to much fanfare and was equipped, as befitted the new industrial age, with all the latest gadgets, including electric lighting. The townspeople were invited to connect with the theatre and hear the opening opera, *La Gioconda*, down their telephone lines. In 1915 fire broke out and rapidly gutted the building. It took four years to restore it and the present theatre, in its third incarnation, opened in 1919. It is named after Crisóstomo de Arriaga, a child prodigy known as the 'Spanish Mozart', who went to Paris and passed away poetically of consumption just before his 20th birthday. After half a century of neglect, the Teatro Arriaga was bought by the city hall and has been thoroughly primped up. Opera, dance, *zarzuela* (a kind of Spanish popular opera) and concerts now take place in the refurbished auditorium, newly equipped with all the latest technological developments. Nearby is the **Café Boulevard**, with its winking neon light, which was built to accommodate the smart audiences attending the opera and has retained a blowsy, Art Nouveau charm. It's one of the city's most popular haunts.

Across the *plaza* stands the imposing, if now rather bleary, **church of San Nicolás de Bari**, built on the ruins of a chapel of the same name and inaugurated in 1756. It is dedicated to the patron saint of sailors, who couldn't save it from the French or the Carlists who ransacked it and used it as a barracks for most of the 19th century. Inside, shiver in the Baroque gloom or admire a handful of sculptures by Basque artist Juan Pascal de Mena. Behind the church, the Casco Viejo metro station and Euskotren

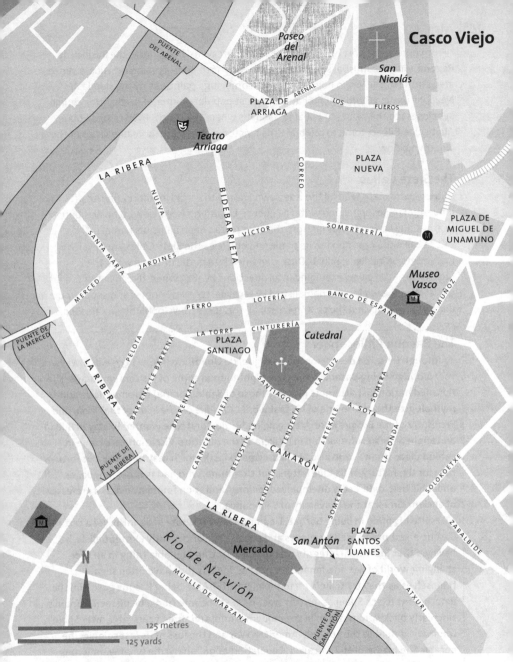

Casco Viejo

Paseo del Arenal

San Nicolás

PLAZA DE ARRIAGA

LOS

FUEROS

ARENAL

🎭 Teatro Arriaga

PUENTE DEL ARENAL

LA RIBERA

NUEVA

BIDEBARRIETA

CORREO

PLAZA NUEVA

SANTA MARÍA

JARDINES

VÍCTOR

SOMBRERERÍA

PLAZA DE MIGUEL DE UNAMUNO

Ⓜ

MERCED

PERRO

LOTERÍA

BANCO DE ESPAÑA

Museo Vasco

M. MUÑOZ

🏛

PUENTE DE LA MERCED

LA TORRE

CINTURERÍA

Catedral

PELOTA

BARRENKALE BARRENA

PLAZA SANTIAGO

SANTIAGO

LA CRUZ

A. SOTA

SOMERA

LA RIBERA

BARRENKALE

J. F. BELOSTIKALE

CARNICERÍA VIEJA

TENDERÍA

ARTEKALE

LE RONDA

PUENTE DE LA RIBERA

CAMARÓN

SOMERA

SOLOKOETXE

🏛

Ⓜ

TENDERÍA

SOMERA

ZABALBIDE

LA RIBERA

Río de Nervión

Mercado

San Antón

PLAZA SANTOS JUANES

N

MUELLE DE MARZANA

PUENTE DE SAN ANTÓN

ATXURI

✝

125 metres

125 yards

station for local services is burrowed into the rock. Head down Calle Esperanza, pausing at the *pelota* court if the players are practising, and you'll find the grimy entrance to the *ascensor* (lift) which will lift you up to the heights of Begoña. It may look like the watchtower of a Soviet labour camp, but your reward will be wonderful views across the old quarter.

From here it's a short but steep walk to the Vizcayans' holy shrine, the **Basílica de Begoña**, with its unusual spire stuck on an early-16th-century church. Inside, a venerated statue of the Virgin holds court with some huge paintings by the slapdash Neapolitan Luca Giordano, probably the most popular painter of his day. This church lies closest to the hearts of Bilbaínos, and it's where the much-loved football team, Atlético de Bilbao, come to celebrate their victories. There are more fine views of the old town below.

The Siete Calles

Steep, worn steps lead all the way down the hill to Plaza Unamuno, named after the influential philosopher and writer Miguel de Unamuno (*see* below), who was born on nearby Calle La Ronda, not far from the little plaza which bears his name.

Calle La Ronda is as good as its name and encircles the **Siete Calles**, the seven original streets of medieval Bilbao. Once contained by a girdle of stone walls, the prosperous little city was bulging in all directions by 1843 when, directly after the first Carlist War, the walls were demolished by royal decree. New homes and shops immediately sprang up, and the centrepiece of all this urban development was arcaded,

The Basque Philosopher

Although he cared deeply for Spain, Miguel de Unamuno (1864–1937) was always very proud of being Basque. More clear-sighted than some of his contemporaries, he ridiculed nationalist attempts (notably those of Sabino Arana) to romanticize and mythologize the race in one of his first works, *Critique on the Issue of the Origin and Prehistory of the Basque Race*. After gaining his doctorate, he wanted to stay in Bilbao and applied for a professorship in Euskera at the Instituto Viscazíano. He came in second place (Arana, who also applied, came in last), which may have been unfortunate for the history of Basque letters, but Unamuno, who had 15 other languages under his belt, didn't stay unemployed for long, and soon found a post as a professor of ancient Greek at the University of Salamanca.

Despite his pride in being Basque, Unamuno always wrote in Spanish. Yet a certain Basque angst permeated his essays and novels. One of the early existentialists, he believed that individual integrity was the only true and reliable thing in an ever-changing world of lies and fanaticism (just as the Basques have often seen themselves as they try to hold on to their identity). Also, being Basque gave him the detachment to see Spain as it really was. In *On Casticismo* (1895) he dissected Spain's singularly backward position in the modern world, and three years later, after Spain's traumatic defeat in the Spanish–American War and the loss of its last colonies, he became the leader of the so-called 'Generation of 98', analyzing what went wrong with Spain, and seeking ways to revitalize it.

In 1901, Unamuno was made rector of Salamanca University, and went on to write one of his most important works, *The Tragic Sense of Life in Men and Peoples* (1913). In spite of the fame it and his novels brought him, he was dismissed from his post as rector for speaking out in support of the Allied cause in the First World War (when

enclosed **Plaza Nueva**, symbol of Bilbao's growth and prosperity, and still the heart of the old town. Edged with cafés, bars and shops stuffed with souvenirs and religious ornaments, it gets especially lively on Sunday afternoons, when families come to eat out on the terraces and stroll around the weekly market, a tradition which has earned the Plaza the nickname of 'the living room'. Known for its antique books, coins and postcards, the market doesn't stop there and has everything from clamouring song-birds (unhappily penned in tiny cages) to dog food and mops.

A couple of blocks south of Plaza Nueva, the recently restored **Catedral de Santiago** sends its graceful spire up over the centre of the Casco Viejo. Begun in the 13th century, most of this understated but elegant grey stone church is 14th–15th-century Gothic (though the façade was added only in the 1880s). The highlight is the magnificent Renaissance portico, constructed in 1581, where town councils were once held under the pale, cool arches.

Around the corner from the cathedral is the delightful **Museo Vasco** (*La Cruz 4; open Tues–Sat 10.30–1.30 and 4–7, Sun 10.30–1.30; adm*), set around a peaceful cloister which once formed part of the city's first Jesuit church and college, established in 1604. In the centre stands the ancient Idolo de Mikeldi, the museum's treasure, which

---

Spain, and Bilbao in particular, was making a fortune from staying neutral). He was so openly opposed to the dictatorship of Primo de Rivera in the 1920s that he was imprisoned on the Canary Islands and became Spain's most famous dissident. A daring rescue led by a Paris newspaper freed him, and in 1931, with the setting up of the Republic, he was re-elected rector at Salamanca.

Unamuno's own integrity led to a most famous incident in the Civil War. Although his opposition to dictatorship had made him a celebrity, Unamuno had come out at first for the Francoist rebels. It wasn't long before he realized that he had made a terrible mistake, but Salamanca was well behind Franco's lines, and in 1936, three months after Franco revolted, the Falange decided to celebrate National Day (Columbus Day) there with a special ceremony. Franco was unable to attend at the last minute, and the unwilling Unamuno had to replace him on the stage. He had to listen as speakers called the Catalans and Basques (both on the Republican side) 'cancers' that needed to be removed from the body of Spain. Then General Millán Astray, the one-eyed, one-armed leader of the Spanish Foreign Legion, set the audience on fire shouting his motto: '¡Viva la muerte!' (Long live death!).

Unamuno's concluding remarks were struck from the official record. Witnesses, however, recalled that he proudly defended his Basque origins, called Astray to account for mutilating the nation in the image of himself, and his parting shot, as the frenzied Astray and his supporters screamed 'Death to the intellectuals!', was: 'You will win, because you have the brute force. But you will not convince.' Surrounded by rabid Falangists, Franco's wife performed the service of a bodyguard and escorted the philosopher safely off the stage; he was placed under house arrest and died of a heart attack two months later.

probably dates back to the Iron Age and looks like the prototype of the cow that jumped over the moon. Gravestones, other funerary pieces and strange stone statues discovered in caves and dating back millennia are also on display. On the first floor, a series of tableaux recreates the old Basque occupations of shepherd, fisherman and whaler, their domestic lives and pastimes, and their religious devotions, all set to a murmuring soundtrack of seagulls, creaking sails and wood being whittled. Photographs document pilgrimages to local churches, and with them are displayed an eclectic range of *ex votos*, including a huge and wonderfully detailed sailing ship found at the Hermitage de Santa María de Olabeaga. Upstairs again, you'll find a scale model of Vizcaya and a reconstruction of the rooms of the Consulate (the old merchants' organization), as well as tools and model ships.

Wander down to the river through the Siete Calles, all but deserted during the afternoon siesta, yet crammed in the evenings with shoppers and strollers taking in the busy bars, cafés and shops, some of which have remained unchanged for generations. The street names often reveal their history: Carnicería was the butchers' street, Tendería was packed with shops, and Barrencalle is named after the Barrondo family in recognition of their staunch support for Pedro of Castile, who lived on this street in a tower which has long since disappeared. The 'Seven Streets' run down to the river, where they join the arcaded Porte de la Ribera, all that remains of the old Plaza Mayor, where stallholders once came to sell their wares. By the beginning of the 20th century they had become such a fixture that it was decided to build them a home, the fabulous Art Deco **Mercado de la Ribera** on the riverfront, the largest covered market in Spain.

Just over the pedestrian bridge of La Ribera is one of Bilbao's oddest museums, the **Museo de Reproducciones Artisticas** (*Conde Mirasol 2; open Mon–Fri 9.30–1.30 and 4–7, Sun 11–2, closed Sat and hols*), a kind of retirement home for hundreds of plaster copies of the world's most famous statues, from the Venus de Milo to the Apollo of Belvedere, all nudging shoulders among the easels. They were made during the 19th century for drawing classes, which you can still take here. The collection was vastly expanded a century ago, when the fashion for drawing classical figures fizzled out and art schools from across Europe shipped their models here.

Back on the other side of the river stands the sturdy **church of San Antón**, shrugging off its grimy coat thanks to an ongoing restoration programme and emerging with a pretty, garlanded portico and bell tower. It overlooks a bridge of the same name, where tolls used to be levied for entrance to the city.

Further upriver, past the ornamental Atxuri train station, is tiny Plaza de la Encarnación. Here, the **Diocesan Museum of Sacred Art** (*open Tues–Sat 10.30–1.30 and 4–7, Sun 10.30–1.30*), occupies the former Convento de la Encarnación and is set around a peaceful Renaissance cloister. It displays over eight centuries' worth of religious art and finery: vestments of gold brocade and embroidery, sculptures and paintings by Basque artists, and a vast silver collection, one of the country's finest, with pieces from across Spain and the Americas.

The Ensanche

Nobody in the 19th century had a sharper sense of urban design than the Spaniards, and wherever a town had money to do something big, the results were impressive. Like Barcelona, Bilbao in its industrial boom years had to face exponential population growth, and its mayors chose to plan for this instead of just letting things happen. The area across the river from Bilbao, the Anteiglesia de Abando, was mostly farmland in the 1870s when the city annexed it. A trio of planners, Severino de Achúcarro, Pablo de Alzola and Ernest Hoffmeyer, got the job of laying out the streets of what came to be known as the **Ensanche**, or 'extension', and they came up with a simple-looking but really rather ingenious plan, with diagonal boulevards dividing up the broad loop of the river like orange sections.

The Ensanche begins across from El Arenal; just over the bridge from the old town, a statue of Bilbao's founder, Diego López de Haro, looks benignly over the massive banks and circling traffic in the Plaza de España, more commonly known as **Plaza Circular**. This has become the business centre of the city, with the big grey skyscraper of the Banco Bilbao Vizcaya, built in the 1960s, to remind us who is the leading force in the city's destiny today. The RENFE station occupies one corner of the square; you'll have to walk around behind it to the riverfront to see one of the city's industrial-age landmarks: the tiny Bilbao–Santander train station, a charming Art Nouveau work with a wrought-iron and tile façade designed by Severino de Achúcarro. The vast desolation of tracks and sidings behind these two stations, wasted space at the heart of the city, is about to be reclaimed as the centrepiece of Bilbao's ambitious facelift – the Intermodal – a huge commercial project to be built on air right over the tracks. A new station under an elliptical glass dome is also envisaged.

Southwest of the Plaza Circular

Plaza Zabálburu marks the beginning of Bilbao's less salubrious quarters, now too in the first stages of gentrification. The artists and funky bars have moved in, but the prostitutes, especially those on Calle la Cortes, are still a going concern. Southwest of Plaza Zabálburu lies the Vista Alegre bullring, carpeted with weird black sand brought from the mines around the city. It is packed during the *Semana Grande*, the week following 15 August every year, when bullfighters quake at the thought of facing the notoriously tough Bilbaíno audience. The **Museo Taurino** (*open Mon–Fri 10.30–1 and 4–6; adm*) holds mementos from over 250 years of bullfighting history, from posters, costumes and photographs to the heads of famous bulls – or in the case of Ofendido, who stands massively at the entrance, the whole beast. Poor Ofendido ('offended') was a magnificent bull who was deprived of his chance for glory because he'd chipped his horns. At least he got a second chance posthumously. The highlight of these exhibits is a magnificent embroidered cape decorated with figures by Goya, which was created for the Enlightenment-era matador Joaquín Rodriguez. The museum also outlines Basque contributions to bullfighting, traditionally regarded as an Andalucían sport, and defiantly points out that the first toreros to face a bull on foot were in fact from northern Navarra and Aragón (they probably had a lot of practice during the Festa de San Fermín; *see* pp.206–7). The most famous Basque bull-fighter was Castor Jaureguibeitia, nicknamed 'Cocherito de Bilbao', who made his debut as a *matador* here at the Vista Alegre bullring in 1905. Fifteen years later it was also the scene of his final performance, given in front of King Alfonso XIII, who awarded him the prized bull's ear as the crowds gave him a roaring standing ovation. In recent years the bullring has not been paying its way, and the city authorities have decided to cover it over so that it can be used for concerts and other performances.

The Gran Vía and the Plaza Moyúa

From Plaza Circular, the main boulevard of the Ensanche extends westwards: the **Gran Vía de Don Diego López de Haro**. Designed to be the city's 'backbone', it was the obvious place in the new city for prominent families and businesses to vie for the most modern and progressive houses. A later addition to the street, but still exhibiting the same pride and optimism, is **El Corte Inglés** department store at Nos.7–9, its façade one vast, high-relief mural evoking the industry and history of Bilbao. Further along is the **Palacio Foral** (the seat of the provincial council), another product of the city's boom times. Completed in 1900, this building was conceived as a means of flaunting the new prosperity, and the façade is a dizzying reminder that less is usually more; swirls, curlicues, garlands and ornamentation of every kind jostle together. The contemporary reaction was horror, particularly from those who had to work in the labyrinthine, impractical interior, but attitudes have mellowed over the years and now its eccentricity earns it an affectionate regard.

The centre of the Ensanche scheme is Plaza de Federico Moyúa, better known as **La Elíptica**. The Hotel Carlton at No.2, still one of the city's posh establishments, served as the seat of the Basque government under the Republic and during the Civil War. At No.5 is the spiky, stripy Chavarri Palace, inspired by a celebrated Brussels hotel; it's famous for the fact that each window is different.

Museo de Bellas Artes

Open Tues–Sat 10.30–1.30 and 4–7.30, Sun 10–2; adm.

From La Elíptica, Calle Elcano takes you to the Museum of Fine Arts on the edge of the large and beautiful Parque de Doña Casilda Iturriza. Although this musuem contains one of the finest art collections in Spain, until recently, few visitors made it to this quiet corner. However, this is set to change as the overflow from the Guggenheim brings more visitors, and the museum is currently being enlarged to accommodate them.

The collection begins in the 13th century with a pair of Catalan Romanesque panels; a simple, striking *Noah and the Ark* surmounted by a monstrous, awkward dove, and a spindly *Descent from the Cross*, in which Christ bears up with an expression of mild bemusement. The early collection is rich in Catalan art, partly because the Catalans themselves were doing very nicely and could afford to grant plenty of commissions. There is a clutch of late-Gothic, Italian-influenced, mannered paintings by another Catalan, Pere Serra (d. 1405), and a remarkable gilded altarpiece by Pere Nicolau. By the mid-15th century, Flemish realism had stamped its imprint across Spanish painting; Bartolomé Bermejo's cold, cruel *Flagellation of St Grace* is unnervingly realistic. There are several Flemish works here, too, including Metsys' *The Money Changers*, some gentle pastoral scenes by Jan Breughel, and a later, unnerving *Lamentation* by Van Dyck, with desperate red-eyed women holding Christ's limp, dead body.

The luminous 16th-century *Piedad* is by Luis de Morales who, despite being dismissed from court by Philip II for being 'too old-fashioned', remained extremely popular and was nicknamed 'El Divino' for his ecstatic saints. They look pallid and contrived next to the intensely emotional canvases of El Greco; the blazing colours of his rapturous *Annunciation* (*c.* 1596–1600) seem to stun even Mary, while in *Saint Francis and the Cross*, the gaunt saint's face gleams palely from the shadows as he contemplates death and resurrection. Another bold colourist was José Ribera, whose *St Sebastian Treated by the Holy Women* depicts the saint tethered by his arm as arrows are drawn from his body in the rather dim heavenly light provided by a couple of angels.

For something a bit fluffier and less intense, there are a few Murillos, including a pudgy-faced Saint Lesmes and a couple of portraits. Untouched by the histrionics of lesser mortals, Zurbarán's sublimely simple still-life paintings reveal a serene, orderly world. *The Virgin with the Infant Jesus*, one of Velázquez's last paintings, is restrained, contemplative and utterly moving. Goya, who started out making designs, or cartoons, for the local carpet factory in Madrid, was appointed Principal Painter to the king in 1799, shortly after being struck with deafness (probably thanks to syphilis). Plunged into silence, he ended by painting vast, apocalyptic visions of a world 'where reason sleeps'. Before these visions became all-consuming, his portraits, such as those here of Martin Zapater and the poet Moratin, provided much of his income and are strikingly frank, acute and utterly unconcerned with rank. But by the 19th century Spanish art had lost its fire, as the smug portraits and bland landscapes attest. There are a few pieces by French artists, among them Cézanne's *Great Bathers* and Gauguin's *Washerwomen at Arles*, and some soft portraits by the American Impressionist Mary Cassatt. Later Spanish works include a bleak portrait of grim-faced prostitutes by Solana, and a touching study of an ineffably *Sad Child* by Moroccan-born Carlos Sárez de Tejada.

The collection of Basque works is very strong and includes wonderful portraits by Echevarría and Zuloaga, particularly his sultry, sloe-eyed *La Condesa Mathieu de Noailles* (1913). The dreamy *Bridge of Burceña* is by Bilbao-born painter Aurelio Areta Errasti, and depicts a silent figure slumped, musing, over the railings. The highlights are, of course, the sculptural pieces, such as *Portrait of a Soldier called Odyssey* by Jorge de Oteiza (*see* box on the next page) and *Around a Void I* by Eduardo Chillida (*see* p.185); both artists were interested in the concept of what Oteiza called 'spatial de-occupation'.

The leafy park itself is an agreeable place to spend an hour or two, with exotic trees carefully labelled, a lagoon and a new light-and-colour bauble called the 'Cybernetic Fountain'.

Jorge de Oteiza

Oteiza, the fiery 5ft-tall *enfant terrible* of the Spanish art world, was born in 1908 in the seaside resort of Orio. He was sent to Madrid to study medicine, but it wasn't long before he abandoned his studies in favour of sculpture and mounted his first exhibition in San Sebastián in 1931. From about 1935, he began his career as a plastic artist with a series of pieces based on found objects, but, disgusted with Francoism and the apathetic dreariness of Spain, he set off for South America, where he spent several years teaching ceramics to students in Buenos Aires and Bogotá. In the 1950s he began to make the pieces for which he is most famous, the 'Metaphysical Boxes', a series of massive forms based on cubes with hollow centres, which reflected his increasing preoccupation with what he described as 'spatial de-occupation'. These works brought him widespread acclaim and recognition, but when he set out the theoretical ideas behind their conception in the *Propósito Experimental* (written 1956–7), the art world reacted with consternation at his radical new ideas.

Otieza was enormously influential on a new generation of sculptors who became known as Equipo 57; this group saw art as a form of behaviour within society and rejected its commercial exploitation. Having riled the critics in the 1950s, Oteiza had another go at goading them in 1963, when he published *Quousque Tandem*, which became the unofficial manifesto of the Escuela Vasca (the Basque School), of which Chillida (*see* p.185) is a long-standing member. He exhorted Basque artists to define their art in terms of the Basque character and bound together his principal theories by stating: 'Rejecting the occupation of space, Basque art is natural, irregular. I reject whatever is not essential, whatever fails to respond to constructive truth. This Basque character is already apparent in the cromlechs, the rings of sacred stones that lead us into the realm of magic, the basis of our tradition.'

Still sculpting and still mischievous in his 90s, Oteiza never passes up an opportunity to throw out a few fireworks. The very suggestion that art should be sold still drives him to distraction – which is why the main body of his work lies stacked in his studio in Zarautz and why he is so contemptuous of 'the other sculptor' (Chillida) who is famously prolific. And rich.

Along the Nervión

When Bilbao's urban planners embarked on post-industrial regeneration in the late 1980s, it was inevitable that the riverbank would be identified as the project's linchpin. The significance of the Nervión (which becomes the Ría de Bilbao) to Bilbao is as much symbolic as practical; for years it has been synonymous in Spain with massive industrial pollution, but clean-up efforts since 1981 have succeeded in making the river habitable to fish for the first time in nearly a century.

Major developments have taken place above water, too, as several kilometres of old rusting jetties and dock installations have been torn out to make room for a riverside park, stretching downstream from the Arenal bridge past the Guggenheim Museum and down to the Palacio Euskalduna. Bilbaínos have taken to the development with gusto – thousands of them pour on to the riverbanks every evening to walk their dogs and eat ice cream – and when the trees grow, and the estuarine pong disappears, it's likely to be a very pleasant space.

Overlooking the river at the Arenal end is the city's Ayuntamiento (town hall), which hasn't followed the big banks and wealthy businesses across the river. It used to sit next to the long-demolished Plaza Mayor on the other side of the Casco Viejo, part of a formidable and powerful trinity along with the church of San Antón and the Trade Court. It was shifted to this spot (where it can keep an eye on everyone) a century ago, and housed in a brand new building with an 'Arab Hall' decorated with Mudéjar-style tiles. The grand houses continue along this side of the river, and it won't be long before the old warehouse district on the opposite bank is full of loft-style apartments and artists' galleries; a few have already moved in among the derelict warehouses.

Halfway along, the glass-floored **Puente Zubi Zuri** ('white bridge' in Basque) was one of the first additions to the riverfront landscape; its nautical theme – the bridge billows out like a great sail – has become a widespread motif in the architecture of New Bilbao. The architect-engineer Santiago Calatrava of Valencia has become a favourite here and was also responsible for the new bridge at Ondárroa and the new airport terminal. Heading off Campo de Volantín into the little *barrio* of Castaños, a funicular glides up from Plaza Funicular to the hilltop park on **Monte Artxanda** (every 15 minutes; *see* 'Getting Around', above), where there are a couple of restaurants and extensive views of the Casco Viejo, the Guggenheim and, on really clear days, the sea, 10 miles to the north. For an authentic cultural experience go up at a weekend, when half of Bilbao squeezes into the rattling cars and hangs out on the mountain, picnicking, chattering and enjoying the view. It's a great place to watch the greening of the city, as lines of turf replace the old freight train tracks which used to run the length of the docks.

Back at the bottom of the hill, cross the river on the Zubi Zuri, which is extended by a zigzag concrete path propped up on scaffolding. It picks its way over the remnants of the warehouses and leads up to the **Alamedo Mazarredo**, where there are several snooty restaurants and the graceful Palacio Ibaigane, which once belonged to the powerful Sota family and is now the seat of Atlético de Bilbao football club. If you can't face that scaffolding, continue your stroll down the Campo de Volantín, past the Guggenheim (*see* below), and into the university district of Deusto. From here, cross the sleek, modern **Puente Euskalduna**, which arches in a broad sideways curve across the river. The bridge is named, like the new concert hall and conference centre, after the old shipyard which once stood here, commemorated by an old shipyard crane, 'La Carola', supposedly named after a pretty girl who crossed the Deusto bridge every day and brought all the workers out to watch and whistle. The great hunk of rusting steel and glass is the high-tech Palacio de Congresos y de la Música Euskalduna (1998), designed by the architects Federico Soriano and Dolores Palacios. An incoherent jumble of metal and concrete, it is supposed to represent the last ship made in the Euskalduna shipyards, churning up the Nervión. More tangible reminders of the old trade will be housed in a new museum devoted to Bilbao's maritime history, currently being constructed downriver towards Olabeaga in the old Euskalduna dry docks, and due to open at the end of 2001.

The Guggenheim Museum

The greatest building of our time.
Philip Johnston

Downstream from the Zubi Zuri, a 6oft tower of steel and golden limestone heralds the presence of Bilbao's new art Mecca and the centrepiece of the city's riverfront redevelopment, Frank O. Gehry's stunning Museo Guggenheim. Gehry's softly glowing titanium clipper ship occupies the Abandoibarra flats, until 1987 home to Bilbao's biggest shipyard and now a worldwide symbol of successful urban renewal. The museum fits into the landscape perfectly, looking utterly futuristic and yet in keeping with the city's industrial past. Its massive popularity and high public visibility have helped to spawn an economic boom, the so-called 'Guggenheim Effect', which has been felt throughout the Basque lands and shows no sign as yet of slowing down. How it all came into being is as intriguing as the building itself.

The Guggenheims

It really looks a good deal like they'd gobble all in sight
On top of earth or under it, so fearful is their might.
They'll gobble all there is to get and turn you inside out.
The Guggenheims will get you if you don't watch out.
Washington Times, 1910

Gobblers? By the 1970s, even most Americans only remembered the Guggenheims for the extraordinary museum in New York that bears their name, forgetting how only a few decades before, their names were splashed regularly across the front pages as one of the dozen richest families in the United States. The one link they have with Bilbao is metals: iron made Bilbao, copper made the Guggenheims. And the fruit of their unlikely marriage, fittingly, is a titanium miracle child.

The Guggenheims were one of the great American sagas of rags to riches. Anti-Semitism in a Swiss ghetto is what pushed Simon Guggenheim the tailor to emigrate to Philadelphia in 1847, where he and his 20-year-old son, Meyer, first worked as itinerant peddlers. Meyer had no formal education, but he realized that his best-selling item was stove polish, and soon began making a better polish at home with the help of a second-hand sausage stuffer. From stove polish Meyer went on to coffee extract, then to food and clothing during the Civil War, spices, lye, Swiss lace and embroideries. The turning point came in 1881, with a haphazard purchase of two waterlogged lead and silver mines in Colorado. Meyer had them drained, and they proved far richer than anyone had imagined. Meyer soon built his first smelter and, like the other robber barons of the era, he did his share to found the American labour movement; starvation wages for miners were the rule, and strikers were clobbered into submission.

Unlike the other robber barons, though, Meyer had seven sons who took over the mining business as a formidable unit. Operations soon expanded to Mexico. In 1900 they battled a Rockefeller-controlled trust for control of America's mines and smelters, and ended up owning 51 per cent of the trust. With JP Morgan they bought Kennecott, a mountain of solid copper in Alaska, and built a $25 million railroad over a moving glacier to exploit it, scooping up much of the rest of Alaska's mineral wealth while they were at it with such assiduity that they also helped to spark the American conservationist movement. They joined with financier Thomas Ryan to exploit the Congo's diamonds and gold mines for its owner-slave master, King Leopold II of Belgium. They expanded into diamond mines in Angola. They acquired a huge copper mine in Bingham canyon in Utah, and then topped that by buying the Chuquicamata mine in Chile, the world's richest copper field. They owned tin mines in Malaysia. By the First World War, the Guggenheims controlled 75 per cent of the earth's silver, copper and lead. The family, however, was beginning to fray. One brother went down on the *Titanic*. The youngest brother sued the older brothers. No one had seven sons; in fact, male heirs interested in the business were exceedingly rare. In 1923 the five remaining brothers sold Chuquicamata to Anaconda Copper, sat back on their multi-millions, and decided it was time to give them away.

The Guggenheims were remarkable for the speed in which they made their fortune, but perhaps are even more so for how quickly and farsightedly they dispersed it. One brother financed the first aeronautics studies in America, the rocket experiments of Robert I I. Goddard, the ancestors of the Jet Propulsion labs at Princeton and Caltech, the masterminds of the US space programme. Another set up a free dental clinic for the children of New York, and left millions to Mount Sinai Hospital and the Mayo Clinic. Another set up a foundation to dispense grants to promising scholars, artists and scientists to do with as they pleased, enabling hundreds of people to start their careers or work on their masterpieces: Linus Pauling, Aaron Copland, Katherine Anne Porter, Vladimir Nabokov, Gian Carlo Menotti, Henry Kissinger, W. H. Auden, Samuel Barber, Thomas Wolfe and Marianne Moore were all Guggenheim fellows.

Then there was brother Solomon, the charmer, who acquired a sudden interest in non-objective art at the age of 65, after meeting a 36-year-old German baroness named Hilla Rebay. Solomon was captivated, and took it to heart when she told him it was his duty to stop collecting Old Masters and patronize the new. Under her guidance he acquired the Kandinskys, Delaunays, Légers, Feiningers and Moholy-Nagys that became the basis of the Solomon R. Guggenheim Foundation. Rebay was the first director. The collection went on tours around America, and with its success Rebay pressed Solomon into building a temple for his collection in New York, and getting American's greatest architect, Frank Lloyd Wright, to design it. Finished in 1959, the Guggenheim Museum was the most controversial, and the most organic, sculpturally beautiful building erected in America in the 20th century.

But even before its completion, the Guggenheims were expanding. In the early 1940s, keen collector Peggy Guggenheim (whose father had gone down with the *Titanic*) wowed the New York art world with her Art of the Century exhibition, displaying her collection of works by Duchamp, Ernst, Mondrian, Tanguy, Arp,

Brancusi, Giacometti and Klee, many of whom were scarcely known in America. Art of the Century was a major force behind abstract expressionism, led by Peggy's protegé Jackson Pollock (who started off as a carpenter in Solomon's museum) and Robert Motherwell. After the war, Peggy bought a *palazzo* in Venice to exhibit her collection, and since her death in 1979 it, too, has been owned by the Guggenheim Foundation.

Expanding into Bilbao

The Guggenheims always knew that mines eventually give out, but the fact that countries like Chile and Angola would nationalize theirs in the 1970s caught them unawares. Share prices collapsed and the Solomon R. Guggenheim Foundation's original endowment, which depended on the dividends, could no longer meet operating costs. Money-spinners like a restaurant and shop were opened, but the Foundation, concluding that its biggest assets were its fabulous permanent collection and its prestigious name, decided that a satellite was in order. In his quest to find a site for another Guggenheim, Thomas Krens, the head of the Foundation, went around the world, to Salzburg, Tokyo, Moscow, Vienna, London and elsewhere, ready to wheel and deal. None of the proposed marriages worked out for one reason or another – until Krens met the Basques, who were ready to come up with the dowry.

At the time, Bilbao's movers and shakers were already well along in their grand scheme for converting the dirty old rust bucket along the Nervión into a magnet for service and high-tech industries. Although a dramatic string of dazzling architectural projects, including Sir Norman Foster's metro, the Calatrava airport terminal and the new congress and performance centre, were under way, they were still casting about for a prestigious state-of-the-art project to anchor their redevelopment schemes, something that would encourage outside investment, something truly bodacious that would give the Basque country headlines that didn't mention the word terrorism. After the huge success of an exhibition of the Guggenheim's permanent works at the Reina Sofía museum in Madrid, the Basques realized a Guggenheim museum was just what they were looking for and boldly suggested Bilbao to Krens.

It just so happened that this was a time when Bilbao city, Vizcaya province and the autonomous regional government were all firmly in the hands of the Basque Nationalist Party (PNV), which enabled them to head off considerable political opposition to the idea. Nor was Krens immediately convinced – although impressed by the PNV's determination to give Bilbao a new direction, he and the other Guggenheim administrators were appalled by the site earmarked for the new museum, a run-down warehouse district punctuated by a brutally ugly bridge, the busiest in Bilbao. Undeterred, the PNV came up with the convincing $100 million (in spite of indignant squawks from the opposition) to ensure that the new museum would be housed in a building of spectacular character, one that would come to identify the city in the same way as the Opera House in Sydney. To this end, Krens provided three names for an architectural competition: Arata Isozaki, the Viennese Coop Himmel-blau and Frank Gehry. They were each given $10,000, one site visit and three weeks.

Fitting in the City

When the design of the museum was put out to competition, both Krens and Bilbao had their own demands. Krens wanted the museum to be thoroughly new, both in form and function: the building itself was to have the same dramatic effect as a cathedral of the Middle Ages; the gallery space should be large enough to accommodate the massive works of modern art which had outgrown traditional museums; and the building should interact with the collection rather than simply provide a blank space for its presentation. The local administration wanted the museum to be a fully integrated part of the city, and Gehry's design was chosen because it fulfilled this condition most completely.

Gehry fell in love with Bilbao, the industrial setting (so very different from the Fifth Avenue Guggenheim) and the city's gritty determination. He wanted the museum to be a link between their 19th and 21st centuries, a building that would be 'a good neighbour'. Surrounded by pools, the museum seems to float by the riverside, echoing the great ships which once made the city's fortune; the materials used – limestone and titanium – evoke the industrial past and the creamy stone of the Deusto university on the opposite bank. The Puente de la Salve bridge, a major access road to the city centre, is embraced by the limestone tower which has no exhibition purpose but exists simply to knit together the city and the museum. A walkway sweeps across the river, around the museum and up a flight of movie-star steps, and gives pedestrian access to the bridge. Instead of an imposing elevated main entrance, visitors *descend* a grand stairway into the main lobby. Even the walls themselves melt into the interior atrium through the glass façade, fuzzing the sense of inside and outside. From within the museum, glass angles frame the university, the new music and conference centre and the old opera house, deliberately embracing the city's landmarks.

Frank Gehry's Titanium Sculpture

He is an architect of immense gifts who dances on the line separating architecture from art but who manages never to let himself fall.
    Paul Goldberger, *New York Times* architecture critic

Gehry, born in Toronto in 1929 but longtime resident of Los Angeles, has often been accused of kookiness, along with an impressive assortment of other labels: postmodernist, cubist, deconstructionist, expressionist, punky, funky, Nouveau Californian or simply 'that chain-link guy', referring back to his first works that caused a stir: his own house in Santa Monica (1978) and the Temporary Contemporary Museum (1983) in a former LA bus garage, made of concrete, plywood, chain-link and corrugated metal. His buildings, made of low cost 'found' materials, resembled 3-D collages, unfinished, spontaneous, even explosive at times.

The leap from 'that chain-link guy' to master of the voluptuous, organic, high-tech Guggenheim Bilbao may seem huge but, according to Gehry's own vision of his work, nothing could be more natural. He believes that architecture itself is art, or sculpture to be precise, because it has three dimensions, and he has made the often-complicated synthesis between the two his territory, trying to match the form and materials to the context of each project. Not bound by any other criteria, his buildings are shot through with an engaging delight and freedom. Architecture as art can serve both life and art, Gehry would argue; it can be poetic, dynamic, sensual, restless, spiritual, lyrical or even irreverent. Unlike many trendy architects who sink into frivolity and kitsch to avoid the cardinal postmodern sin of boring the audience, there's always a method behind Gehry's madness, an inner order to his buildings, an often complex meshing of form and function. His favourite building is Le Corbusier's church at Ronchamp in the Vosges (1955), a sculptural masterpiece by the otherwise supreme rationalist, celebrated for its deeply spiritual spaces. 'I approach each building as a sculptural object, a spatial container, a space with light and air, a response to context and appropriateness of feeling and spirit,' Gehry wrote in 1980, in *Contemporary Architects*. 'To this container, this sculpture, the user brings his baggage, his program, and interacts with it to accommodate his needs. If he can't do that, I've failed.'

In recent years, for his big projects – such as the provocative, swirling Vitra Museum (1988) in Weil-am-Rhein, in Germany, and the Experience Music Project in Seattle (2000) – Gehry the sculptor of buildings has used the latest technology to help him make buildings bend to his will. His preliminary drawing for the Guggenheim was a wildly expressionist sketch, full of verve and rippling energy. He then built a series of models and scanned the final one on CATIA, a computer programme developed in France for designing Mirage jet fighters, which can digitize a sculptural form into a 3-D electronic model. The data translated the undulating curves into numbered sections making it possible to have each piece of steel, stone and glass cut to measure and fitted it on to a swirling skeleton of steel. Gehry has opened the doors of a new architecture without limits, as Richard Serra has said, but it would never have been possible without computers.

Gehry's original idea for the Guggenheim Bilbao was to sheath it in lead and copper, but he realized that lead would slowly leach into the river. He then considered stainless steel, but realized that in the often rainy and cloudy climate of Bilbao it would look dull. As he experimented with ways to make stainless steel somehow warmer, he came across a small piece of titanium in his office. Titanium is a malleable white metal resembling aluminum, a material guaranteed not to rust and used mostly in medical instruments and aircraft design. Intrigued, Gehry stuck it on the wall, and by chance the next day in Los Angeles was rainy and overcast. Yet the titanium still gave off a golden glow. At sunset it had a purple sheen. Gehry was convinced. And thanks to the collapse of the titanium market after the fall of the Soviet Union, prices were low. Also a little goes a long way: on the roof, the titanium panels are only a third of a millimetre thick, but guaranteed, Gehry was told, to last a hundred years.

Most visitors spend as much time wandering around Gehry's enormous sculpture as they do inside it. Like the three blind men and the elephant, your interpretation will depend on which part of the building you are looking at; ships' hulls, truncated fish bodies and palm trees all protrude from the bulging mass in a wonderful juxtaposition of natural forms and 21st-century technology. The curves and titanium

Puppy, or Life Imitates Art, Again

Before you even get a chance to step through the doors of the museum, you'll be mugged by the Guggenheim's first (and biggest) exhibit, a 40ft mountain of flowers and love created by kitsch guru Jeff Koons and answering to the name of 'Puppy' (pronounced 'poopy'). Puppy, presumably a West Highland terrier, is a familiar sight at galleries worldwide – he's made appearances in New York and Sydney, amongst other cities – a kind of vegetarian version of the Littlest Hobo, who wanders from city to city lending his support wherever art exhibitions need him, before turning tail and trotting off into the sunset. But, like the Littlest Hobo, eventually the time came to settle down, and Puppy has put down his roots firmly in Bilbao, to the delight of almost everyone. He's been adopted as the city's *de facto* mascot, his image decorating everything from T-shirts to Vizcaya governmental literature.

Puppy's meteoric rise to mass adulation no doubt amuses his creator. When Koons came across the dog, it was no more than a tacky porcelain souvenir, a mass-produced piece of commercial crassness. Having based a career on taking just this kind of tat and elevating it to the status of High Art, Koons saw potential in Puppy; a couple of months, one CAD program and a few thousand begonias later and, *voila!* a star was born. Yet just as junk can be made into art, art can be made into junk and before long the poor pooch was back where he came from; cuddly Puppys are the hot souvenir in **Bilbao**.

give the building a remarkable sense of movement. Some of the best views are to be had from the Puente de la Salve, a classic lump of 1960s concrete that Bilbao would rather have forgotten but which Gehry's design embraces. One of his skylights looms up towards the bridge, looking for all the world like a giant open-mawed basking shark. The vantage point also looks on to an area of the roof where unsightly brown stains spread across some of the titanium scales to the consternation of the world's press. Apparently, one of the contractors spilled a fireproofing sealant on them during the construction, and the oxide film which coats titanium as soon as it's exposed to oxygen has thickened and dulled like cataracts on an eye. At the time of writing, a new oxide scrubbing foam was being developed, and the management was confident that all would soon be shining again.

A Day at the Guggenheim

Don't underestimate the Guggenheim's popularity. Attendance rates have vastly exceeded projections, and queues of up to an hour to get in have become frequent, especially at weekends. Once you're through the door it's easy enough to wander round the galleries on your own; alternatively, 'audioguides' can be hired (*free*), with recorded information on the key works. Free guided tours cover each installation daily, in English, but there's a definite skill to getting on one – spaces are limited to 20 people and there's no possibility of signing up more than 30 minutes in advance.

Guggenheim Floor Plan

Ground Floor

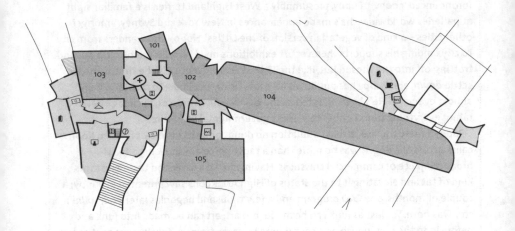

	lift		information	■	exhibition space
	toilets		cloakroom		
	ticket office		auditorium		
	café		bookshop		
	restaurant		wheelchair access		

First Floor

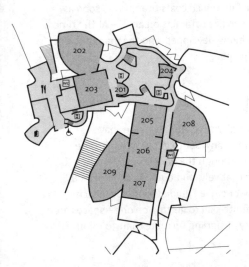

Second Floor

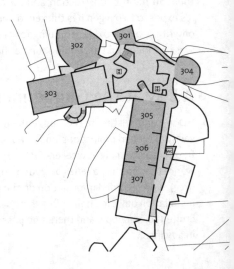

Guggenheim Practicalities

Address: Avenida Abandoibarra 2, 48001 Bilbao, **t** (34) 94 435 90 80, **f** (34) 94 435 90 40. The web site, *www.guggenheim-bilbao.es*, is a good place to see what temporary exhibitions are on and what's coming up.

Opening hours: *Tues–Sun 10–8*. Ticket sales stop 30mins prior to closing.

Information centre: There is a visitor information desk in the main entrance hall. Multilingual staff provide leaflets and information on guided tours, and answer general queries.

Cloakroom: In the main lobby; no charge.

Toilets and telephones: In the basement.

Bank machines: There are two ATMs which accept credit cards by the ground floor entrance closest to the river.

Guided tours: Free guided tours in English, Spanish and Basque take place several times a day. Call **t** 94 435 90 80 for schedule information. It is not possible to pre-book guided tours; you can register for a tour up to 30 minutes before it starts (register at the Information desk in the main lobby). Otherwise, free audioguides are available with recorded information about exhibits.

Group admissions: If the queues get too long, you might consider gathering a group of at least 10 people and heading around to the group admission entrance on the ground floor. This can be quicker than waiting in the main queue. If you already have a group, call **t** 94 435 90 23 (*open Mon–Fri 9am–2pm*) to apply for a group admission.

Shop: The shop is on three levels: on the ground floor you'll find stationery, souvenirs (mugs, posters, puzzles, keyrings, postcards, tapestry kits to embroider your own 'Puppy', T-shirts, calendars, umbrellas, etc.); on the mezzanine level there is a wide selection of handmade jewellery and glassware, hand-painted silk scarves, ceramics, candles, designer sunglasses, handmade paper products and other gift items; on the 1st floor you'll find the bookshop. There are museum guides, monographs on several of the artists featured, art history, design and architectural books, as well as a small selection of local history books.

Café-bar: The small café-bar is on the 1st floor at the entrance to the restaurant. The pale wood panelling, frosted glass screens and wooden furniture in undulating forms are all Gehry-designed. The bar serves simple breakfasts and snacks – good pastries, tortillas and *droquetas* – as well as coffees and drinks, but it is small and it is likely that you will have to stand.

Restaurant: One of the best places to try New Basque cuisine, under the innovative direction of chef Martín Berasategui. The restaurant is extremely popular, so book in advance (**t** 94 423 93 33). There are three *menú degustacións* on offer between 5,300 and 7,200 pts (€32–43.5)and a very good-value lunchtime *menu del día* at 1,500 pts/€9.

The interior spaces are as remarkable as the exterior. The building's heart is a sublime 150ft-high atrium of swooping curves, in every sense the museum's centre – galleries radiate from it on all sides, and you'll inevitably pass through time and again at different levels – but also a sculptural work of art in itself. Light floods in through glass curtain walls and cascades down from skylights in the roof, dancing and jumping yet never finding an absorbent surface to stop its flow. Watch out for Gehry's cheeky nod of the head to Frank Lloyd Wright's famous spiral design; Gehry claims that Thomas Krens egged him on to 'take on the Guggenheim in New York'. It is a worthy successor, but radically different, unrestrained by anything but the imagination, 'a metaphoric visionary city, à la Fritz Lang', as Gehry sees it.

Outside the atrium, the Nervión is incorporated into the design by way of an ingenious raised walkway, rising and curving and creating a union between river and water garden.

Although not a few people end up wandering about the building, enchanted like Alice in Wonderland, Gehry's intention was to provide a perfect and warm setting for contemporary art. Frank Lloyd Wright's spiral ramp, captivating as it is, has always made viewing awkward for many people. Gehry hoped his own non-rational forms would sharpen the visitor's senses and open the mind to the give and take of contemporary art, but he also provided ample space to view it. Even in the more conventional galleries, ceilings are extremely high. The architect has also created some revolutionary gallery spaces, especially the cavernous Fish Gallery, 420ft long by 100ft wide with whalebone-like ribs supporting the ceiling, designed to hold the biggest and heaviest works of modern art without any structural columns getting in the way. Snake, a heavy iron sculpture designed especially for the gallery by Gehry's close friend Richard Serra, throws down the gauntlet to future artists; too heavy to move and too big to fit anywhere else, it's one of the few exhibits that's guaranteed to be on show. This isn't art you look at – you have to participate in it by entering the narrow corridors formed by the six massive undulating steel plates. Serra said that he was trying to reproduce the sensation of a walk through the narrow streets of a medieval city, a feeling underlined by the great iron sides leaning in and swaying out.

The Collection

After Gehry's architectural fireworks and Koons' giant dog, the collection itself has a hard act to follow; whether or not it succeeds will depend on when you go. Thanks to its family connections with New York, Venice and Berlin, the Guggenheim has access to more masterworks of 20th-century art than a museum of its tender age has any right to. Yet the shifting nature of the exhibits means there's no guarantee that the piece you're desperate to see will be on show. However, the site-specific works by Koons and Serra will be there, as will Jenny Holzer's *Installation for Bilbao* (1997), in gallery 101, just off the atrium, a characteristically spiky LED monologue scrolling upwards into a reflective ceiling via nine vertical columns. Very private feelings – expressions of desire, obsession, betrayal, even violence – are emblazoned in public neon signs, shooting searing red words in English and Spanish, and making use of all the effects that neon signs provide: flashing lights, different typography and eye-catching symbols. Step between the vertical posts and the same messages unravel in Basque on the other side in an unearthly blue, dimly reflected in the grey walls.

If the permanent collection is up, look out for a good selection of European avant-garde art: there's a pivotal work by Miró, *The Tilled Field* (1923–4), a bold and relatively accessible prelude to his later, more figurative style; a selection of Kandinskys; some elongated heads by Modigliani and scattered works by Picasso and Klee, mostly on permanent loan from the Guggenheim in New York. Underpinning these is Bilbao's own distinguished collection of abstract expressionists, including pieces by some of the movement's leading figures, among them Robert Motherwell's stark assessment of the Civil War, *Elegy to the Spanish Republic LV* (1955–60), a swirling late-period Pollock (*Ocean Greyness*, 1953) and De Kooning's forceful *Composition* (1955), a gestural riot of primary colours. The polychromatic chaos is balanced by a tranquil Rothko (*Untitled*, 1956) and Yves Klein's *Large Blue Anthropometry* (1960), which the artist created by smearing naked women in paint (the famously patented *International Klein Blue*) and dragging them across the canvas while a 20-piece orchestra played his own *Symphonie Monotone*, a single note sustained for 10 minutes alternating with 10 minutes' silence.

There's a fairly patchy collection of pop art, perhaps best represented by Lichtenstein's unusually subdued *Interior With Mirrored Wall* (1991); some fine pieces by Schnabel, Dubuffet and Basquiat; and a moving monographic exhibition devoted to Anselm Kiefer, one of the artists that the museum has chosen to focus on in terms of their acquisition policy. This juxtaposes the historically laden works of his early period – the notorious faces of Nazi Germany glare down from a chaotic mono-chrome swirl in *The Paths to Worldly Wisdom: Hermann's Battle* (1982–3) – with the unburdened, redemptive inner landscapes that characterize Keifer's work in the 1990s. In *Sun Ship* (1994–5), a dried sunflower glides over devastated landscapes of ash and fallen trees, heading off to a brighter future, a future perhaps realized in the cracked desert colours of *Alone With Wind, Time and Sound* (1997).

Elsewhere, there's a small collection of works by Basque and Spanish artists: sculp-tures by Eduardo Chillida (*see* p.185) and Cristina Iglesias, such as her *Untitled (Jealousy II)* (1997), a strange, seemingly impenetrable 'room' made of Arab-style carved panels; a few textural paintings by Tapiés; and some startling mixed-media still lifes and landscapes from Miquel Barceló – which the museum's directors have pledged to augment with future purchases. They tried hard to get the one work that the Basques feel really belongs here – Picasso's *Guernica* – but Madrid refused to send it even on loan for the opening in 1997, out of fears, they say, that the Basques wouldn't give it back.

Temporary Exhibitions

Nothing draws the crowds to Bilbao like a big new exhibition – until the collection matures, they're the best guarantee of seeing a really strong body of work – and the Guggenheim has achieved a few stunning successes. Temporary features in the past have included a major exhibition of sculpture by Richard Serra, wide-ranging retro-spectives of Chillida and Iglesias, and an assemblage of photography and sculpture by the likes of Picasso, Degas and Rodin.

But nothing so far has been able to compete with the runaway success of 2000's The Art of the Motorcycle exhibition, featuring highly polished machines from an 1894 Hildebrand and Wulfmüller to turn of the millennium superbikes, with a floor plan designed by Frank Gehry in the shape of a Scalextric track. All of a sudden, half the Basque country was in gallery 104 dribbling over the lusty iron horse, and for a time leather, long hair and big beards shared the halls of high culture. Massive public demand bought the exhibition a three-month stay of execution, while art critics wrung their hands and prophesied doom, or at least the conversion of the Guggenheim into a transport museum.

Postscript: The Guggenheim Effect

No new building has been more praised in recent years, and no one disputes that Gehry's massive sculpture marks a significant break with traditional museum models. But there have been some detractors, among them the architectural historian Juan Antonio Ramírez, who describes it as 'a cultural franchise, a sign of the McDonaldization of the universe', and perceives a 'California jokiness at the expense of the tribal tragedy of the Basques'. ETA, seeing it as a symbol of globalization, killed a guard there just before it was opened in 1997 by King Juan Carlos. Security, understandably, remains tight. Others, while marvelling at the building, worry that Guggenheim Bilbao is in the vanguard of the trend of art museums as entertainment centres, with their restaurants, cafés and shops, and that the meaning of the art itself (the serious works at any rate – sorry, Puppy!) is co-opted by the very sort of consumer culture that the avant-garde sought to challenge. The popular appeal of the motorcycle show is used in evidence of this, and the issue has been raised again with an exhibition devoted to fashion designer Georgio Armani which, for all the negative press, was a sell-out in New York and promises to be as good a crowd-puller in Bilbao.

'Cultural tourism' may elicit sneers from architects and art historians, but many other cities gaze enviously at the enormous financial and regenerative benefits that Bilbao has reaped from the Guggenheim. Since opening in 1997, the museum has already recouped every penny invested in it. The city agreed to pay an annual subsidy of around 20 per cent of its budget, but the museum seems well on the way to becoming entirely self-financing long before anyone ever dreamed possible.

The Guggenheim's success has spawned an ambitious series of restoration projects throughout Bilbao, none of which are bigger than the transformation taking place on the Abandoibarra flats, alongside the Guggenheim. Acres of railway sidings and container trucks are set to disappear, making way for a massive new development of office blocks, a luxury hotel, shopping malls and a 30-storey tower block destined for use by the Vizcaya Diputación (provincial council). An extensive park area is also planned, completing the 'green corridor' between Parque de Doña Casilda Iturriza and Paseo del Arenal. The Palacio de Congresos y de la Música, already in place a few hundred yards downstream, completes the project.

The aftershocks of Gehry's masterpiece have reverberated even beyond the confines of Bilbao. The Guggenheim Foundation is so delighted that Gehry has been commissioned to work his magic on a massive new project for New York's own rundown dock area, which has, like Bilbao, looked to the art world to provide a new lease of life, only this time with a $687 million budget. It will hold rotating exhibits from the Hermitage Museum of St Petersburg and the Kunsthistorisches Museum in Vienna – a curious combination of old and new trumpeted as a synergetic *ménage à trois* based on the attraction of opposites. This is on top of the already existing Guggenheim Soho in New York, and the Foundation's flirtation with the Deutsche Bank in Berlin, along with the museum's launch into cyberspace, a Guggenheim Virtual Museum, due to be finished in 2003. 'The Guggenheims will get you if you don't watch out!' Only since Bilbao, cities are fighting to get got; at the time of writing, talks are under way with Brazil about opening a Guggenheim there, too.

Around Bilbao

Only a third of Bilbao's million-odd souls live within the city itself. Bilbao is the heart of a sprawling conurbation which lines the Nervión for 20 miles, with factories and tower blocks squeezing in wherever the terrain permits.

Industrial archaeologists may want to head for **Sestao**, site of the impressive ruins of the Altos Hornos de Vizcaya, once one of the biggest steel mills in Europe, which employed 13,500 in its heyday before it was sold for scrap in 1996; all the bars in the area have evocative photos. As for the fancier suburbs, these are found near the coast, where there are dramatic cliffs and a number of beaches.

The most distinguished suburb is **Getxo** (Neguri, Algorta and Bidezabal metro stations), a combination suburb, marina and beach resort whose waterfront is lined with lovely villas. Getxo claims one of the youngest populations in Vizcaya, and the closest beaches to downtown Bilbao, yet retains a distinctly refined atmosphere; signs politely request that swimming costumes not be worn on the beachfront promenade. A few traces of the town's more earthbound past continue to linger, particularly in the graceful old fishing port of **Algorta**, which cascades down the cliffs from a defiantly modern *urbanisación*. Look out for 19th-century **San Nicolas de Bari**, built in late neoclassical style, where stoups made of giant clam shells prop up the walls by the main door.

Almost everything else in Getxo was built in the 20th century, including the grandiose villas that line the waterfront between Ereaga and Las Arenas beaches. New money from iron and the shipyards paid for these mansions; it couldn't guarantee good taste, but at least in the 1920s it bought a nice view. Nowadays, however, the crumbling old castles look across to the proletarian suburbs of Bilbao's superport, sprawling along the left bank of the estuary from Santurtzi to Portugalete.

The *ría*, and a social chasm, are bridged at the Nervión's mouth by one of Vizcaya's great industrial-age landmarks, the **Puente Colgante**, or 'hanging bridge' (Areeta metro station); the name refers to a system (unique in its day) of transporting people and goods across the river by way of a suspended gondola, allowing free passage to tall ships without the palaver of swinging or raising the bridge. This is Bilbao's proudest monument from the 19th century – locals like to call it 'the Eiffel Tower of Vizcaya' – and was as much a symbol of a vigorous economy in its day as the Guggenheim is now. Modern-day visitors can take a lift to the uppermost span, for a commanding view of the port and estuary.

The beaches continue eastwards along the coast. Though they're jam-packed with Bilbaínos at weekends, they can be fun; both the beaches and the water are surprisingly clean. Two of the most popular are at Sopelanas and **Plentzia**; the latter is an agreeably sleepy town on weekdays, with a handsome medieval quarter. Plentzia lacks any real sights, but It's a good place to wander around when the beach scene gets too frantic; the main monuments are Gothic Santa María Magdalena and the 16th-century town hall, now home to a small Museo Municipal, which has exhibits on Plentzia's fishing history.

If you are spending much time in Bilbao, we might recommend (though not for the faint-hearted) a ride around the mountains that hem in the city. On **Monte Artxandamendia**, or in the hills above Erandio or Portugalete, you will see incredible landscapes of steel mills perched on mountaintops, grazing sheep, Victorian castles, shanty towns and roads on stilts, scenes from some surreal comic book.

Euskadi

Euskadi

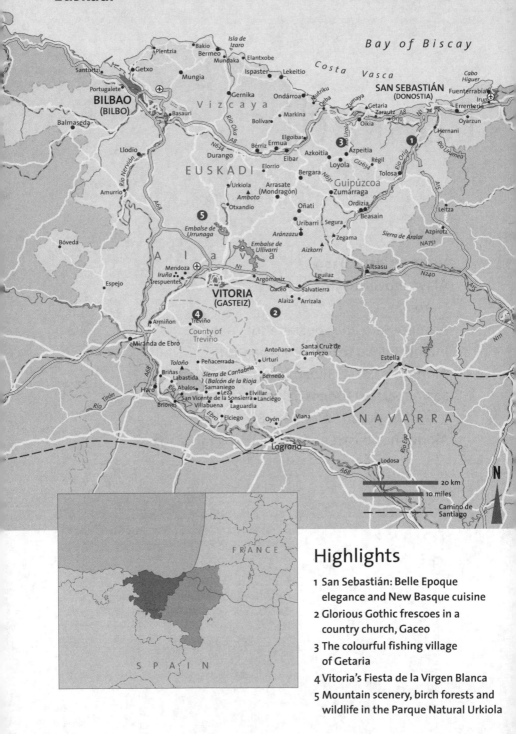

Highlights

1 San Sebastián: Belle Epoque
   elegance and New Basque cuisine

2 Glorious Gothic frescoes in a
   country church, Gaceo

3 The colourful fishing village
   of Getaria

4 Vitoria's Fiesta de la Virgen Blanca

5 Mountain scenery, birch forests and
   wildlife in the Parque Natural Urkiola

Vizcaya (Bizkaia), Alava (Araba) and Guipúzcoa (Gipuzkoa), the three provinces of the autonomous region of Euskadi, are rural and vertical for the most part, lush and green, crisscrossed by a network of rushing mountain streams that meander every which way through steep, narrow valleys in their search for the sea. Pretty Basque houses with long, sloping roofs and floppy-eared Basque sheep decorate the emerald slopes, while below to the north the surf pounds against the wild coast, which relents here and there to admit a busy fishing port or sheltered beach. Signs on restaurants, *tabernas*, and shops are packed full of 'x's 'k's and 'z's, all written in a special Basque fairy-tale font, and add to the otherworldly air. In most places, the industry of Bilbao seem remote.

Basque nationalism, on the other hand, is ever present; every bridge, underpass, and *fronton* has been painted with the Basque flag and slogans of the ETA and Herri Batasuna. Everywhere, big white flags showing Euskadi in silhouette with big red arrows pointing at it demand that Basque prisoners be held in prisons in the Basque country rather than spread throughout Spain and in the Canary Islands, where they are often rotated without notice to families.

With the notable exception of the big cities, San Sebastián and Vitoria, Euskadi is not chock-a-block with 'sights' per se; go there rather for the atmosphere, to pootle about, to take in a *pelota* match at a village *fronton*, or to be on hand as the fishing fleet brings in the catch. Wander down country lanes in search of dolmens, watch a furious game of *mus* in a bar, or try to keep up with Basque trenchermen at the table. But if you like to have destinations to aim for, try the Gothic frescoes at Gaceo and the cartoonish murals at Alaiza; Laguardia and the Rioja vineyards basking in the sun; San Miguel de Arretxinaga with its bizarre Neolithic altar, in Markina; the pagan Basque cemetery of Argiñeta, near Elorrio; the extraordinary Castillo de Butrón; the hermitage-topped islet of San Juan de Gaztelugatxa, near Bakio; the Palaeolithic Cueva de Santimamiñe, near Gernika; the bijou fishing port of Elantxobe and dramatic coast around Deba; picturesque Getaria and its lopsided church; palace-filled Oñati and Bergara; the Jesuit extravaganza at Loyola; and colourful seaside Fuenterrabía, on the French border.

Vitoria (Gasteiz)

Vitoria has style. It also has the air of a little Ruritanian capital – because it is one. The seat of the inland province of Alava and, since 1980, the capital of Euskadi, Vitoria has grown to be one of Spain's modern industrial centres, a phenomenon that has so far done little harm to one of the most surprisingly urbane cities in the nation. Founded as *Victoriacum* by the Visigothic King Leovigild after he smashed the Basques in 581, the name stuck along with the Basque name, Gasteiz, because it recalls the height (*Beturia* in Basque) on which the city was built. In the Middle Ages this was a hot border region between the kingdoms of Navarra and Castile. The Navarrese King Alfonso VI founded a fortress and town here in 1181 and King Sancho IV 'the Wise' granted it a charter of *fueros* (*see* pp.32–3), but the Castilians managed to snatch it away from them soon after. Like everything else in medieval Castile, Vitoria

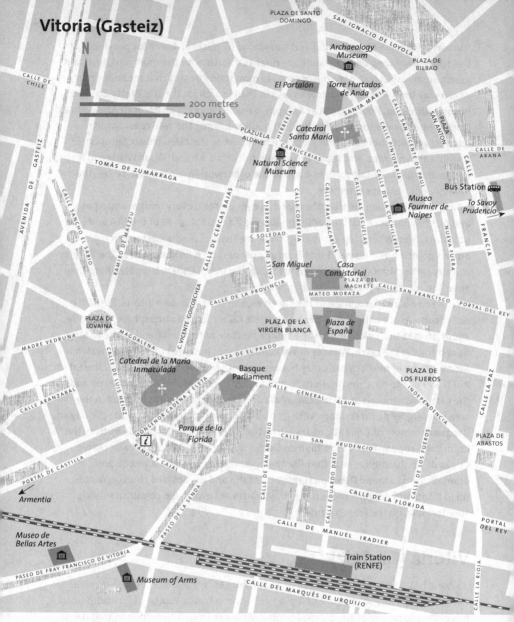

Vitoria (Gasteiz)

N

200 metres
200 yards

PLAZA DE SANTO DOMINGO
SAN IGNACIO DE LOYOLA
PLAZA DE BILBAO
Archaeology Museum
CALLE DE CHILE
El Portalón
Torre Hurtados de Anda
SANTA MARIA
PLAZA SAN ANTON
CALLE DE ARANA
HERRERIA
PLAZUELA ALDAVE
Catedral Santa María
CALLE SAN VICENTE DE PAUL
CARNICERIAS
CALLE PINTORERIA
TOMÁS DE ZUMÁRRAGA
Natural Science Museum
AVENIDA DE GASTEIZ
CALLE SANCHO EL SABIO
RAMIRO DE MAEZTU
CALLE DE CERCAS BAJAS
CALLE CORRERIA
CALLE FRAY ZACARIAS
CALLE DE LAS ESCUELAS
CALLE DE LA CUCHILLERIA
Museo Fournier de Naipes
Bus Station
To Savoy Prudencio
C SOLEDAD
NUEVA FUERA
FRANCIA
CALLE DE LA HERRERIA
San Miguel
Casa Consistorial
PLAZA DEL MACHETE
CALLE SAN FRANCISCO
PORTAL DEL REY
C VICENTE GOICOECHEA
CALLE DE LA PROVINCIA
MATEO MORAZA
PLAZA DE LOVAINA
MAGDALENA
CALLE DE LA PROVINCIA
PLAZA DE LA VIRGEN BLANCA
Plaza de España
PLAZA DE LOS FUEROS
CALLE LA PAZ
MADRE VEDRUNA
CALLE DE LUIS HEINZ
PLAZA DE EL PRADO
Catedral de la María Inmaculada
Basque Parliament
CALLE GENERAL ALAVA
INDEPENDENCIA
CALLE DE LOS FUEROS
PLAZA DE ABASTOS
CALLE ARANZABAL
MONSEÑOR CADENA Y ELETA
Parque de la Florida
CALLE DE SAN ANTONIO
CALLE SAN PRUDENCIO
CALLE EDUARDO DATO
CALLE DE LA FLORIDA
PORTAL DE CASTILLA
RAMÓN Y CAJAL
PASEO DE LA SENDA
Armentia
CALLE DE MANUEL IRADIER
PORTAL DEL REY
Museo de Bellas Artes
Train Station (RENFE)
PASEO DE FRAY FRANCISCO DE VITORIA
Museum of Arms
CALLE DEL MARQUÉS DE URQUIJO
CALLE LA RIOJA

boomed, and extended itself logically in concentric rings of streets – oddly enough, a plan exactly like Amsterdam's, without the canals.

Hard hit by the wars and plagues of the 14th century, Vitoria stagnated for centuries, although one bright spot was the reflected glory of its greatest son, Francisco de Vitoria (1486–1549), an eloquent theologian who lectured at the University of Salamanca. Often called the 'father of international law', he strongly challenged the morality of Europeans colonizing the New World (even the plea of needing to convert the pagans didn't wash with friar Franciso); he defended the human rights of native

Americans, and set forth reasoned discussions on the limitations of war, which under his terms was hardly ever justified. His opinions were highly influential in Renaissance university circles, and even Charles V asked his advice, although history says neither he nor his successors bothered to follow it.

Vitoria next made the headlines when it saw the decisive battle in the Peninuslar War on 21 June 1813, when Wellington, after retreating from his failed siege of Burgos, caught up with the French here and routed them, although his troops, who Wellington himself called 'the scum of the earth', let the French escape over the Pyrenees as they pillaged their baggage in a drunken orgy. News of the victory, however, did rally the Europeans to unite against Napoleon, and the next year the war came to an end with Napoleon's abdication. Vitoria's own recovery as a city came only with the industrial boom of the 1890s. It has preserved itself beautifully throughout, probably an important factor in getting Vitoria named the capital of the Basque autonomous government, the Eusko Jaurlaritza, in 1981. It is also the home of the Euskal Herriko Unibertsitatea (EHU), the University of the Basque Country, established by the government shortly after it took power and now the world's leading centre for the study of the Basque language and its history.

Getting There and Around

By Air
Foronda airport, 9km west of Vitoria, has connections with Madrid and Barcelona (t 94 516 35 00).

By Train and Bus
Vitoria's stylish train station (t 94 523 02 02) is at the head of C/ Eduardo Dato, six blocks from the old town. Trains between San Sebastián and Madrid pass through Vitoria, and Salvatierra is a stop along RENFE's Vitoria–Pamplona run. Otherwise you'll have to take the bus or hitchhike. Generally the more remote the area, the more likely you are to get a ride – friendly locals will often stop and ask you if you want a lift. The bus station (t 94 525 84 00) is at C/ Los Herran 50, a short walk east of the old town. There are regular services to San Sebastián, Bilbao and Logroño, as well as to the provincial villages, and because of the city's position on the main route north from Madrid, you can get a bus to nearly anywhere from here – Bordeaux, Paris, Germany and even London.

By Car
Though small, Vitoria can be a puzzle if you are driving. Most of the centre is a closed-off pedestrian zone, and parking is hard to find.

Tourist Information

Tourist offices: Parque de la Florida, ✉ 01008, t 94 513 13 21. There is a Basque regional office at Dato 11, t 94 516 15 98.

Market Days
Thursday, in Plaza de Abastos. There is also a flea market on Sunday in Plaza de España, and a clothes market on Wednesday and Thursday in C/ Arana.

Where to Stay

Vitoria ✉ 01000

Expensive
★★★★**Hotel Ciudad de Vitoria**, Portal de Castilla 8, t 94 514 11 00, f 94 514 36 16. Has more character than most, with friendly staff and an indoor garden; good discounts are available at weekends and in summer.
★★★**General Álava**, Avda de Gasteiz 79, t 94 522 22 00, f 94 524 83 95. The best value among the several large hotels in the new part of town, with modern, comfortable rooms and TV.

Moderate
★★★**Almoneda**, C/ Florida 7, t 94 515 40 84, f 94 515 46 86, *information@hotelalmoneda*.

The important thing to know about Vitoria is the Fiesta de la Virgen Blanca, on 4 August. It's a typically berserk six-day Basque blowout, with sparkling *cava* everywhere, lots of high-powered fireworks and parties until dawn, but the image of it that sticks in the mind is *Celedón*, a dummy in a beret and workman's clothes. *Celedón* holds an umbrella aloft, which is attached to a wire from the top of the cathedral tower; from this he descends as gracefully as Mary Poppins, gliding across the *plaza* to start the festival. On the morning of 10 August, he glides up the wire and pops magically back into the bell tower, and it's all over for another year.

La Casco Vieja

The old city, with its core of neat, concentric streets, begins with **Plaza de la Virgen Blanca**, a delightful example of asymmetrical medieval town design. Adjacent to it, the enclosed and studiously symmetrical **Plaza de España**, or Plaza Nueva, provides a perfect contrast; this grand neoclassical confection was built at the height of Spain's flirtation with the Enlightenment, in the 1780s, and now houses mostly city offices. Plaza de la Virgen Blanca is the centre of Vitoria's big party on 4 August; it takes its name from the statue in the niche over the door of **San Miguel**, the 14th-century

com. This newly renovated little hotel has simple, tasteful rooms and a pleasant lounge with an eclectic collection of antiques.

Inexpensive

Vitoria offers a wide range of choices for about 7,000 pts/€42, mostly catering for businessmen.

★★Hotel Desiderio, C/ San Prudencio 2, t 94 525 17 99. Functional rooms, but the hotel is close to the old town and very friendly.

★★Dato 28, C/ Eduardo Dato 28 (near the train station), t 94 514 72 30, f 94 523 23 20. Convenient, modern and imaginatively furnished; cheaper than the others, it's a good bargain too. Reserve in advance or you will be sent to the slightly less attractive Residencia Dato 2.

★Achuri, C/ Rioja 11, t 94 525 58 00, f 94 526 40 74. Reasonable and well equipped.

★La Riojana, C/ Cuchillería 66, t 94 526 87 95. Situated in the Casco Viejo, this is one of the cheapest, if a little daunting from the outside.

Two other inexpensive options are:

Savoy Prudencio, C/ Prudencio María de Verástegui 4, t 94 525 00 56.

La Paz, C/ La Paz 3, t 94 513 96 66.

Cheap

Pensión Álava, C/ Florida 25, t 94 523 35 88. Run by a fantastically welcoming old couple, this pension has light and breezy rooms at bargain prices. It's also handily situated between the train station and the Casco Viejo.

Eating Out

Most of the most atmospheric bars and restaurants in Vitoria are in the old town.

El Portalón, Correría 151, t 94 514 27 55. Especially good, with tables on three floors of a 15th-century building and traditional Basque food (*expensive*), such as the house speciality *lautada itzaso*, with meat and fish.

Arkupe, Mateo de Moraza 13, t 94 523 00 80. On the cusp of the old town and the *ensanche*, this attractive restaurant offers good local specialities with a dash of Nouveau Basque flair; try the chard stuffed with wild mushrooms and salmon (*pencas de alcega rellans de setas y salmón*), or the baby squid cooked with potatoes and mussels.

Zaldiarián, Avda de Gasteiz 21, t 94 513 48 22. Smart restaurant serving award-winning traditional cuisine; *suprema de*

church that turns a lovely portico towards the top of the square. An 18th-century arcade called **Los Arcillos**, reached by a stair, runs under some graceful old glass-fronted buildings to connect Plaza de la Virgen Blanca to yet a third connected square on the slope of the hill, **Plaza del Machete**, named after the axe over which city officials would swear their oaths of office.

Behind San Miguel, Calle Fray Zacarías leads north into the medieval streets. This was the high-status street for palaces, as evidenced by two 16th-century Plateresque beauties, the **Palacio Episcopal** and the **Palacio Escoriaza-Esquivel**, built by a local boy who became physician to Charles V; this one has a refined Renaissance courtyard with a marble loggia.

At the top of the street is the old cathedral, **Catedral Santa María** (*t 94 525 51 35, www.catedral-vitoria.com; free guided tours Mon–Fri 11–2, Sat, Sun and hols 11–2 and 5–10; book in advance*), also from the 14th century, with a beautifully carved western doorway and impressive central nave, the aisles lined with the tombs of Vitoria's notables from medieval times. Recent archaeological excavations in the cathedral have unearthed remains of an ancient fortified church and other relics from the 13th century.

mero rustido (sea bass cooked with caramelized onions) and an excellent *lomo de buey* (fillet of beef).

Olarizu, Tomás de Zumarraga 54, **t** 94 524 77 52. Creative, elegant cuisine based on old Alavesa recipes; try the *merluza sobre salsa de mariscos* (hake with a shellfish sauce) and finish up with a delicious 'soup' made from local fruits.

Dos Hermanas, Madre Vedruna 10, **t** 94 513 29 34. A local institution for more than a century, you'll find excellent traditional Basque dishes like *lomo de merluza al vino blanco* (hake with white wine) and *rabo de buey estofado* (stuffed oxtail).

Ikea, C/ Castilla 27, **t** 94 514 47 47. One of the most renowned restaurants in Euskadi, this is where to find truly original cuisine which incorporates international elements from Japanese to French but still manages one of the best versions of *patatas alavesa*, a rustic potato dish, around.

Casablanca 3, C/ Dato 38. An unassuming exterior belies the tasty offerings inside; creamy pumpkin soup and tender roast duck (*inexpensive*).

Dolomiti, C/ Ramón y Cajal, **t** 94 523 34 26. The best and most popular pizzeria in town, run by a former cycling champ named Galdós; it also does Italian dinners (*1,500 pts/€9 for pizza*).

Kintana, C/ Mateo de Moraza 15, **t** 94 523 00 10. Specializes in fresh game dishes.

Mesa, Chile 1, **t** 94 522 84 94. A very popular place (it's worth booking during festivals) serving flavoursome, down-to-earth local dishes (*3–4,000 pts/€18–24*). *Closed Wed.*

Zabala, Mateo de Moraza 9, **t** 94 523 00 09. An old-fashioned spot with simple but delicious regional dishes. (*3–4,000 pts/€18–24*). *Closed Sun and Aug.*

Nightlife

Vitoria has its share of nightlife, mostly in the Casco Vieja, though C/ Dato, near the station, can also be noisy after hours. Some of the clubs (a few on C/ San Prudencio, for example, stay open until 6 or 7am).

Cerveceria Gambrinus, C/ Florida 15. A popular place to begin the evening with a beer and some *pintxos*.

Café Caruso, C/ Enrique de Eguren 9. A coffee house which has occasional concerts and exhibitions.

El Elefante Blanco, Plaza San Antón. Currently the most popular disco.

Salsumba, C/ Tomás de Zumárraga. The place to come for salsa.

Gaztetxe, C/ Fray Zacarías. For alternative music of all sorts (though mostly rock).

A couple of streets west of the cathedral, on C/ del Herrería, the **Torre de Doña Otxanta** is a defensive tower of the 15th–16th centuries. Italian early-Renaissance cities, with their skylines of skyscraper-fortresses, set a fashion that found its way to other countries – fortresses like these were private castles in town, and city officials had to fight hard to keep their owners from acting like rustic barons on their manors, bossing everyone around and generally disturbing the peace of the neighbourhood. Now fully restored, the tower is home to the province's **Natural Science Museum** (*open Tues–Fri 10–2 and 4–6.30, Sat 10–2, Sun 11–2, closed Mon; adm*).

Another conspicuous tower nearby, the **Torre Hurtados de Anda**, lurks just to the north of the cathedral on C/ Correría: this is a blank-walled fort with a half-timbered house planted on top – a proper urban castle. Also on C/ Correría, a rambling brick and timber structure called **El Portalón**, built in the early 16th century, is one of the oldest buildings in town, and it gives an idea of what most of Vitoria must have looked like at the time. Just across the street at Correría 116, the **Archaeology Museum** (*open Tues–Fri 10–2 and 4–6.30, Sat 10–2, Sun 11–2, closed Mon; adm*) occupies a lovely half-timbered house containing Roman finds and Basque discoidal tombstones, as well as some fascinating medieval finds, such as the exceedingly strange *Relief of Marquinez*. There are over a hundred artificial caves in the province of Alava, and exhibits recount the story of the religious hermits who occupied many of them a thousand years ago.

The House of Cards

Palaces are fewer in the eastern quarter of old Vitoria, across C/ Las Escuelas; the houses here are generally plainer, though older, especially those in the former **Judería**, the medieval Jewish ghetto that covered much of this area. On C/ Cuchillería, in the Plateresque Palacio Bendaña, Spain's biggest manufacturer of playing cards (an old Vitoria speciality) has opened the **Museo Fournier del Naipes** (*open Tues–Fri 10–2 and 4–6.30, Sat 10–2, Sun 11–2, closed Mon*). The Fournier Company thinks their collection is the best anywhere; it includes the oldest surviving card (from the 14th century), as well as card-making machinery and paintings. The collection includes plenty of Tarot decks too; originally there was no difference between the cards for fortune telling and those for playing games.

The New Cathedral and the Museum of Fine Arts

The tourist information office shares the pretty **Parque de la Florida**, Vitoria's monumental centre, with the stern, no-nonsense **Basque Parliament** building (*t 94 524 78 00 if you want to sit in the gallery and watch them deliberate*) and the remarkable 'new cathedral', the **Catedral de la María Inmaculada**. Here, the Basques, who don't like anything frumpy but do like the Middle Ages, got together to build a completely 'medieval' building, by medieval methods, beginning in 1907. Most of it is already finished, although there is enough decorative work to do inside to last them another century or two. The style seems to be part English Gothic, part Viollet-le-Duc, and the most endearing feature is the rows of comical modillions around the cornices – lots of satirical and monster faces, including caricatures of the architects and masons.

Vitoria is a city of unexpected delights; one example, completing the park's monumental ensemble, is one of the most resplendent Art Deco petrol stations in Europe, just behind the cathedral. Another, a few blocks southeast on Calle Eduardo Dato, is the fantastical **RENFE station**, done in a kind of Hollywood Moorish style with brightly coloured tiles. The city has just finished constructing a new embellishment, **Plaza de los Fueros**, a square just southeast of Plaza de la Virgen Blanca, designed and decorated by Eduardo Chillida. It's a strange space – part Roman amphitheatre, part basketball court – that the locals haven't quite worked out what to do with yet; it seems to get most use after the bars have closed. At one end, an untitled Chillida sculpture is enclosed within angular walls.

Parque de la Florida, laid out in 1855, retains much of the Romantic spirit of its times, with grand promenades, hidden bowers and overlooks. It was the centre of the city's fashionable district, and a shady walkway from the southern end of the park, the Paseo de la Senda, takes you to the elegant **Paseo de Fray Francisco de Vitoria**, lined with the Hispano-Victorian mansions of the old industrialists. One of these houses, now the **Museo de Bellas Artes** (*open Tues–Fri 10–2 and 4–6.30, Sat 10–2, Sun 11–2; adm*), features a well-displayed collection ranging from early paintings to Picasso and Miró, with a handful of great Spanish masters in between, all in a beautifully restored space with original features such as a Tiffany-style stained-glass skylight.

Some of the finest works are of the type museums here call *Escuela Hispano-flamenca*, paintings from the early 16th century, at a time when the influence from the Low Countries was strong; most are anonymous, and it is impossible to tell which country the artist was from. One of the finest works, a triptych of the Passion by the 'Master of the Legend of Santa Godelina', shows the same sort of conscious stylization as an Uccello; the longer you look at it, the stranger it seems. Medieval painted carved wood figures are well represented, and there are no fewer than three paintings by Ribera, including a *Crucifixion*. As in all Basque museums, Basque painters are more than well represented. Here you'll find some surprises, such as a great early-20th-century landscapist named Fernando de Anarica, or his contemporary Ramon Zubiaurre, whose *Autoridades de mi Aldea* shares the not-quite-naïve sensibility of Rousseau or Grant Wood. The façade of a 13th-century hermitage has been reconstructed in the museum's garden. Back along the Paseo at No.3, the **Museum of Arms** (*open Tues–Fri 10–2 and 4–6.30, Sat 10–2, Sun 11–2; adm*) houses suits of armour, medieval weapons, and dioramas and displays on Wellington's victory at the Battle of Vitoria.

Seeing the last of Vitoria's little secrets means a pleasant 20-minute walk to the southwest (from the Paseo de Fray Francisco, take Paseo de Cervantes and Avenida de San Prudencio; this is part of one of the Santiago pilgrimage routes), to the **Basílica of San Prudencio**, in Armentia, a village swallowed up by the city's suburbs. The church was built at the end of the 12th century, with a fine doorway and curious reliefs and carved capitals inside.

West of Vitoria you can visit Roman ruins, including a long, 13-arched bridge at **Trespuentes**, near the remains of a pre-Roman town, the **oppidum of Iruña** (*open summer Tues–Fri 11–2 and 4–8, Sat 11–3, Sun 11–2; winter Tues–Sat 11–3, Sun 10–3; adm*).

Two kilometres away at Mendoza, near the airport on the A3302, a 13th-century defensive tower with great views over the countryside has been restored to house the **Museo de Heráldica** (*open May–Oct 11–2 and 4–8, Sun 11–2; Nov–April Tues–Fri 11–3, adm*), Spain's only museum dedicated to the origins and graphic styles of heraldic escutcheons. The exhibits give special attention to the histories of the great families of the Basque country.

Alava Province

Just because the Basque capital is located here, you might think that Alava (Araba in Basque) is the Euskadi heartland. In fact, speakers of Basque make up precisely 4 per cent of the population, by far the lowest in the seven Basque provinces. One senses that, having lost ground to the Spaniards for centuries during their long economic decline, the Basques purposely planted their parliament here as part of a careful plan to reclaim the soil. Alava is home to the historical oddity of the County (*Condado*) of Treviño, an enclave of Castilian Spaniards smack in the middle of the province. They are quite happy being part of Castile, just as they were in the Middle Ages, making Alava the only province in Spain, maybe in the world, that is shaped like a doughnut.

Gaceo and Alaiza

There aren't a lot of sights here, but for anyone interested in things medieval the province offers something truly outstanding – and almost totally unknown outside the area. The minuscule village of **Gaceo**, on the N1 east of Vitoria, offers nothing less than one of the finest ensembles of Gothic fresco painting anywhere in Europe. The frescoes are in the simple church of San Martín de Tours (the address of the keyholder is posted on the church door); covered in plaster, they were not rediscovered until 1966.

Research places these works sometime between about 1325 and 1450. The style, a bit archaic with its Romanesque attention to flowing draperies, is distinctive enough for scholars to speculate about an obscure 'Basque-Navarrese' school of artists, perhaps centred in Vitoria. Byzantine influence is also strongly present, though details like the gnarled, rugged cross are uniquely Spanish (such a cross was the symbol of the 19th-century Carlist rebels). Thanks to the plaster, most of the paintings are well preserved, though oddly enough many of the faces have vanished, as in the *Trinity*, with a grand figure of God enthroned, supporting Jesus on the cross, painted on the apse over the altar. True fresco work requires that the plaster underneath the paintings, applied fresh each morning for an artist's day's work, be absolutely right in composition and application. The secrets were just being rediscovered in the 14th century in Italy; artists elsewhere hadn't got it quite right.

The figures around the *Trinity* on the apse seem to be arranged to represent the commemoration of All Saints' Day: various scenes of *Los Bienaventurados*, the Blessed – Apostles, martyrs, confessors, virgins and more – all arranged neatly by category. On the right, note the conspicuous figures of St Michael, weighing souls at Judgement

Tourist Information

Antoñana: Cuesta de Lavadero, t 94 541 02 26 (*summer only*).
Laguardia: Abarca s/n, t 94 160 08 45.

Market Day

Sunday in Laguardia.

Where to Stay and Eat

Argómaniz ✉ 01192

★★★Parador de Argómaniz, on the N1, t 94 529 32 00, f 94 529 32 87, *argomaniz@parador.es* (*expensive*). One of the smaller and simpler *paradores*, with some rooms set in the original building, a 17th-century mansion with iron balconies. Argómaniz is east of Vitoria, near the paintings of Gaceo.

Urturi ✉ 01119

★★★Hotel Borja y Yon Golf, t 94 537 82 32, f 94 537 82 84, *borjagambin@euskalnet.net* (*moderate*). Small new hotel near the golf course, with a comfortable lounge and open fire for après-golf.

Laguardia ✉ 01300

Laguardia, with its reputation for culinary excellence, is definitely the place to stop over if you are passing through La Rioja Alavesa.
Hotel Castillo El Collado, Paseo El Collado, t 94 112 12 00, f 94 160 08 78 (*expensive*). The pick of places to stay, a 1920s palace full of antiques and luscious fabrics, with an incredibly welcoming owner; if you're lucky he'll tell you the story of the 'Love and Madness' suite! The restaurant serves Basque and Navarrese dishes, and magnificent goat roasts.
★★Posada Mayor de Migueloa, C/ Mayor de Migueloa 20, t 94 112 11 75 (*expensive*). In a 17th-century mansion with antique furnishings; also has an excellent but expensive restaurant.
★Pachico Martinez, C/ Sancho Abarca 20, t 94 160 00 09 (*inexpensive*). Has been in the same family since 1806 and is still doing fine.
★Marixa, C/ Sancho Abarca 8, t 94 160 01 65, f 94 160 02 02 (*moderate*). For the best dining in town, with air-conditioned rooms and expensive meals. You might try an unlikely local favourite – *acelga rellena* (stuffed Swiss chard) – which is better than it sounds.
Hotel Palacio de Samaniego, 16km west of Laguardia in Samaniego, t 94 160 91 51, f 94 160 91 57, *jonyana@mediaweb.es* (*moderate*). Well-restored 18th-century mansion, with personalized rooms and a restaurant spread out in three dining rooms, where the emphasis is on primary ingredients and local wines.
Hotel Rural Larrain, 14km east of Laguardia in Lanciego, C/ Mayor 13, t 94 112 82 26, f 94 112 82 51 (*inexpensive*). Refurbished 18th-century mansion, with nine spic-and-span rooms and a warm welcome from Javier and Esther.

Day, and Abraham, gathering the fortunate to his bosom. The choir vault too is entirely covered in frescoes, stock images from the Life of Christ divided by charming borders of trompe l'oeil designs and fantasy architecture. At the bottom right is something no medieval mural picture-book could be without: the souls of the damned getting variously swallowed up in the mouth of hell or cooked in a big pot.

Gaceo is not such an illogical spot for art as it seems. The modern N1 that connects Vitoria to Burgos and Pamplona roughly follows the course of the main Roman road into the north. Enough of this survived in medieval times to keep it an important route, heavily used by pilgrims on their way to Compostela. Perhaps no one ever imagined Gaceo would grow into a metropolis, but it may well have been that the village was a popular pilgrim stop, and some pious gentleman or lady paid for the paintings to edify the sojourners' spirits and give them something to think about as they made their way westwards.

While you're out in Gaceo, you might as well carry on a little further and see some quite different paintings at another tiny hamlet, **Alaiza** (from the N1, take the A3100 south from Salvatierra). The Iglesia de la Asunción here is a barn-like 13th-century building; it too has a painted apse and choir, but the contrast with Gaceo's is like day with night. Instead of flowing Gothic draperies, Alaiza has one-colour cartoons so weird and primitive they might have been done by a Palaeolithic cave artist on a bad day. The central work, on the apse, shows soldiers besieging a castle, while on the choir vault and walls bizarre hooded figures joust, murder or indulge in bodily functions not often seen on church walls. There is a contrastingly precise inscription underneath in Gothic letters, but no one has ever managed to decipher it. The best guess the Spaniards can come up with for this singular work is that these scenes were done *c.* 1367, while Alaiza was under the control of some rough English mercenary soldiers; one of them might have done it.

The closest village of any size in this region, **Salvatierra**, is a pleasant old village of warm stone within striking distance of two of Euskadi's best dolmens – **Aizkomendi** at Eguilaz, visible in a little roadside park off the N1, and **Sorginetxe** in Arizala.

North of the Vitoria, the biggest features on the landscape are the big dams and lakes of **Urrunaga** and **Ullívarri**. The lakes have become popular spots for fishing and water sports; Ullívarri even has a nudist beach. Further north, on the road to Durango, **Otxandio** was the original Basque iron town, a fact commemorated by a statue of the god Vulcan in the main square.

South of Vitoria: the Ebro Valley and La Rioja Alavesa

South of Vitoria, the Castilian fief of the **County of Treviño** looks strangely compelling on the map, but in reality there's plenty of oak woods and good farmland, and that's it. There is one village, Treviño, which has the county's only petrol pump. Just to the east of the county, in the pretty hilly region near Bernedo, is a new public 18-hole golf course at Urturi, designed by Severino Ballesteros.

Some of the best Rioja wines come from **La Rioja Alavesa**, a 40km growing area along the Ebro, facing the autonomous region of La Rioja and extending to Oyón, just north of Logroño. Sheltered from gusts and clouds by the Cantabrian mountains, the climate is midway between Atlantic and Mediterranean and by far the sunniest in Euskadi. The first vines here were introduced by the monastic orders, and the first rules governing the quality go back to 1650; today some 25 per cent of Riojas originate in Euskadi.

Perched high over the river, the key wine town of La Rioja Alavesa is walled **Laguardia** (**Biasteri** in Basque), founded in the 10th century. You can learn all about local wines and their production at La Casa del Vino, and visit the *bodegas*; one, Bodegas Palacio (*t 94 160 00 57*), offers classes on wine appreciation. Another, the Bodegas Ysios, just outside the village, was designed by Santiago Calatrava, the distinguished Spanish architect. This is not the only example of world-class *bodega* design in the area (*see* Elciego, below). Don't miss the 14th-century portal of Laguardia's Gothic Santa María de los Reyes, with the most spectacular sculpted tympanum in Euskadi, still in mint condition and bearing its original bright colours.

In 1935 archaeologists discovered Laguardia's prehistoric ancestor just to the north; the **Poblado de la Hoya** was occupied from the end of Bronze Age until the late Iron Age (about 1500–250 BC). Although the site is not open to the public, you can visit the adjacent small museum (*open May–mid-Oct Tues–Fri 11–2 and 4–8, Sat 11–3, Sun 10–2; mid-Oct–April Tues–Sat 11–3, Sun 10–2*), with a model of what La Hoya may have looked like and finds from the site; explanations are entirely in Castilian and Basque. Some believe it was founded by peoples from the north, who mixed with the indigenous proto-Basques. Further evidence of the importance of this area in prehistoric times are the quantity and quality of its **dolmens**, so many that a dolmen route has been laid out: the most important are the Dolmen della Hechicera, east on the A3228, just beyond Elvillar, while west of Laguardia the A124 leads past two others.

If, like the old song says, you like 'wine, wine, wine, all the time, time, time', La Rioja Alavesa will not disappoint. In **Elciego**, south of Laguardia, you'll find the *bodega* of the Marqués de Riscal (*t 94 160 60 00, www.marquesderiscal.com*), a famous producer who helped establish the reputation of Riojas in the 19th century. The vineyard has a reputation for knowing just how to age wines, and some 30,000 barrels patiently sit in the cellars here, some for as long as 50 years. An added attraction is the new administrative wing, due to open in September 2002, designed by none other than Frank Gehry, architect of the Guggenheim Museum in Bilbao. Gehry has once again used titanium for the undulating roof of the building, which will house a shop, museum and Basque restaurant. To the north in **Leza**, little *bodegas* specialize in *vino de cosechero* (harvester wine) made through 'carbolic maceration' of the whole grape; it ferments in a few days, after which men stomp the grapes to produce a fresh, perfumed, slightly acidic wine, the best of which is 'heart's wine', or *vino de corazón*. Further west, Samaniego, another wine town, is bunched up around the parish church of the Asunción, converted from a 15th-century fortress. Perhaps the most famous *bodega* here belongs to Fernando Remirez de Ganuza, whose exquisite, highly personalized wine is a true *vino de autor*. For the best overview of La Rioja Alavesa, head north of here to the Balcón de la Rioja, at the top of the Herrera mountain pass; if you carry on north, you'll come to **Peñacerrada** (**Urizaharra**), still embraced by perfectly preserved walls.

West of Samaniego, towards Haro and the green Montes del Toloño, **Labastida** has the Romanesque hermitage of Santo Cristo at its highest point, which once belonged to the Monasterio del Toloño. The monks' farm, the 16th-century Granja de Nuestra Señora de Remelluri, is now a prestigious family-run *bodega* open for visits (*t 94 133 18 01*). Others are just west in Briñas (*see* below).

Haro

While here, you might as well slip over the river and visit Haro, the capital of Rioja Alta wines, in the autonomous region of La Rioja. At the confluence of the Ebro and the Tirón, Haro is built around a large arcaded square. Its chief monuments are a handful of noble houses, the attractive **Casa Consistorial** (1775) and the 16th-century

Tourist Information

Tourist office: Plaza Hermanos F. Rodríguez,
t 94 130 33 66.

Market Days

Tuesday and Saturday on Arco de Santa Bárbara.

Where to Stay and Eat

Haro ✉ 26200

★★★★Los Agustinos, C/ San Agustín 2, t 94 131 13 08, f 94 130 31 48 (*expensive*). Superbly restored, occupying a former Augustinian monastery that later served as a prison: note the graffiti carved into the columns of the garden cloister. Rooms are air-conditioned, quiet and equipped with satellite TV.

★★★Iturrimurri, Ctra. N124 Km 41, t 94 131 12 13, f 94 131 17 21 (*expensive*). Along the highway, overlooking Haro, this modern hotel is plain, comfortable and has a pool.

★Hs Aragón, La Vega 9, t 94 131 00 04 (*cheap*). Basic, but your only bet for a cheap sleep.

Terete, C/ Lucrecia Arana 17, t 94 131 00 23. Has filled the centre of Haro with the divine aroma of its famous roast lamb, among a huge choice of other dishes (*moderate*); good 1,500 pts/€9 *menú*. Closed Sun eve, Mon and Oct.

Beethoven I and II, C/ Santo Tomás 3–5 and Pza de la Iglesia 8, t 94 131 11 81. Traditional mushroom, fish and vegetable dishes are the prizes at these two dining rooms (*moderate*).

Briñas ✉ 26200

★★★Hospedería Señorío de Briñas, C/ Travesía Real 3, t 94 030 42 24, hsbrinas@arrakis.es (*expensive*). Has some unique split-level rooms in a carefully restored mini palace, tastefully decorated with antiques.

★El Portal de La Rioja, Ctra. De la Victoria 42, t 94 131 14 80 (*inexpensive*). In addition to rooms with bath, there is an excellent restaurant serving chops grilled on vine cuttings (*chuletas al sarmiento*), a craft shop and a wine museum with century-old bottles.

church of Santo Tomás up in Plaza Iglesia, bearing a handsome, recently restored Plateresque façade with sculpture and reliefs in several registers, paid for by the Condestables of Castile.

The *bodegas* are clustered around the train station. While most welcome visitors, they usually require advance notice. An exception is **Bodegas Bilbaínas** (*C/ Estación 3*, *t 94 131 01 47*), with a pretty façade of *azulejos*, usually open mornings and late afternoons. Along Costa del Vino, you'll find the celebrated cellars of the **CUNE**, or CVNE (*t 94 131 06 50*), home of a fine bubbly; Chilean-owned **López de Heredia** (*t 94 131 01 27*), makers of one of the best Riojas, *Viña Tondonia*; and the vast, French-founded **Rioja Alta**, (*Avda Vizcaya, t 94 131 03 46*), with 25,000 barrels. The even-larger **Federico Paternina** by the Plaza de Toros (*t 94 131 05 50*), founded in 1896, houses 4 million bottles, and welcomes visitors daily except Monday. Another, **Martínez Lacuesta Hnos** (*C/ Ventilla 71, t 94 131 00 50*), is in the old gas works that became obsolete back in 1891, when Haro became the first city in Spain to have public electric street lighting – hence the slogan '*Ya se ven las luces, ya estamos en Haro*' ('We can see the lights already; we've arrived in Haro'). Among the shops, **Selección Vinos de Rioja** (*Pza Paz 5*, *t 94 130 30 17*) offers tastings and a wide variety of different Riojas.

Since 1892, Haro's **Estación Enológica**, C/ Bretón de los Herreros 4 (just behind the bus station), has tested new wine-making techniques and varieties; its **Wine Museum** (*open Mon–Sat 10–2 and 4–8, Sun 10–2*) offers detailed explanations of the latest high-tech processes used for Rioja. For a far less serious initiation, or rather baptism, in Rioja, come to Haro on 29 July, when **San Felices** is celebrated with a *Batalla del*

Vino. Everyone dresses in white, and after Mass, fortified with *zurracapote* (Rioja sangria, made with red wine, citrus fruit and cinnamon) and armed with every conceivable squirter, splasher and sprayer, opposing groups douse one another with 100,000 litres of wine. This Dionysian free-for-all takes place 3km from Haro at the Peña de Bilibio, below the striking rock formation and pass of the Conchas de Haro, the 'Shells of Haro', where Felices, a hermit-follower of San Millán, lived in a cave. Archaeologists have recently discovered a 10th-century church and the ruins of a Roman town, Castrum Bilibium, or Haro la Vieja, just under the rocks.

Around Haro: the Sonsierra

There aren't many landmarks around Haro, but a handful of villages are worth a look if you're trawling about looking for that perfect bottle. A good place to start is the Sonsierra, a pocket of La Rioja on the left bank of the Ebro. **Briñas**, just north of Haro, has a number of noble escutcheoned manors left over from the days when it was the playground of the Haro nobility. These days, wine is the be-all and end-all; there's even a *bodega* under the church.

Don't confuse Briñas with **Briones** to the southeast, where there is a nubbly church tower and a bridge to **San Vicente de la Sonsierra**, a village best known in La Rioja since 1499 for its Guild of Flagellants, *Los Picaos*, headquartered at Ermita de Vera Cruz. During Holy Week, clad in anonymous hoods, the *Picaos* whip themselves across the shoulders, then pique the bruises with wax balls full of crystal splinters until the blood runs. Just outside San Vicente, the curious 12th-century Romanesque **church of Santa María de la Piscina** was founded by Ramiro Sanchez, son-in-law of the Cid, who allegedly brought back a piece of the True Cross from the Crusades. Over the door there's a shield carved with mysterious numbers and symbols. Paintings inside represent the *piscina probática* ('waters of the flock') of Jerusalem and the Holy Grail. Just east, **Abalos** has one of the oldest cellars in Spain, the Bodegón Real Divisa, t 94 133 41 18, owned by descendants of the Cid, and a 16th-century church, San Esteban Protomártir, decorated with dragons.

Inland: Bilbao to San Sebastián

If you drive from Bilbao to San Sebastián along the coast, the narrow, twisting roads will take you nearly a day. The more common routes east are the A8 motorway, with its exorbitant tolls, and the slower, parallel N634, both of which follow some of the more somnolent landscapes of Euskadi before hitting the coast near Deba.

If you avoid the tolls and follow the latter, the first stop is the biggest town in the area, **Durango**, a name that conjures up cowboys and Westerns in the New World (besides the Durango in Colorado, there is another in Mexico, which in colonial times was capital of the province of 'Nueva Vizcaya' – there must have been a lot of Basques about). The original, sadly, has nothing to detain you long; in 1937 the German Condor Legion used it for target practice in a March prelude to Gernika. Colonel Wolfram von Richthofen, a cousin of the Red Baron flying ace, was one of the masterminds behind this new method of warfare, which he promised would terrorize the local population and undermine morale. The Luftwaffe razed Durango's cobblestoned streets and churches, just when the latter were filled for early Mass. In half an hour, 238 civilians were killed. When questioned, Franco claimed that Communist Basque church-burners were responsible for the destruction. What surprised him, and the German theorists, was that Durango's martyrdom only stiffened the Basques' resolve.

Somehow the bombs missed Durango's attractive Baroque centre behind the Portal de Santa Ana, an ornate survival from the old walls. Note the brightly painted Ayuntamiento, and the stone mosaic maze under the portico of Santa María de Uribarri. The most unusual monument is the 19th-century sculpted Kurutziaga Cross, just outside the centre in a neighbourhood of the same name.

South of Durango, the Duranguesado massif juts abruptly out of rolling green hills, creating Vizcaya's most dramatic mountain scenery. Protected as the **Parque Natural Urkiola**, the range offers plenty of opportunities for sweaty assaults on the high peaks or leisurely ambles through birch forest (the park's name means 'place of birch trees' in Basque). Local legends tell that the goddess Mari haunts these hills; one mountain, Amboto, is especially famous for its witches, perhaps as a confused survival of Mari's mountain rituals. More earthly residents include goshawk, peregrine falcon and merlin, all of which can be spotted regularly, as well as two creatures especially associated with witches in Basque, the dragonfly (*sorginorratz*, or 'witch-needle') and butterfly (*sorgin-oilo*, or 'witch-hen').

North of Durango, in the heartland of old Basque traditions, are the minute village and valley of **Bolívar**, from whence came the family of the great liberator of South America, Simón de Bolívar. His Art Deco monument dwarfs the village square, and

Getting Around

Durango and Elorrio are both served by BizkaiBus from Paseo del Arenal in Bilbao, and EuskoTren services between Bilbao and San Sebastián call at Durango.

Tourist Information

Durango: C/ Bruno Maurizio Zabala 2, t 94 603 00 30.
Alto de Urkiola: Caserio Toki-Alai, t 94 681 41 55.

Where to Stay and Eat

Unlike the coast, this is definitely not tourist country, and you'll tend to find only simple accommodation anywhere near the A8.

Durango ✉ **48200**
★★★Hotel Kurutziaga, C/ Kurutziaga 52, t 94 620 08 64, f 94 620 14 09 (*expensive*).

An 18th-century mansion transformed into a modern business hotel, with a decent restaurant.
★★Hs Juego de Bolos, San Agustinalde 2, t 94 681 10 99 (*inexpensive–cheap*). Durango's one *hostal*.
Gaztelua, C/ Herriko Gudarien 1, t 94 681 67 22. There isn't much in workaday Durango, but this is a very friendly local bar and *comedor* serving good local dishes including an excellent fish soup.
Josu Mendizabal, C/ San Antonio, in Bérriz, t 94 622 50 70. Just east of Durango, this local man runs a very popular restaurant with plenty of fresh seafood.

Markina ✉ **48200**
★★Vega, Abesúa 2, t 94 616 60 15 (*moderate*). You can get a good night's sleep at this central place, with large, airy rooms overlooking the main *plaza*.
Niko, San Agustín 4, t 94 616 89 59. Good cooking on a bargain 900 pts/€5.4 *menú*.

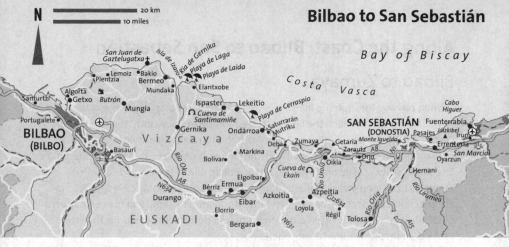

down the village's one lane, the site of his ancestral house has been fixed up as a Museo Bolívar (*open Tues–Fri 10–1, Sat and Sun 12–2, July and Aug also 5–7, closed Mon*). Near the old parish church of Santo Tomás you can see the 'cattle trial yards' and the huge stone weights hauled by oxen at festivals.

Markina, further north, is nicknamed the 'University of Pelota'; its historic *fronton* has produced champions who have made their mark around the world. The town is also famous for its craftsmen, especially those who weave *chisteras*, the handsome elongated wicker baskets used in *cesto punto*, or *jaï-alaï*; if you want to take one home, visit José Egizabal, Okerra Kalea 4, **t** 94 616 64 73, or Ignacio Ugartelxea, Zehar Kalea 11, **t** 94 616 74 87. Take the little bridge over the Río Artibay to visit the uncanny, hexagonal church of San Miguel de Arretxinaga, built around an enormous altar constructed by the giant *jentillaks* (or, according to some, fallen from heaven) that consists of three massive rocks propped against one another. Probably a work of Neolithic times, it now shelters a statue of St Michael, who is almost inevitably associated with old weird places (*see* Aralar, pp.208–9). Another 'cattle trial yard' next to the church only adds to Stone Age ambiance.

Continuing along the N634, you'll get an object lesson in the life of the average Basque, passing through tidy, grey little industrial splotches like Ermua and **Eibar**, a typically peculiar Basque factory town stuffed into a narrow valley, with plenty of tall apartment blocks around what was once Spain's biggest sewing machine plant. **Elgoibar**, the next village up the road, is much the same.

South of the N634, on the BI632, **Elorrio** is an attractive village of grand palaces and impressive little squares adorned with a set of unique crucifixes from the 15–16th centuries. The façade of the Ayuntamiento bears a curious verse from Matthew 12:36: 'I tell you, on the Day of Judgment men will render account for every careless word they utter.' From the centre, it's a lovely walk out to the **hermitage of San Adrián de Argiñeta**, where you can see the 9th- and 10th-century tombs of Argiñeta, carved out of rock, some adorned with Latin inscriptions or pinwheel-like stars that may be sun-signs. Nobody knows to whom these sarcophagi belong; some speculate they are the tombs of some leftover Visigoths or believe the tombs represent pre-Christian burial practices – not one bears a cross. From Elgoibar the road joins the coast (*see* p.170).

Along the Coast: Bilbao to San Sebastián

Bilbao to Zumaya

When passing through the Bilbao suburbs of Getxo (*see* p.145) on the way to Plentzia, turn east to reach the best castle remaining in the vicinity, the 11th-century **Castillo de Butrón** (*open daily 10.30–8; adm*), rebuilt in fairy-tale style in the 19th century and located in the wooded hills. Butrón really deserves a visit; it's Disneyland's Sleeping Beauty's castle on a bad trip, an incredible pile of towers and corbelled ramparts in a gloomy dark stone, built in a style that other countries in the Victorian era generally saved for prisons and asylums. If you aren't careful you may end up on a guided tour; the place is kitted out with props and dummies in costume, to better evoke the fantasy medieval atmosphere.

The main route along the coast beyond Plentzia passes close to **Lemoiz**, near the mouth of the Deba river, which for local fishing collectives and the million residents of Greater Bilbao only 17km away was the site of a real-life bad trip for decades. In 1972 work was begun here on a nuclear reactor, pushed through by Franco, just at a time when nuclear protests were growing around Europe. The usual fears of radiation pollution and an accident, however, went hand in hand with concerns over who would be in charge of it – and there was no doubt in the Basques' minds that it wouldn't be them. Although the project was supported by the PNV and the tycoons of Bilbao (whose companies had been contracted for the work), democracy had no sooner returned than petitions and mass demonstrations showed the depth of

Getting Around

The coast is served by frequent **buses** from Bilbao's Paseo del Arena. The narrow-gauge **Eusko Trenbideak** line runs out of Bilbao to Bermeo via Gernika and Mundaka.

Tourist Information

Bermeo: C/ Askatsun Bidea 2, t 94 617 91 54, f 94 617 91 59, *turismo@jet.es*.
Mundaka: Pza Lehendari Agirre, t 94 617 72 01.
Gernika: C/ Artekale 8, t 94 625 58 92.
Lekeitio: Independentzia Enparantza, t 94 684 40 17, f 94 684 41 67, *www.learjai.com*. Open *in summer only*.

Market Days

Bermeo: Tuesday.
Gernika: Monday, the biggest market in Euskadi.

Where to Stay and Eat

Bakio ✉ 48130
Hotel Joshe Mari, C/ Bentalde 31, t 94 619 40 05, f 94 619 57 03 (*moderate*). This unusual little hotel has only a handful of rooms, each individually decorated with locally gathered antiques; the restaurant offers good food in a relaxing atmosphere.
★★Hotel Arimume, C/ Bentalde 95, t 94 619 40 22 (*moderate*). Right on the beachfront, this is a delightfully old-fashioned place (bathrooms are new), furnished with antiques and with the added bonus of a pretty terrace shaded with trees.
★★Hosteria Senorio de Bizkaia, C/ Jose Maria Cirarda, t 94 619 47 25. Another charming hotel in a 19th-century mansion not far from the beach; it's very popular with the English, and boasts an excellent restaurant.

opposition to the project, culminating in a 1977 protest in Bilbao that gathered an estimated 150,000 to 200,000 people, said to be the largest anti-nuclear demonstration in history. Appeals for a referendum on the plant, however, were ignored by Prime Minister Suárez, who claimed the matter was out of his hands. Soon after, ETA became involved, carrying out 300 attacks in all, including bombs in the plant, that resulted in a dozen dead, among them workers at the plant, ETA militants and special targets (mostly engineers). In 1979 the Basques started to refuse to pay their electric bills, and in 1980, Lemoiz was declared a military zone. In 1982, ETA kidnapped the director of the project and offered to exchange his life for the demolition of the plant; he was killed. When it happened again, the government threw in the towel. Later in the year Lemoiz became one of the few nuclear plants in Europe to be abandoned at such a late stage in its construction, and the whole project was finally scuttled to great rejoicing in 1994.

First stop on the coastal road proper is **Bakio**, a *txakoli*-producing town tucked snugly into a little bay. *Txakoli*, a slightly effervescent and refreshingly tart wine, always flamboyantly poured at arm's length, is made of native hondarrabi zuri and hondarrabi beltza grapes, along with folle blanche and up to 25 per cent chardonnay, sauvignon blanc or cabernet sauvignon, and comes in white (the most common), rosé (or *ojo de gallo*, 'cock's eye') and red. Rated one of Spain's top wines way back in 1571, specialized *tabernas de txakolin* once flourished throughout the Basque country. Laws in many Basque towns banned the importation of other wines, while the General Assembly in Vizcaya took it upon itself to test the *txakoli* put up for sale, under the basic rating of 'drinkable'. Today the greenish, not-quite-ripe grapes are left in open

---

Mundaka ✉ 48360

✶✶Atalaya, Itxaropen Kalea 1, t 94 617 70 00, f 94 687 68 99 (*moderate*). This is one of the loveliest hotels in the region, located right on the river in one of those glorious Basque buildings of a century ago, with glass galleries all around. It has small but lavishly appointed rooms, with satellite TV and minibars.

✶Mundaka, Florentino Larriraga 9, t 94 687 67 00, f 94 687 61 58 (*moderate*). A little more down-to-earth – a sign in the lobby asks surfers to knock the sand off their feet before going up in the lift – but still offers plenty of style.

✶El Puerto, Portu Kalea 1, t 94 687 67 25, f 94 687 67 26 (*moderate*). Has bright and breezy rooms with views over the port and estuary.

Asador Zaldua, Sabino Arana 10, t 94 587 08 71. Serves a wonderful array of fresh fish and succulent steaks grilled to perfection (*moderate*). *Lunch only Nov–Jun*.

Casino, José Mari, C/ Mayor, t 94 687 60 05. Once the local fishermen's guild auction house, this is now a local eating club which has opened its doors to the public. The seafood is superb and is usually caught by a club member.

Gernika ✉ 48300

✶✶Gernika, Carlos Gangoiti 17, t 94 625 03 50 (*moderate*). Accommodation is limited in Gernika; this is one of only two simple places to choose from.

Boliña, C/ Barrenkalle 3, t 94 625 03 00 (*inexpensive*). In the heart of the pedestrian area, this offers rooms with or without bath that are a little basic, but the welcome is charming. The restaurant is very good and offers an excellent *menú de degustastión* at 4,000 pts/€24.

Zimelea Etxea, Carlos Cangoiti 57, t 94 625 10 12. The best choice in town (*expensive*).

Zallo Berri, C/ Juan Calzada 79, t 94 625 18 00. A delightful, simple restaurant

steel vats from one to six weeks, sealed once they ferment, and bottled according to tradition after two February frosts.

Nearby, the islet of **San Juan de Gaztelugatxa** is linked to the mainland by a pretty arched bridge. In the old days, the isle supported a castle, but now the only building is a hermitage. On three dates in the summer – 24 June, 31 July and 29 August – big processions make their way there. According to legend, St John the Baptist, who must have been a first cousin to the *jentillaks*, took only three hops to get here from Bermeo; his footprint may still be seen near the top of the 232 steps to the sanctuary. The magnificent views along the dark coastal cliffs are worth expending the puff to get there.

Bermeo and Mundaka

Continuing round the coast from Bakio, **Bermeo** is Euskadi's largest fishing port, a colourful, working town that makes few concessions to tourism, especially since the fishing fleet has recently benefitted from new EU fishing regulations. Bermeo and its neighbour Mundako have the special distinction of racing in the first ever recorded regatta, in 1719, in a contest of fishing launches, or *traineras*, very like the popular regattas run today. Nor do seamen here waste any time with mermaids: the town is famous for the burning of an effigy of one named Xixili on 16 September, the day of its patron saint, Nuestra Señora de Alboniga.

Bermeo celebrates the long history of Basque seafaring in the Museo del Pescador (*open Tues–Sat 10–1.30 and 4–7.30, Sun 10–1.30, closed Mon*), which relates stories of whaling expeditions from the Bay of Biscay, where the Basques first nabbed the so-

---

(*moderate*) serving traditional, regional food (excellent value *menú del día*), although the young chef likes to throw out a few surprises.

Lezika, near Gernika's Santimamiñe caves. This fine restaurant (*moderate*) is located in an 18th-century Basque chalet in a charming woody grove.

Baserri Maitea, Ctra. B1635 (on the way to Bermeo), Km2, t 94 635 34 08. A wonderful restaurant in a 300-year-old farmhouse with wooden beams; the very fish is particularly good (*moderate*).

Lekeitio ✉ 48280

★★★**Emperatriz Zita**, C/ Santa Elena Etorbidea s/n, t 94 684 26 55, f 94 624 35 00, *rlekeitio@usa.net* (*moderate*). A recently opened modern palace of a place, complete with a thalassotherapy centre, built over the ruins of the home of the last Austro-Hungarian empress.

★★★**Zubieta**, Portal de Atea, t 94 684 30 30, f 94 684 10 99, *hzubieta@line-pro.es* (*moderate*). Charming hotel on the grounds of a castle, in the former gatehouse, with lovely rooms and lovely owners.

★★**Beitia**, Avda Abroa 25, t 94 684 01 11, f 94 684 21 65 (*moderate*). Adequate.

Hosteria Señorio de Bizcaya, José María Cirarda 4, t/f 94 619 47 25 (*moderate*). A noble old palace, lovingly restored and surrounded by gardens with beautifully restored rooms.

Piñupe, Avda Abaroa 10, t 94 684 29 84, f 94 684 07 71 (*inexpensive*). Very simple rooms, but a fine little place nonetheless.

Zapirain, Igualdegui 3, t 94 684 02 55. Serves good, abundant fish dinners (*moderate*).

Méson Arropain, Ctra. Marquina Ispaster, t 94 684 03 13. Five kilometres from Lekeitio, this friendly restaurant (*expensive*) cooks up excellent fish dishes smothered with bubbling *salsas*, and has good *txakoli* to wash it all down with.

called Basque whale (*Eubalaena glacialis*) – beginning with the ones who ran aground or came too close to shore – and then by the year 1000 pursuing them to the Arctic, perhaps reaching North America long before Columbus, although there is no solid proof. For centuries, whale hunting was a great Basque secret, and in the early Middle Ages Bermeo and other whaling ports made fortunes trading the ivory from the teeth, the oil rendered from the blubber, and the meat, which was red yet permitted during Lent and the many other fast days on the Church calendar, as it came from the sea. The better cuts (most notably the tongue, which the local bishops claimed as their tithes) were eaten fresh or preserved in salt, while the less prestigious bits were dried and exported around Europe. In the 13th century, Bermeo incorporated this seagoing gold mine on its seal. Whale hunting expanded to cod, and by the early 16th century the Basques were fishing around the mouth of the St Lawrence, to such an extent that pidgin Euskera became an important trading language, remembered for generations among the native people.

The route from here skirts the broad, flat Ría de Gernika estuary, and takes a detour south along the Río Oka to Gernika. Near the mouth of the inlet lie the **Pedernales** and **Mundaka**, the latter famous among surfers for having the longest left-hand break in Europe. If this means nothing to you, there's plenty of enjoyment to be had in wandering Mundaka's labyrinthine alleys and soaking up the views from its charming waterfront promenade. In the estuary's mouth, the tiny island of Izaro used to be home to a band of hardy monks. On the opposite shore are two more pretty beaches at **Laida** and **Laga**.

Gernika (Guernica)

Guernica is without doubt the most powerful and driving symbol in the entire Basque political culture. For an American, it would be Pearl Harbor, the Alamo and Bunker Hill combined in a single, searing metaphor.
Robert Clark

The ancient, sacred city of the Basques is mostly rebuilt now, and the majority of the inhabitants are too young to remember the horror that occurred one market day in 1937, when some 1,645 people were killed in a concentrated 3-hour aerial bombardment by state-of-the-art German aircraft. But other than the beautiful setting in the Mundaka valley near the sea, and the oak tree by the 19th-century Basque parliament building (*Las Casas Juntas*), there's not much to see.

The **Tree of Gernika**, the seedling of an ancient oak, is the symbol of Basque democracy; under it the representatives of the Basque provinces met in assembly from the early Middle Ages on, and proclaimed the laws that governed them. After 1300, the kings of Castile would come Gernika's oak to swear to uphold Basque *fueros* and ancient laws. The tree is the subject of one of the best-loved Basque songs, *Gernikako Arbola*, written in 1853 by José Maria Iparragirre, a veteran of the first Carlist War and itinerant folk singer. The song was so successful in the Basque country that Iparragirre was sent by Madrid into exile to Argentina. In 1876, after the

Basque *fueros* were abolished, a community group demanded Iparragirre's return. The first verse goes:

Gernikako arbola
da bedeinkatua,
euskaldunen artean
guztiz maitatua.
Eman da zabal zazu
munduan frutua;
adoratzen zaitugu,
arbola santua.

(The tree of Gernika/is a blessed symbol,/held dear by all the Basque people/with deep love./Let your fruit fall/over all the world;/we adore you,/sacred tree.)

When the tree died in 1860, it was immediately replanted with a sapling from one of its acorns; remnants of the original's 300-year-old trunk can be seen under a nearby pavilion. The young tree somehow survived the bombing, and serves as a potent symbol of freedom and hope, not only for the Basques but for everyone – Gernika shocked the world because it was the first time modern technology was used as a tool of terror, a prelude to our own greatest nightmares.

Gernika was rebuilt in the Franco era, though neither the planning nor the architecture win any prizes. The **Museo de la Paz** is a solemn reminder of Gernika's past and the current world climate. The museum carefully documents the bombing through photographs, essays and art (including an inferior copy of Picasso's masterpiece; the Basques, who not surprisingly feel that they are the rightful owners, have been lobbying Madrid to send them the original to hang in the Guggenheim, but so far without result); it also highlights the absurdity of the destruction that continues in other lives and cities worldwide. There are also two modern memorials to commemorate the bombing: *Gure Aitaren Etxea*, 'our father's house', is an eloquent contribution by Chillida, dedicated to peace and sighted on the Tree; behind it is an amorphous work by Henry Moore, *Large Figure in a Shelter*.

Surrounding Gernika is the 220 sq km **Urdaibai Biosphere Reserve**, created in 1984 to prevent the destruction of fragile habitats in the Ría de Mundaka. The reserve is hardly a pristine wilderness – besides Gernika it counts 18 towns within its boundaries – but the sympathetic interaction between the inhabitants and their environment has led it to be considered an embodiment of that most elusive of eco-ideals: sustainable development. Farms and factories share Urdaibai with wetlands and lush oak forests; greenshank and bar-tailed godwit stalk the mud flats, while lucky observers may get a glimpse of the nocturnal genet, an odd mixture of raccoon and tabby cat with enormous eyes.

About 5km northeast of Gernika, the **Cueva de Santimamiñe** (*guided tours Mon–Fri 10, 11.15, 12.30, 4.30, 5.30 – note that due to the fragility of the art, only 15 people at a time are allowed in; get there early*) has Euskadi's best Upper Palaeolithic art: two rooms with engravings of bison, horses, arrows, a bear and a deer, and geometric

Experiments in Saturation Bombing

Gernika in 1937 became the kind of symbol for its times that Sarajevo was for the 1990s, a civilized little place that a band of thugs had chosen to flatten. Almost as soon as it happened, the Nationalist propaganda machine began sending out stories that the Communists had really destroyed the town by placing bombs in the sewers. It may have been the only time in his life that Francisco Franco was actually embarrassed. Just how much responsibility the Generalísimo had for Gernika will probably never be known, but there is nothing in his long, shabby career that suggests he was capable of such a stunt – Franco could massacre prisoners and stuff prisons with priests and professors, but Gernika, and Durango, which preceeded it (*see* pp.161–2), were evil on a Nazi scale.

Hitler had sent his 'Condor Legion' to Spain not only to give Franco a hand, but to test the new Luftwaffe's theories of terror bombing, and his commanders coldly determined Gernika to be the site of lesson number two (on a market day too). Though the town had no military significance whatsoever, as a symbol of Basque nationhood it was the perfect spot for a bombing designed especially to destroy the enemy's morale – by breaking their hearts, perhaps. While Gernika had little effect on the Civil War – the isolated Basque pocket was bound to fall anyhow – the Nazis were pleased enough with the results and the notoriety they gained from them to make such bombing the centre of their strategy; after Gernika came Warsaw, Rotterdam and Coventry, among many others.

Picasso's great painting, resting safely in New York during the Franco years, did as much as the bombing itself to catch the world's attention when it was displayed the following year in the Republic's pavilion at the Paris World's Fair. Since 1981 it has been proudly displayed in Madrid, perhaps the ultimate exorcism of the War and the General. The *Guernica* that seemed so mysterious and revolutionary in its time now seems quite familiar and eloquent to us, so much have our ways of seeing changed since that distant age. The black and white gives it the immediacy of a newspaper photo. Picasso's preliminary sketches show that the central figures in the painting, the fallen horse and rider, were in his mind from the beginning. We can see in them the image of Gernika's destroyers: the eternal bully on horseback, the *caudillo*, the conqueror. In a way, *Guernica* may have been Picasso's prophecy – with such an atrocity as this, the man on horseback may finally have gone too far.

designs; they are rather faint, as only some of the black paint of the outlines has survived. It is said that these caves are also the home of the Beigorri, a huge hairy red bull with a militant stare, the protector of the goddess Mari (*see* pp.53–4). A path leads from the cave entrance into the **Forest of Oma**, where local artist Agustín Ibarrola has fused art with nature by painting luminous multicoloured bands and symbols on the trees, to achieve an array of perspective tricks.

From Gernika, a detour off the main road to Lekeitio leads northwards to **Elantxobe**, huddled beneath sheer cliffs, an immaculate little fishing village that funnels down to a bijou harbour, so steep in fact that the bus has to be spun around on a mobile turntable, like a San Francisco cable car. Geographical challenges have helped the village retain its remote atmosphere – there's only one way in, down the serpentine main street – and traditional fishermen's houses adorn the narrow lanes down to the little port. Above loom the cliffs of Cabo Ogoña, highest on the Basque coast.

Lekeitio to Deba

Next along the coast is **Lekeitio (Lequeitio)**, with its beaches, Isuntza and Carraspio, further out. Isabel II preferred the beaches here to San Sebastián; she was holidaying in Lekeitio in September 1868 when rebellion broke out under Marshal Prim, whose *pronunciamento* deposed the dynasty, forcing Isabel into exile in France. The well-preserved palaces in Lekeitio's old quarter stand as testimony to its Belle Epoque popularity, but the elegant old port still catches more fish than tourists. Don't miss the early-16th-century Gothic church of Santa Maria and its impressive Flemish *retablo mayor*, an intricate explosion of gilded wood and polychrome carvings. Lekeitio is famous for its *antzareguna*, which takes place during the San Antolines festival in early September. This goose rodeo, however, is not an event for the faint-hearted. A rope is stretched over the port, held on either side by strong tug-of-war veterans. In the middle a goose is suspended by its feet over the port. Competitors, not allowed to weigh more than 70kg, are rowed up under the goose. One by one they grab the bird by the neck, and tuck its head under their armpit. The goose takes wing, but the weight is too great, so it only gets about 30ft high before it crashes into the sea. Then the goose tries again, and again; the man is like a human yoyo and hangs on as long as he can. The winner breaks the goose's neck.

Crossing into Guipúzcoa province at **Ondárroa** used to mean paying duty at the provincial customs house near the medieval stone Puente Vieja. The village is another pretty fishing port, one of Vizcaya's busiest and a popular spot on sunny weekends, though quieter than Lekeitio. **Mutriku** is a quiet village set back on a narrow inlet 3km from the quiet beach at **Saturrarán**. Mutriku is linked with Deba and Zumaya by a clifftop path which passes through green fields and tiny hamlets, affording magnificent views. The coastal scenery between Deba and Zumaya is the best in Euskadi, cliffs arcing gracefully from a choppy ocean in great vertical bands of pink and golden sandstone, and this is a good way to explore it. **Deba**, a favoured resort at the turn of last century, nowadays lies happily in the shadows of the other coastal centres. The local church, Santa Maria la Real, is of late Gothic construction and has a painted portal; somewhat older are the Palaeolithic scratchings in the nearby **Cueva de Ekain**.

Zumaya to San Sebastián

Zumaya

Zumaya is a pleasant town set at the mouth of the Urola river. A kilometre out of town on the other side, keep an eye out for the town's chief attraction, the **Museo Zuloaga** (*open Jan–Sept Sun only 10–2; adm*), a cosy villa set in a small park of ancient trees, surrounded by a wall. This was the home of the Basque painter Ignacio Zuloaga (1870–1945), and it holds not only a selection of his own works, but the masterpieces

Getting Around

The coast is served by frequent **buses** from Bilbao. The narrow-gauge **Eusko Trenbideak** line stops four or five times a day at Durango, then Deba, Zumaya and Zarautz on the way to San Sebastián.

Tourist Information

Zumaya: Pza Zuloaga, t 94 314 33 96. *Open summer only*.

Getaria: Parque Aldamar 2, t 94 314 09 57. *Open summer only*.

Zarautz: Nafarroa Kalea, t 94 383 09 90, f 94 383 56 28.

Where to Stay and Eat

Zumaya ✉ 20808

Some of the bars in the main square have inexpensive rooms, and cheaper food can be found on C/ Erribera.

***Zelai, Itzurun s/n, t 94 386 51 00, f 94 386 51 78 (*expensive–moderate*). Has comfortable rooms in a brand-new building high up on the cliffs. There's a good restaurant, and a thalassotherapy pool for natural healing.

Agroturismo Iesuskoa, in Zumaya's Barrio de Oikia, t 94 386 17 39 (*inexpensive*). Has horses to rent and six rooms in a restored farmhouse just outside town; at weekends most of Zumaya comes out to sit under the trees and eat good grilled fish meals.

Asador Bedua, Barrio Bedina, t 94 386 05 51. Although a bit pricey, serves excellent grilled surf and turf in a friendly atmosphere.

Getaria ✉ 20808

Pensión Guetariano, C/ Herrerieta 3, t 94 314 05 67 (*inexpensive*). In the cheerful green and yellow house at Getaria's main crossroads; a friendly place with magazines in the lounge and comfortable rooms with bath.

Pensión Iribar, C/ Nagusia 34, t 94 314 04 06 (*inexpensive*). May lack a bit of character, but is well located on the quiet street leading down to the port, and has a good restaurant.

**Hs San Prudencio, t 94 314 04 11 (*cheap*). Bargain lodgings (for the area) by the beach; rooms without bath.

Kaia Kaipe, Gral. Arnao 10 (upstairs), t 94 314 05 00. With good Basque seafood and views, this is one of many restaurants crowding the harbour where you can drink txakoli wine grown in the nearby hills (*expensive*).

Elkano, Herrerieta 2, t 94 314 06 14. Boasts the best grilled fish on the harbour (*expensive*).

Iribar Jatexea, Kale Nagusia 38, t 94 314 04 06. Another excellent *asador* (grillhouse) with good-value fresh local meat and fish.

Talaipe, Puerto Viejo s/n, t 94 314 06 13. Right on the tip of the old port, this place has wonderful views and marine-themed décor to go with the delicious fresh fish dishes.

Zarautz ✉ 20800

Zarautz can be as pricey as San Sebastián.

****Karlos Arguiñano, Mendilauta 13, t 94 313 00 00, f 94 313 34 50 (*luxury*). A formidably expensive modern hotel, but its restaurant is one of the best dining places along this stretch of coast, with sophisticated seafood dishes and a warm, welcoming atmosphere (*closed Sun eve and Mon*).

Pensión Txiki-Polit, Musika Plaza s/n, t 94 383 53 57, f 94 383 37 31 (*inexpensive*). The most interesting budget option, an unusual circular 1950s building with decent rooms and a very popular restaurant; the *menú del día* is a great deal for 1,100 pts/€6.5.

Camping Talai-Mendi, Monte Talai-Mendi, t 94 383 00 42 (*inexpensive*). A quiet camp site near the beach.

Otzarreta, Santa Klara 5, t 94 313 40 95. One of the finest restaurants in town, an elegant and traditional establishment with cuisine to match. The seafood is especially good.

Aiten-Etxe, Elkano 3, t 94 383 25 02. Fine, uncomplicated seafood dishes (*expensive*) accompanied by magnificent views along Zarautz's main beach. *Closed Sun eve and Tues*.

Orio ✉ 20810

Orio is known for its bream, safely nabbed far from its dirty river.

Itsas Ondo, C/ Kaia 7, t 94 313 11 79. Has good, up-to-date cuisine (*moderate*).

Katxiña, Barrio San Martín s/n, t 94 383 14 07. A very pretty place tucked into the side of the hill, this *asador* (grillhouse) offers particularly good local fish and meat.

he collected over the years: several El Grecos, Goyas, Moraleses, two saints by Zurbarán and an excellent collection of medieval statues and *retablos*. Adjacent, the little 12th-century **church and cloister of Santiago Etxea** was a stop for pilgrims taking the coastal route to Compostela. Below stretches the pine-rimmed beach named after the painter, **Playa Zuloaga**.

There's more art in the centre of Zumaya, in the 15th-century **church of San Pedro**: two triptychs on either side of the altar, the one on the right Flemish, and a dark, Gothic *St Christopher* on the back wall. There's another beach to the west at **San Telmo**, a dramatic swathe of sand under sheer red cliffs, known for its pounding surf.

Getaria

East of Zumaya, the N634 ascends dramatically over the sea before reaching **Getaria**. The shipbuilders of Zarautz (*see* below), the next fishing town to the east, built the *Vitoria*, the first ship to circumnavigate the globe; Getaria, now a petite and utterly charming resort, produced the man who captained it, Juan Sebastián Elcano.

From the coastal road, you wouldn't think there was much to Getaria at all, but once you're there you will find one of the loveliest villages of Euskadi, hugging the steep slope down to the harbour, sheltered by a narrow peninsula and an islet known for its shape as El Ratón, 'the mouse'. Whenever the Getarianos go to Mass in the **church of San Salvador**, in the centre of the old town, they step on Elcano's grave, located just inside the door, though Elcano died of scurvy in the Pacific in 1526, so there probably isn't much of him in there anyway. Once you're beyond Elcano's tomb, this church has other surprises up its sleeve. Founded in the 13th century, it was rebuilt in 1429 in a curious off-kilter fashion: the wooden floor lilts as if on rough seas and the choir vaulting is just as tilted. No one knows why. Along the right wall, near the suspended *ex voto* of a ship, is something you rarely see in a church: a menorah. A double flight of stairs rises in the back, and the crypt and another chapel lie along the alley descending to the port. The crypt contains the remains of the ancestors of the same Queen Fabiola who made nearby Zarautz a resort. Getaria doesn't mind; although it has two small beaches of its own, it picked up all of Zarautz's fishing business. From the port, with its brightly painted boats and seafood restaurants, a path leads up to the top of Mouse Island, a nice natural area with flitting birds and fine views.

Besides hauling in the fishy ingredients for a *ttoro*, Getaria is also the epicentre of *txakoli* production in Euskadi (*see* pp.69–70). Demand for the tangy wine, which is closely identified with the Basques, has soared since autonomy; whereas in 1981, Getaria had a mere 16 hectares of vines, there are now a hundred, especially since *Txakoli de Getaria* was given its Denominación de Origen credentials in 1989.

Zarautz and Orio

Big waves and a mile-and-a-half of sand draw surfers to nearby **Zarautz**. Whaling and shipbuilding in the Middle Ages put Zarautz on the map, while more summering royalty – this time Belgium's King Baudouin and Queen Fabiola – inaugurated its international reputation as a resort in the 20th century. Now the second biggest resort in Euskadi after San Sebastián, Zarautz is especially popular among well-to-do

The First Man to Sail Around the World

In the Age of Discovery, no Spanish or Portuguese captain worth his salt would set out without a Basque pilot, the heirs of centuries of experience in whaling boats off Europe's westernmost shores, and who may actually have found the American coast in the Middle Ages, but kept the knowledge a closely guarded secret. Basques were deeply involved in all four of Columbus' voyages, from building the ships to outfitting them and providing the crews. One Basque who accompanied Columbus, Juan de la Cosa (or Juan Vizcaino) later explored the Caribbean on his own and in 1500 drew the first world map showing America.

Elcano, like many sea men in Getaria, started off as a deep-sea fisherman and smuggler to French ports, but he sought even greater adventures, and went on to fight with the Grand Capitán of Córdoba against Naples and explore some of the coast of Africa. He was in Seville in 1519, and got a job on an expedition backed by Charles V to send Portuguese navigator Ferdinand Magellan on what they hoped would be a quick western shortcut to the Indies by sailing southwest around America to the spice laden Molucca Islands. Charles supplied five ships and 239 men, and in August they set out. As they wintered on the coast of Brazil there was a mutiny against continuing any further. By then Magellan and Elcano avidly hated one another, and most of the blame fell on Elcano, who was chained up and forced to do hard labour. One ship turned back before attempting the turbulent straits that took Magellan's name (October 1520).

If already dismayed by the distances involved just crossing the Atlantic, the expedition must have been appalled at the extent of the Pacific. Even worse, by the time Magellan's little fleet made it to the Philippines in 1521, a civil war had just broken out, which soon numbered Magellan among its dead. After several other Portuguese leaders fell victim to the intrigues of the war, Elcano took over the helm of the expedition and sailed halfway around the world from the Moluccas to Seville in the only surviving ship, the *Vitoria*, with the 17 surviving members of the crew. He arrived in October 1522, some 1,124 days after setting out (Elcano was surprised to realize he had lost a day somewhere according to the ship's log, the first inkling of an international date line). Charles V later received Elcano, granting him a pension of 500 *ducados* and a coat of arms with the legend *primus circumdedisti me*. It was a feat that no one would try to equal for a long time; the one lesson of the expedition was that the eastern route around the Horn was in fact much quicker.

In spite of his singular feat, Elcano was destined to remain forever in Magellan's shadow – except of course in the eyes of his fellow Basques. The Getarianos erected a statue of Elcano just outside the gate of the old town, and stage a historical re-enactment of his landing every four years on 7 August.

Basque nationalists – hence summer courses in Basque language and folklore events, to go with the golf course, riding stables and good food (with some harder-to-swallow prices). In the historic centre of Zarautz, look for its trio of tower houses, especially the Torre Luzea in Calle Mayor and the one incorporated into the 16th-century Palacio de Narros. The most important church, Santa María la Real, has a half-Plateresque, half-Renaissance *retablo*; the campanile was added atop yet another medieval tower house in the 18th century.

The last stop on the coast before the cliffs take all roads inland is **Orio**, a venerable fishing village that looks like an industrial town at the mouth of the Río Orio, one of the most polluted rivers in Spain. Although the beach by Orio's very popular camp site is clean enough, rough seas can bring out the no-swimming flags. If you're planning a picnic, drive up to the lush hilltop **Parque de Pagoeta**, signposted along the N634.

San Sebastián (Donostia)

Sebastian bat ba da zeruan
Donosti bat bakarra munduan

(There's only one St Sebastián up in heaven/And there's only one Donostia here on earth)

from the *March of St Sebastian*, 1861

At the beginning of the 21st century, it is difficult to imagine that a place like San Sebastián (Donostia in Basque) could ever exist. The Belle Epoque may be a hundred years away, but in San Sebastián the buildings still seem to be made of ice cream, with trim in Impressionist colours and florid brass streetlights; people still dress up instinctively for the evening *paseo*. This confection embraces one of the peninsula's most enchanting bays, the oyster-shaped **Bahía de La Concha**, protected from the bad moods of the Atlantic by a wooded islet, the **Isla de Santa Clara**, and by **Monte Urgull**, the hump-backed sentinel on the easternmost tip of the bay. It looks a bit like Rio de Janiero, and it's a movie set when the sun's shining, which is most of the time.

San Sebastián has probably been around as long as the Basques, but the earliest mention of it is as a Roman port called *Easo*. The town resurfaced in the Middle Ages; in the 12th century, when the Navarrese controlled this part of the coast, they built the first fortress on Monte Urgull, one that has been rebuilt and reinforced many times since. The first recorded tourist came against his will – François I, king of France, was locked up in the fortress for a time by Charles V after being captured at the Battle of Pavia in 1527. In the 19th century, the city found a new role as the cynosure of fashion; a century before there were any such thing as '*costas*', wealthy Spaniards were coming here to spend their summers bathing. In the 1850s it was blessed by the presence of Queen Isabel II, who brought the government and the court with her in summer. It was during her reign that San Sebastián was made capital of the province and the Paris–Madrid railroad was completed, making the city convenient to holiday-makers from both capitals.

Queen Regent María Cristina again made San Sebastián the rage in 1886 – following the example of Empress Eugénie of France, who had popularized nearby Biarritz (*see* pp.246–50) The sister city of Reno, Nevada, it's still a classy place to go, a lovely, relaxed, seaside resort in a spectacular setting. And the Donostiarrak, as the inhabitants are known, know how to throw a party. The wild 24-hour non-stop *Tamborrada*,

Getting There and Around

By Air

San Sebastián's airport to the east, near Fuenterrabía (t 94 365 88 00), has connections to Madrid and Barcelona. The bus to the airport, Fuenterrabía and Irún (t 94 364 13 02) departs from Pza Guipuzkoa every 12 minutes – note that this is really the bus for Fuenterrabía, and lets you off across the road from the airport.

By Train

RENFE trains depart from the Estación del Norte (t 94 328 30 89) on Paseo de Francia. There are frequent connections with Irún and Hendaye, Paris, Burgos and Madrid; and less frequent trains to Barcelona, Pamplona, Salamanca, Vitoria, Zaragoza and León. *Talgos* whizz all the way to Madrid, Málaga, Córdoba, Algeciras, Valencia, Alicante, Oviedo and Gijón.

Topo trains (t 94 347 08 15), and Eusko Trenbideak-Ferrocariles Vascos (Feve-Eusko Tren, t 94 345 01 31) depart from the Estación de Amara. Topo run to Hendaye, going by way of Oyarzun, whilst EuskoTrens leave for Bilbao, stopping everywhere on the way.

By Bus

A bewildering number of small bus companies leave from the station on Pza de Pio XII. at the southern end of town, a block from the river. The ticket office for **Pesa**, which runs the services to Bilbao, Biarritz and Bayonne, is nearby at C/ Sancho el Sabio 33, though some lines (including La Roncelesa, t 94 346 10 64, for buses to Pamplona and Vitoria) have their offices on Paseo de Vizcaya. There are five buses daily to Oviedo, seven to Burgos and five to Galicia. Within Euskadi, buses depart every half-hour to Bilbao and Vitoria, and up to 10 times a day to Pamplona.

There are 19 bus lines in San Sebastián itself (t 94 328 71 00); no.16 goes to Igueldo and the funicular (*daily in summer 10–10, every 15 minutes*).

By Bike

Cycling is a great way to explore San Sebastián, especially along the 12km seafront promenade; it's possible to get from one end of the city to the other without having to cross a road. Bikes can be hired from Paseo de la Zurrida 22, t 94 327 92 60.

Motor Boats

Boats make excursions out to the Isla de Santa Clara every half-hour from the pier (*muelle*), where you can also rent a rowing boat to do the same yourself.

Tours

Walking tours: Every Thurs, Fri and Sat in July and August with Guitour, t 94 343 09 09 (2,000 pts/€12, not including admission fees).

Bus tour: A guided tour bus, t 69 642 98 47, departs from in front of the municipal tourist office every hour, picking up and dropping off at all the major sights (1,500 pts/€9).

Hot air balloons: There are balloon tours over San Sebastián and surroundings from nearby Pasajes, t 94 352 71 42.

Tourist Information

Tourist offices: The municipal office is on the river, C/ Reina Regente, t 94 348 11 66. The Basque government office as at Paseo de los Fueros 1, t 94 342 62 82.

Post office: C/ Urdaneta, behind the cathedral.

Internet access: Two good places are **Easonet Comunicaciones**, C/ Usandizaga 2, and **Net Line**, C/ Urdaneta 8.

Shopping

Along with the tourist shops in the Parte Vieja, there are a number of more original places that sell a range of items from surf-punk paraphernalia to exquisite home-made chocolates. The Centro Romántico has a wide range of fashionable boutiques, from chains like Zara and Mango to individual establishments selling Spanish designers.

Bilintx, C/ Fermín Calbetón 21. Another shop with books in English; they also stock a good range of maps and guides. There is a vast selection of books about the Basque lands in the basement, although mainly in Spanish or French.

Casa Angelita, C/ Claudio Delgado (near Plaza del Txofre). The place to hire a Carnival costume.

Casa Erviti, C/ Loiola, near the cathedral. Manufacturers of traditional Basque instruments, including the drums of the Tamborrada.

Casa Ponsol, C/ Narrica 4. An institution in the world of Basque berets, in business since 1838.

Chocolates Saint Gerons, C/ Etxaide 6, t 94 342 48 04. Try the oranges coated with chocolate.

Hontza, C/ Okendo 5. If you're inspired by all the sumptuous seafood you've been eating, this place sells books on Basque cooking in English.

Oddyti, C/ San Martín 24, t 94 342 29 21. Come here to wrap yourself up in the latest of clubland street styles.

Pasteleria Otaegui, C/ Narrica 18. Probably the most popular pastry shop in San Seb, makers of an excellent *pantxineta* (flaky pastry filled with frangipane)

Saski-naski, C/ Fermín Calbetón 45, t 94 342 28 91. A delightful boutique run by kindly staff specialising in handmade Basque gifts, including ceramics, sculpture, linens and jewellery.

Markets

The central **Mercado de la Brecha** has been given a glass roof and a string of fast-food outlets, but underneath you'll find immaculate stalls selling all kinds of fresh produce. The **Mercado de San Martín** in the Centro Romanticó is more traditional and devoted entirely to local produce.

Where to Stay

San Sebastián ✉ 20000

San Sebastián is not the place to look for bargains, and many of the cheaper *hostales* and *fondas* are packed full of university students most of the year. In general, the further back you are from the sea, the less expensive the accommodation will be.

Luxury–Expensive

★★★★★**María Cristina**, C/ Okendo 1, t 94 342 49 00, f 94 342 39 14, *hmc@sheraton.com* (*luxury*). For a touch of Belle Epoque elegance, this old grande dame is one of Spain's best hotels; it looks onto the Río Urumea's promenade, a short walk from La Concha.

★★★★**Hotel Londres y Inglaterra**, C/ Zubieta 2 (on La Concha beach), t 94 344 07 70, f 94 344 04 91, *h.londres@paisvasco.com* (*luxury*). The city's other most luxurious address, with splendid views, first-class service, and plenty of charm, as well as one of the city's best restaurants (*meals around 3,500 pts/€21*).

★★★★**Mercure Monte Igueldo**, on the top of the mountain, t 94 321 02 11, f 94 321 50 28 (*expensive*). Peace and quiet and absolutely stunning views over the bay.

★★★**Gudamendi**, Pza de Gudamendi, Barrio de Igueldo, t 94 321 40 00, f 94 321 51 08, *gudamendi@interplanet.es* (*expensive*). Quiet, comfortable and attractive, located halfway up Monte Igueldo.

★★★**La Galeria**, C/ Infanta Cristina 1–3, t 94 321 60 77, f 94 321 12 98, *hotel@hotellagaleria. com, www.hotellagaleria.com* (*expensive*). A couple of minutes from Playa Ondarreta on a lovely quiet street, this French-inspired turn-of-the-last-century *palacete* has rooms full of antiques and individuality.

★★★**Niza**, C/ Zubieta 56, t 94 342 66 63, f 94 344 12 51, *niza@adegi.es, www.adegi.es/hotel-niza* (*expensive*). Another classic hotel from the Belle Epoque, this doesn't have quite the range of services of its more upmarket sisters, but makes up for it with a fantastic, beach-front location and charming staff.

Moderate

San Sebastián being the posh resort it is, most *hostales* here fall into the moderate price category, and there are plenty of chances for a simple double room between 6,000/€36 and 10,000 pts/€60.

★★**Pensión Bikain**, C/ Triunfo 8, t 94 345 43 33, f 94 346 80 74. Has four-star facilities at a very good price, close to the beach and the Parte Vieja, as well as spotless rooms, parking facilities and a very helpful owner.

★★**Pensión Donostiarra**, C/ San Martin 6, t 94 342 61 67, f 94 343 00 71. Light, airy rooms with either a little balcony of flowers or a glassed-in *solana* full of pot plants.

★★**La Estrella**, Plaza de Sarriegi 1, t 94 342 09 97. On the edge of the Parte Vieja, a short walk from the bay.

★★Pensión Kaia, C/ Puerto 12, **t** 94 343 13 42. Situated in the old town, this has little going for it but the price; rooms with bath or without.

Inexpensive

The best you'll find will be at the higher end of the inexpensive range, and there are a fair number of them both in the Parte Vieja and in the centre.

★★Hs Eder II, Alameda del Boulevard, **t** 94 342 64 49. A well-run place at the edge of the Parte Vieja, right in the centre.

★★Ozcariz, Fuenterrabía 8, **t** 94 342 53 06. In a noisy location, but very welcoming.

★★Pensión La Perla, C/ Loiola 10, **t** 94 342 81 23. An old-fashioned budget choice, handily located between the cathedral and market.

★Pensión Urgull, C/ Esterlines 10, **t** 94 343 00 47. This is a delightful, inexpensive choice; there are only four immaculate rooms with two shared bathrooms. The charming owners are kind, friendly and more than happy to help out with local information.

★Pensión Easo, C/ San Bartolomé 24, **t** 94 345 39 12. A good bargain choice.

Pensión Añorga, C/ Easo 12, **t** 94 346 79 45. Well worn but friendly; all rooms with shower.

★Hotel Record, Calzada Vieja de Ategorrieta, **t** 94 327 12 55, **f** 94 327 85 21. A little family-run hotel in a villa by the beach at Gros.

Camping de Igueldo, Paseo Orkelaga, **t** 94 321 45 02. The best camping option, up on Monte Igueldo, though it's quite expensive.

La Sirena, **t** 94 331 02 68, *udala-youthhostel@ donostia.org*. A youth hostel situated at the end of Ondarreta beach, at the foot of the road up Monte Igueldo; it's the cheapest place in town.

Eating Out

As eating is the local obsession, it's not surprising that the city can claim several of Spain's most renowned, award-winning restaurants – cathedrals of Basque cuisine. For something cheaper, follow the crowds through the *tapas* bars of the Parte Vieja (*see* below).

Expensive

Arzak, Alto de Miracruz 21, **t** 94 327 84 65. This is often described as the finest restaurant in Spain and offers a constantly changing menu of delights (its *11,000 pts/ €66 menú de degustación* may be the best choice in this book for a big splurge). Chef Juan Mari Arzak is often at hand to make suggestions, as dishes change with the seasons and market availability. Among the specialities that you might see is *cola de rape enveulta de hierbes* (monkfish encrusted with herbs). Book weeks in advance. *Closed Sun eve and Mon, most of June, and the first fortnight in Nov.*

Akelarre, in the Barrio de Igueldo, **t** 94 321 20 52. This restaurant is celebrated for its mixture of some of the most remarkably innovative New Basque cuisine with a delicious array of traditional local dishes – look out for the wonderfully prepared langoustines. This is the place to see and be seen during the city's film festival – and there's a beautiful mountain-side setting with views over the sea to boot. *Closed Sun eve and Mon.*

Casa Nicolasa, Aldamar 4, **t** 94 342 17 62. Another culinary shrine, founded in 1912, it specializes in classic Basque cookery and offers a large choice of dishes, among them *almejas gratinadas* (gratinéed clams) and a fabulous range of desserts. Eat for around 7,500 pts/€45. *Closed Sun eve and Mon.*

Panier Fleuri, Paseo de Salamanca 1, **t** 94 342 42 05. A throwback to the Belle Epoque, this classic restaurant near the Basilica de Santa María offers superb New Basque cuisine and a fabulous wine list. Delicate dishes like *filetes de salmonete en emulsión* (salmon in a feather-light sauce) characterize the cooking here, as does the exquisite attention to detail. *Closed Sun night and Wed.*

Urepel, Paseo de Salamanca 3, **t** 94 342 40 40. Just up from the Panier Fleuri, this is another of San Sebastián's most eminent restaurants, serving classic Basque cuisine with original touches. The house speciality is the *sopa de pescados* (fish soup), a rich, flavoursome dish that won't leave much room for the dessert list. *Closed Sun, Tues, Christmas, Easter and three weeks in July.*

Rekondo, Paseo de Igueldo 57, t 94 321 29 07.
A superb choice, specializing in grilled fish
and meat and with a huge wine cellar; come
here for elegant dining at around 6,000 pts/
€36.

Moderate

Beti Jai, C/ Fermín Calbetón 22, t 94 342 77 37.
Bang in the middle of 'Restaurant Walk',
this is one of the city's finest and liveliest
seafood restaurants, although there are
plenty of other things on the menu and a
hectic bar if you don't want to sit down
(see below). The salpicón de mariscos (a
refreshing seafood salad) is excellent.
Closed Mon, Tues, Christmas and end
June–early July.

Salduba, Arrandegui 6, t 94 342 56 27.
At this wooden-beamed retreat from the
crowds in the heart of the Parte Vieja,
you'll find traditional dishes and attentive
service.

Casa Urola, C/ Fermín Calbetón 22, t 94 342
11 75. This is a wonderful old favourite, a
good, refined restaurant with a decently
priced menú del día, and a less expensive bar
area packed with locals. The wine list is
particularly good.

Bodegón Alejandro, C/ Fermin Calbetón 4,
t 94 347 77 37. This delightful establishment
offers popular, traditional cooking based on
the freshest produce and accompanied by
an excellent selection of wines.

Cheap and Vegetarian

Casa Tiburcío, C/ Fermin Calbeton, t 94 342
31 30. A popular choice in the Parte Vieja for
an unusually varied menú and an excellent
choice of pintxos.

Makrobiotika, Intxaurrondo Kalea 52. San
Sebastián's best vegetarian restaurant,
serving a variety of cereal-based dishes. Take
bus nos.13 or 24 from the centre, as it's a bit
of a trek.

Ttun Ttun Taberna, C/ San Jeronimo 25,
t 94 342 68 82. This unassuming tavern
is an enclave of Basquedom, serving a
wonderful soul-satisfying menú for
900 pts/€5.5.

Sagardotegiak Plaza Berri, C/ Nueva 18,
t 94 329 30 00. A rare sidreria (see pp.71–2)
in the city limits.

Tapas/Pinchos/Pintxos

Parte Vieja

The Parte Vieja is proud of its reputation for
having more bars per square metre than
anywhere else in the world. Every street is
lined with dozens of bars, each with a
groaning counter.

Perhaps the gastronomic heart of the Parte
Vieja are Calle Mayor and C/ 31 de Agosta, the
only streets to withstand the destruction of
the city in 1813, and filled with the most traditional bars, restaurants and the famous
gastronomic societies which feast in secret
(see p.66).

The Plaza de la Constitución, with its freshly
painted balconies and cool arcades, is a lovely
place to while away an hour or two, and the
Fermín Calbetón is sometimes known as
'Restaurant Walk', thanks to the virtually
unbroken string of busy establishments.

Clery, Plaza de la Trinidad 1, t 94 342 34 01.
Tucked away near the Santa María Basilica,
this is one of San Sebastián's most well-
loved restaurants, with an attractive bar
and terrace where you can sample tasty
pintxos like little fried balls of cod with a
green pepper sauce. It's a great place to
eat during the spring jazz festival, when
concerts take place in the Plaza de la
Trinidad.

La Cepa, C/ 31 de Agosto 9, t 94 342 63 94. With
a ceiling dripping with cured hams and a
liberal splashing of taurine memorabilia,
this is one of the most down-to-earth of the
local bars. Among its classic pintxos are the
gildas, anchovies with tuna and mild green
chillies, a perennial favourite.

Martinéz, C/ 31 de Agosto 13, t 94 342 49 65.
A classic old town bar with a broad counter
piled staggeringly high with delicious
pintxos. Try the champis, wild mushrooms
which are sometimes stuffed with a
pungent slice of cured sausage, or the delicious fresh prawns tossed in breadcrumbs
and fried.

Ormazabel, C/ 31 de Agosto 22, t 94 342 99 07.
A little, family-run bodega with an excellent
selection of local wines to accompany the
unusual spinach croquetas, or the
chiperones, baby squid, which have been
everyone's favourite for more than 40 years.

Gaztelu, C/ 31 de Agosto 22, **t** 94 342 14 11. Next to the Ormazabel, this friendly, neighbourhood bar where everyone seems to know everyone else has got a big reputation for its classic *pintxos*; even a simple dish like *tortilla de patatas* is mouth-wateringly rich and buttery.

Gambara, C/ San Jeronimo 21. A tiny bar with a big reputation for its wide array of *pintxos*: excellent prawns, fresh asparagus in season, a good selection of cured meats, all washed down with some of the best *txakoli* (the sharp, local wine; *see* pp.69–70) in town.

Aselena, C/ Iñigo 1 (just off the Plaza de la Constitucíon), **t** 94 342 62 75. This is the city's hot spot on the feast of St Tomás in December, when the Plaza fills up with revellers. The *pastela de merluza* (hake 'cake') here is said to have inspired Juan Mari Arzak to create one of the signature dishes of Nouveau Basque cuisine – *krabbaroka*.

Txepetxa, C/ Pescadería 5, **t** 94 342 22 27. This bar has become a 'temple of anchovies', and you can get them prepared in every imaginable way, from classic anchovies with black olives to an exotic dish prepared with coconut and Polynesian spices.

Tamboril, C/ Pescadería 2, **t** 94 342 35 07. All kinds of *banderillas* (mini *tapas* skewered on toothpicks) are on offer here, but the house speciality is the stuffed mushrooms (*champis*), which are served up on a slice of crusty bread.

Borda Berri, C/ Fermin Calbetón 12, **t** 94 342 56 38. An elegant, historic bar with a range of innovative *raciones* – stuffed peppers with tuna and a light red capsicum mousse among them – and, unusually for this part of town, a refined cocktail list.

Bar Beti Jai, C/ Fermin Calbetón 12, **t** 94 342 77 37. If you can't manage a big splurge in the restaurant (*see* above), try some of the exquisite seafood specialities as *raciones* in the bar. The food is all so fresh that it doesn't require any fancy sauces; try the sublimely simple marinated anchovies or the baby squid (*chiperones*).

Casa Alcade, Calle Mayor 19, **t** 94 342 62 16. Walls lined with bullfighting memorabilia and hanging hams are the backdrop for the food at this bar which has remained virtu-

ally unchanged for 80 years. The wafer-thin slices of cured Spanish ham make a fine accompaniment to many of the excellent Riojas on offer.

Gros

Surprisingly few tourists make it across the river to this pleasing neighbourhood which has its own lively bars and nightlife.

Aloña Berri, C/ Berminghan 24, **t** 94 329 08 18. Some of the best and most imaginative *banderillas* in the city are to be had here, all beautifully arranged; the cod, this time served as a *brandada de bacalao*, is exceptionally good.

Bar Bergara, C/ General Arteche 8, **t** 94 327 50 26. A spacious, attractive bar with all manner of lightly fried titbits skewered on cocktail sticks and an excellent selection of wines and spirits. Try the delicious *txalupa*, langoustine gratinéed with wild mushrooms, or the delicious cod baked with garlic and herbs (*bacalao ajoarriero*).

Joxean, C/ Secundino Esnaola 39–41, **t** 94 327 85 15. A lively bar with a young crowd and a small restaurant. The *pintxos* are imaginative twists on old favourites, like *mollejas encebolladas*, a rich sweetbread dish, or *hojaldre de pimientos rellenos*, flaky pastry with stuffed peppers.

Entertainment and Nightlife

The centre of the serious party action is the streets of the Parte Vieja. Late-night bars and clubs are also found around the end of Ondarreta beach. For listings, check out the back pages of *El Diario Vasco*, the local newspaper.

Akerbeltz, C/ Mari. A tiny bar with a popularity that far exceeds its size, so everyone just congregates outside to enjoy the view of the bay with their beer.

Be Bop, Paseo de Salamanca. One of several bars in the area with live music. This one's a jazz venue.

Café Remember Rock, C/ Republica Argentina s/n. Live rock shows.

Etxekalte, C/ Mari 1. Has two floors of dance music and is almost always chock-full.

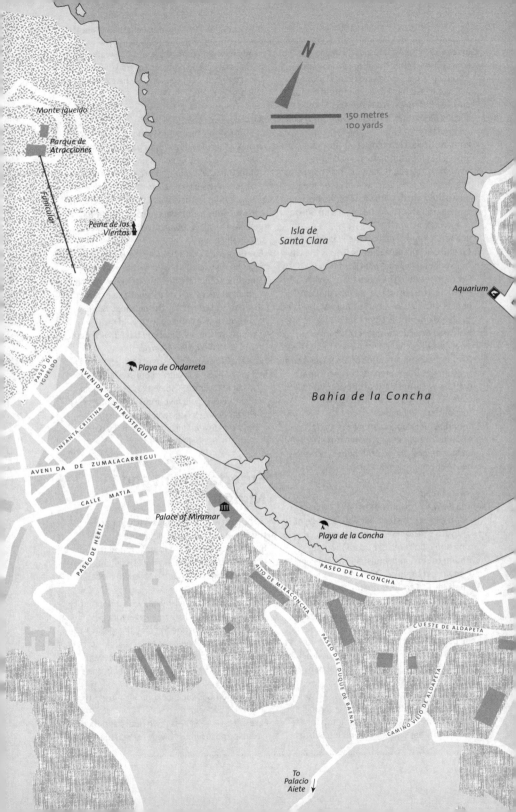

N

150 metres
100 yards

Monte Igueldo

Parque de
Atracciones

Funicular

Peine de los
Vientos

Isla de
Santa Clara

Aquarium

Paseo de Igueldo

Avenida de Satrústegui

Infanta Cristina

Playa de Ondarreta

Bahía de la Concha

Aveni da de Zumalacarregui

Calle Matía

Paseo de Heriz

Palace of Miramar

Playa de la Concha

Alto de Miraconcha

Paseo de la Concha

Cueste de Aldapeta

Paseo del Duque de Baena

Camino Viejo de Aldapeta

To
Palacio
Aiete

San Sebastián (Donostia)

Mar Cantábrico

British Cemetery

Monte Urgull

PASEO NUEVO

Castillo de la Mota

Museo Naval

Santa María del Coro

Museum of San Telmo

PLAZA DE LA TRINIDAD

CALLE 31 DE AGOSTO

San Vicente

PASEO DE SALAMANCA

LA PARTE VIEJA

PASEO DE SALAMANCA

MARI

CALLE MAYOR

PUERTO

CALLE SAN JERÓNIMO

PLAZA DE LA CONSTITUCIÓN

IÑIGO

PESCADERÍA

ALDAMAR

FERMÍN CALBETÓN

El Muelle

PUENTE DE ZURRIOLA

Playa de Gros

Playa de Zurriola

Palacio de Congresos Kursaal y Auditorio

AVENIDA DE LA ZURRIOLA

ALAMEDA DEL BOULEVARD

Ayuntamiento

PASEO REPÚBLICA ARGENTINA

Parque de Alderdi Eder

PEÑA FLORIDA

PLAZA DE GIPUZKOA

CALLE OKENDO

CALLE ANDÍA

PASEO DE COLÓN

CALLE DE ZABALETA

BERMINGHAM

CALLE DE SAN FRANCISCO

GEN ARTECHE

CALLE MIRAMAR

CENTRO ROMÁNTICO

C NUEVA

GROS

SECUNDINO ESNAOLA

CALLE MIRACRUZ

PUENTE DE SANTA CATALINA

PLAZA DE EUSKADI

PLAZA DE CERVANTES

AVENIDA DE LA LIBERTAD

CALLE LOIOLA

CALLE DE SAN MARCIAL

ETXAIDE

PASEO DE LA CONCHA

FUENTERRABÍA

PLAZA DE ZUBIETA ZARAGOZA

CALLE DE SAN MARTÍN

Mercado de la Brecha

PASEO DEL DUQUE DE MANDAS

CALLE DE EASO

CALLE DE SAN BARTOLOMÉ

Catedral de Buen Pastor

CALLE DE URBANETA

CALLE REYES CATÓLICOS

CALLE DE PRIM

PASEO DEL ÁRBOL DE GUERNICA

PASEO DE LOS FUEROS

PASEO DE FRANCIA

PUENTE DE MARÍA CRISTINA

Estación del Norte

PLAZA EASO

CALLE MORAZA

Estación de Amara

Río Urumea

Parque de Cristina Enea

To Bus Station

Río Urumea

beginning at midnight on 19 January, honours the town's patron saint with a mad tattooing of drums and barrels, recalling how the town's laundresses mocked the occupying Napoleonic troops by following their drummers about, banging away on their washtubs; now the roles are played by the *txokos*, or gastronomic societies, who dress up as soldiers and chefs. Carnival here is Rio style, with plenty of Basque transvestites to liven things up. A major jazz festival takes place in July, followed by a week of city-wide partying for the *Semana Grande* (8–15 August), coinciding with an International Fireworks Festival. The International Film Festival takes place in September, along with ocean-going fishing boat races, the Regatas de Traineras de La Concha (on the two first Sundays), one of the most closely followed events on the Basque sports calendar.

Playa de la Concha and the Comb of the Winds

Sheltered within the bay is the magnificent golden crescent of the **Playa de la Concha**, San Sebastián's centrepiece and its largest beach, beautifully hemmed by the Paseo de la Concha, an elegant promenade with flouncy balustrades, dotted with creamy Belle Epoque cafés and the matronly bathhouse. On its western end stands a promontory topped by the mock-Tudor **Palace of Miramar of María Cristina**, built as a summerhouse for the royal family and the scene of a raging battle on the day that the Spanish Republic was declared in 1931. It is now owned by the city and used for receptions and special exhibitions, but you can sit in the gardens. A tunnel under the Miramar leads to the **Playa de Ondarreta**, a traditional society retreat, with a smart tennis club and graceful old houses. Ondarreta beach itself comes to a dead end at seaside Monte Igueldo, crowned by a **Parque de Atracciones**. You can get to the top by road or by the delightful, rickety old funicular from the end of the beach, and the reward is a spectacular view over San Sebastián, the **Bay of Biscay** (Bizkaiko Golkoa) and the Cantabrian mountains. Back on the shore, beyond the beach and the funicular stands one of the most talked-about monuments of modern Spanish sculpture, Eduardo Chillida's **Peine de los Vientos**, the *Comb of the Winds*. The work is a series of terraces, built into the rocks that guard the entrance to the bay, decorated with cast-iron constructions, the 'teeth' of the comb that smooths the winds coming from the sea towards the city. Chillida is a native of San Sebastián (he was once goalie for the local football side), and his house is on the cliffs above the monument.

The Centro Romanticó

Nearly all the city behind the beaches of La Concha and Ondarreta dates from the 19th century; San Sebastián is an ancient place, but it has been burned to the ground 12 times in its history, lastly by Wellington's drunken soldiers, who celebrated the conquest of the town with their accustomed murder and mayhem. The city was rebuilt and even expanded soon after, in a neat neoclassical grid now called the Centro Romanticó, with the **Catedral del Buen Pastor**, completed in the 1880s, at its centre. The Mercado de San Martín squats nearby, with stalls packed with fresh produce from the sea and the surrounding mountains. At the heart of this district is the arcaded Plaza de Gipuzkoa, sternly overlooked by the neoclassical **Palacio Foral**.

Heading towards the river, the Plaza de Okeando is flanked by the grand María Cristina hotel, with its pretty swathes of colourful tiles, and the prim Victoria Eugenia Theatre, inaugurated in 1912, and host to the Quincena Musical, a fortnight-long programme of classical music. This trim neighbourhood is the main shopping district of the city, with several swanky designer shops and a swathe of classy teashops.

A promenade-lined river, the Urumea, divides 19th-century Sanse (as the city is affectionately known) from the newer quarter of Gros, once the workingmen-student-bohemian enclave, a lively place full of bars and restaurants and endowed with its own beach, the Playa de Gros, which is always less crowded but lies outside the sheltered bay, subject to the wind, waves and filthy debris. Still, it's great for surfers, who come in droves. The beachfront landscape here has just received a new adornment: a rather fearsome, angular convention centre called the Kursaal, of which guided tours are inexplicably offered. Of the three charming bridges that span the Urumea, the María Cristina (near the station) most resembles a cream pastry.

The Parte Vieja and Monte Urgull

Most of the action in town takes place under Monte Urgull in the narrow streets of The Parte Vieja, or old town. From La Concha beach, its entrance is guarded by a beautiful, well-manicured square, the **Parque de Alderdi Eder**, and the enormous 19th-century **Ayuntamiento**, or town hall, formerly the casino that María Cristina built (the new one is in the Hotel de Londres). Behind it, the swanky yacht club, set in a beautiful white rationalist building from the 1930s, looks like something from an Agatha Christie novel. What remains of the city's fishing fleet may be seen in the harbour behind the Ayuntamiento, a picturesque tumble of whitewashed cottages rimmed by souvenir shops, pricey tourist restaurants – although it's worth trying the freshly grilled sardines – and a pair of salty museums: the recently refurbished **Museo Naval** (*open summer Tues–Sat 10–1.30 and 5–8.30, Sun 11–2; otherwise 10–1.30 and 4–7.30, Sun 11–2*), devoted to the Basques' proud naval history, with models, photographs and a reconstruction of a carpenter's workshop, and, at the far end of the port, the **Aquarium** (*open July–Sept 10–10, rest of the year 10–8; adm*), stuffed with model ships, the skeleton of a Basque whale that went belly-up in San Sebastián's port and, downstairs, tanks of fish and other sea creatures from around the world, visited by means of a glass corridor.

From here you can stroll along the outer edge of **Monte Urgull** on the Paseo Nuevo, a splendid little walk between turf and surf. In the late afternoon, when the light is best, stroll up one of the numerous paths to the summit of the rock; Monte Urgull is really the city's park, closed to traffic and including surprises along the way such as a peaceful British cemetery from Wellington's campaign, and some of the old bastions and ancient cannons of the city's defences. Up at the top is the half-ruined **Castillo de Santa Cruz de la Mota** (16th century), with a small but excellent museum of local history inside. It's topped with an ungainly kitsch statue of Christ (from the Franco era) called the **Sagrado Corazón**, which keeps an eye on the holiday-makers on La Concha beach below.

The centre of the Parte Vieja is the arcaded **Plaza de la Constitución**, which once did double duty as the local bullring, when spectators would cram onto the numbered, crisply painted balconies for the best view. Within a few blocks of this local centre of Basque nationalism stand San Sebastián's three best monuments. From Calle Mayor, the distant neo-Gothic spires of the Catedral del Buen Pastor outstare the hyper-ornate façade of **Santa María del Coro** (18th century), on Vía Coro, topped with a writhing statue of San Sebastian full of arrows. It's gloomy inside, with dark, monstrous retablos half-hidden in shadows, but the main altarpiece is well lit and surmounted by the church's treasure, a statue of the Virgin which is said to have been found up the sleeve of a priest who was trying to smuggle it out and placed in its present position to discourage further attempts. Don't miss, at the back of the church, a limpid alabaster Greek cross by Eduardo Chillida in a pale arc of light. Dense cubes interlock and the shape of the cross is formed by the central hollow. Next to the church is the Plaza de la Trinidad, focus of the city's celebrated jazz festival in July and a popular spot for skateboarders during the rest of the year.

At the other end of the Calle 31 de Agosto, the only street left standing after the great fire of 1813, is the solid Gothic **church of San Vicente** (16th century) on C/ San Vicente, the oldest building in the city. Inside there's a dramatic *retablo* by Basque painters Bengoechea and Iriarte, but the moving *Pietá* (1999) by Oteiza and José Ramon Anda on the exterior walls is infinitely more affecting. Nearby, the old Dominican monastery of San Telmo, is now the fascinating **Museum of San Telmo** (*open summer Tues–Sat 10.30–1.30 and 5–8.30, Sun 10–2; winter Tues–Sat 10.30–1.30 and 4–8, Sun 10–2; adm*). The monastery's church is adorned with golden murals by the Catalan artist Josep Sert (1930) on the history of the Basque people. Old Basque discoidal tombstones, adorned with geometric patterns and star-like solar symbols, are lined up in the cloister; upstairs, the museum contains three El Grecos, two bear skeletons, Basque lucky charms and amulets, Basque sports paraphernalia, the interior of a Basque cottage and more. It's about to be expanded into a new glassy complex which will take over one side of the *plaza*.

The main attraction of the Parte Vieja is its countless bars, where the evening crowds hasten to devour delectable seafood tapas and Basque goodies. Here in the homeland of the Basque gastronomic societies (*see* p.66), eating is the greatest obsession. A fun excursion is to gather up some of that good food and row it out to **Isla de Santa Clara** for a picnic (*in summer there's also a regular ferry to the island from El Muelle, the dock behind the Ayuntamiento; boats run from 10am to 8pm*).

Around San Sebastián

There are several lovely parks in the hills around the city. The **Parque Monte Ullia** once had its own amusement park and funicular, but these have long disappeared. Nowadays, you have to clamber up under your own steam from Sagües station on the edge of Gros for dramatic views of the thrashing Cantabrian Sea. A mile inland from La Concha is the graceful **Aiete Palace**, built in the late 19th century for the duke and duchess of Bailén, and surrounded by breezy woods and pretty landscaped gardens with a lake.

Eduardo Chillida

Creator of a slew of monumental sculptures adorning boulevards and museums across the world, Chillida has long been the international standard-bearer of the Escuela Vasca (Basque School) founded by Jorge de Oteiza (*see* p.132), who exhorted Basque artists to define an aesthetic rooted in the Basque character. Chillida's use of iron, granite and wood follows the same tradition as the Basque ironworkers, shipwrights and their predecessors who worked in stone, leaving dolmens and cromlechs in the mountains and finely worked tools in the caves.

Born in San Sebastián in 1924, Chillida studied architecture in Madrid for four years before abandoning his studies for sculpture, and the Spanish capital, then ruled by the repressive Franco, for the French one. Chillida's earliest works were figurative, including sculptures in clay or plaster, but he soon rejected them in favour of purely abstract pieces forged from iron, 'drawings in space' reminiscent of the work of the great Catalan sculptor Julio González. These early pieces were often spiky, penetrating or spearing, and yet retained an impression of lightness, fluidity and airiness. Chillida was interested in the contrast 'between the solidity of the iron and its sudden endings in space', an interest which became clearer after his return to Hernani (near San Sebastián) in 1951. The later works are often solid pieces, created from interlocking cubes of iron or granite; others are formed entirely from a single strip of metal, the flow of form unbroken. He has begun to construct a series of monolithic sculptures, hewn from Galician granite, their massiveness and weight deliberately counterbalanced by a sense of airy grace, so that stone can sometimes seem liquid and weightless. He has been notoriously prolific, and few Basque towns can't boast of a Chillida or two – if only on the plaques at their local branch of the Kutxo bank. Chillida designed the logo.

About 5 miles from town, the brand new **Chillida Museum** is devoted to the works of San Sebastián's favourite son (*t 94 333 60 06, www.eduardo-chillida.com; open 10.30–2; take the N1 from San Sebastián and turn off onto the GI2132 to Hernani, or get the half-hourly bus from Calle Oquendo*). Eduardo Chillida restored this 16th-century cottage with its old oak beams, lit by a sheet of natural light which pours in from a great glass wall and illuminates works spanning half a century. The lawns, shaded by enormous old trees, are dotted with more than 40 massive pieces, sculpted mostly from iron and granite, yet paradoxically light and graceful.

Inland from San Sebastián

Tolosa and Ordizia: Beans and Cheese

Guipúzcoa, San Sebastián's province, is the most densely populated rural part of the Basque country, where plenty of fat villages bear unpronounceable, unimaginable names. There being only one fast route through the area, from San Sebastián to Tolosa (following a branch of the Compostela road), you'll have to invest a lot of time on some lovely, lazy back roads if you want to see any of them. Despair will probably

Tourist Information

Tolosa: C/ Nafarroa Etorbidea, **t** 94 365 49 72.
Oñati: Foru Enparatza 11, **t** 94 378 34 53.

Market Day

Tolosa: Saturday in Plaza del Tinglado.

Where to Stay and Eat

Tolosa ✉ 20400

★Oria, Oria 2, **t** 94 365 46 88 (*moderate*).
Modern, cosy and located in the centre.
Hs Oyarbide, Plaza Gorriti 1, **t** 94 367 00 17
(*cheap*). Simple rooms equipped with
a sink.
Frontón, San Francisco Ibiltokia 4, **t** 94 365
29 41. Longstanding classic from the 30s
with an Art Deco interior and New Basque
cuisine (*expensive*) – try *lomo de merluza
alvapor sobre salsa de piquillos*. Also likely
to have the town's famous beans on
the menu.
Casa Julián, Santa Clara 6, **t** 94 367 14 17.
Tolosa's oldest restaurant, and still one of
the best, specializing in grilled steaks,
pimientos del piquillo and *tejas de Tolosa*,
with a good list of Rioja wines (*moderate*).
Closed Sun.
Nicolás, Zumalacárregui 6, **t** 94 365 47 59. Does
delicious things with fresh and dried cod, as
well as charcoal-grilled steaks (*moderate*).
Closed Sun and Aug.
Sausta, Paso Belate 78, **t** 94 365 54 53. The
young chef has trained with some of the
region's most formidable chefs, and for
some of the most innovative New Basque
cuisine at very decent prices, this attractive
restaurant is a must (*moderate*). Try the
mero a la planch sobre salsa de marisco (sea
bass with shellfish sauce) and top it all off
with a wonderful chocolate soufflé with
passion fruit.

Oñati ✉ 20400

You couldn't find a nicer spot to stay in this
part of Guipúzcoa.
★Etxe Aundi, Torre Auzo 10, **t** 94 378 19 56,
f 94 378 32 90, *cu37993@cempresard*
(*inexpensive*). Has all modern comforts and a
good restaurant in a lovely old building.
★Etxeberria, R. M. Zuazola 14, **t** 94 378 04 60.
A pleasant place in the middle of town.
Soraluze Ostatua, Carretera Aranzazu, Barrio
Uribarri s/n, **t** 94 371 61 79, **f** 94 371 60 70
(*inexpensive*). Seven kilometres up the road
to Aránzazu, 12 comfortable rooms, fine
views and a babysitting service.
Hospedería de Aránzazu, **t** 94 378 13 13 (*cheap*).
A large place for pilgrims at the Sanctuary of
Aránzazu; simple, clean doubles with bath.
Txopekua, Barrio Uribarri, **t** 94 378 05 71. A
good restaurant in Oñati, in a Basque home-
stead on the road to Aránzazu (*moderate*).
Iturritxo, Atzeko Kale 32, **t** 94 371 60 78. A well-
loved local establishment which is always
full; the secret is the excellent regional
cooking and the very reasonable prices.

Azpeitia ✉ 20730

★Izarra, Avda de Loyola s/n (near the basilica),
t 94 381 07 50 (*moderate*). An upmarket
place with a swimming pool.
★Hs Uranga, Pza de Loyola 7, **t** 94 381 25 43
(*inexpensive*). Nearby, with bathless rooms
and a restaurant.
Etxeberri, **t** 94 372 12 11. In Zumárraga, on the
main road to Azpeitia; extremely cosy and
welcoming, specializing in Basque game
dishes (*moderate–inexpensive*). *Closed
Sun eve.*
Juantxo, Loiola Blde 3, **t** 94 381 43 15. A
welcoming, old-fashioned spot with an
excellent reputation for its fine traditional
cuisine made with market-fresh local
produce, washed down with a pungent local
txakoli wine. The home-made desserts are
especially good.

set in at a corner with signs pointing you to Aizarnazabal, Azpeitia, Azkoitia,
Azkarate, or Araiz-Matximenta; you'll begin to think the Basques are doing this
just for you.

One of the first Basque towns to join the industrial revolution, **Tolosa** (named after
Toulouse) is the largest town on the Oria river, thriving on paper mills (which explain
the aroma), although of the 23 that rolled during the Franco era, only a handful are

still in operation. Tolosa also makes wicker *chisteras* for *pelota*, and sweets, especially *tejas* (almond biscuits) and *delicias*. You can learn all about them in the Museo de Confitería at Lechuga 3, next to the Plaza del Ayuntamiento, or taste them in Tolosa's *pastelería* of renown, Gorrochategui, in Calle Arbol de Gernika. Dining out is the other main reason to stop (*see* the box on the left).

To a Basque, however, Tolosa means beans, or more precisely *Tolosako Babarruna Elkartea* or *alubias de Tolosa*, a native of Venezuela introduced in the 18th century by the Real Compañia Guipúzcoana de Caracas. Even the method of planting them between rows of maize is continued here, by the 40 official bean growers; like *txakoli*, red peppers, sheep's cheese and so on, they are strictly Denominación de Origen. Dry beans are almost black, oval and plump, but once cooked they turn red. The proper way to cook them is in an earthenware crock with garlic, onion and olive oil, which helps them conjure up a delicious thick sauce. For a truly filling meal, the Basques pile them on top of boiled cabbage and serve them with ribs and blood sausage.

Southwest of Tolosa on the N1, there's **Ordizia**, a medieval new town founded as Villafranca de Oria in 1256. Ordizia's special privileges, designed to promote the production of ewe's milk cheese (*ardi gasna*), were ratified by Juana the Mad in 1512, and ever since then it has been the cheese capital of Euskadi. The cheese, more precisely, is Idiazabal, made with the milk of an ancient race of Basque sheep, the *laxta*, a handsome, black-faced breed with curling horns and dainty grey dreadlocks. Since Neolithic times, shepherds have herded them up to summer pastures in the mountains, then down the paths of transhumance into the valleys each winter; some 800 shepherds still keep up the good work, a quarter of them producing their own cheese and, since 1904, competing in Ordizia's September cheese contest.

The pretty mountain village of **Segura**, further down the N1, has a main street lined with the palaces of a locally powerful family, the Guevaras, and other nobles. Up in the mountains beyond Zegama, bits of the original Roman road to Vitoria are still visible, and traditionalist pilgrims to Compostela still ascend the Aizkorri massif through the narrow, pedestrian-only San Adrián tunnel, before descending into the dry ochre plains of Alava.

Oñati and the Sanctuary of Aránzazu

For motorists, however, this valley has become something of a dead end. Before Segura, at Beasain, the main road branches westwards for **Oñati (Onate)**, beautifully set in a rich, rolling valley, dominated in the distance by the bluish pointed peaks of Mount Amboto and Udalaitz. It served as the capital of the pretender Don Carlos in the Carlist Wars and was one of the few towns in Euskadi to be ruled by a noble; and it retained a degree of independence until 1845. For many years the town had the only Basque university, founded in 1540; Oñati's landmark, it has a beautiful Plateresque façade and a plain but distinguished arcaded courtyard. The parish church of San Miguel (15th century) contains a number of treasures, including the alabaster tomb of the university's founder, Bishop Zuázola de Ávila, attributed to Diego de Siloé, and an attractive Plateresque cloister. Other noteworthy buildings include the Ayuntamiento and the Franciscan Convento de Bidaurreta.

Oñati is known also for its well-preserved medieval palaces, one of which saw the birth in 1511 of the conquistador Lope de Aguirre, perhaps best known these days as the deranged 'Wrath of God' in the film by Werner Herzog. The limping, mad-eyed Klaus Kinski was perfectly cast for the real man, who sailed from Sevilla at the age of 21, not long after Pizzarro arrived with the first fabulous shipments of treasure from the New World. Aguirre fought up and down South America in all the wars of the day, with a rare obsessiveness; at one point, after a judge had him publicly whipped for a minor infraction, Lope pursued the judge 6,000km, barefoot through Peru, to kill him in revenge. Somewhere along the way he acquired a daughter, and in 1560 the two of them accompanied Pedro de Ursúa's expedition down the Amazon in search of El Dorado. Aguirre mutinied, had Ursúa killed and, although he remained the real power, proclaimed Guzman, the ranking nobleman of the expedition, the Prince of Peru, in an act signed by 186 soldiers, 'the first act of American Independence'. Although in the film, Herzog has the members of the expedition die one by one on their raft, the real expedition reached the Atlantic in July. Aguirre took the port there by surprise and wrote a famous letter to King Philip II, surely the most astonishing one the royal bureaucrat ever received, informing him that he was going straight to hell for the misdeeds of his vassals in the New World, and signing it 'Son of your loyal Basque vassals, and I, rebel until death against you for your ingratitude, Lope de Aguirre, the Wanderer.' Although the Spaniards in Venezuela were terrorized by Aguirre's approach, his men by then had had enough and deserted him. When the troops of the governor of Venezuela closed in, Aguirre killed his daughter to keep her from being captured, and was cut to pieces.

A scenic road up from Oñati climbs 9km to the **sanctuary of Aránzazu**, usually filled with tour buses and pilgrims. Here, in 1469, a shepherd found an icon of the Virgin by a thorn bush and a cow bell, and the Virgin of Aránzazu became the patron saint of Guipúzcoa. The church that houses the icon has been rebuilt innumerable times since, lastly in 1950. This curious temple of Basque modernism is striking in its lonely and rugged setting, its two towers covered with a distinctive skin of pyramidal concrete nubs, creating a waffle-iron effect – a reference to an eccentric Renaissance conceit popular in Spain, seen in many buildings from Salamanca to Naples. Some of the best-known Basque artists contributed to church: there are sculptures on the facade by Jorge Oteiza, the main doors are by Eduardo Chillida, and the crypt holds paintings by Nestor Basterretxea.

Arrasate (Mondragón) and Bergara

The only town of any size in the region has two names: Basques call it **Arrasate**, Spaniards Mondragón. Though a nondescript industrial town these days, Arrasate used to be a spa – a Spanish prime minister, Antonio Cánovas del Castillo, was murdered here by an anarchist in 1897 while taking a cure. Arrasate still has some of its medieval walls and gates, along with the 14th-century Gothic church of San Juan.

It's under the name of Mondragón that the town has made its mark, synonymous with one of the most successful and innovative co-operative ventures in the world, one that is often pointed out as proof that the hard-working and egalitarian virtues of the Basques are still a force to be reckoned with. It all started with a young, inspired priest, José María Arizmendiarrieta, who arrived in town in 1941 to find it like the rest of Euskadi, severely depressed both economically and emotionally after the Civil War. A firm believer in the ability of people to control their own destiny, no matter how hard the circumstances, he founded in 1943 the Mondragón Eskola Politeknikoa, open to any young person in the area who wanted to attend and learn a useful skill. In 1956 five graduates formed the first co-operative manufacturing company, producing oil stoves and paraffin heaters. In 1959 they helped to create the Caja Laboral Popular savings bank, a co-operative credit company that became the keystone in the creation of scores of new co-operatives in the area. During the 1970s a technological research centre was founded, in the 1990s a private business university. Now the eighth largest firm in Spain, Mondragón has since gone international, and employs a fifth of all workers in Euskadi.

Further north, as a contrast, pretty **Bergara** offers a step back in time, with its palaces, churches and other monuments from the 16th and 17th centuries; note the Palacio Arrese, with its cut-out corner window in the best Spanish Renaissance style. Bergara is closely linked with another great Basque initiative, the Real Sociedad Bascongada de Amigos del Pais (Royal Basque Society of Friends of Bascongadas), founded by aristocrats in Azkoitia in 1764 to 'cultivate the learning and the taste of the Basque nation for the sciences, the fine arts and the arts; to correct and refine its customs, banish idleness, ignorance and their fatal consequences, and further tighten the union of the Three Basque Provinces of Alava, Vizcaya, and Guipúzcoa.' Its motto was *Irurak Bat*, 'the Three are One' (the inspiration for the nationalist slogan, *Zazpiak Bat* 'the Seven are One'), and it became the model for similar societies in Spain under the one enlightened king Charles III (1759–88). In 1767 the Real Socieded Bascongada founded the University of Bergara, the first secular university in Spain. It taught experimental physics, chemistry, mineralogy, humanities, mathematics, philosophy, ethics, religion, poetry, design, statistics, history of the Basque country and the *fueros*, Euskera (taught as a museum-piece even back then, a telling sign of 18th-century bourgeois attitudes), Latin, Spanish, French, English, Italian, vocal and instrumental music, gymnastics, fencing and dance. If not for the University of Bergara, in fact, you would be reading this by candlelight. Here, in 1783, the Elhuyar brothers from the French Basque country isolated tungsten, the element used in the filaments of lightbulbs.

East of Bergara, near the village of Zumárraga, is the unusual 15th-century fortress **church of Santa Maria**, popularly known as La Antigua. The hewn-oak interior is rustic and spartan with carved geometric patterns running along the balustrades and beams, punctuated by the occasional female bust.

Loyola: St Ignatius' Home Town

From Zumárraga the GI631 heads north, passing through Azkoitia before reaching the ancient village of **Azpeitia** and the nearby hamlet of **Loyola** (**Loiola**), birthplace in 1491 of Ignatius or Íñigo López de Loyola, and now home of the **Sanctuary of St Ignatius**.

The First General

Among the most Catholic of Catholics, the Basques are very proud that 'their' saint's Company of Jesus is today the largest of all religious orders (unless you count their new rivals for the pope's affections, the Opus Dei; see p.199). In the past, however, the Loyolas weren't always so popular, at least locally: not only were they exceptionally warlike, but they fought for Castile against their fellow Basques, and were ennobled by Alfonso XII in 1331. From their castle in Azpeitia, they got into the habit of raiding their neighbours, even the Church. Iñigo's grandfather wasn't very good at it, and got caught and sentenced to fight the Moors in Andalucía. His son, Iñigo's father, fought for Ferdinand and Isabella.

Iñigo was the last of 13 children born into this family of warriors. His mother died when he was an infant, and there was a vague idea of raising him to be a priest, although he would have none of it. At 16, he was made a page to Juan Velazquez, the treasurer of Castile, where he adopted all the vices court life – womanizing, gambling and brawling – with great gusto. In a family feud, he and his one brother who actually became a priest ambushed some clerics belonging to the rival family, killing one. When they were finally brought to justice, Iñigo argued that he too had a right to clerical immunity; the case dragged on, and the Loyolas seem to have been influential enough to get the charges dropped. But by all accounts, Iñigo was a strong-minded, persuasive force to be reckoned with.

After his patron died, he went to Pamplona to serve the viceroy of Navarra, his cousin. In 1521, when François I's huge army marched into Navarra and was welcomed in Pamplona as liberators from Castile, Iñigo got into the citadel and convinced the commander to hold out against all the odds for the honour of Spain. Just when Iñigo was ready to fight to the finish, a cannon ball hit him in the legs, breaking one. The French, in honour of his bravery, set his leg and carried him back to the family home in Loyola on a litter.

Iñigo suffered all the tortures 16th-century medicine had in its little black bag. His leg failed to heal, so the surgeons rebroke it and reset it. He nearly died, the leg finally healed, but the bone protruded below the knee and one leg was shorter than the other. Wanting to continue to wear the high boots of the courtier, Iñigo ordered the doctors to saw off the offending knob of bone and lengthen his shorter leg by stretching it on a kind of rack. The pain was excruciating, and it didn't work. During the long weeks of recovery the patient became so bored that he asked for romances to read. All they had in the house was the *Lives of the Saints*, so he read that. He was especially impressed by St Francis, who like himself had fought and been wounded in battle. And like Francis, as he recuperated, he found a new calling.

The actual birth house, built by the saint's grandfather after his four-year exile among the Moors, is a fortress-like Mudéjar structure, redesigned inside as a museum with solemn chapels and over-the-top gilded ceilings. Next to it stands the **basilica**, one of the outstanding Baroque works in all Spain. Carlo Fontana, a student of Bernini who had worked on many of the great Baroque building projects in Rome, was the main architect, and the costs were borne by a Habsburg queen of Austria; her family's

In March 1522, when he was well enough to walk, he went to Barcelona and its otherworldly holy of holies, Montserrat, where he knelt all night in vigil before the Virgin's altar, according to the rites of chivalry. He would be her knight, and leaving his sword at the altar, he gave away all his fine clothes and dressed himself in rough clothes with sandals and a staff. He had his first mystical experience, living as a hermit in a nearby cave. He sailed to Rome, had an audience with the pope, went to the Holy Land and returned to Spain determined to become a priest.

First, however, he had to go back to school to learn Latin. While there, he began to preach; the Spanish Inquisition arrested him twice, questioned him for weeks, and finally banned him from holding forth. So he went to Paris, where he attended university, and gathered his first followers. In an old crypt in Montmartre, seven of them took vows of poverty and chastity and to travel to Jerusalem, where Ignatius (as he now called himself) hoped they could be hospital porters. Discussions with the pope and Inquisition in Italy led in another direction, to forming a community, the Company of Jesus, which began to teach in Rome. Well educated and disciplined to total obedience, the Company was like no other religious order: it had no routine of offices to perform, no special dress or habits. In Its military-style hierarchy, its General was answerable only to the pope.

For Pope Paul III, this middle-aged Basque soldier of Christ, with his special skills of persuasion and organization, was exactly the right man in the right place at the right time, the undaunted warrior he needed to lead the counterattack at the front lines of dogma. The Reformation was in full swing and the rest of Europe was in danger of sliding into the Protestant camp. As bullying had failed to do the job, education seemed to be the answer and, for the first time ever, the Catholic church began to take it seriously. Ignatius had his orders: teach the people.

The Jesuits, in fact, would turn the tide and become the Church's greatest single weapon in the Counter-Reformation. By the time of Ignatius' death in 1556, they had 100 establishments throughout Europe and over 1,000 members, talented, educated and ready to go wherever they were called to set up seminaries and advise on religious issues – somewhat like a modern consultancy firm. Although the original intention was to serve the poor, they were so successful that they soon became closely associated with the elite (purely for practical reasons, it was claimed, as the elite decided which church their subjects attended).

'Obey and you will be saved', was the brunt of the Jesuit message, nicely linking the secular and sacred, and all beautifully packaged with grandeur and pageantry in their vast new 'Jesuit-style' or Baroque churches, offering tempting previews of heaven's delights.

coat of arms in stone hangs over the main door. Begun in 1689, this circular temple with its 211ft-high dome took almost 50 years to complete. To give an Italian building the proper Spanish touch, the ornate rotunda is flanked by two plain, broad wings of monastery buildings, making a façade almost 500ft wide – creating the sharp contrast of vast, austere surfaces and patches of exuberant decoration that marks so many of the best Spanish buildings. At the entrance, a monumental stairway guarded by stylized lions leads up to a porch under three arches; in it are five niches with statues of early Jesuit heroes, including Ignatius' fellow Basque St Francis Xavier (*see* pp.221–4). Nothing on the exterior, however, prepares you for the overwrought stone carving that covers every part of the dome inside, designed by a group of masters that included Joaquín de Churriguerra, one of the three brothers whose taste for ornament gave Spanish architecture the word *churrigueresque*. As in most Jesuit monuments, no expense was spared, from the fine Carrara marble frieze around the rotunda to the elaborate pavement in coloured stone. Over the main altar, a life-size statue of St Ignatius is covered with silver sent by the Basques of Caracas, Venezuela.

On the way back east to Tolosa, the twisting GI2634 passes through **Régil**, a pretty mountain town with beautiful views from the Col de Régil, the 'Balcón de Guipúzcoa'.

Along the Coast: San Sebastián to France

If you're driving to France, there is a choice of routes: either the A8 motorway, which is expensive though occasionally dramatic, or the old routes through Fuenterrabía to Hendaye. Just east of San Sebastián on the coastal road, the long ribbon town of **Pasajes de San Juan** (**Pasai Donibane** in Basque) lines the east bank of an estuary, with picturesque old houses. Victor Hugo lived in one for a while, and the Marquis de Lafayette lodged in another before sailing off to aid Britain's American colonists in their revolution. Philip built part of the Invincible Armada here, although now all such business affairs are handled by San Juan's ugly stepsister on the San Sebastián side of the estuary, **Pasajes de San Pedro**. From here the road goes along Monte Jáizkibel, offering superb views over the **Bay of Biscay**, the French coast and the Pyrenees.

Fuenterrabía and Hendaye stand either side of the sandy ford of the Río Bidasoa, which has endowed it with a spacious protected sandy beach. **Fuenterrabía** (**Hondarribia** in Basque, with an aspirated H that apparently neither the French nor Spanish can get right) often gets overlooked with all the border confusion, but this is

A Border Anomaly

In the Río Bidasoa between Fuenterrabía and Hendaye, there is a small island called the Isla de la Conferencia, or Ile des Faisans. This was a traditional meeting place for French and Spanish diplomats from the 15th century. In 1659 the Treaty of the Pyrenees was signed here, ending the long wars between France and Spain; the following year, representatives of both sides returned to plan the marriage of Louis XIV and the Spanish infanta (*see* p.243). A special pavilion was erected for the occasion, and the king of Spain sent his court painter, Velázquez, to decorate it. Unfortunately, the artist caught a bad cold here that eventually killed him.

Even today, the island is owned jointly by both countries, and there is a solemn agreement in a cabinet somewhere that details how the Spanish police shall look after it from April to October, and the French for the other six months. But really, there isn't anything to watch over; the island at present is uninhabited and completely empty.

Getting Around

It's only 20 minutes by bus from San Sebastián to Irún or Fuenterrabía on the frontier; connections are frequent by bus and train, and not a few people watching their pesetas stay in Irún (or in France) rather than in the more pricey resort. If you're not in a hurry, take the narrow-gauge 'El Topo' for a leisurely ride through fine scenery.

Tourist Information

Fuenterrabía: Javier Ugarte 6, t 94 364 54 58, f 94 364 54 66, *www.bidasoaturisimo.com*. Offers guided tours of Fuenterrabía and the surrounding area.
Irún: Puente de Santiago, Barrio de Behobia s/n, t 94 362 26 27, and in the train station, t 94 361 67 08.

Where to Stay and Eat

Fuenterrabía ⊠ 20280

In the moderate and inexpensive ranges there are few choices (actually, rooms are a better bargain across the border in Hendaye, though Fuenterrabía makes a more pleasant stay). If you like staying in converted historic buildings, however, Fuenterrabía has more choices than any town in the Basque country.

★★★**Parador Imperador Carlos V**, Pza de Armas 14, t 94 364 55 00, f 94 364 21 53, *pilardemiguel@parador.es* (*luxury*). Prettily situated at the very top of town, in the castle of Charles V that later housed so many kings and dukes on French business over the centuries. The decoration is medieval, including fine tapestries on the walls. Don't miss having breakfast or a drink on the terrace, high over the Bidasoa river.
★★★**Pampinot**, Kale Nagusia 5, t 94 364 06 00, f 94 364 51 28 (*expensive*). A smaller, but just as noble, historical monument, with eight rooms in a restored 15th-century mansion in the heart of the old quarter.
★★★**Hotel Obispo**, Pza del Obispo, t 94 364 54 00, f 94 364 23 86 (*expensive*). A 14th-century mansion, this one in the old residence of the Bishop of Fuenterrabía, built on the Bastion San Felipe, with sumptuously refitted rooms, splendid views and Internet facilities.
★★**San Nicolás**, Pza de Armas 6, t 94 364 42 78 (*moderate*). A little mauve-and-pink hotel with attractive, functional rooms right on the *plaza*.
★★**Hostal Alvarez Quintero**, C/ Alvarez Quintero 7, t 94 364 22 99 (*cheap*). In the old fishing quarter, one of a small number of *hostales*; dependable and relatively good value, and 500 yards from the beach.
Pension Zaragoza, Javier Ugarte 1, t 94 364 13 41, f 94 333 00 60 (*cheap*). Clean rooms, many with a sea view.

one of the most agreeable destinations on the coast; the village glows with colour – in its brightly painted houses, especially along Calle San Nicolás and Calle Pampinot, in its balconies loaded with flowers, and in its fishing fleet, which has not been afraid to take on France in the EU's battles over fishing rights. The town has had its share of sieges – you can still see the ancient walls and a castle of Charles V, now a *parador* – and every summer sees an invasion of French tourists (the local defensive measure of raising prices has had little effect in repelling them). In the evening, head out towards the lighthouse on **Cabo Higuer** – the northeasternmost corner of Spain – for views of the sunset over the bay.

If you come on Good Friday, the old streets around the church of the Assumption are the scene of an atmospheric procession after the symbolic entombment of Christ: Roman soldiers, the Archangel Michael and the Apostles, each bearing their attributes (in real life most of them old fishermen). On Easter Day they gather again, and when the priest declares '*Gloria in Excelsis Deo*', the Romans all fall over at once, as if struck by a bolt of lightning.

Restaurant Sebastian, C/ Mayor 9, t 94 364 01 67. Offers intimate dining in an ancient grocery store; try the wonderful pheasant stuffed with wild mushrooms (*expensive*). Chosen as Spain's best restaurant in 1999. *Closed Sun eve and Mon, and Nov.*

Alameda, C/ Alameda 1, t 94 364 27 89. Rustically furnished, this is a fine restaurant serving imaginative and award-winning New Basque cuisine with a strong local flavour, such as *manitas de cerdo braseadas* (braised pigs' trotters) or a scrumptious lasagne with squid and pumpkin (*expensive–moderate*). *Closed Tues and Sun eve.*

Beko Errota, C/ Barrio de Jaizubia, t 94 364 31 94. Traditional Basque dishes are on offer here, with a particularly good selection of fish dishes (*expensive–moderate*). An elegant restaurant with two dining rooms, it's everyone's favourite spot to celebrate family occasions at the weekends, so book ahead.

Arraunlauri, Paseo Butrón 3, t 94 364 15 81. The best bet next to the sea, offering simple fish dishes and other scrumptious seafood (*moderate*).

Hermandad de Pescadores, C/ Zuloaga 12, t 94 364 27 38. Restaurant run by the fishermen's confraternity, with typical marine décor (*moderate*).

Yola Berri, C/ San Pedro 27, t 94 364 65 11. Renowned for the huge range and excellent quality of its *pintxos* (*cheap*). There's a good choice of similar bars along the street.

Irún ✉ 20300

Cheaper rooms in Irún are no longer the bargain they once were, and very little is available for under 6,000 pts/€36.

★★★**Alcazar,** Avda Iparralde 11, t 94 362 09 00, f 94 362 27 97 (*expensive*). Top of the range.

★★**Lizaso,** C/ Aduana 5–7, t 94 361 16 00 (*inexpensive*). Possibly the best deal in Irún, with decent rooms.

Mertxe, C/ Francisco Gainza 9, t 94 362 46 82. A pretty chalet-style building with a winter garden, this is one of the finest restaurants in the region (*expensive*). Delicate but assured New Basque dishes such as an oyster and artichoke salad with squid ink dressing or *salteado de mollejas y sesas* – a rather alarming dish of lamb sweetbreads and brains.

Ramon Roteta, Villa Ainara, Irún 1, t 94 364 16 93. Gracious dining in a lovely villa with a garden; grand cuisine and superb desserts (*expensive*). *Closed Sun eve and Thurs.*

Labeko Etxea, Barrio Olaberria, t 94 363 19 64. In a rural setting, offering Basque dishes prepared with a knowing touch (*expensive–moderate*).

Romantxo, Pza de Urdanibia, t 94 362 09 71. Good home cooking (*moderate*).

Larretxipi, Larretxipi 5, t 94 363 26 59. Excellent fish, though a number of places nearby are cheaper.

Take the faster N1, which runs alongside the A8 from San Sebastián, and you end up in **Irún**, further up the Bidasoa and known to all as the grim border stop of endless, pointless waits, with *ventas* selling tasty snacks as compensation. This sad state comes courtesy of Franco and his German friends, who bombed it to smithereens in the Civil War after Gernika. One thing to do in Irún is visit the Porcelenas Bidasoa, Avda Elizatxo 60, makers of prestigious ceramics. Inland you can climb **Monte San Marcial** for a memorable view over the Bay of Biscay (there is a road to the top), or else flee the bustling coast for the serene **Valley of Oyarzun**, one of Euskadi's rural beauty spots, with the pretty villages of Oyarzun, Lesaka and Vera de Bidasoa. There are plenty of Neolithic monuments all through this region, on both sides of the border; the place where the Pyrenees meet the sea seems to have been a particularly holy spot. A site called **Oianleku**, off the main road near Oyarzun, includes some small stone circles among the dolmens.

Navarra

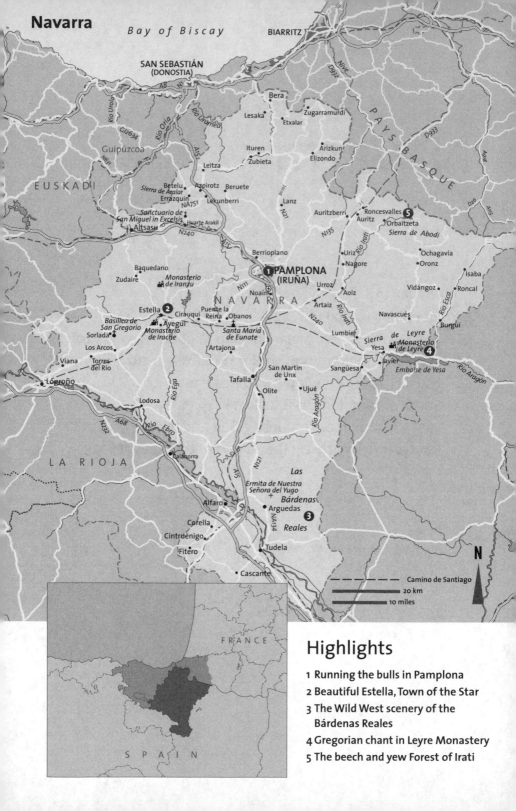

Navarra

Highlights

1 Running the bulls in Pamplona
2 Beautiful Estella, Town of the Star
3 The Wild West scenery of the Bárdenas Reales
4 Gregorian chant in Leyre Monastery
5 The beech and yew Forest of Irati

Europe's traditional front door to Spain, Navarra (Nafarroa in Basque) combines a sizeable, often nationalistic, Basque minority up in the misty western Pyrenees with a conservative, non-Basque Navarrese majority tending the sunny vineyards and gardens of the Ebro valley flatlands to the south. The combination (both sides are known as proud tough cookies lacking polish) hasn't always been comfortable, and only now that much of the population has abandoned the countryside have tensions between the two groups loosened up. As everyone must know by now, much of this 'loosening up' is concentrated in Pamplona, the capital both groups share, into an ecstatic week-long bacchanalia of inebriated recklessness, bull running and partying known as the Sanfermines. There is plenty to see at other times, much of it old and strange, and much of it up in the Basque strongholds of the Pyrenees or along the *camino francés* to Santiago. 'To come…is to go back' is the Navarrese tourist board's ambivalent slogan in English, promising at least a safe passage home for visitors, which wasn't always the case in the past.

Navarra: The Flea Between Two Monkeys

Navarra (perhaps the name of the ancient Basque tribe who lived here; no one knows) has played a standoffish, James Dean role in history since 605, when the Franks tried to harness it as part of the duchy of Vasconia, a huge untenable territory that extended from the Garonne to the Ebro. Charlemagne himself came down in 778, either to discipline the unruly duchy or to force it to join his fight against the Moors, and after razing the walls of Pamplona he went stomping back to France – except for his rear guard, which the furious Basques of Pamplona ambushed at the pass of Roncesvalles.

Charlemagne taught the Navarrese (who were all Basque back then) that the best policy was to owe nothing to nobody, and within a few years of his unlamented passing they created the independent kingdom of Navarra. It was the generally democratic Basques' one experiment in monarchy, and for a brief period it was a wild success under the gifted Sancho III 'the Great' (1004–34). Sancho worked hand in hand with Cluny's abbots to establish the *camino francés* to Santiago through Navarra. He controlled much of French Basque country, appointing his relatives as viscounts and inviting in French Gascon settlers to boost the population (and beginning the long trend towards diluting Navarra's Basqueness), and he ruled Galicia itself, at the end of the pilgrims' road, and then pocketed Castile and León after the death of its last count, setting up his son Fernando I as the first to take the title of 'King of the Spains'. Sancho's creation was too precocious to hold, and by the time of Sancho IV (1054–76) Navarra was once again a fierce rival of Castile, but avoided entanglements – marital or martial – by playing the French card.

'The Flea between Two Monkeys', as it became known, was ruled by three different French dynasties from 1234, when the Basque line died out. The last dynasty was the d'Albrets of Foix, one of whom, Germana, married Ferdinand the Catholic after the death of Isabella. This link, however, did not keep Ferdinand from slyly demanding that Navarra's rulers, Jean and Catherine d'Albret, let his armies march through to France in 1512. His request, as he expected, was refused, and he used the refusal as an excuse to grab Navarra south of the Pyrenees and annex it to Castile. Ferdinand kept the Navarrese happy by maintaining their *fueros*, which in practice gave the region an autonomy enjoyed by no other in Spain; it was ruled by a viceroy, minted its own coins and had its own government. But the Basques, who remembered their centuries of true independence, soon grew restless, and wanted the Castilians out.

Meanwhile, the d'Albrets were left with only Basse-Navarre, a thimble-sized realm north of the mountains. When François I became king of France and archrival of Ferdinand's grandson Charles V, he took on the cause of Henri d'Albret and sent a huge French and German army through Roncesvalles. After taking Pamplona (many of the population of which welcomed the French as liberators), the army marched on to take Castile. It stopped along the way to sack the Navarrese town of Los Arcos, and in revenge the Basques and Castilians united to defeat the French. The d'Albrets would never rule a united Navarra, but they went on to give France a long line of kings with the accession of Henri IV (1589–1610).

Napoleonic and Liberal attempts to do away with the *fueros* turned the Navarrese into fierce reactionaries and the most ardent of Carlists who thoroughly distrusted the Left, so much so that in the 1930s Navarra rejected the Republic's offer of autonomy. Instead, the Navarrese *requetés* in their distinctive red berets became some of Franco's best troops, fighting for their old privileges and Catholicism – just as the Basques were, only on the Republican side. Franco rewarded Navarra by leaving the *fueros* intact, making it the only autonomous region in Spain until his death, while culturally oppressing the Basques in the northern valleys. Today, Navarra is officially the *Comunidad Floral de Navarra*, all on its own; the fact that a referendum was never held in Navarra, allowing it to vote on whether it wanted to join with the other three Basque provinces, remains a bone of contention with nationalists to this day.

Pamplona (Iruña)

Whether you call it Pamplona, the town founded by Pompey in 75 BC, or by its older name Iruña, which means simply 'the city' in Basque, the capital of Navarra sits on a strategic 1,400ft pimple on the beautiful fertile plain, its existence as inevitable as its nickname, the 'Gateway of Spain'. For a few years in the 730s, the Arabs used it in reverse, as the gateway to France, until their dreams of Europe were hammered at Poitiers.

Over the next decades the Basques regained control of Pamplona, clobbered Charlemagne after he burnt their walls, and set up their own king. In 918 the Moors came back and razed Pamplona to the ground again. To encourage rebuilding, Sancho the Great invited his subjects over the Pyrenees in what is now Basse-Navarre to come and start trades in what became the two new districts of Pamplona, San Cernín and San Nicolás. The fact that the three districts of the city were practically independent and had their own privileges led to violent rivalry between them, so much so that in 1521 the French, coming to the rescue of the French Navarrese, unsuccessfully besieged Pamplona in an effort to regain San Cernín and San Nicolás. Wounded while

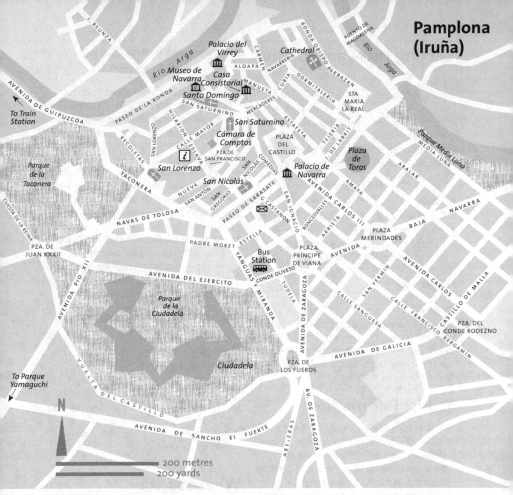

Pamplona (Iruña)

fighting for Castile was a certain Captain Íñigo López de Recalde (or Loyola), who got religion in a militant way and founded the Jesuits (*see* pp.190–1).

Pamplona seems to have been naturally conducive to that sort of thing, with a reputation for being crazily austere, brooding and puritanical. For anyone who knows the city only for throwing the wildest party in Europe, this comes as a shock of *desfase*, or maladjustment, a word that means (and gleefully celebrates) the unresolved contradictions that coexist in post-Franco Spain. Stern Catholicism (*'Qui dit basque, dit catholique'*, say the French) is part of the city's fabric. 'From the top to the bottom of Pamplonese society, I have found the whole place poisoned by clerical alkaloid,' grumped Miguel de Unamuno. 'It oozed out of every corner...one drop in the eye is enough to infect you forever.' In the 1950s, the secretive Opus Dei, Christianity's ultra-conservative fifth column (known as Octopus Dei or the Holy Mafia by detractors), chose Pamplona to build their Universidad de Navarra, their most important educational institution in Spain, especially since Pope John Paul II's recent beatification of the founder, Josemaria Escriva; today, the head prelate of the order is a Basque, Bishop Javier Echevarria.

Getting There and Around

By Air

Pamplona's airport (t 94 816 87 00) is 9km south of the city, with connections to Madrid, Barcelona and Santander. The cheapest way to get to the airport is to take a Beriainesa bus from the bus station (every half-hour) to Noaín, which drops you a few hundred metres from the airport.

By Train

The train station is 2km out of town on Avda San Jorge. Bus no.9 makes connections with the centre every 10mins (t 94 813 02 02). Tickets and information can also be had at the railway office in town at C/ Estella 8, t 94 822 72 82.

By Bus

The bus station (t 94 822 38 54) is in town, near the citadel, at C/ Conde Oliveto 8. Besides provincial connections, there are six buses daily to Vitoria, four to Bilbao, seven to San Sebastián and six to Zaragoza.

Tourist Information

Tourist office: C/ Eslava 1, Plaza San Fransisco, t 94 820 65 40, f 94 820 70 34, *oit.pamplona @cfnavarra.es*. The staff here operate a **booking service** for *casas rurales* throughout Navarra, t 94 820 65 41, f 94 820 70 34, *central.reservas@cfnavarra.es*. For up-to-date information on the Sanfermines and events, see *www.sanfirmin.com*.

Post office: Just off Paseo de Sarasate.

Internet access: Email can be checked at **IturNet**, C/ Iturrama 1, a long hike away in the new part of town.

Shopping

Abáruza, C/ Santo Domingo 29. A local book-shop with an excellent selection of titles covering all aspects of Navarrese and Basque culture.

Artesanía Popular San Antón, C/ San Antón 3. Combine shopping with altruism; you'll find souvenirs, ceramics and crafts made by local people sold in aid of families in need.

Botería Roncesvalles, Avda Roncesvalles 2. Traditional handmade goatskin wine containers.

Casa Casla, C/ Calceteros 8. Justly famous for its *chorizo de Pamplona*; you can't miss this old-fashioned little shop bristling with cured sausages.

Markets

Mercado de Santo Domingo, next to the town hall in Plaza de los Burgos. The oldest and most popular market in the city with a wide array of local produce on offer (*Monday–Saturday*).

Mercadillo de Landaben, Polígono Landaben. This Sunday-morning open-air market (*not July and August*) has everything from clothes and shoes to fresh fruit and vegetables.

Sports and Activities

All kinds of adventure sports are on offer in the surrounding mountains and valleys. Tour agencies offer a range of different trips:

Mirua, t 94 846 48 31. Mountain-biking, rock-climbing and hiking.

Nattura, Naturaleze y Aventura, t 94 813 10 44. Rafting, pot-holing and hiking.

Pottoka Tours, t 94 822 22 75. Horse-riding, hang-gliding and plane tours.

Where to Stay

Pamplona ✉ 31300

During the Sanfermines, hotel prices double and often triple, supplemented by scores of overpriced rooms in *casas particulares*, adver-tised weeks ahead in the local newspapers, *Navarra Hoy* and *Diario de Navarra*. If you end up sleeping outside, any of the gardens along the walls or river are preferable to the noisy, filthy, vomit-filled citadel. Keep a close eye on your belongings (petty criminals, unfortu-nately, go into overdrive along with everyone else during the fiesta) and check in what you don't need at the *consigna* in Plaza San Fransisco, next to the tourist office; everyone else does too, so get there early. Two free camp sites are set up along the road to France, but again, don't leave anything there you might really miss. If you stay outside Pamplona and drive into town, beware that breaking into cars is widespread but discerning: thieves took our toothbrushes, tampons and travel iron but left everything else.

Luxury

****Iruña Palace Los Tres Reyes, Jardines de la Taconera, t 94 822 66 00, f 94 822 29 30, *www.hotel3reyes.com*. Conveniently located a short walk from the old town, this modern hotel pampers its well-heeled guests with every possible convenience, including an indoor heated pool and tennis.

Expensive

***Maisonnave, C/ Nueva 20 (next to Pza San Francisco), t 94 822 26 00, f 94 822 01 66. This gleaming modern edifice offers comfort, prestige and a peaceful garden at the back. It also has a restaurant (*see* below).

***NH El Toro, Berrioplano (5km from Pamplona on the Guipúzcoa road), t 94 830 22 11, f 94 830 20 85. Has quiet rooms in a traditional-style mansion, overlooking a statue group of the *encierro*.

Moderate

***Europa, C/ Espoz y Mina 11 (just off Pza del Castillo), t 94 822 18 00, f 94 822 92 35, *heuropa@cmn.navarra.net*. One of Pamplona's prettiest choices with its flower-bedecked balconies, some overlooking the *encierro* action in Estafeta. The restaurant, one of the city's finest, is run by the same management as the Alhambra's (*see* below).

***Yoldi, Avda San Ignacio 11, t 94 822 48 00, f 94 821 20 45, *www.webs.navarra.net/hyoldi*. Has long been the favourite of *toreros* and aficionados in general.

**Eslava, Pza Virgen de la O, t 94 822 22 70, f 94 822 51 57. Small, quiet and cosy, with views over the walls of Pamplona.

*La Perla, Pza del Castillo, t 94 822 77 06, f 94 821 15 19. Hemingway always stayed at this, Pamplona's oldest hotel, at least as long as room 217 was available; the others, recently renovated, still have their high ceilings and plaster mouldings from 1880.

Inexpensive

*Hs Bearán, San Nicolás 25, t 94 822 34 28, f 94 822 34 28. One of the few decent

hostales, where all doubles come with baths. Rooms have been recently refurbished and it is charmingly run by a pleasant family.

**Hs Príncipe de Viana I and II, Avda Zaragoza 4, t 94 824 91 47, f 94 824 91 46. Clean but faded rooms with baths; run by a pair of sisters in the same building.

**Hostal Navarra, C/ Tudela 9, t 94 822 51 64, f 94 822 34 26. Has been miraculously revived by a lick of paint and some flowering plants on the balconies. It's convenient for early-morning bus departures and is 5 minutes' walk from the Casco Viejo; all rooms have bath.

Pensión Sarasate, Paseo Sarasate 30, t 94 822 30 84. Small and personal; the decent but unspectacular rooms all have private bath.

Pensión Lambertini, C/ Mercaderes 17, t 94 821 03 03. Has a comfy living room stuffed with books and knick-knacks, and balconies overlooking the route of the encierro. Ask for one of the lovely rooms at the back, which boast extensive views across the Cuenca de Pamplona.

Cheap

Cheaper *hostales* and *fondas* are mostly on C/ San Gregorio and C/ San Nicolás.

*Pensión Casa García, C/ San Gregorio 12, t 94 822 38 93. Offers 10 double rooms without bath, and a very decent *menú del día* in its restaurant.

Casa Santa Cecilia, C/ Navarrería 17, t 94 822 22 30. Located in an 18th-century palace, and providing one of the nicest cheap sleeps under lofty ceilings in huge rooms.

Otano, San Nicolás 5, t 94 822 50 95. Has been popular for years for its nice rooms with baths, and a good, inexpensive restaurant-bar.

Excaba, t 94 833 03 15. The nearest camp site, 7km to the north.

Eating Out

Expensive

Josetxo, Plaza Príncipe de Viana 1, t 94 822 20 97. Has been a local gourmet institution in Pamplona for 40 years. Try to book one of the small Belle Epoque dining rooms upstairs, and choose between delicacies such as *ajo arriero con langosta* (seafood casserole with lobster) or the chef's prize *solomillo a la broche con salsa de trufa* (steak fillet on a spit with truffle sauce). *Closed Sun and Aug.*

Hartza, C/ Juan de Labrit 19, t 94 822 45 68. Very close to the bullring, this is a traditional, welcoming establishment serving up fresh Basque-Navarre dishes made with ingredients selected daily by the Hartza brothers themselves. It's famous for its *bonito encebollado* (tuna with onions), hake dishes and home-made desserts. *Closed Sun eve, Mon, and mid-July to early Aug.*

Alhambra, C/ Francisco Bergamín 7, t 94 824 50 07. Look out for more imaginative dishes at this fashionable place: potatoes stuffed with truffles and scampi and home-made desserts. Good *menú degustación* at 4,400 pts/€26.5. *Closed Sun and mid-July to early Aug.*

Rodero, C/ Arrieta 3, t 94 822 80 35. Here you'll find modern variations on Navarrese, Basque and French recipes prepared with the finest seasonal ingredients. Try the *corona de alcachofas fritas* (lightly fried artichokes) to start, followed by the *canelón de bacaloa con ajo* (cod baked with garlic). The wine list is excellent. *Closed Sun and Aug.*

Europa, C/Espoz y Mina 11, t 94 822 18 00. Indulges diners with refined service and classic Navarrese meat and game dishes; try the stewed breast and thigh of pigeon, smothered in rich gravy. *Closed Sun.*

Restaurante del Rey Noble (Las Pocholas), Paseo de Sarasate, t 94 822 22 14. This has been one of the city's finest and most exclusive restaurants since 1938. The food is very traditional and very fresh; *rabo estofado* (stuffed bull's tail) and *ajoarriero de langosta* (langoustines cooked with garlic, parsley and chilli). *Closed Sun and Aug.*

Restaurante del Mirador, Hotel Maisonnave, C/ Nueva 20, t 94 822 26 00. This modern hotel restaurant serves excellent Navarrese cuisine, like the *merluza a la koskera*, or tangy fresh artichokes in season. It's on the very top floor and offers wonderful views of the old city.

Don Pablo, C/ Navas de Tolosa 19, t 94 822 52 99. This is the place to come for imaginative French-Navarrese cuisine in classic surroundings; on the menu, there's *filletes de lenguado con hongos* (sole with wild mushrooms), *hojaldre de frutas y foie* (a butter pastry filled with fruit and foie gras) and the house speciality is fresh fish grilled to perfection over charcoal. *Closed Sat and mid-July to mid-August.*

Moderate

Sarasate, t 94 833 08 20. At weekends half of Pamplona drives 11km out towards Irún to dine on the imaginative home cooking served at this traditional *caserío*, with a fireplace for winter dining and a terrace in the summer. *Closed Sun eve and Mon.*

Chalet de Izu, Avda Baja Navarra 47, t 94 822 60 93. Near Parque Media Luna, with plenty of swish atmosphere and good *menús.*

Asador Olaverri, C/ Santa Marta 4, t 94 823 50 63. Come here for a big grilled-meat-and-wine feast. *Closed Sun eve and mid-July to mid-Aug.*

Erburu, C/ San Lorenzo 19, t 94 822 51 69. This is a quiet, wooden-beamed retreat at the height of the *marcha*; it serves Navarrese-style seafood and excellent beef. *Closed Mon and last two weeks of July.*

Casa Sixto, C/ Estafeta 81, t 94 822 51 27. Well known for its succulent home-cooked game dishes. *Closed Wed and Oct.*

La Chistera, C/ San Nicolás 20, t 94 821 05 12. Another popular spot for local dishes; try the *lenguado en salsa de gambas* (sole with a prawn sauce) and finish up with the divine fruit tarts.

Enekorri, C/ Tudela 14, t 94 823 25 47. This is traditionally where Pamplonans come to celebrate New Year; it has an attractive mixture of old and new furnishings, echoed in the food, a creative mix of traditional recipes with new twists. The *merluza enekorri*, hake in a delicate sauce, is especially good and the wine list has a big reputation.

Baserri, C/ San Nicolás 32, t 94 822 20 21. Hard to beat for *cocina en miniatura*; this restaurant's fine creations have repeatedly walked away with top honours at Pamplona's annual *Concurso de Pinchos*. You can try a selection of them, and delicacies such as fresh rocket and smoked cod salad, on the excellent 3,000 pts/€18 *menú especial*.

Cheap

La Campana, C/ Campana 12, t 94 822 00 08. The chef here takes special pride in preparing unusual recipes such as chicken in champagne.

Casa Paco, C/ Lindatxikía (behind San Nicolás church), t 94 822 51 05. A favourite for lunch since the 1920s.

Sarasate, C/ San Nicolás 19, t 94 822 57 27. Come here for the best vegetarian meals in Pamplona. *Closed Sun and evenings, except Fri and Sat.*

Tapas/Pinchos/Pintxos

As well as elegant cafés, Pamplona had some 700 bars at the last count, or one for every 280 inhabitants, many of whom seem to be always in them, day and night.

Café Iruña, Plaza del Castillo 44. You can tuck into inexpensive light meals until 2.30am at this famous 1888 *modernista* place.

Baviera, Plaza del Castillo 10. Another of the old stalwarts on the *plaza*; plenty of atmosphere and one of the best selections of Navarrese *pintxos* to boot.

Nueva Casino, Plaza del Castillo 44. Hugely popular during the Sanfermines, when it holds the *baile de la alpargeta* – only beautiful people are allowed entry, but thankfully they have broad ideas of what constitutes '*guapa*'.

Café El Kiosko, Plaza del Castillo 14. A local favourite with a lively ambience, decent *pintxos* and a large terrace.

Mesón del Caballo Blanco, near the cathedral in Redín. An atmospheric old stone house with a terrace – a delightful place to linger; in winter, sandwiches are served around the fireplace.

Roch, C/ Comedias. Small, lively and usually packed at the start of *la marcha*, thanks in part to their superb *fritos de pimiento pintxos*.

El Cordovilla, in the Casco Viejo. A bar which claims to make the biggest *pinchos morunos* (kebabs) in the world.

Mesón del Pirineo, C/ Estafeta 14. Set in a beautiful old building, this is a very lively spot on the main bull-running street.

Fitero, C/ Estafeta 58. Another classic bar with a good range of *pintxos*; the *croquetas* are the best in town.

Monasterio, C/ Espoz y Mina 11. The best place in Pamplona for *fritos calientes*, fried morsels of everything from cod or wild mushrooms to capsicums.

Café Niza, C/ Duque de Ahumada 1. Graceful *modernista*-style bar by the Teatro Gayarre – a great place to while away an hour or two.

Bodega San Martín, C/ Aldapa 4–6. The house speciality is *cazuelicas de caracoles y ajoarriero*, baked snails with garlic, accompanied by a drop of something from the extensive range of wines and liqueurs.

Entertainment and Nightlife

Theatre

Teatro Gayarre, Avda de Carlos III, t 94 822 01 39. Besides drama, the Teatro hosts several music concerts, including performances by the Sinfónica de Euskadi.

Cinema

For undubbed films (marked 'v.o.'), check local newspapers or ask at the tourist office.

Cinés Príncipe de Viana, C/ García Castañon 6, t 94 822 19 39.

Golem Yamaguchi, Plaza Yamaguchi 9, t 94 825 19 03.

Nightclubs and Bars

Subsuelo, Plaza de Castillo 44. A popular underground bar on different levels.

Sector, C/ Abejarras 11. Young university students pack this place out.

ONB, C/ Abejarras 11. Latin-American dancing from salsa and merengue to tango for an enthusiastic mixed crowd.

Reverendos, Monasterio de Velate 5. A popular, laid-back club for 30-somethings.

O'Connors, Paseo de Sarasate 13. Irish pub with curious Irish-Basque *pintxos* and a noisy, cheerful atmosphere.

In the 1960s, Pamplona's new tennis club still built separate swimming pools for men and women. Forty years on, the city now prides itself on setting up Spain's first shelter for battered women, the first city workshops for training disadvantaged youth and the first urban rubbish recycling programme. It is also the seat of the Udako Euskal Unibertsitaea (Basque Summer University), which has led the way in higher education in Euskera, and has promoted the printing of over 180 university text books in Basque.

'Pamplona is a city that gives much more than it promises,' said Victor Hugo. It certainly will if you come in the second week of July for the Sanfermines, but expect it also to take your money, your watch, your sleep and a lifetime's supply of adrenaline.

A Walk through the Casco Viejo

Pamplona was squeezed into a tight girdle of walls until the early 1900s, when the city spread in all directions and accumulated around 185,000 inhabitants in the process. But for all its 20th-century flab, the vital organs in the historic Casco Viejo remain intact, beginning with the city's heart, **Plaza del Castillo**, shaded by the knitted boughs of the plane trees, circled by too many cars and framed by arcades sheltering stylish cafés. Off the southwest corner extends the **Paseo de Sarasate**, populated by stone kings and queens and the overwrought **Monumento a los Fueros**, erected by popular subscription after Madrid tried to mess with Navarra's privileges back in 1893. The bronze allegory of Navarra holds a copy of the *Ley Foral*, or Fueros' Law, surrounded by the broken chains from the Battle of Las Navas de Tolosa, symbolizing freedom; these also feature on Navarra's coat of arms. Historical frescoes decorate the neoclassical **Palacio de Navarra** at one end of the Paseo; its archives contain one of the best caches of medieval documents in Spain and the garden boasts a massive sequoia.

Off the eastern end of Plaza del Castillo, the narrow streets jammed with shops and bars were once the *Judería*, where Pamplona's Jews, 'a gentle and reasonable race' according to the king of Navarra, lived unmolested until Navarra was gobbled up by the intolerant, Inquisitor-infested Spain of Ferdinand and Isabella. Behind these, tucked up near the ramparts, the gracious 14th–15th-century Gothic **cathedral** hides behind a dull-witted neoclassical façade, slapped on in the 18th century by a misguided do-gooder; a shame because the original front, according to travellers' descriptions, was ribald and lusty, almost verging on the obscene.

When completed, this was the second-largest cathedral in Spain after León's, and suitable shelter for the beautiful alabaster tombs of the cathedral's sponsors, big-nosed Charles III 'the Noble' and his big-nosed queen Leonora de Trastámara, sculpted in the 15th century by Jean de Lomme of Tournai. The kings of Navarra were crowned before the Romanesque statue of *Santa María La Real*, carved and gilded in silver in the 12th century, who peers out from beneath a spidery neo-Gothic canopy in the presbytery. The cathedral was at the cutting edge of ecclesiastical fashion: the Renaissance choir benches are the work of the region's finest sculptors and the lacy Gothic grille was one of the first of its kind in Spain. The door to the cloister, the *Puerta del Amparo* (Gate of Succour, 1335), has a sad but busy little polychrome gathering mourning the Virgin's death in the tympanum, and a host of miniature carvings depicting scenes of succour encrusting the door frame.

The delicacy of the Gothic **cloister** (1280–1472) approaches gossamer in stone and reaches a climax of decorative bravura in the justly named **Puerta Preciosa** (1350–60), carved with a superb *Dormition of the Virgin*. The Garro family are buried in the northeast corner beneath a jolly band of cavorting musical angels. Off the cloister, the vain archbishop of Barbazán built the Barbazana Chapel in the 14th century to house his tomb, and now lies contented beneath a stunning, star-strewn vaulted roof and a Gothic carving of the Virgin of Consolation. The **Museo Diocesano** (*open Mon–Fri 10–1.30 and 4–7, Sat 10–1.30; adm*) occupies the kitchen and refectory, where pilgrims once dined. It contains two remarkable reliquaries – the 1258 *Relicario del Santo Sepulcro* and the 1401 *Relicario del Lignum Crucis*, adorned with precious stones, along with sweet-faced 12th–15th-century carvings of the Madonna and Child, and the cathedral's glittering 16th-century silver shrine and processional monstrance. The kitchen displays old plans and engravings of the cathedral, but is mainly remarkable for its enormous chimneys, one in each corner with a huge lantern-chimney in the middle.

The narrow old lanes around the cathedral belong to the **Navarrería**, the original Basque quarter, populated in the Middle Ages by cathedral builders and farmers who tilled the bishop's lands. Here on the promontory, on the Rincón del Caballo Blanco, you'll find the most impressive segment of the surviving **walls** built by Philip II, with a reputation for impregnability so powerful that no one challenged it until the French tried to hole up here against Wellington; the views stretch for miles over the plain. Just west, the 13th-century **Palacio del Virrey** started out as the royal palace and is now being completely refurbished and expanded.

Past the attractive **Portal de Zumalacárregui** (16th-century, but renamed after the heroic Carlist general who died at the siege of Bilbao), the **Museo de Navarra** (*t 94 842 64 95, www.cfnavarra.es/cultura/museo; open 10–2 and 5–7, Sun 11–2, closed Mon; adm*) occupies a huge 16th-century hospital and contains everything from Navarrese prehistory to contemporary art, with Roman mosaics, Gothic wall paintings, carved capitals from Pamplona's original Romanesque cathedral (minus the naughty bits), an ivory coffret from Leyre made in Córdoba in the 11th century and a fine portrait of the Marqués de San Adrián by Goya.

Just below the museum, wooden barricades remind you that this is the start of the *encierro*; the bulls leave their corral near Plaza Santo Domingo and head up C/ Mercaderes and C/ Estafeta. Follow their route and you'll come to Plaza Consistorial and the colourful Baroque **Casa Consistorial**, topped with jaunty allegorical figures. Pamplona's nobles built their finest escutcheoned palaces just off this square, along C/ Zapatería and C/ Mayor. Plazas de Consejo and San Francisco, set diagonally opposite each other, are also worth a look, the latter with a *modernista* (Art Nouveau) hotel converted into a bank. Nearby in C/ Ansoleaza, the well-preserved Gothic **Cámara de los Comptos Reales** (*open Mon–Fri 9–2*), the kings' mint in the 12th century, has a magnificent porch opening onto a vault and patio with some original decorations intact.

Pamplona's Annual Meltdown: Los Sanfermines

Before Hemingway there was Fermín, son of a Roman senator and first bishop of Pamplona. His family had been converted by San Saturnino (or Sernin, or Cernín) of Toulouse, who was martyred by being dragged about by a bull. Fermín, for his part, travelled as a missionary to the Gauls and was beheaded in Amiens for his trouble. Some time between then and 1324, when Pamplona held its first fiesta, Fermín decided to take bullfighters under his saintly cape; by 1591 his festival had found its current dates and form.

Although it's the insanely dangerous running of the bulls that has made Los Sanfermines world-famous, this is only a tiny portion of the nine days of nonstop revelling when 'Pamplona becomes the world capital of happiness', a state of hyper-bliss fuelled by 3 million litres of alcohol. Each year.

There is some order to the madness. The Sanfermines officially open at noon on 6 July, when thousands of Navarrese in their festival attire (white shirts and white trousers or skirts, red sashes and red bandanas) gather in front of the town hall to hold their bandanas aloft as a rocket called *El Chupinazo* is fired off the balcony and a city councillor cries in Spanish and Basque: 'People of Pamplona! Long live San Fermín!' The city explodes with a mighty roar, while popping tens of thousands of champagne corks (and smashing the bottles on the pavement, usually causing the first casualties).

In the afternoon, the giants and big heads (*gigantes y cabezudos*) – as essential to the fiesta as the bulls – leave their 'home' in the bus station. The eight 13ft plaster giants supported by dancers date from 1860 and represent kings and queens, whirling and swirling the minuet, their sweeping skirts flowing in the air. They are accompanied by the *cabezudos* and *kilikis*, big-headed figures in tricorn hats, with names like Napoleon and Patata, who wallop children on the head with foam rubber balls tied to bats. This is also the prerogative of the *zaldikos*, the colourfully dressed men wearing cardboard horses around their waists; all are accompanied by dancers, *txistularis* and *gaiteros*.

At four o'clock a massive scrum, the *Riau Riau,* begins when members of the Corporación de San Fermín dressed in all their finery try to proceed 400m down the Calle Mayor to the chapel of San Fermín at San Lorenzo for vespers, but everyone else tries to prevent them in a gung-ho defiance of authority, to the extent that it's often late at night before the Corporación achieves its goal. The mayor of Pamplona has tried for several years to ban the chaotic *Riau Riau,* but it seems to be unbanable. After a first night of carousing and dancing in the streets, the dawn of 7 July and every following day is welcomed with the *dianas*, a citywide wake-up call performed on screeching pipes.

The *encierro*, or *zezenketa*, the running of the bulls, begins daily at 8am, but if you want a good place to watch, wedge yourself into a spot along the route – Cuesta de San Domingo, Mercaderes and Estafeta – at least an hour earlier. Before running, the locals sing a hymn to Fermín and arm themselves with a rolled-up newspaper to distract the bull's attention, since the animals – 1,200lbs of muscle and fury – charge at the nearest moving object, ideally at a flung newspaper instead of a falling runner. A rocket goes up as the first bull leaves the corral; a second rocket means that all are released, and a third signals that all have made it to the bullring – on a good run the whole *encierro* only lasts 3 minutes.

The most dangerous moments are when the runners and bulls have to squeeze into the runway of the bullring, or when a bull gets loose from his fellows and panics. People (and not all of them tourists) get trampled and gored every year; if you run you can hedge your bets by running on weekdays, when it's less crowded, and by avoiding the *toros* of the Salvador Guardiola ranch, which have the most blood-stained record.

The spirit of abandon is so infectious that, even if you come determined not to run, you may find yourself joining in on a self-destructive spur of the moment. Women do defy the authorities and run, although the police try to pull them out. During the *encierro* the lower seats of the bullring are free (again, arrive early), except on Sunday; from here you can watch the bulls and runners pile in and, afterwards, more fun and games as heifers with padded horns are released on the crowd in the ring. The traditional breakfast is huge (bull stews, lamb's sweet-breads, ham and eggs in tomato sauce, washed down with gallons of chilled rosé and *patxaran*).

The bullfights themselves take place daily at 6.30 in the evening – tickets sell out with the speed of lightning and are usually only available from scalpers. The *sombra* seats are for serious aficionados, while members of the 16 *peñas* (clubs devoted to making noise and in general being as obnoxious as possible) fill up the *sol* seats and create a parallel fiesta if the action in the ring isn't up to snuff or create pandemonium if it is. Afternoons also see other bull sports that are bloodless (for the bull, at any rate): the dodging, swerving *concurso de recortadores* and leaping *corrida vasca-landesa*.

Between the bullfights there are concerts, Navarrese dance (*jotas*) and Basque dances, processions of the relics of San Fermín and other religious services, parades and activities for young children and senior citizens. At night, fireworks burst over the citadel and the *toro de fuego*, or 'fire bull', carried by a runner and spitting fireworks, chases children down the route of the *encierro*. Then there's the midnight *El Estruendo de Irún*, led by an enormous drum called the *bomba*, in which hundreds of people – just about anyone who can lay their hands on anything that makes a sound – gather and let loose in an ear-bashing sonic disorder.

At midnight on 14 July, Pamplona winds down to an exhausted, nostalgic finale, a ceremony known as the *Probe de mí*; everyone gathers in front of the town hall (or in the Plaza del Castillo for the livelier, unofficial ceremony), with a candle and sings: 'Poor me, poor me, another San Fermín has come to an end.' As the clock strikes 12 everyone removes their red scarves and agrees, like Hemingway, that it was 'a damned fine show' and promises to do better and worse next year. Die-hards party on until 8am the next day, and perform one last feat, the *encierro de la villavesa*: the bulls are all dead so they run in front of a bus.

The not always tremendously popular *francos* invited to Pamplona by Sancho the Great lived just to the east in their two rival quarters named after, and defended by, 13th-century churches that doubled as fortresses when their fellow citizens went on the war path. These are **San Saturnino** (or San Cernín) in C/ San Saturnino and **San Nicolás** in lively, bar-lined C/ San Nicolás; a plaque by the former marks the site where the first Pamplonans were converted by San Saturnino. To the west, **San Lorenzo** is best known for its chapel dedicated to San Fermín, built by the city in 1717, where his bust reliquary quietly resides 51 weeks of the year, presiding over weddings; so many Pamplonese want to be married under his protective eye that there's a two-year waiting list.

Pamplona is well endowed with parks: good for naps during the fiesta. The oldest, the French-style **Parque de la Taconera**, closes the west end of the Casco Viejo and has one of the city's nicest cafés, the **Vienés**, in a charming old kiosk. Just south, the star-shaped **Ciudadela**, built on the orders of Philip II, now has a green park inside and outside the steep walls. The immaculate new **Parque Yamaguchi** is named after Pamplona's Japanese 'twin', and has a neat Japanese garden complete with lakeside wooden house for the tea ceremony. Also here is one of Pamplona's newest attractions, a tall, fat red-and-blue tower containing the **Planetario** (*open Aug–Sept 11.30–1.30 and 6–9, Oct–June 9.30–1.30 and 5.30–9; adm*). The city's prettiest garden, **Parque Media Luna**, lines the river east of the city and has a path ending at the medieval bridge, the Puente de Magdalena, used by the pilgrims. The park in front of the **Plaza de Toros** – the third bullring largest in the world – was renamed Paseo Hemingway and has a grizzled bust of the writer whose *The Sun Also Rises* (1926) made Pamplona a household word.

West of Pamplona:
Aralar and San Miguel in Excelsis

Navarra's magic mountain, **Aralar**, is a favourite spot for a picnic or Sunday hike from Pamplona, gracefully wooded with beech, rowan and hawthorn groves. It has been sacred to the Basques since Neolithic times, when they erected 30 dolmens and menhirs in the yew groves around Putxerri, the biggest concentration of Neolithic monuments in all Spain. On top is Navarra's holy of holies, the **Sanctuario de San Miguel in Excelsis** (*open 9–2 and 4 to sunset*), on a panoramic north–south road that climbs over Aralar between Huarte Arakil and Lekunberri.

The gloomy stone chapel, built by the count of Goñi, was consecrated in 1098. Traditionally guarded by mastiffs (although we didn't see any), the chapel has had an empty air ever since French Basques plundered it in 1797, when they knocked off St Michael's head (or so say apologists who find the crystal head too weird); the hands of the desecrators were chopped off before they were put to death and nailed over the chapel door. You can see the chains worn by Teodosio de Goñi (*see* box on p.210) and the hole through which the dragon appeared; pilgrims still stick their heads into it, although no one remembers why. A high-tech alarm system protects the recently

Getting Around

Most **trains** between Pamplona and the main junction of Altsasu stop at Huarte Araquil.

Tourist Information

Lekunberri: Plazaola 21, t 94 850 72 04, *oit.lekunberri@cfnavarra.es.*
Altsasu: Plaza de los Fueros, t 94 846 83 43.

Where to Stay and Eat

**Hs Ayestarán II, C/ Aralar 22, Lekunberri, t 94 850 41 27 (*inexpensive*). Has a pleasant old-fashioned atmosphere, as well as tennis, children's recreational facilities, a pool and garden; *menús* feature home-cooked stews, stuffed peppers and cod with almonds.

San Miguel de Aralar, t 94 856 10 66. The pilgrims' hostel next to this church is rugged and comfortable enough, but isn't famous for its food.

*Hs Basa Kabl, Leitza, t 94 851 01 25, *basakabi@ jet.es* (*inexpensive*). You can sleep and eat reasonably at this place right in the centre.

Asador Betelu, t 94 851 30 26. Between Betelu and Azpirotz; attracts hordes of hungry diners. *Closed Thurs eve.*

Taverna Oilade, Leitza. Functions as the town beanery, bar, mess hall and gambling den; good fish soup and other filling dishes (*inexpensive*).

Restaurant Iru-Bide, Avenida Pamplona, Altsasua t 94 846 77 16. Small local bar with a *comedor* at the back; the TV is on all the time, but the food is excellent (*inexpensive*).

stolen, but recently recovered, enamelled Byzantine *retablo*, showing the Virgin on a rainbow in a mandorla with the Christ Child; the only comparable work in Europe is the great altarpiece in St Mark's in Venice. Tentatively dated 1028, it was probably originally stolen from Constantinople by a Crusader and sold to Sancho the Great, who donated it to the chapel.

Around Aralar

Of the villages under the mountain, **Lekunberri** is the most orientated to tourism, but **Leitza**, just north, is a prettier choice, besides being the home of Basque legend Iñaki Perurena, the *arrejazotzale*, or champion heavy-stone weightlifter. Along the road to Tolosa, **Betelu** not only bottles Navarra's mineral water, but has a fun little roadside swimming hole with slides where the stream has been dammed.

Zudaire, south of Aralar, is the head town in a broken terrain called **Las Améscoas**, the refuge of the Carlists and delight of speleologists: most of the caves are located above Zudaire around **Baquedano**, with its craggy ravine and streams.

Aralar is hardly the only mountain in Europe dedicated to heaven's Generalíssimo: there's Mont-Saint-Michel in France, St Michael's Mount in England, Monte Sant'Angelo in Italy, to name a few. In art, Michael is often shown with a spear, not slaying as much as *transfixing* dragons to the earth: these are sources of underground water. And sure enough, the Sierra de Aralar is so karstic as to be practically hollow; under the sanctuary there's an immense subterranean river that makes moaning dragonish sounds, feeding an icy lake under a domed cavern.

Altsasu (Alsasua), below Aralar on the road to Vitoria (Gasteiz), is a typical Navarrese town 364 days of the year, but on Carnival Tuesday it goes atavistic with one of the most spectacular rural carnivals to survive in modern Europe, suppressed under Franco but revived in 1982. As the light fails, men appear dressed as *momotxorroaks*,

The Knight, the Dragon and the Archangel

In the 9th century, Count Teodosio de Goñi went off to fight the Saracens with his Visigothic overlord King Witiza. He was returning home when he met a hermit (the devil in disguise) who warned him that his wife was unfaithful. Seething with rage, the knight stormed into his castle, saw two forms lying in his bed and without hesitation slew them both (this was endemic in the Middle Ages; the same thing happened to St Julian the Hospitaller). When Teodosio ran out he met his wife returning from Mass, who told him, to his horror, that she had given his own aged parents the bed. Horrified, Teodosio went to Rome to ask the pope what penance he could possibly do to redeem his soul, and after three nights the pope had a dream that he should wear heavy chains in solitude until God showed his forgiveness by breaking them.

Binding himself in chains, Teodosio went up to the top of Mt Aralar and lived as a hermit for years. One day, when he was sitting next to a cave, a scaly green dragon emerged, smoke billowing from its nostrils. Teodosio implored the aid of St Michael, who suddenly appeared with his sword in hand and spoke to the dragon in perfect Basque: '*Nor Jaunggoitkoa bezaka?*' ('Who is stronger than God?'). The dragon slunk back into its cave and the archangel struck off the knight's chains and left a statue of himself – an angelic figure with a large cross on its head and an empty glass case where the face ought to be. Every year between March and August the figure goes on a fertility-blessing tour through a hundred Navarra villages; on Corpus Christi pilgrims walk or cycle up to the chapel to pay their respects.

half-demonic creatures bearing sharp wooden pitchforks, dressed in sheep skins, headdresses that cover their faces sprouting huge horns, and white aprons. A vat of bull's blood is brought out, and they cover hands, arms and apron with it, then set about each other with their pitchforks while the *heriotsaks*, the 'deaths', join in with their sickles, and witches and sorcerors dance around the *akerbeltz*, a great black billy goat, all to the sound of the *gaïtas*. As it gets increasingly violent, the leader of the *momotxorroaks* suddenly blows a horn, and all dance a mad, frenetic, high-kicking dance. And then it's over, and all the creatures retire to the bar. Visitors are not welcome, however, and could get hurt.

West of Pamplona: the Camino de Santiago

Few places in Europe can boast such a concentration of medieval curiosities as this stretch of the famous road (*see* **Culture**), where the mystic syncretism of the Jews, Knight Templars, pagans and pilgrims was expressed in monuments with secret messages that tease and mystify today.

From Pamplona to Estella

A short turn off the N111 (about 15km from Pamplona) leads to the old village of **Obanos**, and 1.6km beyond that village to a lonely field and **Santa María de Eunate** (*open 10–1 and 4.30–7, closed Mon*), a striking 12th-century church built by the Templars. The Templars often built their chapels as octagons, but this one was purposely made irregular, and is surrounded by a unique 33-arched octagonal cloister – hence its name 'Eunate' ('the hundred doors'). Many knights were buried here, and it's likely that its peculiar structure had deep significance in the Templars' initiatory rites. There are only a few carved capitals – some little monsters, and pomegranates on the portal, which oddly faces north. During its restoration, scallop shells were discovered along with the tombs – the church also served as a mortuary chapel for pilgrims. The lack of a central keystone supporting the eight ribs inside hints that Arab architects were involved in the building. The Romanesque Virgin by the alabaster window is a copy of the one stolen in 1974.

The *camino francés* from Roncesvalles (*see* p.228) and the *camino aragonés* converged at the 11th-century bridge in **Puente la Reina**, which hasn't changed much since the day when pilgrims marched down the sombre Rúa Mayor, where many houses preserve their coats of arms.

The pilgrims traditionally entered Puente la Reina through the arch of another Templar foundation, El Crucifijo, a church with scallops and Celtic interlaced designs on the portal and two naves. The smaller one was added to house a powerful 14th-century German crucifix left by a pilgrim, where the Christ is nailed not to a cross, but the trunk and branches of a Y-shaped tree. Towards the bridge, the church of Santiago has a weathered Moorish-style lobed portal and, inside, two excellent polychrome

Getting Around

By Bus
La Estellesa buses (t 94 821 32 25) from Pamplona stop at Puente la Reina and Estella (with a fancy neo-Moorish station) en route to Logroño five times a day.

Tours
Navark, t 94 855 39 54, t 94 855 50 22, f 94 855 17 45, *basaura@accesocero.es*. Guided tours of Estella and the district: monasteries, abandoned villages and archaeological sites.

Tourist Information

Puente la Reina: Casa Consistorial, t 94 834 08 45.
Estella: San Nicolás 1, t 94 855 63 11, *oit.estella@cfnavarra.es*.
Los Arcos: In the Casa Consistorial, t 94 844 10 04.
Viana: Plaza de los Fueros, t 94 844 63 02.

Where to Stay and Eat

Puente la Reina ✉ 31100
**Mesón del Peregrino, on the Pamplona road, t 94 834 00 75, f 94 834 11 90 (*moderate*). This stone and timber place isn't as old as it looks, but it has cosy, air-conditioned rooms and a pool, and serves up excellent meals with a French gourmet touch in a split-level dining room. *Closed Sun eve and Mon*.
**Hôtel Jakue, Calle Irunbidea, t 94 834 10 17. At the northern end of town, this modern, functional hotel has decent, comfortable rooms and a surprisingly good restaurant.
Fonda Lorca, in the main plaza. The cheapest option of all.

Estella ✉ 31200
***Irache, Ayegui (3km away on the Logroño road), t 94 855 11 50, f 94 855 47 54, *hotelirache@tsai.es* (*moderate*). The largest and most comfortable hotel, set in a 1970s *urbanización*, offering air conditioning and a pool.

14th-century statues. From Puente la Reina, the path (although not the road) continues up to atmospheric old **Cirauqui** propped on its hill, where the church of San Román has another multi-foiled portal framed in archivolts with geometric designs. The ancient road to the west of Cirauqui, paved with Roman stones, predates even the pilgrims.

Estella (Lizarra): the Town of the Star

A stop at Estella, known as Estella la Bella for its beauty, was much looked forward to by the pilgrims. It owes its foundation in 1090 to a convenient miracle: nightly showers of shooting stars that always fell on the same place on a hill intrigued some shepherds, who investigated and found a cave hidden by thorns, sheltering a statue of the Virgin. Returning from the siege of Toledo the same year, King Sancho Ramírez founded Estella on the opposite bank of the Río Ega from the old settlement of Lizarra (coincidentally the Basque word for 'star') and populated it with *francos*, or freemen: artisans, merchants and others who owed allegiance to no feudal lord (although, confusingly, most of these *francos* were also Franks from Gascony, who fought in the Reconquista for pay or piety's sake). Thanks to them, Estella has numerous fine medieval buildings; if many have been cropped, thank the Grand Inquisitor of Castile, Cardinal Cisneros, whose troops literally cut Navarra down to size in 1512 for Ferdinand the Catholic.

★Hôtel Yerri, Avenida Yerri 35, t 94 854 60 34, f 94 855 50 81. Another modern and well-equipped if rather bland establishment; it's a little bit of a walk from the centre.

★Pensión San Andrés, C/ Mayor 1, t 94 855 04 48 (*inexpensive*). Clean and central, this is a good bet for something a little less, with good-value family rooms.

★Hs Cristina, C/ Baja Navarra 1, t 94 855 07 72 (*inexpensive*). Run by a kindly woman.

Fonda Izarra, C/ Caldería, t 94 855 06 78 (*cheap*). The doubles here are the cheapest of all.

La Cepa, Pza Fueros 8, t 94 855 00 32. Specializes in Basque and Navarrese cuisine (*moderate*), with *menús degustación* at 3,000 and 4,000 pts/€18 and 24. *Closed all day Wed and most eves except Fri and Sat.*

Bar La Moderna, Calle Mayor 54. Lively, youthful bar with a little terrace serving excellent *pintxos*.

La Navarra, Gustavo de Maeztú 16, t 94 855 00 40. Another good bet, perhaps more for its medieval atmosphere than food, which is good if a bit pricey. *Closed Sun eve and Mon.*

Los Arcos ✉ **31210**
★★Hotel Monaco, Pza del Coso 22, t 94 864 00 00 (*moderate*).

★★Hs Ezequiel, La Serna 14, t 94 864 02 96, f 94 864 02 78 (*moderate*). Slightly dearer, though pilgrims get a 10% discount.

Viana ✉ **31230**
La Granja, Navarro Villoslada 19, in the centre, t 94 864 50 78 (*moderate–inexpensive*). Has rooms with bath and average cooking.

Hôtel Casa Armendariz, t 94 864 50 78, f 94 844 63 45. This is a cosy little spot in the centre of town; the rooms are small but the management is charming.

Borgia, Serapio Urra, t 94 864 57 81. Avant-garde décor is the setting for Aurora Cariñanos' temple of personal, imaginative cuisine, where you can dine on delectable dishes such as *pochas con caracoles al tomillo* (fresh haricot beans with snails and thyme) (*expensive–moderate*). The cellar is excellent. *Closed Sun eve and Aug.*

The most exciting time to visit Estella is the Friday before the first Sunday in August, when it holds the only *encierro* where women are welcome to join in the run, even if the bulls are really heifers with padded horns.

The arcaded main square, **Plaza de Santiago**, is on the newer, Estella side of town, where for pious pilgrims the most important monument is the **Basílica de Nuestra Señora de Puy**, built on the overlook where the stars fell on Navarra that night. The Virgin is still there, but the old basilica was replaced in 1951 with a concrete and glass star-shaped church. South of Plaza de Santiago, the highlight for art pilgrims is 12th-century **San Miguel**, the parish church of the *francos*, set on a craggy rock atop its original set of steps. Don't hesitate: march right up them for the magnificent portal, where Christ in Majesty holds pride of place among angels, Evangelists and the Elders of the Apocalypse, the favourite theme on church tympanums all along the *camino francés* in both France and Spain. On the left, St Michael pins the dragon and weighs souls; on the right, an angel shows the empty tomb to the three Marys. The top, sadly, fell to the Cardinal's tower-bashing squad, but the brackets are good, especially the man-eating wolf.

Near San Miguel you'll find Estella's medieval bridge, which pilgrims crossed to the Lizarra side to visit the 12th-century **San Sepolcro**, with a fascinating façade added in 1328 but again truncated by Cisneros. The tympanum has an animated Last Supper, Crucifixion, Resurrection and what looks to be the Harrowing of Hell; statues of the 12 Apostles flank the door; one of them appears to be holding a stack of pancakes. To the right of the bridge is the piquant centre of old Lizarra, with churches and palaces bearing proud coats of arms, most now occupied by antiques shops, along Calle de la Rúa ('street of the street'). The finest palace is the Plateresque brick **Casa Fray Diego**, now used as the *Casa de Cultura*. Off to the left was the *Juderia*, or ghetto, its 12th-century synagogue converted into **Santa María de Jus del Castillo**, where the apse is decorated with a rich assortment of Romanesque modillions. The church is dwarfed by the adjacent 13th-century **monastery of Santo Domingo**, recently converted into a retirement home. Further up, near the new bridge, a 16th-century fountain under a canopy of linden trees in **Plaza de San Martín** makes a delightful place to linger.

A curving flight of stairs leads up to the 12th-century **San Pedro de la Rúa** (*open in summer 10.30–1.30, and at 4.30, 5.30 and 6.30; adm*), defended by a skyscraper bell tower. The Moorish-inspired foiled arch of the portal is crowned by a relief of St James in a boat with stars, blessed by a giant hand emerging from the water. Inside, the church has its share of curiosities: a unique column made of three interlaced 'serpents', and the black Virgen de la O, a cult figure of the masons, who left their marks all over the church. The Baroque chapel to the left houses St Andrew's shoulder blade; the story goes that the bishop of Patras took it with him for good luck while making the pilgrimage in 1270. Luck failed him in Estella, where he died and was buried in San Pedro's cloister, along with his relic. The holy shoulder blade wasn't going to have any of this, and made itself known by a curious light that appeared over the tomb; in 1626, the day when Andrew was proclaimed patron of Estella, a burning vision of his X-shaped cross hovered over the church. Of the cloister, only two galleries survive, reconstructed after the castle above was blown up in 1572 and crashed down on top of it. The capitals are excellent, carved with the Lives of the Saints and the Apocalypse: the twisted column is a copy of a famous one in Santo Domingo de Silos in Burgos.

Over the years, Estella became a favourite residence of the kings, whose 12th-century **Palacio de los Reyes de Navarra**, opposite San Pedro, is one of the best-preserved civic buildings from the period. Prominent at street level, a capital bears the oldest known depiction of Roland, clad in scaly armour, fighting the equally scaly giant Ferragut; further up, another capital shows a scene of devils and animal musicians, including a donkey playing a harp. The palace now houses the **Museo Gustavo de Maeztú** (*open Tues–Sat 11–1 and 5–7, Sun 11–1, closed Mon; adm*), devoted to works by Estella's best-known painter (1887–1947). In the tourist office next door, take a look at the model showing the evolution of Estella between 1090 and 1990.

Around Estella

Estella is an important producer of DO Navarra wine, and the most interesting *bodega* to visit just happens to be the Benedictine **Monasterio de Irache**, 2km south at Ayegui (*open weekdays 10–2 and 5–7, Sat and Sun 9–2 and 4–7, closed Mon and Tues pm*). First recorded in 958, it later received a generous endowment from Sancho the Great, who helped finance one of the very first pilgrims' hospitals here. In 1569, Philip II moved the university of theology here from Sahagún (near Léon), where it remained, enjoying the same privileges as Salamanca until it closed down with the expropriation of monasteries in 1824. The complex is a handsome mix behind an eclectic façade. The entrance is through an elegant Plateresque door, leading into an austerely beautiful Romanesque church with three apses under a Renaissance dome, stripped of centuries' encrustation of altarpieces. The original Romanesque north door is decorated with hunting scenes, while the sumptuous Plateresque cloister has a bevy of grotesque and religious capitals. The small wine museum preserves Irache's 1,000-year-old custom of offering free drinks to pilgrims.

Twelve kilometres up the San Sebastián road, the **Monasterio de Iranzu** (*open daily 10–2 and 4–8; adm*) was founded in the 11th century by Cistercians, who chose to live in a dramatic ravine true to their preference for remote settings in the wilds. It was recently restored by the government of Navarra and given to the Theatine order. The monks will show you around their medieval kitchen and Romanesque-Gothic cloister with a hexagonal fountain and church.

South of Estella on the Ebro, **Lodosa** is famous for its *appellation contrôlée* red peppers, *pimientos del piquillo* (similar to the *piments d'Espelette, see* p.267), which are dried in long garlands over the white façades of the houses. Its church, San Miguel, has an immense rococo *retablo*.

Los Arcos, Sorlada and Torres del Río

After Estella, the pilgrims walked to **Los Arcos**, where, tucked off the N111, there is an arcaded *plaza* and a 16th-century church, Santa María, with a pretty cathedral-size Gothic cloister, carved choirstalls and frantic Baroque *retablos*. Seven kilometres north of Los Arcos at **Sorlada**, a grand 18th-century Baroque basilica belongs to **San Gregorio**

Ostiense, a once immensely popular saint who lost much of his influence to modern fertilizers. His story is told in the basilica's naïve paintings: back in 1039 locusts plagued the region so badly that a group of farmers walked to Rome and asked the pope for help. The pope had a dream that Cardinal Gregory of Ostia was the man for the job, and off he went to Navarra, where he preached and dispersed the locusts, an exertion that killed him after five years. He was buried at Sorlada and forgotten, until a light redirected farmers to his tomb. Remembering his good juju against the locusts (and their ancestral Celtic head cult), they would cart his skull reliquary around their fields, pouring water through the hole which made it into 'holy Gregory water'. Philip II had gallons of it sent down to water the orchards of the Escorial. Farming is so big that you can take an agricultural tour of the local *bodegas*, ostrich farm, preserve-makers and distilleries, t 94 844 11 42.

West of Los Arcos, **Torres del Río** has a striking, tall octagonal church, **Santo Sepolcro**, built in the late 12th or early 13th centuries by the Knights of the Holy Sepulchre, or some say the Templars; like Santa María Eunate, it may have been a mortuary chapel for pilgrims. The rather majestic cross-ribbed vaulting in the dome, with additional ribs springing from the four corners of the building, is exactly like that in the churches built in Córdoba under the Caliphs, all said to be ultimately modelled on the second mihrab in the Great Mosque there. The large windows of the exterior only admit a minimum of light inside. Hopefully restoration work will have been completed by the time you get there.

Viana: Where Cesare Borgia Bit the Dust

Viana, the pilgrims' last stop in Navarra, fits a lot of monumentality into a small space. Founded by King Sancho VII 'the Strong' in 1219 to defend his frontier with Castile, it became the hereditary principality of the heir to the throne of Navarra in 1423. Although its once-proud castle fell to Cardinal Cisneros' demolition programme, nobles and courtly hangers-on stayed on and built themselves splendid mansions with big coats of arms, the elegant 17th-century **Casa Consistorial**, crowned with an escutcheon the size of an asteroid, and the 13th–14th-century **church of Santa María**, hidden by a magnificent concave Renaissance façade based on a triumphal arch, with a coffered ceiling designed and carved by Juan de Goyaz (1549). Inside, the Gothic interior is quite airy and lovely, culminating in an intricate gilded Baroque retable.

The façade could be considered the tombstone of Cesare Borgia (1475–1507), whose memorial, all that is left of his desecrated remains, lies buried under the marker in front of the church. Now how did Pope Alexander VI's son and Machiavelli's hero end up in Viana? With the papacy and central Italy in his pocket by 1502, married to Charlotte, sister of the king of Navarre, and supported by France, Cesare had just embarked on a brilliant career as a ruthless Renaissance prince-assassin. When his father pulled the rug out from under him by dying suddenly in 1503, Cesare himself was too ill to get to the Vatican and influence the conclave to elect a Borgia candidate; according to Machiavelli's *The Prince*, it was the only political mistake he ever made. It proved to be fatal. Once Julius II, archenemy of the Borgias, was elected in late 1503, Cesare's conquests in Italy were frittered away in anarchy, the French turned against him, and he went from being on top of the world to a man whose life was in danger. He fled to Aragón, the cradle of the Borgias, only to be imprisoned by Ferdinand. The still-independent kingdom of Navarra proved to be his only refuge, and he died in a skirmish in Viana, fighting Castilian rebels.

From here the pilgrim's road continues to Logroño in La Rioja.

South of Pamplona to Tudela

The green Basque hills are a distant memory south of Pamplona; here the skies are bright and clear, the land arid and toasted golden brown after the last winter rains, except for the green swathes of vineyards in La Ribera, cradle of Navarra's finest, freshest rosés.

Getting Around

By Train

Trains linking Pamplona and Zaragoza call at Tafalla, Olite and Tudela.

By Bus

Conda buses (t 94 822 10 26) stop at Tafalla, Olite and Tudela on the way to Zaragoza.

By Bicycle

Hire a bicycle or mountain bike from **Chiquibike** in Tudela and Arguedas, t 94 882 52 01, t 689 695 660.

Tourist Information

Olite: Plaza Carlos III, t 94 874 17 03, *oit.olite@cfnavarra.es*.
Tudela: Plaza Vieja 1, t/f 94 884 80 58, *oit.tudela@cfnavarra.es*.

Market Days

Tafalla: Friday, on Plaza Navarra.
Olite: Wednesday, Paseo del Portal.
Fitero: Tuesday and Friday, on Plaza San Raimundo.

Sports and Activities

A number of firms offer excursions into the Bárdenas Reales in a 4x4 or on horseback: **Novotur**, t 94 826 76 15 and **Sietesuelas**, t 94 882 79 63, t 608 574329 (which also offers other nature tours and excursions to archaeological sites).

Erreka, t 94 822 15 06, *http://webs.navarra.net/erreka*. Half-day programmes to 3- or 5-day study trips of Las Bárdenas, with a chance to do adventure sports.

Doshaches Riding Club, t 94 872 60 49. Horse-riding through the dessert.

Camello Bizco, t 94 884 74 90, t 609 431 121, *camellobizco@mx3.redestb.es*. Mountain-bike tours.

Club Ippico Arbayœn and **Dos Haches**, t 94 888 02 71, t 608 084398, organise 5-day excursions on horses to visit the surrounding beauty spots, including the Bárdenas Reales.

Where to Stay and Eat

Tafalla ✉ 31300
**Hs Tafalla, on the Zaragoza road, t 94 870 03 00, f 94 870 30 52 (*inexpensive*). Has nice rooms and food, especially when the dishes involve asparagus, lamb and hake. *Closed Fri.*
Túbal, Plaza de Navarra 2, t 94 870 08 52. Chef Atxen Jiménez draws in diners from Pamplona and beyond with her delicious variations on classic Navarrese themes – *menestra de verduras* and innovations such as crêpes filled with celery in almond sauce (*expensive–moderate*). *Closed Sun eve, Mon and late Aug.*

Olite ✉ 31390
***Parador Príncipe de Viana, t 94 874 00 00, f 94 874 02 01 (*expensive*). Next to

Tafalla and Olite

In the 17th century, a Dutchman named E. Cock described Tafalla and Olite as the 'flowers of Navarra', and both have determinedly crowed Cock's sweet nicknames ever since. Old **Tafalla** has wilted a bit over the centuries and grass grows between the cobbles, but it still has an impressive Plaza Mayor and claims one of the finest and biggest *retablos* in the north: a masterpiece by Basque artist Juan de Ancheta tucked away in the austere church of Santa María.

Northwest of Tafalla, **Artajona** has the air of an abandoned stage set: majestic medieval walls with startlingly intact crenellated towers defend little more than the 13th-century fortress church of San Saturnino. This has a tympanum showing the saint exorcising a woman, watched by Juana the Mad and Philip the Fair of France, while the lintel shows Saturnino's martyrdom with the bull (*see* p.206). The Hispano-Flemish *retablo mayor* dates from 1515. This is the second church on the site.

the castle of Carlos III in the converted 13th-century Castillo de los Teobaldos. A garden, air-con and beautiful furnishings make castle-dwelling a delight, as do delicious Navarrese gourmet treats in the dining room.

★★Hotel Merindad de Olite, Rúa de la Judería 11, t/f 94 874 07 35 (*moderate*). Has pleasant rooms decorated in a quirky faux-medieval style. The restaurant, which boasts a huge fireplace, serves particularly good fish dishes, and a tasty lamb with *chilindron*, a kind of Navarrese ratatouille.

★★Casa Zanito, Rúa Mayor 16, t 94 874 00 02, *zanito@cmn.navarra.net* (*inexpensive*). Offers simple, cheerful rooms and excellent meals, based on market availability, topped off with good home-made desserts.

Gambarte, Rúa del Seco 13, t 94 874 01 39. A pleasant place serving the most reasonably priced food in town. *Closed last two weeks Sept.*

Ujué ✉ 31390

Accommodation in this area is restricted to *casas rurales*.

Casa El Chofer 1, t 94 873 90 11 (*cheap*). Come here for good rooms with private bath.

Mesón las Torres, t 94 873 81 05. This has long been *the* place to dine, with Navarrese taste treats and Ujué's special candied almonds (*moderate*).

Tudela ✉ 31500

★★Hs Remigio, C/ Gaztambide 4, t 94 882 08 50, f 94 882 41 23 (*moderate*). Because there is nowhere to stay in the old town, and prices are high elsewhere, this is likely to be your best bet. It's not far from the Plaza de Fueros, and is decorated with an old-fashioned rusticity.

★Hs Nueva Parrilla, Carlos III el Noble 12, t 94 882 24 00, f 94 882 25 45 (*moderate*). The only other moderately priced place to stay in Tudela.

Casa Ignacio, C/ Cortaderos 11, t 94 882 10 21. Tudela is the chief producer of the ingredients of Navarra's famous *menestra de verduras*: delicious asparagus, artichokes, peas, celery and lettuces. Book a table here to taste them at their freshest (*moderate*). *Closed Tues and 15 Aug–15 Sept.*

Iruña, Calle Muro 11, t 94 882 10 00. Another great place to try the local *menestra de verduras* (*moderate*).

Choko, Pza de los Fueros, t 94 882 10 19. An alternative with pretty views (*moderate*). *Closed Mon.*

La Estrella, C/ Carnicerías 14, t 94 841 11 21. Serves up good home cooking based on garden vegetables (*inexpensive*). *Closed 16–30 Sept.*

Cintruénigo ✉ 31592

Maher, C/ La Ribera 19, t 94 881 11 50. The most seductive reason to stop in the village is to dine at what is probably Navarra's best restaurant (*expensive–moderate*). Delicious Navarrese dishes with an imaginative *nouvelle cuisine* touch are served: traditional *menú* 3,000 pts/€18, or for a splurge opt for a *menú degustación*.

Artajona's walls, redone in the 14th century, were first built between 1085 and 1103 by the Templars and canons of Saint-Sernin (San Saturnino) of Toulouse, at a time when the counts of Toulouse were among the chief players in Europe, leading the First Crusade and fighting side by side with the Cid.

Near Artajona, the **Ermita de la Virgen** shelters a lovely bronze and enamel 13th-century Virgin holding a bouquet of roses and has two megalithic gallery tombs nearby.

Olite, south of Tafalla, is dwarfed by its huge, battlemented, lofty-towered **Castle of Charles III** (*open Mon–Sat 10–2 and 4–7; adm*), built for the king of Navarra in 1407. Each of its 15 towers and turrets has its own character, and restorers have made the whole thing seem startlingly new. Inside, the décor is Mudéjar; hanging gardens were suspended from the great arches of the terraces, and there was a *leonera*, or lion pit, and a very busy set of dungeons; the Navarrese royal families led messy, frustrated lives. At night the whole complex is illuminated with a golden light, creating a striking backdrop to performances in the summer Festival of Navarra. The castle's Gothic chapel, Santa María la Real (*open 9.30–12 and 5–8*), has a gorgeous 13th-century façade, and the Romanesque church of San Pedro (*same hours*) has an octagonal tower and portal adorned with two large stone eagles, one devouring the hare it has captured (symbolizing force) and the other, more friendly, representing gentleness.

East of Tafalla and Olite, **San Martín de Unx** has a superb crypt under its 12th-century church. From here a byroad branches south for the striking medieval village of **Ujué**, set on a hill corrugated with terraces, where a shepherd, directed by a dove (*ujué*), found the statue of the black Virgin now housed in the powerful 13th-century Romanesque-Gothic church of Santa María. The doorway has finely carved scenes of the Last Supper and the Magi, and the altar preserves the heart of King Charles II of Navarra. Every year since 1043, on the first Sunday after St Mark's day (25 April), the Virgin has been the object of a solemn pilgrimage that departs from Tafalla at 2am.

Tudela

Founded by the Moors, Tudela, the second city of Navarra and capital of La Ribera region, was the last town in Navarra to submit to Ferdinand the Catholic, and it did so most unwillingly. Before the big bigot, Tudela had always made a point of welcoming Jews, Moors and heretics expelled from Castile or persecuted by the Inquisition, and it was no accident that its tolerant environment nurtured three of Spain's top medieval writers: Benjamin of Tudela, the great traveller and chronicler (1127–73); the poet Judah Ha-Levi of the same period; and doctor Miguel Servet (1511–53), one of the first to write on the circulation of the blood.

Don't be disheartened by Tudela's protective coating of dusty, gritty sprawl, but head straight for its picturesque, labyrinthine Moorish-Jewish kernel, around the elegant 17th-century **Plaza de los Fueros**; the decorations on the façades recall its use as a bullring in the 18th and 19th centuries. The Gothic **cathedral** (*open daily 9–1 and 4–7, closed Mon and Sun afternoon; adm*) was built over the town's Great Mosque in the 12th century and topped with a pretty 17th-century tower. It has three decorated doorways: the north and south portals have capitals with New Testament scenes, while the west portal, the *Portada del Juicio Final*, is devoted to the Last Judgement, depicted in 114 different scenes in eight soaring bands. The delightful choir, behind its Renaissance grille, is considered the finest Flamboyant Gothic work in Navarra, carved with geometric flora, fauna and fantasy motifs; note, under the main chair, the figures of two crows picking out the eyes of a man – the dean who commissioned the work but refused to pay the sculptors the agreed price. The main altar has a beautiful Hispano-Flemish *retablo* painted by Pedro Díaz de Oviedo, and yet more chains from Las Navas de Tolosa. There's an ornate Gothic *retablo* of Santa Caterina and a chapel of Santa Ana, patroness of Tudela, with a cupola that approaches Baroque orgasm. The 13th-century **cloister**, with twin and triple columns, has capitals on the Life of Jesus and other New Testament stories, while the Escuela de Cristo, off the east end of the cloister, has Mudéjar paintings and decorations.

Among the best palaces are the **Casa del Almirante**, near the cathedral, and, in the C/ de Magallón, the lovely Renaissance **Palace of the Marqués de San Adrián**. An irregular, 17-arched, 13th-century **bridge** spanning the Ebro still takes much of Tudela's traffic, with help from a new ultra-modern suspension bridge.

Around Tudela: a Desert, Water and Wine

Just east of Tudela is a striking desert straight out of the American Far West known as the **Bárdenas Reales**, where erosion has sculpted steep tabletops, weird wrinkled hills and rocks balanced on pyramids. The best way to see it (and not get lost) is by the GR13 walking path, which crosses its northern extent from the Ermita de Nuestra Señoro del Yugo. An easier way, however, is to go along on an organized excursion, by horse, mountain bike or 4x4 (*see* 'Sports and Activities', above).

South of Tudela, **Cascante** is known for its wines and church of the Virgen del Romero (Our Lady of the Rosemary Bush), built in the 17th century and reached by way of an arcaded walkway from the village below. The small spa town of **Fitero** (the waters are used in treating tuberculosis) grew up around the 11th-century Cistercian monastery of Santa María la Real, whose abbot, San Raimundo, founded the famous Order of the Knights of Calatrava in 1158. Don't miss the Romanesque Sala Capitular, a monumental *retablo* from the 16th century, the ornate 18th-century chapel of the Virgen de la Barda and, among the treasures, a 10th-century ivory coffer from the workshop of the Caliph of Córdoba. **Cintruénigo** and **Corella**, just north, are important producers of DO Navarra wine, with a good dozen *bodegas* in the environs.

East of Pamplona: Sangüesa, Javier and Leyre

Pilgrims to Santiago from Mediterranean lands would cross the Pyrenees at Somport in Aragón and enter Navarra at Sangüesa, home of one of the very best Romanesque churches and one of the craziest palaces in all Spain, but these days, if the wind's wrong, the pong of the nearby paper mill hurries visitors along; note that

Tourist Information

Aoiz: t 94 833 65 98.

Sangüesa: C/ Mayor 2, t 94 887 14 11, oit.sanguesa@cfnavarra.es. Guided tours of the monuments (a good way to be sure to find them open) are organized by El Claustro, t 94 843 04 97.

Javier: t 94 888 03 42.

Where to Stay and Eat

Aoiz ✉ 31430

*Hs Beti Jai, Santa Agueda 4, t 94 833 60 52 (*inexpensive*). Has a few rooms and an excellent restaurant (*moderate*), a soul-satisfying, good-value mix of the best regional traditions with the most modern techniques; the hake in langoustine sauce is especially good. Lovely riverside views. *Closed Mon.*

Sangüesa ✉ 31430

**Yamaguchi, on the road to Javier, t 94 887 01 27, yamaguchi@interbook.net (*inexpensive*). A cosy place with a pool and nice restaurant.

**Hs Las Navas, C/ Alfonso El Batallador 7, t 94 887 00 77 (*inexpensive*). Another small place, slightly cheaper.

Mediavilla, C/ Alfonso El Batallador, t 94 887 02 12. A Basque *asador* serving delicious charcoal-grilled fish and meat with excellent local wine (*moderate*). *Closed Mon.*

Javier/Leyre ✉ 31411

****Hotel Señorio de Monjardín, Ctra. de Leyre s/n, t 94 888 41 88, f 94 888 42 00 (*expensive*). A brand new hotel 3km from Leyre on the N240 with some luxurious suites and a restaurant featuring Navarrese cuisine and seasonal game dishes.

***Xavier, t 94 888 40 06, f 94 888 40 78 (*moderate*). You can stay and eat next to the castle at this antique place.

*El Mesón, t 94 888 40 35, f 94 888 42 26 (*inexpensive*). Also next to the castle but rather more basic.

**Hospedería de Leyre, t 94 888 41 00, f 94 888 41 37, info@monasterio-de-leyre.com (*moderate*). This charming former pilgrims' hostel at Leyre is the perfect antidote to stress; its restaurant specializes in traditional Navarrese cuisine. *Open Mar–Nov.*

if you go by bus from Pamplona (La Veloz Sangüesina, t 94 822 69 95), there are only three a day and you'll be stuck with the stink longer than you might like. If you're driving, there's enough of interest in the area to make a day's excursion.

Aoiz (Agoitz)

The area due east of Pamplona, crossed by the Río Irati, gets few tourists, but if you're driving, the undulating landscapes and nearly deserted villages make an interesting alternative to the more direct N240 to Sangüesa. Aoiz itself has fine old houses, a medieval bridge and the 15th-century **church of San Miguel Arcángel**, worth a look for its excellent *retablo mayor* (1580) by Basque master Juan de Achieta and its unusual 12th-century painted stone font. Romanesque connoisseurs should go out of their way to **Artaiz**, a tiny blip to the southwest (due south of Urroz), where the church of San Martín has the finest sculpture in rural Navarra, including some not too scary monsters.

Sangüesa

Sangüesa was a direct product of the pilgrimage, purposely moved from its original hilltop location in the 11th century to the spot where the road crosses the Río Aragón. In 1122, Alfonso el Batallador, king of neighbouring Aragón, sent down a colony of *francos* to augment Sangüesa's population, and 10 years after that ordered the

Knights of St John to build a church well worth stopping for: **Santa María la Real**. This possesses one of the most intriguing and extraordinary portals anywhere (unfortunately the street in front is quite busy, so you have to look at it between the cars), so strange that some writers believe that its symbols (knotted labyrinths, mermaids, two-headed beasts symbolizing duality, etc.) were sculpted by Cagots (*see* pp.222–3), or by a brotherhood of artists onto something deeper than orthodox Catholicism; even the damned are laughing in the *Last Judgement* on the tympanum, presided over by a Christ in Majesty with a secret smile and vigorous Evangelists almost dancing around the throne. Below, the elongated figures on the jambs show stylistic similarities to Chartres cathedral, although again the subjects are unusual: on the left the three Marys (the Virgin, Mary Magdalene and Mary Solomé, mother of St James), on the right Peter, Paul and Judas, hanged, with the inscription *Judas Mercator*. The upper half of the portal is by another hand altogether, crossed by two tiers of Apostles of near-Egyptian rigidity and another Christ in Majesty, surrounded by symbols of the four Evangelists. If the church is open, ask the sacristan to show you the capitals in the apse, hidden behind the Flemish Renaissance *retablo*. Note the well in the corner: not something you find every day inside a church. Walk around to see the beautiful carved corbels on the apse and the octagonal tower.

When Sangüesa came to be part of Navarra, the kings made it one of their several residences. Sangüesa's arcaded Rúa Mayor is lined with palaces, including the **Casa Consistorial**, built over the old royal patio of arms, today a charming leafy square; behind this is the austere 12th-century, twin-towered Palacio del Príncipe de Viana. The 12th-century **church of Santiago** has a huge battlemented tower and carved capitals, and conserves a large stone statue of St James, discovered buried under the floor in 1965. The slightly later, Gothic **San Salvador** has a pentagonal tower and a huge porch, sheltering a carved portal; its Plateresque choir stalls come from Leyre. Just around the corner, in C/ Alfonso el Batallador, the brick **Palacio Vallesantoro** catches the eye with its corkscrew Baroque portal and the widest, most extraordinary wooden eaves in Spain, carved with a phantasmagorical menagerie that makes the creatures on Santa María look tame.

Javier

Sanguesa is the base for visiting two of Navarra's holy sites. **Javier**, 13km away, is topped by a picturesque if over-restored battlemented castle, the birthplace in 1506 of Francisco de Javier (Xavier). In the complicated politics of Navarra, the Javiers were Basques who had supported the French d'Albrets and fought against the Castilians and Basques; Francis' father had died in battle and he went to live in exile, attending the University of Paris, where he met and roomed with a much older, war-scarred fellow Basque named Iñigo from Loyola, whose family had fought against his. Nevertheless, the two got along, at least socially; the charming, tall, athletic Francisco found his roommate's religious ardour and vows ridiculous and argued with him for two years before Iñigo won him over, and he became one of the seven founders of the Company of Jesus in 1534 (*see* pp.190–1). Francisco was the most talented and courageous of the early Jesuits, and in 1540, Iñigo sent him on a mission to the Indies and

Europe's Untouchables: The Cagots

Navarra, Basse-Navarre and Gascony are especially dense with reminders of the Cagots. At the back end of a village, or set outside it, there will be a quarter that the locals call the *ancien Cagotérie*. Or a parish priest will show you the special door in the side of the church, the only one they were allowed to use, or the *bénitier des Cagots*, the holy-water stoup reserved for them alone. Most of them were carpenters by trade, and wherever you see a really old market *halles*, or a wooden church steeple or a half-timbered house, chances are it was the Cagots who built it. The last full-blooded Cagot in Gascony died in the 19th century, although small communities of them were reported in obscure corners of the Basque country as late as 1902. But even as this mysterious people was fading away, French, Spanish and Basque writers and scientists were becoming interested in the strange story of these outcasts and who they really were.

The Cagots, under a number of different names, are mentioned in documents dating back to the 11th century: Crestias, Capots, Agots (in Basque), Ladres (Gascon for lepers), Gafets, Gézitains. People believed them to be lepers and forced a stringent code of apartheid on them: Cagots could not farm, or enter a mill or a tavern, or drink out of public fountains save the ones reserved for them; they were kept at the back of the church, and served Communion separately. Often they had their own church, and they always were buried in separate cemeteries. Although what remains of Cagot houses does not differ much from other dwellings, they were constrained to live apart, either in closed-off quarters of towns or in separate hamlets on the outskirts. In some localities they were forced to wear distinctive clothing, such as a goose's foot pinned to their tunics. There was an elaborate etiquette in everyday life to stop them coming into close contact with anyone else (in Navarra they had to play castanets at all crossroads and public places to warn people of their presence) and Cagots by law always married amongst their own kind. Although exceptions are recorded, almost all Cagots worked with wood; besides the master carpenters, they chopped trees for firewood, and made furniture, wooden plates and utensils. Back then it was believed that wood did not transmit diseases (a notion born out by modern science: bacteria survive much longer on plastic, for example).

One thing is certain – lepers they were not. Leprosy, though a continuing scourge in the Middle Ages, is not a hereditary disease, and the Cagots made up a caste that lived its separate life for centuries, without any evidence of chronic ill health – even though country people believed that even the touch of one would burn your skin. Plenty of guesses have been put forward as to their origins. Some held them to be descendants of Visigoths, caught behind after the Frankish conquests and reduced to servitude. Others claimed the first Cagots were Moorish slaves, brought back by the many Gascon lords who went to Spain to hire themselves out in the battles of the Reconquista. Miscellaneous conjectures include refugee Cathar heretics after the Albigensian crusade, Jews, religious excommunicates, or even Gypsies.

Others believe, using Sangüesa's church as a prime example, that the Cagots were only symbolic lepers, kept at a distance for the stigma of their heresies (curiously, one of their alternative names, Crestias, or Christians, seems only to emphasize that they were still, really, in the fold). This heresy may have been a highly contagious kind of universal mysticism practised by the Templars or the Order of the Knights of St Lazarus, an order founded in the East before the Templars and devoted to the care of lepers, using Lazarus as their symbol of death within life.

The most reliable contemporary accounts of Cagots suggest they really didn't look much different from anyone else. And as for their origin, the correct answer might be 'all of the above, among others'. The most plausible hypotheses have the children of lepers still living apart, by habit or by force, in the old leper colonies that were once found all over the region. Over the centuries, they were possibly joined by any and every sort of vagabond and refugee seeking a new life in this more tolerant, semi-autonomous, out-of-the-way corner of Europe. The main pilgrimage routes to Compostela converged in Navarra – the last stop before the difficult crossing over the mountains – and a huge number of people made the trip each year (many of them forced to do it as penance or punishment for crimes); more than a few would be likely to stay. To these, add the people attracted by the huge land-clearing and building programmes of the 13th century (most of which welcomed criminals and anyone else willing to work) and it is easy to imagine all the loose ends of Europe piling up here on the Pyrenees. Neighbouring French-controlled Languedoc had no Cagots, but it did see several massacres of Jews and vagabonds in the 14th century (in medieval times, the lands of the king of France were never a very healthy place for minorities of any sort). Perhaps the stigma of being a Cagot was a worthwhile trade for a peaceable life for some people. Still, the mystery will probably never be solved. Why, for example, were they called Crestias (Christians), and why, in the Middle Ages, were they exempt from civil law and taxes, subject only to Church laws and courts?

The end of the story is as remarkable as the beginning. On the French side, the Cagots themselves seem to have undertaken an epic civil rights struggle and, incredibly enough in the context of *ancien régime* France, they eventually won. Although in 1479 a medical inquest by the Parlement of Toulouse concluded that they were not diseased in any way, it still took until 1627 to get the Parlement to publish an ordinance prohibiting local officials from persecuting the *maîtres charpentiers* (as they preferred to be known). From 1680 onwards, they fought for the right to be buried in common ground; decades later, men began marrying Cagot women, and finally a prototypical Rosa Parks, a Cagot named Michel Legaret, got fed up one Sunday and stepped right up to the front of the church. He got a hundred days in the jail for that, an outrage that finally moved the Bordeaux Parlement to outlaw all segregation.

Winning in court proved much easier than raising the consciousness of their fellow men. Throughout the 18th century, Parlements and church officials often had to intervene in remote villages, where peasants resisted the new laws and sometimes resorted to violence. By then the Cagots' numbers were on the decrease, as men found they could take their skill and make a living elsewhere or move to the colonies where no one had ever heard of a Cagot, let alone knew how to discriminate against one. The definitive end of Jim Crow came with 1789 and the Declaration of the Rights of Man; in return, grateful Cagots signed up for the army in large numbers to defend the Revolution. After that, there were no more Cagots, only Frenchmen.

Japan, where in the face of all obstacles (notably from European traders) he became the Church's most successful missionary since St Paul. He died en route to China in 1552, was canonized at the same time as St Ignatius, in 1622, and was later declared the apostle of Japan and the Indies, the patron saint of missionaries.

Although the castle is now a Jesuit college, you can take the tour (*open 9–1 and 4–7; adm*) and learn a lot, about both St Francis and castles – this one dates back to the 11th century, was wrecked in 1516 by Cardinal Cisneros' troops, and was restored after 1952. Perhaps most fascinating is the fresco of the *Dance of Death*, a grim reminder that the Pyrenees were especially hard hit by the plague.

Leyre

Just north of Javier, at **Yesa**, the Río Aragón has been dammed to form the vast **Yesa Reservoir**. A road from Yesa leads up into the beautiful Sierra de Leyre and to the **Monasterio de San Salvador de Leyre** (*open daily 10.15–2 and 3.30–7; adm*). *Leyre* in Basque means 'eagerness to overcome'. The monastery's foundation predates the Moors, and its abbots served as the first bishops of Pamplona. In the 8th century its most famous abbot, San Virila, so constantly prayed to heaven for a peek into infinity that he was granted his wish, by the lovely warbling of a bird. To the abbot, the vision was a sublime moment, but when he went down to tell his monks about it he found that all had changed – his eternal second had lasted 300 years. This means he missed the precarious 9th century, when Leyre temporarily served as a refuge for the king of Pamplona from the Moors; the first kings of Navarra were buried there.

Located on the pilgrimage road branching in from Aragón, Leyre essentially dates from the 11th century, when Sancho the Great reformed the rule according to that of Cluny and declared it 'the centre and heart of my realm'. Abandoned in the 19th century, the monastery was reoccupied in 1950 by the Benedictines, who began a restoration programme that unfortunately obscures much of the older building. Visits begin in the startling, 11th-century **crypt**, where the first impression is that the church is sinking into the ground. The columns are runty little stubs of columns of unequal height weighed down by heavy block capitals, carved with simple geometric designs that stand at about chest level. The architect, it appears, was torn between the desire for ennobling capitals and columns and the need to provide the vaulting to support the chancel area above; a compromise, perhaps only possible for an architect who never studied his classical proportions, although to us it may look like some postmodernist Romanesque Expressionist having fun with our perceptions. The chancel above was consecrated in 1057, modelled on a French Romanesque design from the Limousin, and supplemented two centuries later with a single-aisled nave; the effect is harmonious, light and austere, providing the perfect setting for the Benedictines' beautiful 7th-century Gregorian chants, still sung at matins and vespers (*t 94 888 41 50; Mon–Fri 7.30am, 9am, 7 pm and 9pm, Sun and hols 8am, midday, 7pm and 9pm*). The bones of the first 10 kings of Navarra lie in a simple wooden casket behind a fine grille; the 13th-century statue of the Virgin of Leyre sits on the altar. The west portal, the **Porta Speciosa**, is finely carved with a mix of saints and monsters.

If Rip Van Winkle legends don't faze you, it's a 10-minute walk up to the **Fountain of San Virila** for the magnificent view of the artificial lake and the Navarrese countryside that the abbot contemplated during his prayers, although the warbling birds have been replaced by hang-gliding Spaniards. Nature is a big attraction in eastern Navarra. The Sierra de Leyre divides the Roncal and Salazar valleys (*see* below), but there are two splendid gorges quite close at hand. The **Hoz de Lumbier**, formed by the Irati river, has a pleasant riverside trail for walking or cycling, and is a breeding site for griffon vultures and the rare red-beaked variety of chough. The even more spectacular, sheer-sided, 6km **Hoz de Arbayún** (*see* p.228) lies further to the north along the Río Salazar, with more griffon and a few Egyptian vultures; both gorges are accessible from Lumbier.

Routes Into France:
Up the Valleys of the Pyrenees

The Navarrese Pyrenees don't win altitude records, but they're green, wooded and shot through with legends, many lingering in the mists around Roncesvalles, for centuries the pass most favoured by French pilgrims to Santiago. Much of Navarra's Basque population is concentrated in the three valleys of Roncal, Salazar and Baztán (confusingly divided in the *ley del vascuence*, or 'Basque law', of 1986 into three different linguistic zones). Seemingly every house in every hamlet is emblazoned with a coat of arms – for the Basques have traditionally considered themselves all equal and therefore all noble.

The Eastern Valleys: Valle del Roncal and Valle de Salazar

Like many Pyrenean valleys, the Roncal was so remote for centuries that the central authorities were content to let it run its own show. Time has changed a few things: timber logged on its thickly forested slopes now travels by truck instead of careering down the Esca river, and the valley's renowned sheep's cheese, *queso de Roncal*, is now made in a factory (but according to farm traditions). Mist often envelops **Isaba**, the Valle del Roncal's biggest town, gathered under its fortress-church of San Cipriano (1540). Every 13 July since 1375, at stone frontier-marker no.262, the mayor of Isaba and his colleagues don traditional costume, march up to meet their counterparts from the Valle de Baretous in France, and ask them three times for the 'Tribute of the Three Cows' in exchange for the right to graze their herds in the Valle del Roncal in August – something both sides used to kill for before the annual tribute was agreed on. Isaba provides an excellent base for exploring the magnificent mountain scenery: hike up the region's highest peaks, **Pic d'Anie** (8,200ft) and **Mesa de los Tres Reyes** (7,900ft), or make the most beautiful walk of all, into the Parque Natural Pirenáico to the **refugio de Belagua**, set in a stunning glacial amphitheatre.

Roncal, once the capital of the valley, is a pretty village surrounded by pine forests. The great, amiable Basque tenor Julián Gayarre (1844–90) was born here and lies buried in a suitably high-operatic tomb just outside town; the **Casa-Museo Julián**

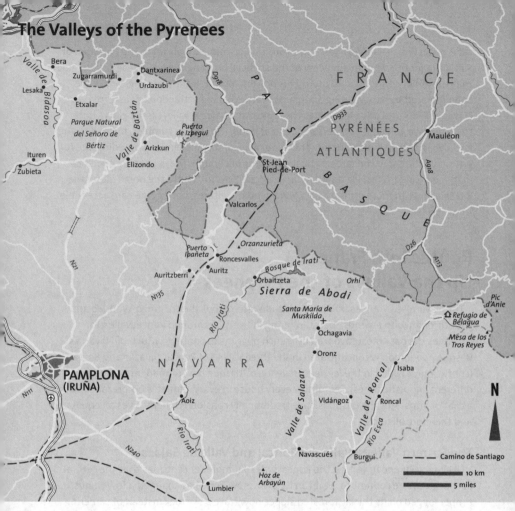

Gayarre (*open Tues–Sun 10–1.30 and 5–7, 4–6 in winter; adm*) contains costumes and photos from his glory days. **Burgui**, south, has a Roman bridge and two roads that cut over to the Valle de Salazar: an easy one westward to Navascués and a narrow one northward by way of the remote village of Vidángoz.

The sparsely populated **Valle de Salazar** is much less visited but just as lovely, abubble with trout streams, beech forests and old white stone Basque *caserónes*, or mansions, with their pompous coats of arms. The best line the riverfront and cobbled lanes in **Ochagavía**, the local metropolis and another good base for walks. An easy one is up to the 13th-century **chapel of Santa María de Muskilda**, topped by an unusual square tower with a round roof: its *romería* (pilgrimage) on 8 September is celebrated with some of Navarra's most ancient dances.

To the north, a road twists through the Sierra de Abodi to the snow-white **hermitage of Nuestra Señora de las Nieves** (1954): from here, trails of varying length and difficulty lead into the vast beech and ancient yew **Forest of Irati** (Bosque de Irati), the largest primeval forest in Spain, with majestic Mt Orhi (6,618ft) as a backdrop. This

Getting There and Around

By Bus

There are no trains here, and in most cases the buses from Pamplona go only once a day.

La Tafallesa (t 94 822 28 86) and **La Roncalesa (t** 94 830 02 57) both serve the Valle del Roncal; they stop at Yesa, near the lake, and 4km from the monastery of Leyre (*see* below).

For the Valles de Salazar and Aezkoa, **Río Irati (t** 94 822 14 70) has one bus daily to Ochagavía, and one to Orbaitzeta.

For Roncesvalles, you can go as far as Auritz (Burguete) and walk 3km (**La Montañesa, t** 94 821 15 84).

La Baztanesa (t 94 822 67 12) serves the Valle de Baztán.

Tourist Information

Roncal: Calle Gayarre, **t** 94 847 52 56, **f** 94 847 53 16, *oit.roncal@cfnavarra.es*.
Ochagavía: On the main road, opposite the river, **t** 94 889 06 41, **f** 94 889 06 79, *oit.ochagavia@cfnavarra.es*.

Where to Stay and Eat

Navarra as a whole has made efforts to improve the provision of reasonably priced accommodation in rural areas. Traditional houses have been restored as *casas rurales,* or bed and breakfasts: write to the Pamplona tourist office for their *Guía de Alojamientos de Turismo Rural.*

A central reservation office, **t** 94 822 93 28, **f** 94 821 20 59, will book beds for pilgrims along the Camino de Santiago.

Valle del Roncal ⊠ 31680

★★★Isaba, Ctra. Roncal s/n, Isaba, **t** 94 889 30 00, **f** 94 889 30 30, *hotelisaba@ctv.es* (*moderate*). New, luxurious and with the most modern rooms in the valley, as well as a sauna and gym.

★Hs Lola, Mendigatxa, Isaba, **t** 94 889 30 12, *www.hotelesruralesnavarra.es* (*inexpensive*). Provides good rooms and a restaurant.

Pensión Txiki, Mendigatxa, Isaba, **t** 94 889 31 18 (*inexpensive*). Offers reasonable half-board rates.

Pensión Txabalkua, Izargentea 16, Isaba, **t** 94 889 30 83. One of the cheapest options for half-board rates.

★Hotel Ezkurra, Ezkurra, **t** 94 889 33 03, **f** 94 889 33 02 (*inexpensive*). Tucked away down a back street, this classic mountain *hostal* has comfortable rooms and a cosy top-floor sitting room, complete with fireplace and stunning mountain views.

Venta de Juan Pito, Puerta de Belagua (at the mountain refuge), **t** 94 889 30 80. You can try inexpensive local dishes here, such as *migas pastor* (fried bread) and Roncal cheese. *Open July–Sept; rest of year weekends only.*

In Roncal itself choose between:

★Hs Zaltua, Castillo 23, **t** 94 847 50 08 (*moderate–inexpensive*).

Pensión Begoña, Bº Castillo 118, **t** 94 847 50 56 (*inexpensive*).

Ochagavía ⊠ 31680

Most accommodation in the Salazar valley is in *casas rurales.*

Casa Ballent, t 94 889 03 73 (*inexpensive*). One of the best, with cosy bedrooms, a welcoming owner and views from the terrace over the Pyrenees and the communal vegetable patch.

★Hs Ori-Alde, t 94 889 00 27 (*cheap*). A 12-room place featuring Basque cooking in the kitchen. *Open July–Oct.*

Auñamendi, Pza Guarpide 1, **t** 94 889 01 89, *auniamendi@jet.es* (*moderate–inexpensive*). As well as offering rooms, this place serves trout with ham and a good asparagus and prawn pudding.

★★Hs Salazar, C/ Mayor s/n, Oronz, **t** 94 889 00 53, **f** 94 889 03 70 (*inexpensive*). Just south of Ochagavía, with a pool and pretty views.

Orbaitzeta ⊠ 31670

There are no hotels here, and only a handful of *casas rurales.*

Casa Mujurdin, t 94 8/6 60 46 (*cheap*). Has just two rooms with shared bath in a classic Basque stone house.

Casa Sastrarena, t 94 876 60 93 (*cheap*). Offers rooms with private bath at a slightly higher price.

is one of the richest wildlife habitats in the Pyrenees, full of red squirrels, deer and wild boar, with lesser populations of wild cat and beech marten. The area also contains a couple of real rarities: the white-backed woodpecker, found only where there are plenty of insect-ridden beech trees, and the endemic Pyrenean Desvan, an aquatic shrew with a nose like a dragon's snout.

Besides the usual Basque fairy folk, the forest is haunted by a rather unexpected ghost: that of Jeanne d'Albret, queen of French Navarre and mother of Henri IV, a nasty, diehard Protestant fanatic. Poisoned in 1572, Jeanne tours her old domain on windy nights with an escort of lovely Basque *lamiaks*, the mischievous nymphs with whom she never would have been caught dead while still alive.

On the other side of the forest, the picturesque village of **Orbaitzeta** makes a good base for explorations; nearby, a dolmen called **Azpegi I** is surrounded by a circle of 123 stones.

In the south of the valley, the spectacular 1,000ft sheer-sided limestone gorge, the **Hoz de Arbayún**, extends for 10km below the road, home to Spain's largest colonies of rare griffon vultures (*buitres*), with their 8ft wing span, and an assortment of smaller eagles; you can nearly always spot them floating majestically around the roadside belvedere between Navascués and Lumbier.

Roncesvalles (Orreaga)

Of all the passes over the Pyrenees, introverted Roncesvalles ('Bramble Valley') is the most renowned, thanks to the *camino frances* to Compostela (*see* pp.57–9). French pilgrims would mumble verses from the *Chanson de Roland* as they paid their respects to the sites associated with Charlemagne and his nephew Roland, then say their first prayer to another gallant knight, Santiago. From Roncesvalles' Colegiata it's 781km to Compostela, a distance the fittest pilgrims could cover in 20 days.

Not so long ago the Colegiata had a sad, has-been look. Although in the 18th century, Roncesvalles still counted 30,000 passing pilgrims a year, numbers fell dramatically in the 19th century. Most of the monasteries and churches along the route were closed forever with the national confiscation of church lands in 1837; many were converted into stables or pillaged for their building stone. By the 1970s, the medieval floods of pilgrims had dried to a trickle of eccentrics.

But just when it seemed that the pilgrimage was ready to be pushed into Europe's closet of forgotten traditions, it came roaring back. A number of factors seem to be involved – modern disillusionment with conventional religion, the restless search for something beyond the routine of over-organized day-to-day lives and, more prosaically, the growth of ecological and alternative tourism. In 1982, John Paul II became the first pope ever to visit Santiago; in 1985, UNESCO declared it the 'Foremost Cultural Route in Europe', helping to fund the restoration of the churches that punctuate the trail. Although modern roads have changed the face of the *camino frances* forever, efforts have been made to create alternative paths for pedestrians, marked with scallop shells, and new inexpensive *hostales* have sprouted along the way for walkers or cyclists. No one predicted that in the 1990s the number of pilgrims who stopped to have their documents stamped in Roncesvalles would grow

Tourist Information

Roncesvalles: Antiguo Molino, t 94 876 03 01, oit.roncesvalles@cfnavarra.es.

Where to Stay and Eat

Roncesvalles ✉ 31650

If you have no luck at any of the places listed below, then try one of several *casas rurales* in the vicinity.

**Hs La Posada, t 94 876 02 25 (*inexpensive*). If you want to stay in comfort there are 18 spacious rooms in the Colegiata, with a fine restaurant located in the medieval inn that formerly served the pilgrims.

*Hs Casa Sabina, t 94 876 00 12 (*moderate*). Next to the monastery gate, with six pleasant rooms and good Navarrese cooking.

**Hs Loizu, in Auritz (3km from Roncesvalles), t 94 876 00 08, f 94 879 04 44, hloizu@cmn.navarra.net. Pretty little hotel-restaurant which offers plenty of atmosphere for its moderate rates.

**Hostal Burguete, Auritz, t 94 876 00 05 (*inexpensive*). Whenever Hemingway decamped to the Pyrenees he stayed here; though its elegance is mostly faded, this antiques-bedecked old place is still a great choice for slumming it in style.

by thousands each year. The pilgrims' quest is back in business; even Shirley McLaine has done it and written a book about her experience.

The three main pilgrims' routes through France converged at Saint-Jean-Pied-de-Port and then continued up to the busy frontier town of **Valcarlos**, the 'carlos' in its name referring to Charlemagne, who was camped here when he heard the dying Roland's horn blast. From here, the road winds up through lush greenery to Roncesvalles, where the 12th-century **church of Sancti Spiritus** (the 'Silo de Charlemagne') is said to have been first built as Roland's tomb. According to legend, by the time the emperor arrived, not only were Roland and the peers dead, but so were all the Saracens; since he couldn't tell who was who (poor Charlemagne – his legends always make him seem as thick as a pudding), he asked heaven for a sign to make sure he gave all the Franks a Christian burial, and all at once the Christian corpses looked up to heaven, with red roses sprouting from their lips. Equally unlucky pilgrims were laid in the 7th-century **ossuary** underneath the church; according to Aymeric Picaud (*see* p.59), many of these were done in by 'false pilgrims', most of whom were the locals. Adjacent, a 13th-century **church of Santiago** is neglected and nearly always locked.

Set back from the road, at the foot of the pass, the **Colegiata de Roncesvalles** is a French-style Gothic church consecrated in 1219, which replaced the first Colegiata, built up at Puerto Ibañeta in 112 and abandoned by the frostbitten monks after five ghastly winters. What was originally the front of the Colegiata caved in under the snow in 1600 (hence the incongruous corrugated zinc roof on the rest) and was replaced by a **cloister**, from where you can pop into the 14th-century chapterhouse to see the stained glass (1960) showing a scene from the 1212 Battle of Las Navas de Tolosa, where Sancho VII 'the Strong' led the Navarrese to their great victory over the Moors. The chains in the chapel are among those that bound 10,000 slaves at the ankle and wrist, forming a human shield around the emir's tent, a scurvy tactic that failed to prevent the Christians from leaping over and carrying off the tent as booty. The chapterhouse holds the **tomb of Sancho the Strong**. Apparently, in life

Roland the Rotter

All over the Pyrenees, you'll find memories of Roland – from the Brèche de Roland in the High Pyrenees, hewn with a mighty stroke of his sword Durandal, to a menhir on Mt Aralar that he tossed like Obelix. From here, his fame spread across Europe, remembered in everything from Ariosto's Renaissance epic *Orlando Furioso* to the ancient, mysterious statue of 'Roland the Giant' that stands in front of Bremen city hall.

But who is this Roland really? Outside of the *Chanson de Roland*, information is scarce. The chronicler Eginhardt, writing *c.* 830, mentions a certain Roland, duke of the Marches of Brittany – who perished in the famous ambush in the Pyrenees in 778 – without according him any particular importance. Two hundred years later this obscure incident had blossomed into one of the great epics of medieval Europe.

Here is the mighty hero, with his wise friend and companion-in-arms Oliver. Here is the most puissant knight in the army of his uncle Charlemagne, come down from the north to crusade against the heathen Muslims of Spain. Charlemagne sweeps all before him, occupying many lands south of the Pyrenees and burning Pamplona to the ground before coming to grief at the unsuccessful siege of Zaragoza. On their return, Roland and Oliver and the peers of the rearguard are trapped at the pass of Roncesvalles, thanks to a tip from Roland's jealous stepfather Ganelon. Numberless hordes of Muslims overwhelm the French; though outnumbered, they cut down

the king was exactly as tall as his 7ft 4in effigy: pilgrims used to think that his battle maces, now in the museum, belonged to Roland. Sancho financed the Colegiata, which over time has been stripped of its costly gifts, with the exception of a much revered 13th-century image of the Virgin under her baldachin. Its jumbled, anachronistic, pious legend goes that after the battle at the pass, Charlemagne founded a monastery up at Ibañeta. When the Moors poured through to attack France in 732, the monks hid the statue, and it remained hidden until 1130, when the hiding place was revealed to a Basque shepherd by a red stag with a star shimmering between its antlers.

The fascinating **museum** (*open Easter–Oct 10.30–1.30 and 4–6; Nov–Easter 10–2 and 4–7; adm*) contains such rarefied medieval treasures as the emerald which fell from the emir's turban when giant King Sancho burst into his tent at Las Navas de Tolosa (surely it was a sight enough to scare the emerald off anybody); an 11th-century *pyx*, or golden box used to hold the Host; and a reliquary of gold and enamel called 'Charlemagne's chessboard' (*c.* 1350) for its 32 little cases, each designed to hold a saintly fingertip or tooth. Among the paintings there's an excellent 15th-century Flemish triptych and a *Holy Family* by Morales, and two books on Confucianism, purchased in India in the time of St Francis Xavier.

An easy and beautiful path from the monastery leads up in half an hour to the **Puerto Ibañeta** (3,150ft), from where the Basques, hidden on Mounts Astobizkar and Orzanzurieta, dropped boulders on the heads of the Franks. A modern chapel replaces the monastery of San Salvador, where the monks would toll a bell to guide pilgrims

Moors by the thousands, like General Custer or John Wayne against the savage Injuns. Finally Roland, cut with a thousand wounds, smites his sword Durandal against the rock, meaning to keep it from the hands of the infidels (although in the *Chanson* he ends up heaving it into the air, whereupon it finally ends up stuck in the cliff at Rocamadour, a major site on the pilgrims' road in southwest France). He then sounds his horn Oliphant to warn Charlemagne, alas too far away to rescue them, puffing so hard that he blows his brains out, as Michael and Gabriel appear to escort his soul to heaven. History says it wasn't a Muslim horde at all, but rather the Navarrese Basques who did Roland in. And why shouldn't they get their revenge on these uncouth Franks who were devastating their land, trying to force this democratic nation to kneel before some crowned foreign thug who called himself their king? We might excuse a people who did not even have a word in their language for 'king' if they were not much impressed with Charlemagne.

How this affair metamorphosed into an epic at the turn of the last millennium, or how the caterpillar Roland of history re-emerged as the mythological butterfly in the *Chanson* is murky, but as with most epics it involved a modicum of propaganda. The immediate source of the *Chanson* is said to have been a famous vision of Roland given to an 11th-century archbishop of Pamplona, which transformed Basque farmers into infidel knights (just in time for the Crusades). For the French there was another bonus: glorification of Carolingian imperialism provided poetic justification for the expansionist dreams of the Capetian kings.

through the mists and snow storms. Heading south, the pretty villages of **Auritz** (**Burguete**) and **Auritzberri** (**Espinal**) were the pilgrims' next stops and are still good places to stay.

Western Valleys: Valle de Baztán and Valle de Bidasoa

Frequent rains off the Atlantic make these valleys so lush that they're called the 'Switzerland of Navarra'. Both are dotted with well-preserved, unspoiled white Basque villages, trout streams and quietly beautiful scenery. One of the best-known smugglers' routes ran from the caves of Sare, just over the border in France, to the caves of Zugarramurdi; it still makes a pretty and easy walk today. But what Zugarramurdi is most famous for is its role as the Salem of the Basque lands.

The **Valle de Baztán** once had Spain's largest Cagot population (*see* pp.222–3) and perhaps not entirely coincidentally a supposed colony of witches in the early 17th century, based in **Zugarramurdi**, 'the Hill of Elms', a pretty place just in from the French frontier. As in Salem, the witchcraft scare began with the dubious confessions of a young woman in 1608, and spread like wildfire from denunciation to denunciation in a kind of mass hysteria. It wasn't long before 10 witches had confessed to a whole slew of heinous crimes, taking responsibility for nearly every death and trouble in Zugarramurdi that occurred over the past 50 years. According to Basque law, they were tried and pardoned. Then the Inquisition, based in Logroño, got wind of it. Thirty-one hapless souls, mostly women and children, were arrested and 'put to the question' in 1609; of those condemned, 13 died under torture and six,

Tourist Information

Elizondo: C/ Jaime Urrutia, t 94 858 12 79.

Sports and Activities

The old **smugglers' path** to Sare is easy to follow and waymarked with silhouettes of the little Basque horse, the *pottok*. **Orbela**, at Beintza-Labaien ✉ 31753, t 94 845 00 14, organizes full- or half-day guided excursions into the mountains of Baztan-Bidasoa; they also offer mountain bike tours down the old Bidasoa railway line, and spelunking excursions into one of the local caves, Lezealde-Labaien. **BKZ**, at the Albergue Bertiz Aterpea in Narbarte, t 94 859 23 22, t 94 859 21 16, f 94 859 21 02, *bidasoa@teleline.es*, offers white-water rafting and canoeing trips at all levels.

Where to Stay and Eat

Zugarramurdi ✉ 31710

Alzatenea, in the village centre, t 948 59 91 87. A charming little restaurant, specializing in roast meat cooked over a wood fire, served under an arbour (*inexpensive*).

Urdazubi ✉ 31711

Hostal Irigoienea, C/ Salvador, t 94 859 92 67, f 94 859 92 43, *hoirigoienea@jet.es* (*inexpensive*). This old Navarrese farmhouse furnished with a handful of antiques is a charming place to stay.

Menta, on the Dantxarinea road, t 94 859 90 20. Sitting out on the terrace, you can feast on a superb mix of French and Navarrese dishes, with game dishes in season (*moderate*); good wine list too. *Closed Mon eve and Tues.*

Elizondo ✉ 31700

★★★Baztán, on the main road, t 94 858 00 50, f 94 845 23 23, *hotelbaztan@biaipe.net* (*moderate*). Modern, with panoramic views, a pool and a garden. *Closed Dec–Mar.*

★★Hs Saskaitz, M. Azpilijueta 10, t 94 858 06 15, f 94 858 09 92, *hotelelizondo@biaipe.net* (*moderate*). Cosy enough, this has been tastefully refurbished. It's calm despite being in the centre of town.

Pensión Eskisaroi, t 94 858 00 13 (*moderate*). A cheaper option, which also does inexpensive dinners.

Casa Galarza, C/ Santiago 1, t 94 858 01 01. A rival to Roncal's offerings, this haven of traditional Baztanian cuisine and cheese serves *txuri-tabeltz*, a stew of lamb's tripe for which Elizondo is famous (*inexpensive*). *Closed Tues.*

Casa Rural Urruska, 10km away in Barrio de Bearzún, t 94 845 21 06. Simple but solid home cooking (*inexpensive*) is served while livestock baa and moo on the ground floor. It attracts hungry clients from all down the valley.

who refused to confess, survived to be burned alive at an *auto-da-fé*. Another 11 were burned the following year. That year, the Inquisition claimed to have discovered 1,590 witches in Navarra alone. No one really knows how much they suffered, or how many died.

Just outside the village, carved out of the mountain by the *Infernuko Erreka* ('Hell's Stream'), the vast **Cuevas de Zugarramurdi** (*open daily 9–7; adm*) were the scene of black sabbaths, or *akelarres*, in which the participants smeared themselves with an unguent made of human brains and bones – mixed with belladonna, toads, salamanders and snakes – and flew through the night to join in outrageous orgies with a Satanic black billy goat, *akerbeltz* – at least according to the confessions extracted by the Inquisitors.

Basque witchcraft enjoyed a revival in the post-Franco 1970s, when the cult was seen either as a feminist revolt against an oppressive male-dominated society and religion, or as an instance of pocket survivals of the old pagan beliefs, demonized by the Church, perhaps even practised as underground rituals of Basque solidarity.

Whatever the case, the inhabitants of Zugarramurdi have decided that it was all a splendid excuse for a hugely popular *Sorginak Besta* (Fiesta of Witches), to dress up and party on the Saturday closest to the summer solstice, and thousands gather in the caves for an old-fashioned re-enactment of an *akelarre*, complete with all kinds of philtres and magic potions.

Even older magic was built into the **cromlechs of Mairuillarrieta**, dedicated to the Basque goddess Mari, reached by a path from the village. There are other caves, the lovely stalactite **Cuevas de Urdax** just south at Urdazubi/Urdax, where fish-tailed *lamiak* once frolicked in the stream, or perhaps still do when no one's looking; guided tours run roughly every 20 minutes in the summer.

Elizondo, the chief village in the Baztán valley, has an informal tourist office where you can pick up a map that pinpoints the historic houses: those along the river are especially impressive.

Arizkun, 7km northeast, has the fortified stone house of one of Spain's busiest conquistadores, Pedro de Ursúa, leader of the search for El Dorado up the Amazon in 1560 when he was killed by rebel leader Lope de Aguirre (*see* p.188). The parish church has a striking Baroque façade. Further north a road turns east to France by way of the spectacular **Izpegui pass** (summer only).

Navarra's westernmost Pyrenean valley, the Valle de Bidasoa, embraces streams filled with salmon and trout and, more prosaically, the main San Sebastián–Pamplona road. Bus services in the area offer a chance to visit charming old Basque villages such as **Bera** (**Vera**) **de Bidasoa**, only a couple miles from the French frontier, where there's an ethnographic museum (*t 94 863 00 20 for an appointment*) in the former summer home of Basque novelist and doctor Pío Baroja (1872–1956). A member of the Generation of 98, Pío Baroja was a firm supporter of the Republic from the beginning, (*Memorias de un hombre de acción*), but he was also fascinated by Basque witchcraft, and made it a feature of one of his novels, *La Dama de Urtubi*. **Lesaka**, equally pretty, claims one of the best-preserved fortified feudal houses in Navarra. Tiny **Etxalar** (**Echalar**), a hamlet that time forgot, is on a stream on the pretty, seldom-used road to Zugarramurdi – seldom used except in October, during the annual wild pigeon and woodcock holocaust. The church at Etxalar is surrounded by 100 Basque funerary steles with their distinctive solar symbol discs.

Further south, the **Parque Natural del Señoro de Bértiz**, a former private estate, has foot, bicycle and riding paths through thousands of acres of oak, beech and chestnut forests; the gardens near the manor boast over 120 species of exotic trees (*garden open Mon 4–6, Tues–Fri 10–2 and 4–6, Sat and Sun 10–2 and 4–7*). Note the coat of arms of the lord of Bértiz, showing a mermaid holding a mirror and comb; Charles III ordered her to be placed there in 1421 in honour of the persuasive powers of his ambassador, Micheto de Bértiz.

Two villages just west of here, **Zubieta** and **Ituren**, are famous for a late-January ritual ushering in spring that could have been invented by Dr Seuss: young unmarried men and boys (starting as young as five) called *joaldunaks* dress up in striped dunce's caps and lacey smocks or sheepskins and fasten a pair of copper *polunpaks* (giant bells) to their backs with an intricate network of laces. Thus arrayed, for two days the *jouldunaks* make a *zanpantzar*, a group of 20 or so, who dance and march from village to village across the frosty land, their *polunpak* banging and clanging with deep resonance as they go along. It is all very serious, and this is one of those occasions when the Basques show their great age. The *joaldunaks* with their sheepskins and bells have a very close counterpart in the Mamuthones of Mamoiada, who perform a similar function in Sardinia, whose people are nearly as long in the tooth.

The Pays Basque

11

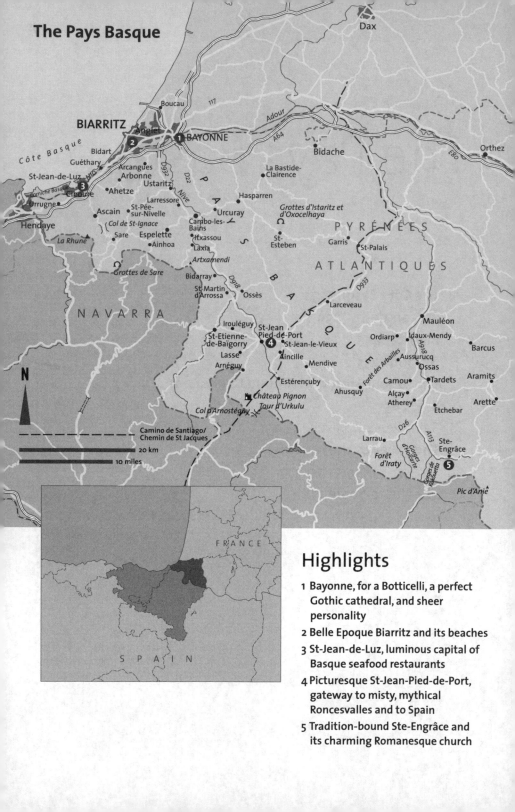

The Pays Basque

Highlights

1 Bayonne, for a Botticelli, a perfect Gothic cathedral, and sheer personality

2 Belle Epoque Biarritz and its beaches

3 St-Jean-de-Luz, luminous capital of Basque seafood restaurants

4 Picturesque St-Jean-Pied-de-Port, gateway to misty, mythical Roncesvalles and to Spain

5 Tradition-bound Ste-Engrâce and its charming Romanesque church

Of all the *départements* of France, number 64 is the one with the most remarkable split personality. Béarn, occupying the eastern half, is a resolutely Gascon province, redolent of garlic and castles and good Jurançon wine. But cross the Gave d'Oloron, a national boundary that does not appear on any map, and you're entering an entirely different world, where each village church has a *fronton* next to it and everything except the dog is painted white, green and red: specifically, the Pays Basque, or North Euskadi as the Basques prefer to call it.

The three little provinces in France are laid out in vertical stripes across the western half of the Pyrénées-Atlantiques: first, coastal Labourd (from *Lapurdum*, the Roman name of Bayonne), a delightful land full of beautiful villages, which also includes Bayonne and Biarritz where Basques have long been a minority, and with a string of resorts that the French tourist office has dubbed the Côte Basque; next, inland, Basse-Navarre (Behe-Nafarroa), with Pyrenean valleys in the south and hard-working farmers in the humble lowlands; and finally, the even humbler Soule (Zuberoa) around Mauléon, the most isolated Basque province, with a mere 14,000 inhabitants, last guardian of a unique dialect and old folk ways lost elsewhere.

The Basques, whose territory once extended to Bordeaux, have been losing ground in France ever since Roman times, and they worry that unless drastic measures are taken, especially in teaching Euskera to the young, they may vanish altogether. If the results of a recent survey, taken after the government's unprecedented proposal to grant an autonomy statute to Corsica, are any indication, two centuries of centralization policies and the comforts of the French social system have succeeded in dividing opinion on the future direction of the Pays Basque. A majority still favour their own *département basque* (as promised by Mitterand two decades ago) and mandatory bilingual schooling, yet the survey also found that only 22 per cent of the Basques considered themselves Basque first, before French or European.

Whether this might change thanks to the recent revival of Basque culture and media inspired by the renaissance over the border remains to be seen. Nationalist feeling remains strongest in the countryside, where the percentage of Euskera speakers remains high. We met one nationalist supporter in Basse-Navarre, a young mechanic on his way to a ping-pong tournament. With an earnest look in his eyes, he told us: 'They'll never let the Basque lands unite, because together we would be stronger than either France or Spain.' A marvellous people.

The Côte Basque

Hendaye and Urrugne

A booming resort at the crossing point into France, **Hendaye** is divided into two distinct units, the old town and **Hendaye-Plage**, on the coast. Hendaye's border location on the Bidassoa river puts it in the news every century or so, thanks to a small, uninhabited island in the Bidassoa called the **Ile des Faisans** (also known as Ile de la Conférence) that belongs to neither country (*see* p.192). In October 1940, Hendaye's

Tourist Information

Hendaye: 12 Rue des Aubépines, t 05 59 20
00 34, f 05 59 20 79 17, *www.hendaye.com*.
Urrugne: Maison Posta, Place René Soubelet,
t 05 59 54 60 80, f 05 59 54 63 49.

Market Days

Hendaye: Wednesday and Saturday.

Where to Stay and Eat

Hendaye ✉ 64700

Rather less attractive than Biarritz or St-
Jean, Hendaye is correspondingly less posh.
***Hotel Serge Blanco, Bd Mer, t 05 59 51
35 35, f 05 59 51 36 00 (*expensive*). Named
after the famous Basque rugby star who is
the proprietor and whose empire features a

thalassotherapy centre and a restaurant on
the beach.
**Lafon, 99 Bd de la Mier, t 05 59 20 04 67,
f 05 59 48 06 85 (*inexpensive*). A hotel
serving menus at 110–170F/€17–26.
**Santiago, 29 Rue Santiago, t 05 59 20 00 94,
f 05 59 20 83 26 (*cheap*). One of the least
expensive hotels around, and stays open
all year.

Urrugne ✉ 64122

Chez Maïté, Place de la Mairie, t 05 59 54 30 27.
Handy if you're stopping for lunch after a
visit to the Parc Floral Florenia gardens. Try
seafood, *poulet basquaise* and a choice of
very special home-made desserts. There are
100–140F/€15–21.5 menus, but it's worth
paying a little more for the specialities
à la carte.

train station was the scene of the famous meeting between Hitler and Franco. Hitler
had come down in his private train carriage (where the meeting took place) to bluster
the Caudillo into joining the war, seeing it as a tit-for-tat matter, since Germany had
very much helped Franco win his war. No one knows what actually passed between
the two, although Hitler would later comment that he would rather have his teeth
pulled than have to talk to the 'Sphinx' again. Franco, although he had little to say at
the time, would later boast how he saved Spain from the disaster of another defeat at
Hendaye. Perhaps he did, and it's an interesting point that during the war, Franco,
while occasionally paying lip service to Hitler, let Spain in fact become one place
where Jews were safe.

The **beach** is long and broad, though as a resort Hendaye can't match the charm of
the other towns along the Côte Basque. The area surrounding the sands is a bland
place lined with old villas, gradually being replaced by concrete hotels, the preserve of
family vacations. The old town offers nothing particularly special to draw you out of
your way, although you may want to take a tour of the **Château Antoine d'Abbadie**
(*t 05 59 20 04 53; open April–May and Oct daily 10–noon, June–Sept daily 10–2; 1hr tours
April–May and Oct on Tues, Thurs and Fri 3pm, June–Sept Mon–Sat 11am and 3, 4 and
5pm; 1½hr tours June–Sept Mon–Sat 10am; adm*), an eccentric Disneyland-Gothic
castle on a hill at the southern end of the beach, in a lovely area set aside as a natural
reserve. It was built in the 19th century by Viollet-le-Duc for an Irish-born traveller son
of a Basque family named Antoine d'Abbadie, who spent a lot of time in Ethiopia.
There's a large collection of mementos from that country, an observatory, and **Le
Domaine**, t 05 59 20 37 20, an exotic 110-acre park. The villa is covered with inscriptions
in Amharic and Gaelic.

Frisbees were invented in the 1950s during a pie-pan toss in a bakery in Connecticut,
but the idea may have been Basque all along. After all, they've been wearing the
felt equivalent of a frisbee on their heads since the early 19th century, and in

summer, Hendaye hosts the World Beret Tossing Championships (contact the tourist office for dates). The record so far is just over 86ft, perhaps nothing next to a tournament frisbee toss, but still a distance that one imagines other hats would find hard to beat.

Heading into the Pays Basque from Hendaye, you have a choice of either the coastal road, the scenic Corniche Basque (the D912), or the more inland N10 or the motorway; these two pass through **Urrugne** ('*la village à la rime qui repugne*', as Théophile Gautier rather unkindly put it), where the church of St-Vincent has a Renaissance portal with some excellent reliefs, damaged somewhat by English artillery in 1814. Note the famous inscription on the tower's sundial: *vulnerant omnes, ultima necat*, referring to the hours – 'each one wounds, the last one kills'. Inside, there is more good sculptural work, notably on the bishop's chair, supported by a figure the locals call 'Samson'; they say if you pull his nose you will grow strong, and you can bet all the aspiring Basque wagon-lifters and tug-of-warriors stop in to visit. The **Château d'Uturbie** (*t 05 59 20 82 72; tours offered April–Oct Wed–Mon at 11am and from 2–7pm; adm*), was the home of the medieval viscounts of the Labourdan, the first of whom was appointed by Sancho the Great of Navarra in the 11th century. The castle in its present incarnation dates from the 1340s, though each century up until the Revolution added its bits and pieces. Wellington made it his headquarters briefly in 1814. The interior has some impressive 17th–18th-century furnishings, and a fine set of Flemish tapestries.

From the village, a winding road leads up to the pilgrimage **chapel of Notre-Dame-de-Socorri**, with views over the mountains; it's a lovely spot for a picnic – although it may be disconcerting to know that nearly all the souls sleeping in the chapel's oak-shaded cemetery were victims of cholera epidemics.

Just outside Urrugne, anyone who likes gardens won't want to miss the 30,000 trees and million flowers of the **Parc Floral Florenia** (*open 5 Feb–5 Mar and Oct–5 Nov Tues–Sun 2–6; April–Sept Tues–Sun 10–7; closed Mon except hols; adm*). It may seem hard to believe, but Florenia opened only in 1993. An official of the Pyrénées-Atlantiques council named François Girard was on a mission to Canada. Visiting the famous Butchert Gardens in Vancouver, he was inspired to create something like it back home. With determination and persistence, Girard got everyone else in the area involved with the project, lined up 20 million francs in financing and made his dream come true in only three years. The park covers 45 acres and, young as the plantings are, it's already quite impressive.

St-Jean-de-Luz

For those who do not naturally gravitate towards the sun and fun of the beach, a seaside resort needs a certain special, intangible quality. Like the theatre, a good resort must be able to make one suspend one's disbelief. In all of southern France, there are very few places that can do this: one is Collioure on the Mediterranean, another St-Jean-de-Luz. The name is perfect. Light and colour can be extraordinary here, illuminating an immaculately white Basque town and the acres of glistening rose-silver seafood its restaurants roll out on tables to lure in customers. Even in the Basque lands, St-Jean's cooks are renowned for their skill and imagination. The beaches are fine and, best of all, this is not the sort of town to have entirely succumbed to the tourist tide; the fishermen on the quay still strut around as if they own the place. What more could you ask?

Unfortunately, the name really has nothing to do with light (*luz* in Spanish). Gradgrind etymologists have traced it back to a Celtic or Latin word *louth* or *lutum*, meaning mud, the same as Paris' original name, *Lutetia* – Mudville. St-Jean, or rather Donihane Lohitzun, as the Basques know it, grew up in a swampy nowhere that coincidentally happened to have a good harbour. It began to thrive as a fishing port when the river Adour started silting up the harbour of Bayonne in the Middle Ages. The Luziens shared fully in the French Basques' whaling and bucca-neering adventures up until the Revolution. It's tuna and sardines they're after now, and tourists.

Tourist Information

St-Jean-de-Luz: Place M. Foch, t 05 59 26 03 16, f 05 59 26 21 47, www.saint-jean-de-luz.com. **Ciboure**: 4 Place du Fronton, t 05 59 47 49 40.

Market Days

St-Jean-de-Luz: Tuesday and Friday, and also Saturday in summer. There are also markets Monday–Saturday year round in Les Halles, and on Sunday from July to mid-September. **Ciboure**: Sunday.

Sports and Activities

Sea excursions are big here. Two boats offer **cruises** or **deep-sea fishing**: the *Mary Rose* in the Port de la Ville, t 05 59 26 39 84, t 06 08 25 49 74; and the *Nivelle III*, from the Port du Pêche, t 05 59 35 45 37, t 06 09 73 61 82. You can also go up the Nivelle in an old-fashioned launch, *Cap Nature*, t 06 81 20 84 98. The Ecole Nationale de Voile, at Socoa, t 05 59 47 06 32, offers courses in **windsurfing**.

Where to Stay

St-Jean-de-Luz ✉ 64500

If St-Jean has one drawback, it's finding a reasonably priced place to stay – rates here are even higher than in Biarritz. The top spots are not by the beach; be warned that you may be required to take half board (*demi-pension*) at the height of summer.

****Chantaco**, Route d'Ascain, t 05 59 26 14 76, f 05 59 26 35 97 (*luxury–expensive*). The emphasis is on golf, with the area's most famous course next door. The hotel, in a villa, with a patio covered in vines, is set in a lovely park, and offers tennis courts and a pool in addition to golf. Here you'll find de luxe rooms and service, with prices to match. *Closed Dec–April*.

****Parc Victoria**, 5 Rue Cèpe, t 05 59 26 78 78, f 05 59 26 78 08 (*expensive*). A gracious mansion on the outskirts of town. It's a beautifully decorated, intimate place (only eight rooms and four suites), and has its own park with a pool.

****Helianthal**, Place Maurice-Ravel, t 05 55 51 51 51, f 05 59 51 26 38 (*expensive*). A big, slick thalassotherapy centre with modern luxurious rooms overlooking the bay in the centre of the pedestrian quarter, and all the seaweed treatments you could want, along with other special programmes from slim-ming to a stress-free break for young mothers. It has its own excellent restaurant, L'Atlantique, which serves classic French cuisine with deft modern touches and, of course, a special *menu diététique* for those taking the cures.

***Devinière**, 5 Rue Loquin, t 05 59 26 05 51, f 05 59 51 26 38 (*moderate*). In a narrow

The Port

A casual visitor could walk around St-Jean all day and never notice it had a beach, but it's a good one, long and deep, tucked away on the northern side of town, protected by a jetty and very safe for swimming. At its centre is the lavish **casino**, built in 1924. As in Biarritz, the 20s and 30s were a holiday boom time, and both have a sprinkling of Art Deco villas; one in St-Jean, the **Villa Leïhorra**, is open for tours by appointment, t 05 59 47 07 09.

St-Jean naturally turns its face to the port, lined with blue, red and green fishing boats, and a broad quay where the fishermen spread their nets. St-Jean is home to the biggest tuna fleet in France, and number of boats offer excursions (*see* 'Sports and Activities', below). Behind the port is the town hall and the adjacent **Maison de Louis XIV** (*Place Louis XIV, t/f 05 59 26 01 56; open June and Sept–mid-Oct Mon–Sat 10.30–12 and 2.30–6.30, July–Aug Mon–Sat 10.30–12.30 and 2.30–6.30; closed Sun and hols; adm*), a typical Basque town house of 1643 where the Roi Soleil stayed for his wedding. The nearby **Pavillon de l'Infante**, where the bride boarded, has been turned

pedestrian street, this charming hotel with just eight rooms is filled with antiques and curiosities. There is also a pretty little garden, where you can have breakfast.

★★★De la Poste, 83 Rue Gambetta, t 05 59 26 04 53, f 05 59 26 42 14 (*inexpensive*). Right in the centre.

★★Hôtel de la Plage, 33 Rue Garat, t 05 59 51 03 44, f 05 59 51 03 48 (*moderate*). A comfortable hotel, white with bright red shutters, right on the beach. Some rooms have private terraces. The brasserie downstairs is pretty decent and also enjoys sea views.

★★Ohartiza, Rue Garat, t 05 59 26 00 06, f 05 59 26 74 75 (*moderate*). Flower-filled balconies greet you at this likeable little place tucked between the church and the sea; inside there are more flowers and twittering birds. Upper floors have good views.

★★★La Marisa, 16 Rue Sophie, t 05 59 26 95 46, f 05 59 51 17 06 (*moderate*). Newly revamped, the Marisa is in an old Basque stone house partly furnished with antiques. It's centrally located close to the beach, the port and the pedestrian area.

★★Le Trinquet Maïténa, 42 Rue du Midi, t 05 59 26 05 13, f 05 59 26 09 0 (*inexpensive*). A tidy and very friendly Basque house on a quiet street right in the heart of town.

Le Petit Trianon, 56 Bd Victor Hugo, t 05 59 26 11 90, f 05 59 26 14 10 (*inexpensive*). A simple, centrally located hotel, with spotless if basic rooms and a small private terrace.

Ciboure ✉ 64500

★★★Lehen Tokia, 1 Chemin Achoharreta, t 05 59 47 18 16, f 05 59 47 38 04 (*moderate*). This romantic hill-set old villa overlooks the bay and is surrounded by rose gardens, with a small swimming pool. The house is a mixture of Art Deco and traditional Basque and the rooms are delightful. *Closed mid-Nov–mid-Dec*.

★★La Caravelle, Bd Pierre Benoît, t 05 59 47 18 05 (*inexpensive*). By the Ravel house, with sweet, personalized rooms.

Bakea, 9 Place Camille Julian, t 05 59 47 34 40 (*inexpensive*). Twelve rooms.

Eating Out

St-Jean-de-Luz

Everyone knows St-Jean as the capital of Basque cuisine in France, and there is a marvellous collection of restaurants around the centre – though it may be a tourist town, competition keeps the quality high. Rue de la République, just off main Rue Gambetta near the port, must be counted among the sights of the Basque coast no one should miss. It's almost entirely lined with seafood restaurants, each one with its beautifully arranged table of *fruits de mer* out front.

Auberge Kaiku, 17 Rue de la République, t 05 59 26 13 20. The oldest house in St-Jean (1540)

into a wax museum of characters from Louis' time, a branch of the **Musée Grévin** (*7 Rue Mazarin, t 05 59 51 24 88; open July–Aug daily 10–12.30 and 2–8, April–June and Sept–Oct 10–12 and 2–6.30, Nov–March Sat–Sun and school hols 2–6; adm, with half-hour tours*).

From the port, the main street, pedestrian Rue Gambetta, takes you to **St-Jean Baptiste**, largest and greatest of all Basque churches in France, where Louis XIV and Maria Teresa of Spain were married. It is a lesson in Basque subtlety, plain and bright outside, and plain and bright within; any Baptist or Methodist would feel at home here. The aesthetic is in the detail, especially the wonderful wooden ceiling formed like the hull of a ship, and the three levels of wooden galleries around both sides of the nave, carved with all the art and sincerity the local shipwrights could manage. The church was begun in the 14th century, but such wooden galleries do not last forever, no matter how well made; this latest version, probably much like those that preceded it, was done in the 1860s. Another feature, also typical of Basque churches, is the ornate gilded altarpiece, dripping with Baroque detail. The main door of the church

rolls out one of the most sumptuous tables (*expensive*); no fixed menus here, but you can negotiate your way to a fine marine repast between 200F/€30.5 and 300F/€45.5. *Closed Mon lunchtimes year-round, 12 Nov–22 Dec, and Wed 15 Sept–15 June.*

Chez Pablo, 5 Rue Mademoiselle-Etcheto, **t** 05 59 26 37 81. This has been going since 1928 and is a favourite place to celebrate family occasions; traditional Basque home cooking featuring cod *a la vizcaina*, *piballes* (elvers), squid cooked in its own ink and a hearty Basque omelette, all served on old-fashioned waxed tablecloths (*expensive–moderate*).

Vieille Auberge, 22 Rue Tourasse, **t** 05 59 26 19 61. For a filling Basque meal in the company of Luziens in the heart of the old town; menus usually include grilled fish and sometimes paella (*expensive–moderate*).

Taverne Basque, 5 Rue de la République, **t** 05 59 26 01 26. Another delightful spot on this busy street; the menus offer exception-ally good value and you can try out dishes like asparagus with Serrano ham, or fresh pan-fried cod with caramelized onions (*moderate*). *Closed Mon, Tues (except in summer), Jan and Mar.*

Pasaka, 11 Rue de la République, **t** 05 59 26 05 17. A cosy interior and two terraces, where you can feast on local grilled sardines, or *ttoro*, a satisfying Basque fish soup with potatoes and saffron (*moderate*).

Le Kayola, 18 Rue de la République. Oysters, salmon for starters, a satisfying *ttoro* and grills (*moderate*).

Chez Pantxua, Port de Soccoa, **t** 05 59 47 13 73. A long-established local favourite decorated with Basque paintings, serving *fruits de mer* and fish according to the catch of the day (*moderate*).

Le Patio, Rue de l'Abbé-Onaïndia, **t** 05 59 26 99 11. A place with a Spanish accent that serves up a very gratifying *parillada* (seafood mixed grill) with just about everything you can imagine, including lobster (*moderate*).

Le Peita, Rue Tourasse, **t** 05 59 26 86 66. All the Basque seafood favourites (*moderate*).

Ciboure

Bakea, 9 Place Camille Julian, **t** 05 59 47 34 40. Has outside tables right on the port; a local favourite for *ttoro* and grills (*moderate*).

Chez Mattin, 51 Rue Evariste Baignol, **t** 05 59 47 19 52). Old taverna famous for its *ttoro*, a recipe passed down from father to son (*moderate*).

Bars

Le Majestic, Place Louis XIV. One of the oldest in St-Jean; offers *pintxos* with your apéritif.

Chez Kako, in Les Halles. Friendly *bodega* with *pintxos* for shoppers and evening revellers; light meals available.

Pantxua, 7 Rue Tourasse. Favourite rendezvous of fishermen, with tasty *pintxos*.

St-Jean – Petit Paris

It was a party to remember, and without its tourists St-Jean would be left only with the memory of that one glorious month when it seemed the centre of the world. In 1659, Spain and France signed the Treaty of the Pyrenees, putting an end to a century and a half of almost continuous hostility. To ice the deal, a marriage was arranged between Louis XIV and the Spanish infanta, María Teresa. Preparations went on for a year, and this obscure whaling and fishing port, roughly halfway between Paris and Madrid, was chosen as the venue. In May 1660, *everybody* came to St-Jean, including nearly the entire French court. 'Monsieur' (Louis' neurotic uncle) and Cardinal Mazarin were there; the 'Grande Mademoiselle' (Louis' flamboyant cousin) and her lover floated down; and all the dandies and popinjays of Versailles followed in their wake. Louis himself arrived last, in a gilded carriage. One observer, Madame de Motteville, marvelled at how everyone was covered in lace and feathers and tassels. So were the horses. It reminded her of King Cyrus and ancient Persia.

Years before, a Gypsy fortune-teller had predicted that peace between France and Spain would finally come 'with a whale'. And on the day that María Teresa and the Spaniards arrived in St-Jean, a great whale was sighted just off the harbour. The courtiers rushed to the shore to watch the town's seamen give chase. Young Louis, however, took the opportunity to barge in on his future bride in her chambers; he surprised her *en déshabillé* and they had an intimate lunch together. For the wedding, there were Basque dancers, mock naval battles offshore, a bullfight and a grand ball in the main square, now Place Louis XIV, illuminated with thousands of candles and torches. Louis and his bride lived happily ever after (although the France Louis ruled suffered greatly); when the queen died, Louis remarked that her death was 'the only chagrin she ever caused me'. The peace with Spain has lasted up to the present, save for the unfortunate interlude of Napoleon. As for the whale, they caught it, and the bishop of Bayonne, who performed the wedding ceremony, took the tongue and fat back to Bayonne with him.

was sealed up after Louis and Maria Teresa passed through it on their wedding day. These days on special occasions, the church hosts a *messe de Corsaires*, not a service sponsored by pirates, but by St-Jean's confraternities dedicated to 'the defence of the sardine, tuna and anchovy'. There's nothing fishy about the Mass, however, which is famous for the beauty of its Basque choral music (the tourist office has the dates).

On the edge of the town, just off the RN10, you can find out about Basque traditions, language, costumes, music and local crafts at a Basque theme park, the **Ecomusée de la Tradition Basque** (*open Mon–Sat 10–12.30 and 2.30–7 outside school holidays, no break during school holidays; adm*). There's a shop, a restaurant and visits finish up with a tasting of the local herb-based liqueur, Izarra.

Ciboure

Right across the port from St-Jean, over a little bridge, this is the less-touristy, working member of these twin towns. Ciboure was the home of Maurice Ravel, who was born at No.12 Quai Ravel of a Basque mother and French father, and who once started a concerto based on Basque themes and rhythms (called *Zaspiak Bat* or 'Seven are One', after the nationalist motto), but never finished it.

The town has a mirror-image of St-Jean's picturesque port, though this side is mostly used by pleasure boats. Behind the port, there are pretty streets of old Basque houses such as **Rue de la Fontaine**, and the simple **St-Vincent**, a 16th-century fortified church with an octagonal tower. On the northern end of town, facing the coast, is the quarter of **Socoa** with its **castle**, begun by Henri IV and now housing a surfing and windsurfing school.

Guéthary and Bidart

If St-Jean-de-Luz is too frenetic and Biarritz is too big and cosmopolitan, you've got two very amiable choices in between, Guéthary and Bidart. Both are perfect Basque villages, with church, *mairie* and *fronton*, and both have good beaches. Even if they do get a bit crowded at the height of summer, it's too early to call them spoiled yet.

Tourist Information

Guéthary: Rue du Comte Swiecinsky, t 05 59 26 56 60, f 05 59 54 92 67, *www.guethary-france.com*.

Bidart: Rue de la Plage, t 05 59 54 93 85, *www.bidarttourisme.com*.

Where to Stay and Eat

Guéthary ✉ 64210

*Choko-Ona, Av Harispe, t 05 59 26 51 01, f 05 59 54 81 59 (*inexpensive*). One of the nicer hotels in this sleepy resort.

Madrid, right in the village centre on Place Toulet, t 05 59 26 52 12, *thierry.listre@wanadoo.fr*. Cheery and homey and blue-and-white, with rooms overlooking the ocean. The restaurant serves mostly seafood (*moderate*).

Kandela, also in the centre. A tiny restaurant with a terrace, specializing in grills, fish and seafood, and with a good local wine list (*moderate*).

Héteroclito, Chemin de la Plage, t 05 59 54 98 92. A wonderful palace of utter kitsch, originally a souvenir bazaar. For live music, dinner on the terrace, a young, cool crowd and a lively atmosphere in the bar. Also popular with the surfing fraternity.

Bidart ✉ 64210

***Villa l'Arche, Chemin Cambonoea, t 05 59 51 65 95 (*moderate*). This charming Basque-style farmhouse on a cliff has eight sun-filled rooms with terraces and its grounds lead directly onto the beach. There are also two apartments, and gourmet breakfasts.

Laminak, Route de Saint-Pée, t 05 59 41 95 40 (*moderate*). Outside town is this converted 17th-century Basque farm, with beautifully decorated rooms in frilly '*Style Anglais*'. It's less than three miles from the beaches and within sight of the Pyrenees, which you can gaze at while you breakfast out on the terrace or in the winter garden.

Elissaldia Hotel, Place de la Mairie, t 05 59 54 90 03 (*inexpensive*). A cheap, authentic place to stay within a *pelote* ball's throw of the church and *fronton* court. It's a snip, with sea views thrown in. There's also a bar and restaurant.

Masion d'Hôte Irigoian, Quartier Ilbarritz, t 05 59 43 83 00 (*inexpensive*). Conveniently located near the beach and the golf courses, a charming bed and breakfast in a 17th century Basque farm.

Table des Frères Ibarboure, Route Ahetze, t 05 59 54 81 64. One of the region's most celebrated restaurants (*expensive*). The cuisine is predictably perfect and abstrusely *soignée*, from the *encornets farcis* (stuffed squid) and oysters with caviar to the rich and extravagant desserts.

La Parrilla, on the N10, t 05 59 54 78 94. Worth a little splurge for a *parilla* (mixed grill) of five different kinds of fresh seafood (*moderate*).

Sleepy **Guéthary** comes first, a resort for as many years as Biarritz, though it never made it big. It has a pretty, Basque-style *mairie*, which must get a window broken every now and then from the *fronton* right in front of it, along with a tiny port and a beach. On the outskirts of the village is the **Musée d'Art Contemporain** (*open April–Oct Wed–Mon 3–7; adm*), set in a late-19th-century Basque mansion built by a local boy who made good in Argentina before returning to spread his largesse among his townspeople. It features a number of ponderous works by a Romanian sculptor, Swiecinski, among other more recent local works, but the real highlight is the beautiful tree-filled park which overlooks the ocean.

Bidart has a grand view across the coast from the pilgrimage chapel of Ste-Madeleine. Bidart's parish church, in the centre, has some painted altarpieces and a quite unusual Slavic baptismal font – a gift from Queen Natalie of Serbia, who spent a lot of time here before the First World War in a palace called the Pavillon Royal, above the beach.

Biarritz

Les vents, les astres et la mer me sont favorables.

town motto

For their 1959 season, the designers at Cadillac came up with something special: a sleek and shiny convertible, nearly 25ft long, with the highest tailfins in automotive history (22 inches). They called it the *Biarritz*, a tribute to the Basque village that was chosen by fortune, for a few decades at the end of the 19th century, to become the most glittering resort in Europe. Nowadays, there's still enough Ritz in Biarritz to support six luxury hotels (among 65 more modest establishments). But, freed from the burden of being the cynosure of fashion, the resort has become a pleasantly laid-back place, where anyone, wealthy or not, can have an unpretentious good time.

Come in the off season and you'll notice the otherwise inconspicuous phenomenon of Biarritz today – it's becoming the retirement capital of France, a Gallic Bournemouth or Florida. Already 34 per cent of the population are retirees, and the number goes up each year. Another statistic: 45 per cent of all the housing is holiday homes; you'll certainly notice that after September, when Biarritz declines into an overgrown village. Then everybody knows everyone else; they shake hands and exchange pleasantries on street corners, or lounge in the bar talking about how nice and quiet it is.

History Under the Palms

Local historians claim that both Biarritz and its landmark, the Atalaya, are names bestowed by the ancient Phoenicians, who may well have used the port as a stage on their trade routes to Britain. Biarritz is said to mean something like 'safe harbour', and Atalaya a kind of tower (like the *talayots* of Minorca, an important landmark visible to the early, coast-hugging sailors).

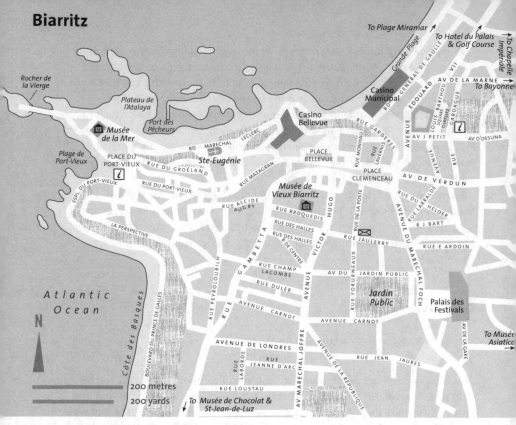

Biarritz

Map labels:

To Plage Miramar ↗
To Hotel du Palais & Golf Course ↗
To Chapelle Impériale
Grande Plage
BD GÉNÉRAL DE GAULLE
AVENUE EDOUARD VII
AV DE LA MARNE →
To Bayonne
Rocher de la Vierge
Plateau de l'Atalaya
Casino Municipal
RUE GARDÈRES
Casino Bellevue
SQUARE LOUIS-BARTHOU
GARDAGUE
AVENUE J PETIT
AV D'OSSUNA
Musée de la Mer
Port des Pêcheurs
BD MARECHAL LECLERC
RUE DU GROËLAND
Ste-Eugénie
PLACE DU PORT-VIEUX
Plage de Port-Vieux
PLACE BELLEVUE
RUE MONNAU
RUE LAVERNIS
AVENUE D'ETCHEVERRY
RUE
AVENUE DE VERDUN
PLACE CLEMENCEAU
Musée de Vieux Biarritz
RUE MAZAGRAN
ESPL DU PORT-VIEUX
RUE DU PORT-VIEUX
LA PERSPECTIVE
RUE ALCIDE AUGRY
RUE BROQUEDIS
RUE DE LA POSTE
AV DE VERDUN
RUE DU LARRALDE
RUE HELDER
R J BART
VICTOR HUGO
RUE DES HALLES
RUE DES HALLES
RUE JAULERRY
AVENUE DU MARECHAL FOCH
RUE E ARDOIN
RUE DE CENTRE
GAMBETTA
RUE CHAMP LACOMBE
RUE DULER
AV DU JARDIN PUBLIC
RUE FOURNEAUX
Jardin Public
Palais des Festivals
RUE PEYROLOUBILH
RUE
AVENUE CARNOT
AVENUE
AVENUE CARNOT
To Musée Asiatico
Atlantic Ocean
Côte des Basques
BOULEVARD DU PRINCE DE GALLES
AV DE LA GARE
AVENUE DE LONDRES
AV MARECHAL JOFFRE
AVENUE DE LA RÉPUBLIQUE
RUE JEAN JAURES
RUE LABORDE
RUE JEANNE D'ARCH
RUE LOUSTAU
To Musée de Chocolat & St-Jean-de-Luz
200 metres
200 yards
N

Before the 1860s, Biarritz was never more than a simple fishing village. But in the Middle Ages, even more than Bayonne it was the heart of the Basque whaling fleet. *Cachalots*, Basque whales, and other species of whale were once common in the Bay of Biscay. A permanent watch was kept on the Atalaya, and whenever one was sighted, the entire village would row out and try to nab it; the Biarrots were probably the inventors of the harpoon, and a harpooner once figured on the village's coat of arms. When the whales caught on and started avoiding the area, the Biarrots and the other Basque whalers bravely sailed out into the open sea after them. By 1800, Basque whalers couldn't keep up with the British and Americans, but Biarritz was beginning to make part of its living from a new and unprecedented phenomenon, the desire of northerners to come and spend a holiday beside the sea.

Eugenia Maria de Montijo de Guzmán, to whom Biarritz owes its present status, came from a minor Spanish noble family a bit down on its luck. But even as a young girl, fortune-telling Gypsies and nuns forecast a brilliant future for her; 'an eagle will carry you to the heavens and then drop you,' one of them supposedly said. Eugenia also had a scheming, social-climbing mother, who by hard work and cleverness got her daughter as far as the court of the new Emperor Napoleon III in Paris in 1852. The striking 26-year-old blonde was more than capable of doing the rest of the job herself. A brilliant horsewoman who affected an easy familiarity in the company of males, and who liked to smoke a cigar now and then, she made quite an impression. But there was a cold, unapproachable side to her too, and she used it to win the Emperor's heart by being the only girl in Paris the old rogue couldn't have. It is claimed he found his way into her bedroom one night; meeting a chilly reception, he asked the way to her heart. 'Through the church,' she replied.

As Empress Eugénie, she helped inaugurate the cult of fashion in Paris, making the fortune of Worth, first of the celebrity couturiers. With a political outlook somewhat to the right of Attila the Hun, and a near-total control over Napoleon, she was able to exert a tremendous influence over the policies of the government, presiding gloriously over the orgy of greed, corruption, décolletage and waltzes that was the Second

Getting There and Around

By Air

Biarritz's **airport**, the Aérogare de Parme (t 05 59 43 83 83) has four or five flights a day to Paris Orly with Air France (t 08 02 80 28 02) and three a day to Charles de Gaulle. **Ryanair** (t 05 59 43 83 93) flies to London Stansted daily. The no.6 bus from Biarritz goes to the airport.

By Train

Biarritz is a stop on the main rail line from Paris through Bordeaux and down to the Spanish border. There are plenty of trains along this run; most of them also stop at Bayonne. There are a few TGVs each day which also stop in Bayonne. **SNCF information** in Biarritz, t 05 59 50 83 07; in Bayonne, t 05 59 55 20 45. Other lines from Bayonne go up the Gaves to Orthez and Pau in Béarn, and down the valley of the Nive to St-Jean-Pied-de-Port.

By Bus

There is a parallel and equally convenient **bus** service down the coast run by the ATCRB line (t 05 59 26 06 99) – about a dozen a day from Biarritz and Bayonne to St-Jean-de-Luz and Hendaye, and buses for San Sebastián, Spain, on Tues, Thurs and Sat. The Spanish bus line, PESA, runs a twice-daily service along the coast to St-Jean-de-Luz and on to San Sebastián, leaving from just outside Bayonne's tourist information office (which holds time-table information – buy tickets on the bus).

Public Transport

Public transport in the Biarritz–Bayonne area is run by an aggressive-sounding line called STAB (info and tickets: Biarritz, Av J. Petit, t 05 59 24 26 53; Bayonne, Place du

General de Gaulle, t 05 59 59 04 61; Infobus provides information on all local services, t 05 59 52 59 52). Regular **city buses** connect the two cities, from the Hôtel de Ville in Biarritz to the Hôtel de Ville in Bayonne – line 1 or 2, or faster, the Express BAB. Biarritz's SNCF **station** is far from the city centre; the no.2 bus terminates here.

Tours

Walking tours: These can be arranged through the tourist office and are available during July and August only unless pre-booked. Tours leave at 10am on Mondays and 6pm on Fridays.
Petit train: Every tourist town in France seems to have one and Biarritz is no exception. If you can't take another step, hop on for a guided tour of the town from the Grande Plage to the Côte des Basques via the Port des Pêcheurs.
Boat tours: The *Bayonne* offers 2-hour trips up the Adour, t 05 59 47 77 17.

Tourist Information

Tourist office: Square d'Ixelles (next to the town hall), t 05 59 22 37 00, f 05 59 44 14 19, *www.tourisme.fr/biarritz. Open Mon–Sat 9–6, Sun 10–5; July and Aug 8–8.* There's another office at the Jardin Public. The city's web site, *www.villeobiarritz.fr*, also has masses of information on events and holiday rentals.

Shopping

Arosteguy, 5 Av Victor Hugo, t 05 59 24 00 52, *www. maison-argosteguy.com*. Celebrated

Empire. It took a woman historian, Edith Saunders, to notice this strangely significant bit of the world's secret history. In her lovely book, *A Distant Summer*, she wrote:

> ...*Eugénie had risen like a brilliant star, to create not only new fashions but a new taste in beauty, a new type of woman. The old type, which had lingered on in England and was represented in the pages of Dickens, belonged to Europe's Romantic period and was open-mouthed, angelic and mawkish. The new type, with its predilection for blonde hair and its hard expression, is still with us. The Empress set the modern standard of highly polished perfection which is maintained today by Hollywood film stars and mechanically transmitted to entranced millions who follow in the*

grocer's selling the finest Basque products, and lots of imported delicacies, too.

Bookstore, 27 Place Clemenceau. With a good selection of books in English if you have run out of holiday reading for the beach.

Boutique 64, 16 Rue Gambetta. A wide choice of Basque clothes and other items.

Cazaux Céramistes, 10 Rue Broquedis, t 05 59 23 15 01. This ceramic workshop has been going since the end of the 18th century, and in the last century produced some of France's top Art Deco pieces. Guided visits of the workshop can be arranged in advance but the shop is open all year.

Chailla, Halles Centrales (central market). For a wide range of local cheeses and cured meats – this is just one of many amazing stalls.

Chez Paries, 27 Place Clemenceau. For marzipan fantasies and *mouchous* (macaroon kisses)

Chocolat Henriet, Place Clemenceau. Delicious chocolates filled with oranges and almonds.

Rodon, 1 Rue Mazagran. Excellent Basque jewellery.

Sports and Activities

Golf

Golf thrives in Biarritz. There are 10 courses around the town and several more in St-Jean-de-Luz, ranging from lush, professional-length links with an ocean view to dinky 3-par places to practise your iron shots. At least one important tournament is held in Biarritz each season. Serious courses include the **Golf de Chiberta** in Anglet, Bd des Plages; **Golf d'Arcangues** in Arcangues, south of Biarritz; **Golf de Chantaco**, Route d'Ascain, St-Jean-de-Luz; and **Golf de la Nivelle**, Place Sharp,

Ciboure. All are at least par 69, and have a daily ticket from 200 to 400F/€30.5 to 70.

Water Sports

If you should feel a sudden desire to take up **surfing**, there are five schools in Biarritz and Anglet, and lots of places to rent equipment. Useful contacts include: **Biarritz Surf Training**, 4 Impasse Hélène Boucher, t 05 59 23 15 31, t 05 59 43 74 25; and **Ecole de Surf Moraiz**, 4 Place Bellevue, t 05 59 24 22 09, t 05 59 22 16 28.

Thalassotherapy

You may not have heard of thalassotherapy – the use of seawater for aiding stress, fitness or recovery from diseases – but in France it is big business; Biarritz has two of the most modern and up-to-date establishments, the **Institut Thalassa**, 11 Rue Louison Bobet, t 05 59 24 20 82, and **Les Thermes Marine**, 80 Rue de Madrid, t 05 59 23 01 22, and there's a third in the Hotel Atlanthal in Anglet (*see* below).

Gambling

If you have any money left, you can fritter it away on the *tiercé*, *quarté* and *quinté* at the Hippodrome de la Cité des Fleurs on Avenue du Lac Marion, still one of France's premier racing venues.

Where to Stay

Biarritz ✉ 64200

Don't let Biarritz's past fool you into thinking there's no place for the likes of you and me here. In fact, the vast majority of people who come these days are looking for a bargain, and they have little trouble finding

measure allotted by their circumstance. To look like a film star is the dream of the present day woman of the industrial age; in 1855 everyone dreamed of looking like Eugénie.

As a girl, Eugénie and her mother had often vacationed at the just 'discovered' village of Biarritz. As Empress, she dragged Napoleon back down with her and established the summer court on the beach. Having invented the new woman, Eugénie now made some great contributions to the modern concept of the seaside resort. The imperial couple didn't stay in a hotel; Eugénie had a palace – the Villa Eugénie – built on the most prominent spot along the beach in 1854. Everybody who was anybody in

one, although Biarritz is somewhat lacking at the lower end of the scale – if you arrive without a reservation in July or August you might get pushed up into the higher brackets. The tourist office on Place d'Ixelles can help find a room even during rush hour in August.

Luxury

★★★★Hôtel du Palais, 1 Av de l'Impératrice, t 05 59 41 64 00, f 05 59 41 67 99. *www.cote basque.tm.fr/palais*. Probably the most prestigious address on France's west coast. Built in Biarritz's glory days on the site of Napoleon and Eugénie's villa, this compound on the beach, where the amenities even include a private putting green, has a circuit of old wrought-iron fences to separate you from the rest of the world. For a while in the 1950s, the Palais was closed, but the city got it fixed up and reopened, under a determined mayor who had campaigned under the simple slogan: 'No Palace, No Millionaires.' Some of the rooms are palatial, many with period furnishings. *See* also 'Eating Out'.

★★★★Miramar, 13 Rue Louison Bobet, t 05 59 41 30 00, f 05 59 24 77 20. The younger contender for the luxury prize. Modern and up to date, this hotel may not have the panache of the Palais, but compensates with very high standards in every respect: one of Biarritz's best restaurants (*see* below), a pool, sauna, and even its own thalassotherapy centre.

Expensive

★★★★Café de Paris, 5 Place Bellevue, t 05 59 24 19 53, f 05 59 24 18 20. A chic alternative close to the sea. It is one of Biarritz's best restaurants but also has rooms above, all with

magnificent sea views, some with huge terraces.

★★★★Hôtel Régina et Golf, 52 Av Imperatrice, t 05 59 41 33 00, *H9990@accor-hotels*. A plush – if slightly soulless – option near the golf course, with large modern rooms set around an indoor courtyard, and all the amenities including a swimming pool.

★★★Plaza, Av Edouard VII, t 05 59 24 74 00, f 05 59 22 22 01. Built in 1928, with a touch of restrained Art Deco elegance. It has retained much of its original decoration, and a quiet sense of decorum to match.

Moderate

★★★Maison Garnier, 29 Rue Gambetta, t 05 59 01 60 70, f 05 59 01 60 80. Currently fashionable and set in a 19th-century Basque house. There are seven exquisitely restored rooms, all with antique furniture.

★★★Hôtel Windsor, Av Edouard VII, t 05 59 24 08 52. Just a short walk from the Grande Plage, this is a very pleasant hotel, particularly if you can get one of the rooms on the upper floors with balconies offering views across the ocean.

★★★Louisiane, Rue Guy Petit, t 05 59 22 20 20, f 05 59 24 95 77. Worth a try, despite its unprepossessing modern exterior. A conveniently located, well-managed chain hotel with its own swimming pool, a boon for those who want to swim rather than surf.

★★★Château de Clair de Lune, 48 Av Alan Seeger, t 05 59 41 53 20, f 05 59 41 53 29. An alternative far from the centre. It's in a Belle Epoque villa in a delicious park, with tranquillity assured, and lovely rooms, though it's a bit expensive.

★★Le Petit Hôtel, 11 Rue Gardères, t 05 59 24 87 00. Centrally placed very near the Grande

Paris soon followed, along with grand dukes, petit dukes, every sort of count and baron, and plenty of factory owners with marriageable daughters. The royal families of Spain and Belgium came; the English were already here, laying out golf courses, while Count von Bismarck canoodled with the wife of the Russian ambassador.

The Fall of France in 1870 put an end to the Second Empire, and to Eugénie's fairy tale. In 1881 the government of the Third Republic demolished the Villa Eugénie after a fire and divided the estate into building lots. But you can't keep a good princess down; Eugénie lived a romantic if somewhat melancholy life in exile, an object of fascination wherever she travelled. She died in Madrid in 1920, at the age of 94.

Plage, this is also a charming choice. Rooms 4 and 5 have the best views and are a bit less pokey than some of the others.

★★Hôtel Romance, 6 Allée des Acacias, t 05 59 41 25 65. This is a prettily restored old house in a quiet, residential district; it's difficult to find but worth it, particularly for the rooms which open out into the peaceful garden. It is very reasonably priced at the bottom end of this category. *Closed Jan and Feb.*

Inexpensive

★★Hostellerie Victoria, 11 Av Reine Victoria, t 05 59 24 08 21. In a delightful villa from the old days, close to Grande Plage.

★★Hôtel du Rocher de la Vierge, 13 Rue du Port-Vieux, t 05 59 24 11 74. At the centre of the action in the old town.

★★Palacito Hotel, 1 Rue Gambetta, t 05 59 24 04 89, f 05 59 24 33 43. A traditional small hotel in the middle of town.

★★Hôtel Gardenia, 19 Av Carnot, t 05 59 24 10 46, f 05 59 24 41 31. Recently refurbished, this is a very welcoming little hotel painted a rosy pink and conveniently placed for the Grande Plage and local nightlife.

★★Maïtagaria, 34 Av Carnot, t 05 59 24 26 65, f 05 59 24 27 37. Another comfortable establishment a little further away from the centre (but still less than a 10-minute walk to the beach). It's been thoroughly redecorated in cosy, fussy French style and offers very good value for money.

★Palym, 7 Rue du Port-Vieux, t 05 59 24 16 56, f 05 59 24 96 12. A family-run, old-style place popular with surfers.

Auberge de Jeunesse, 28 Rue Philippe Veyrin, t 05 59 41 76 00, f 05 59 41 76 06. Youth hostel, close to the Lac Mouriscot.

Camping

While every other town on the coast has a huge choice of places, Biarritz doesn't. You'll do better looking in nearby Bidart, which has 12 of them around the beach and coastal highway. In Biarritz, try **Biarritz Camping**, 28 Rue Harcet, t 05 59 23 00 12.

Eating Out

Expensive

La Rotonde, Hôtel du Palais, t 05 59 41 64 00. This may be the southwest's ultimate trip in luxurious dining: a magnificent domed room with its original decoration, and views over the beach and sea. They've just changed chefs and the personality of the cuisine is as yet unclear – only expect it to remain first-rate. There is a formidable wine list (*menus start at 290F/€44 for lunch; the full treatment will set you back 350–600F/ €53–91*).

Le Relais, Miramar Hotel, t 05 59 41 30 00. Without the posh ambience of the former (without any ambience at all, in fact, though there is a sea view), but you can eat as well for a bit less. Seafood is the main attraction, cooked with a delightful lightness and savour: a *fricassée* of sole and langoustines, or lobster ravioli with *cèpes*.

Les Jardins de l'Océan, Hôtel Régina et Golf, 52 Av de l'Impératrice, t 05 59 41 33 00. Good for a slightly more modest seafood extravaganza (the *grand plateau de fruits de mer*, includes lobster).

Les Platanes, 32 Av du Beausoleil, t 05 59 23 13 68. This utterly delightful restaurant is set in an old Basque farmhouse in an undiscovered part of town; the cuisine – Gascon with

Even without her, Biarritz carried on. More Russian princes and even Queen Victoria came to visit (in 1889); the Prince of Wales left so much money in the casino that they named two different streets after him. The Belle Epoque brought a tidal wave of building: grand hotels, the casino, a salt-water spa and acres of wealthy villas in every imaginable style.

It wasn't a wild scene like the Côte d'Azur in the 1920s. The swells followed a respectable and rather bland daily schedule, starting with a morning promenade past the shop windows on Rue Mazagran at 10, followed by an hour on the beach, dressing for lunch at 11.30, and so on. The First World War started Biarritz's fall from

some fresh, modern touches – has been much lauded recently and with very good reason. The house speciality is foie gras, but you should also taste the pigeon or the fresh local fish, which is always cooked to perfection. If you have any room left, finish up with a chocolate marvel: *chocolat aux chocolats*.

Café de Paris, 5 Place Bellevue, t 05 59 22 19 53. Stylish brasserie and restaurant specializing in southwestern cuisine, with excellent crab and lobster.

Campagne et Gourmandise, 52 Av Alan Seeger, t 05 59 41 10 11. In a Basque farmhouse in the grounds of the Château de Claire de Lune (*see* 'Where to Stay', above). You can dine on a terrace with splendid panoramic views of the Pyrenees. Typical dishes include *fricassée de champignons en cappuccino d'herbes*, *queue de bœuf à la tranche de foie gras*, and pigeon tart.

Moderate
Goulue, 3 Rue E. Ardoin, t 05 59 24 90 90. A Belle Epoque-style restaurant with attentive service of classic local dishes; try a plateful of baby squid or monkfish cooked with bacon.

Le Clos Basque, 12 Rue Louis Barthou, t 05 59 24 24 96. An authentic little bistro with stone walls and Spanish tiles inside, and a charming terrace outside. Local specialities such as squid with peppers and pigs' trotters with lentils are served.

L'Auberge, Rue du Harispe 22, t 05 59 41 01 41. This is a peaceful spot away from the crowds where you can dine out on the flower-filled terrace; the food is Gascon and the *menu du terroir* is a great way to try out the highlights. *Eves only, closed Sun out of season.*

L'Operne, 17 Av Edouard VII, t 05 59 24 30 30, f 05 59 24 37 89. An elegant seafood restaurant right on the seafront; try the simply grilled fish of the day.

Le Galion, Bd du Général du Gaulle 17, t 05 59 24 29 32. Another sumptuous seafood restaurant, with wonderful ocean views.

Chez Albert, Port des Pêcheurs, t 05 59 24 43 84. This may at first glance look like a typical tourist restaurant, but it's popular year-round with visitors and Biarrots alike for quality seafood at reasonable prices. Squid in its own ink is a speciality.

Café de la Grand Plage, 1 Av Edouard VII, t 05 59 22 77 88. 1930s-style brasserie-café, facing the ocean and overlooking the Grand Plage, serving a wide range of drinks, snacks and light meals.

Le Surfing, 9 Bd Prince de Galles, t 05 59 24 78 72. Overlooking the Plage des Basques, this is the place for fashionable surfers to peel off their wetsuits and enjoy a décor of surfboards and Hawaiian shirts. It specializes in fish but serves a variety of good salads too.

Blue Cargo, Villa Itsasoan, Av Ibarritz, t 05 59 24 36 30. In a villa perched right on the beach of Ibarritz, on the outskirts of Biarritz. It's perfect for sunset-over-the-sea drinks or simple seafood meals.

Bistrot des Halles, Rue du Centre, t 05 59 24 21 22. Usually crowded for both lunch and dinner. As in any French town, you won't go wrong looking around the market, and for 75F you won't do better than the daily special (usually a grilled fish or steak) here.

Cheap
The Players, Esplanade du Casino de Biarritz, t 05 59 24 19 60. Can't be beaten for

fashion; In the 20s everybody started shifting to Nice and Cannes where life promised a bit more excitement.

In the past decade, Biarritz has begun to shake off its dusty image with dramatic refurbishment of its hotels and fine buildings, in architectural styles ranging from Belle Epoque to Art Deco and Art Nouveau. These include the splendid **Casino Municipal**, which dominates the Grande Plage, with its restored casinos, entertainment centres and an old-style grand café overlooking the beach.

Despite its hordes of retirees, Biarritz is hardly behind the times. France Telecom has made it the experimental city for the communications of the future, wiring up the

good cheap seafood and vast pizzas. It's right next to the Grand Plage, with views out to sea.

Le Taïtu, 54 Av Edouard VII, t 05 59 24 32 42. Corny pirate décor but good pizzas, served until late.

Pâtisserie Miremont, Place Clemenceau. This is the place to go while you're waiting for dinner: today, as in the Belle Epoque, an essential part of the Biarritz experience is to drop in at four in the afternoon for a coffee and a little pastry that's much too pretty to eat. The pâtisserie retains its original décor, with rooms overlooking the sea.

Port des Pêcheurs is the site of several good *tapas* places.

Anglet ✉ 64600

A seaside suburb of Biarritz.

★★★Atlanthal, 153 Bd des Plages, t 05 59 52 75 75, f 05 59 52 75 13 (*moderate*). Beachside hotel equipped with its own thalasso-therapy centre.

Auberge de Jeunesse, 19 Rue des Vignes, t 05 59 58 70 00, f 05 59 58 70 07 (*cheap*). A favourite of young surfers, a few minutes from the waves.

La Mama Nature, Av de la Chambre d'Amour, t 05 59 03 37 21. Favourite surfer bar, with affordable pizzas and plates of pasta.

Entertainment and Nightlife

Theatre, Dance, Classical Music

There is always something going on in Biarritz. The tourist information office distributes a leaflet called *Kulturaldia*, which gives details. They also provides a central ticket

service for all events, t 05 59 22 44 66, f 05 59 24 97 80.

Bars and Clubs

There isn't much worth mentioning besides the little bars in and around the Port des Pecheurs which get jam-packed with surfers and young people in summer. There are a few decent *tapas* bars, including:

Bar Jean, 5 Rue des Halles, t 05 59 24 80 38. A Biarritz classic; the place to go for superb fresh *tapas*, oysters and a good choice of wines in a traditional Spanish-tiled *bodega*.

El Callejon, 5 Rue Monhau, t 05 59 24 99 15. Another old-fashioned spot, which serves good *tapas*.

Le Bodegon, 5 Av de la Gare, t 05 59 24 60 09. *Jambons de Bayonne* hanging from the ceiling and cocktails poured around a large U-shaped bar.

There is a handful of nightclubs, although none stand out. Try:

Le Caveau, 4 Rue Gambetta.

Le Copacobana, 24 Av Edouard VII.

Le Flamingo Casino Municipal, Av Edouard VII.

Play Boy Club, Résidence Grand Hotel, 15 Place Clemenceau.

Le Cayo Coco, 3 Rue Jaulerry. A Cuban place with free salsa dance lessons every Thursday and Friday night.

If that isn't your scene, head for a civilized *Thé Dansant* complete with orchestra at the Casino (call the tourist information office for details). Bayonne (*see* p.260) is better for live music and clubs.

Cinema

Cinema Le Royal, 8 Av du Marechal Foch, t 05 59 24 21 72.

town with a single fibre optic cable to provide cable TV, telephone, '*visiophone*', '*télétel* ', 'interactive communications' and God knows what else. And plenty of young people still come in the summer for one unexpected reason – surfing. Stuck in its odd angle of coastline, Biarritz provides what many claim are the only perfect waves on the Atlantic; French hot-doggers and surf bunnies have made it the modest Malibu Beach of Europe. Lots of good Frenchmen who have never heard of surfing, and who would never dream of sitting on a beach, know Biarritz for its crack rugby squad – the great Serge Blanco played here until his retirement in 1992 (now the local hero runs a thalassotherapy centre down in Hendaye).

The Atalaya

Here, on the tip of old Biarritz's little peninsula, is the height where in the old days the watch would send up smoke signals when whales were sighted. To the right, the Port des Pêcheurs now holds only pleasure craft, although in 1981 its surviving fishermen (mostly Gascon, rather than Basque) managed to get it the status of a *comune libre*, a village within the town, with its own mayor. To the left is the old fishing port, long ago unusable and filled up with the beach of Port-Vieux, and also the best place in Biarritz for a stroll, the **Rocher de la Vierge**. Napoleon III and Eugénie were responsible for this system of causeways and tunnels, connecting a number of crags and tiny islands into a memorable walk just above the pounding surf, although storms decimated Napoleon's ambitions for another port here. The biggest rock, all that remains of Napoleon's jetty, carries a marble statue of the Virgin Mary, erected after the tragic end of *La Surprise* and her crew, who were drowned in a massive storm within sight of the port in 1893.

Up on top of the Atalaya, the **Musée de la Mer** (*t 05 59 22 33 34; open daily 9.30–12.30 and 2–6, plus evenings in summer, closed first week of Jan; adm; the seals are fed at 10.30 and 5*), in a clean Art Deco building, contains an imaginatively decorated old aquarium for a look at what's down below the surface of the Bay of Biscay. Two floors are devoted to interactive exhibits on the natural history of the sea, whales and whaling, fishing and navigation, with models and skeletons; a whole room awaits ornithologists, with all kinds of regional birds. There's a Shark Cave to give you the shivers and a Seal Pool where you can watch the inmates clowning around for the crowds and getting fed. The pretty terrace café has wonderful views out over the Rocher de la Vierge.

South from the Atalaya on Avenue Beaurivage, you'll reach the **Musée du Chocolat** at Nos.14–16 (*open 10–12 and 2.30–6, until 7pm during July and Aug*), which has plenty of exhibits on the history of chocolate-making in the area (*see* p.256) and plenty more chances to gorge yourself. Descending eastwards from the Atalaya, the Bd Maréchal Leclerc takes you to the church of **Ste-Eugénie**, another modest contribution of the Empress'; the big organ inside won a prize at the 1900 Paris World's Fair. The church faces one of the centres of resort life in the old days, the beautifully restored **Casino Bellevue**, now converted to residences and exhibition and conference rooms. Not far away, by the city marketplace on Rue Broquelis, is the **Musée de Vieux Biarritz** (*open Fri–Sat and Mon–Wed 10–12 and 2.30–6; adm*); set in a former Anglican church, this is a small exhibition of photos and mementos of the good old days. Deep in the web of residential streets, there is also a museum of Oriental art, **Asiatica** (*1 Rue Guy Petit, t 05 59 22 78 78; open Tues–Sat 10–12.30 and 2.30–7, Sun 2.30–7; adm*), with a vast and earnest collection which includes jades, bronzes and porcelain from China, Nepal and India, and many Tibetan *thangkas* (paintings on silk).

Beaches and Villas

Below the Atalaya, the shore straightens out into the long, luscious expanse of the **Grande Plage**, which before Eugénie was called (for reasons not entirely clear) the Plage des Fous, the 'beach of the mad', dominated by the magnificently restored casino. Further up the beach, behind the wrought-iron fences, is Biarritz's stately landmark, the sumptuous **Hôtel du Palais**. This is the spot where Eugénie built her palace, destroyed by fire in 1881. The present hotel, begun in 1905, is the successor to an even grander one that also burned down. Across the street, the Russian aristocrats built their onion-domed **church of St-Alexandre-Nevsky** (1908).

Avenue Edouard VII, which becomes Avenue de l'Impératrice further on, was the status address of Belle Epoque Biarritz, lined with ornate hotels and residences now largely converted to other uses. In the shady streets behind them, all originally part of the imperial estate, scores of wealthy villas still survive, in a crazy quilt of styles ranging from Art Nouveau to neo-Moorish to Anglo-Norman. Some of the best can be seen on and around Avenue Reine Victoria. Also in this area, you can have a look at what passed for piety in the Second Empire – another creation of Napoleon and Eugénie, the 1864 **Chapelle Impériale**, on Avenue Reine Victoria at Rue Pellot. Built at the height of Napoleon's megalomaniacal campaigns in Mexico, it was dedicated to the black Mexican virgin, Notre-Dame de Guadalupe. Unfortunately the lavish neo-Byzantine interior is rarely open (*mid-Sept–mid-July Thurs 2.30–5.30; mid-July–mid-Sept Tues, Thurs and Sat 3–7*).

At the end of Plage Miramar stands the other landmark on this stretch of the coast, the 143ft **Phare St-Martin** (*t 05 59 22 37 10; open Sept–June Sat–Sun 3–7, July–Aug Tues–Sun 10–12 and 3–7*), a rare example of an old-fashioned lighthouse, built in 1834 and little changed since. It's only 249 steps to climb.

As for beaches, there is a wide choice of places to plant your towel, and you should be able to find a spot that's not too crowded even in the height of summer. From south to north: at Biarritz's southern limits are the broad expanse of the Plage de la Milady, Plage Marbella and the Côte des Basques, a favourite of the surfing set. Below the old town is the tiny but pleasant Plage du Port-Vieux. The Grande Plage and Plage Miramar, the centre of the action, are lovely, if often cramped, but further out, stretching miles along the northern coast in the suburb of Anglet, there are plenty more. When the beach traffic's too terrific in summer, take the special Navette des Plages bus from Place Clemenceau or Avenue de l'Impératrice (*summer only, otherwise the no.4 or 6 lines*) to the above-mentioned beaches, or go north and take your pick among the Plage de la Chambre d'Amour, the Plages des Corsaires, de la Madrague, de l'Ocean and des Dunes, or Plage des Cavaliers. The first one takes its name from a number of caves, now mostly submerged, that served for lovers' trysts long ago. Plenty of different stories have grown up around the place – about pairs of lovers who took refuge here and were tragically drowned with the tide – but the notorious French witch-hunter de Lancre, who wrote a report on witchcraft in the Labourd in 1609, said that this was known locally to be none other than the birth-place of Venus, where the goddess rose up from the foam of the sea.

For a break from the city and the beaches, in 10 minutes you can drive to **Arcangues**, a lovely village on a height south of Biarritz. In the centre, the serene, light-filled 16th-century church has one of the oldest carved double galleries in France and a delicate painted roof in the choir. The church shares space with the *fronton* and a bust of Arcangues' son Luis Mariano, celebrated singing star of some really excruciating French film musicals of the 1940s and 50s. He's buried nearby in a simple grave always thickly covered with flowers; the terraced cemetery itself leads into the lovely Bois de Saint Pée, a great place to get lost. There are more quiet 17th-century churches and tranquil town squares at the Basque villages of **Arbonne** (the church here has a special holy water font for the Cagots; *see* pp.222–3) and **Ahetze**, famous for its flea market held on the third Sunday of every month.

Bayonne

Arthur Young, the famous English traveller of the 1780s, called it the prettiest town he'd seen in France. Young had a good eye; even today, Bayonne is as attractive and lively an urban setting as you'll find in the southwest. Despite a remarkable history, a majestic cathedral and a delicious medieval centre full of brightly painted old half-timbered buildings, Bayonne doesn't attract much attention these days, lost as it is in the sprawling conurbation that includes Biarritz, the ports and industry of Boucau and the dormitory community of Anglet. Nevertheless, if you enjoy good cities or if you need a break from the beaches, spend a day in Bayonne.

History

Bayonne began in the 3rd century AD as a Roman *castrum* called Lapurdum, home to the cohort that guarded *Novempopulania*, which encompassed Aquitaine and much of southwest France. Although *Lapurdum* left its name to the province Labourd, nothing else was heard from Bayonne until the booming 12th century, when it adopted its present name and grew into an important port town. Even then, Bayonne was not Basque but in fact a predominantly Gascon town; the two peoples have been getting on well enough ever since. From 1151 until 1452, it was ruled by the English, an arrangement agreeable to both sides; Bayonne gave the Plantagenets a strong base at the southern end of their continental empire, and the town enjoyed considerable privileges and freedom, not to mention a busy trade with Britain.

All that ended when King Charles VII and the French marched in at the end of the Hundred Years' War. Not long after, an even bigger disaster hit – the river Adour suddenly picked itself up and moved to a new bed, leaving the port high and dry. But Bayonne, close to the border with Spain, was important to the French; in 1578 they

Chocolate City

While the Basques were among the first to recognize and profit from New World plants such as corn, tobacco and rubber (which put the bounce in their *pelota* balls), their history as chocolatiers came in a more roundabout way. The fad for drinking chocolate began with Hernan Cortés, who tried *xocoatl* during his conquest of Mexico in 1519 and brought back some beans and recipes. The Spanish court fell for the stuff, and so did the Basques, but the Spanish and Portuguese (who independently discovered chocolate in Brazil) were savvy enough to keep its secrets to themselves. Jewish refugees from the Spanish Inquisition who had settled in Portugal learned how to make it, and when Philip II inherited Portugal and extended the Inquisition there, the *chocolatiers* took refuge in Bayonne's ghetto, the Quartier St-Esprit. When Louis XIV passed through on his way to marry the Spanish *infanta* Maria Teresa in 1659, he and his courtiers succumbed to the delights of chocolate; Maria Teresa herself was a cup-a-day girl, in spite of popular wisdom that condemned chocolate along with tobacco as evil and ruinous to the health.

In the 18th century, a Basque pirate captain named Sopite thoughtfully provided something to sprinkle on top of one's morning dose – bringing the first cinnamon to France from Sumatra in a daring trip ordered by royal command in the middle of a war (his ship, *La Basquaise*, met five English vessels on the way home and beat them all). After the French Revolution put an end to discrimination, Bayonne's Jewish *chocolatiers* moved out of the ghetto into the centre and built up a reputation as the best in France – there are still quite a few in the old town who keep up the tradition. Two of the best are Daranatz and Cazeneuve, both located under the arcades of the Hôtel de Ville.

sent down engineers to dig a canal and redirect the Adour, and the port was back in business. A century later, Louis XIV dispatched his famous military engineer, Vauban, to make Bayonne an impregnable stronghold; the sprawling, state-of-the-art fortifications he designed, along with the Citadelle, are a striking feature of the cityscape even today.

Bayonne's military vocation flourished in the 18th century. An armaments industry grew up and gave the world the word 'bayonet', while Basque and Gascon corsairs, with letters of marque from the king, sallied out to snatch what they could from the Spanish, the English and North Africans. Besides weapons, the city's other passion was sweets, in particular chocolate (*see* above).

Bayonne lost its status as a free port and most of its trade with the Revolution, and there were more troubles to come. Vauban's walls proved their worth in the Napoleonic Wars. Coming up from Spain, Wellington's army twice besieged the city, in 1813 and 1814; they took it on the second try, by stringing a bridge of ships across the Adour and dragging artillery across it to bombard the city from both sides. Recovery came only with the arrival of the railway from Paris in 1854. Industrialization proceeded apace after that, and now Bayonne's little jewel of a historic centre is wrapped in the 'BAB' (Bayonne, Anglet, Biarritz), a metropolitan area of over 100,000 people, counting Biarritz and smaller towns.

Grand Bayonne and the Cathedral

Bayonne's main street is a river, the little Nive, and it is one of the most delightful centrepieces a city could ask for, lined on both sides with busy quays and tall old houses with trim painted in bright colours (mostly red and green, but no prizes for guessing that).

The Nive also marks the division between the two old quarters of the walled town, Grand Bayonne and Petit Bayonne. The former is the business end, jammed with animated, pedestrian-only shopping streets.

Cathédrale Ste-Marie

One of these streets, narrow Rue Argenterie, will take you from the quays to Bayonne's landmark and symbol, the **Cathédrale Ste-Marie**. It is also a symbol of the coming of French control – one of the few examples of the northerners' Gothic style in the southwest, and certainly one of the best. Begun in the 12th century, most of the

Getting There and Around

See p.247 under 'Biarritz' for all bus and train information in these twin cities.

Boat Tours

Two-hour boat trips with commentary along the Nive depart daily throughout the year. For reservations, call **t** 05 59 47 77 17.

Tourist Information

Tourist office: Place des Basques, **t** 05 59 46 01 46, **f** 05 59 59 37 55. *Open Mon–Fri 9–6 and Sat 10–6*. Ask them about their guided historical tours of the city.
Internet and email: **Centre Tim's France**, Le Forum, **t** 05 59 57 11 00 (*open Mon–Fri 10–12 and 2–7*), and **Cyber Net Café**, tucked behind a café-bar on Place de la République in the Quartier de St Esprit (*open 7am–2am*).

Market Days

Monday to Saturday mornings in Les Halles and all day Friday. Place des Gascons holds a market on Wednesday and Saturday mornings; Quais de la Nive has one on Tuesday, Thursday and Saturday mornings; Rue Ste-Catherine has one on Friday and Sunday mornings; and Polo Beyris holds one on Friday morning. There's a *marché à la brocante* (flea market) on Friday mornings at Place Montaut.

Shopping

Chocolat Cazenave, 19 Rue du Port-Neuf, **t** 05 59 59 03 16. Founded in 1854, one of the best and longest-established of the dozens of *chocolatiers* along this street. Buy some chocs to take home, after sipping one of their famous cuppas.
Conserverie Artisanale de Jambon de Bayonne, 41 Rue des Cordeliers, **t** 05 59 25 65 30. Tastings and tours of the workshop, with a shop where you can buy fine local hams.
Fabrique de Makilas, 37 Rue Vieille Boucherie, **t** 05 59 59 18 20. One of the last three makers of the traditional *makila*, a carved Basque walking stick with a hidden sword inside.

Sports and Activities

Pelote: There are several *pelote* courts in the town. Check with the tourist office for details of dates and times, or contact the **Fédération Française de Pelote Basque**, **t** 05 59 59 22 34.
Rugby: The local team, Aviron Bayonne, is enormously popular and usually among the best in France. Games take place most Sundays during the season at the Stade Jean-Duager; again, the tourist office will have details.
Bullfighting: *Corridas* take place between 14 and 21 July, and during the Feria des Fêtes in early August, the Feria de l'Assomption in mid-August and the Feria de l'Atlantique in early September. Tickets and information can be obtained from the tourist information office.

Where to Stay

Bayonne ✉ 64100

If you're not too concerned about proximity to a beach, the animated streets of Bayonne

work was done in the 13th. Some was still going on in the 16th century, when the south tower went up and the arms of the king of France were added to the sculptural decoration of the portal in honour of Bayonne's new rulers. Throughout, the building was largely financed by Bayonne's whalers. The bishops exacted a tenth of the profits from them, also claiming 'by divine right' the most prized parts of each whale for themselves – the tongue and the fat (the tongue, fresh or salted, was considered the ultimate delicacy; the blubber was rendered down into an oil used for fuel). Despite all the city's loot from whales, piracy and chocolates, however, the cathedral still wasn't finished until the 19th century, when followers of Viollet-le-Duc oversaw a thorough restoration and added the matching north tower.

might make a nice, cheaper alternative to staying in Biarritz.

★★★Best Western Grand Hôtel, 21 Rue Thiers, **t** 05 59 59 62 00, **f** 05 59 59 62 01 (*expensive–moderate*) All the city can offer in terms of luxury; it has managed to retain some of its former stately character, with large, well-equipped rooms and an 'English Bar'.

★★★Hôtel Frantour-Loustau, 1 Place de la République, **t** 05 59 55 08 08, **f** 05 59 55 69 36 (*moderate*). Part of a French chain but, although formulaic, it does offer pretty views of Vieux Bayonne and the Pyrenees and good facilities for the price.

★★Hôtel Ibis, 44–50 Bd Alsace-Lorraine, Quartier St-Esprit, **t** 05 59 50 38 38, **f** 05 59 50 38 00 (*inexpensive*). A functional chain hotel with a small garden and a restaurant.

★★Hôtel Adour, 13 Place Ste-Ursule, Quartier St-Esprit, **t** 05 59 55 11 31, **f** 05 59 55 86 40 (*inexpensive*). Overlooking the Nive, this hotel has seen better times. Still, it has a certain faded charm, the rooms are spick and span and there is a decent restaurant.

★★Hôtel Basses Pyrénées, 1 Place des Victoires, **t** 05 59 59 00 29 (*inexpensive*). An old, family-run hotel worth a visit for the wonderful views across the old city ramparts; rooms overlooking the square are quieter, but lack the charm of those with a view.

★★Hôtel Côte Basque, 2 Rue Maubec, **t** 05 59 55 10 21, **f** 05 59 55 39 85 (*inexpensive*). A very friendly place near the station with a decent café-restaurant underneath; it's worth getting a room at the back as those over-looking the street can be noisy.

★Monbar, 24 Rue Pannecau, **t** 05 59 59 26 80 (*inexpensive*). Well-kept little hotel furnished with antiques on a lively street in Petit Bayonne, across the Nive.

★Des Arceaux, 26 Rue du Port-Neuf, **t** 05 59 59 15 53 (*inexpensive–cheap*). One of the best options in the heart of Vieux Bayonne near the cathedral. It's good for local nightlife but can get a bit noisy in the high season.

★Le Port-Neuf, 44 Rue du Port-Neuf, **t** 05 59 25 65 83 (*inexpensive–cheap*). Another popular little cheapie in Vieux Bayonne with a pretty breakfast terrace.

Eating Out

Like other cities on the coast, Bayonne does much better with restaurants than with hotels. Many of the best inexpensive places can be found in Petit Bayonne, either on the quays along the Nive or in the back streets behind them.

Le Cheval Blanc, Rue Bourg-Neuf, just round the corner from the Musée Bonnat, **t** 05 59 59 01 33, **f** 05 59 59 52 26. At the top of the heap, by popular acclaim. Even though the Tellechea family has been running this place for a long time, they never get tired of finding innovative twists to traditional Basque cooking: stuffed squid or *poulet basquaise* with *cèpes* (*expensive–moderate*).

Francois Miura, 24 Rue Marengo, **t** 05 59 59 49 89. A stylish small restaurant just by the Nive with modern furniture and contemporary paintings set against the old stone walls. The cuisine is an equally good mix of old and new; try *chipirons farcis au pied de porc* (squid in ink stuffed with pork) followed by a light tart with seasonal fruits (*expensive–moderate*).

Le Saint Simon, 1 Rue des Basques, **t** 05 59 59 27 71. An elegant, intimate restaurant in a beautiful old Basque house, serving a

So far from the Ile-de-France and so long in building, it isn't surprising that there are no unusual stylistic departures here. What is surprising is how well it all fits together; this is a truly elegant building. Best of all, it still enjoys the sort of setting a Gothic cathedral should have – among narrow streets and tightly packed tall buildings, where its presence and verticality can make exactly the impression its designers intended.

Individual details worth calling attention to are few; this cathedral was thoroughly trashed in the Revolution. Inside, there's no need for detail; the rise of the slender pilasters that carry the rib-vaulted nave permit a lofty interior that no church in the southwest save the Jacobins in Toulouse can match. There is some good Renaissance

thoughtful menu of regional delicacies, such as fresh squid lightly fried with garlic and served with fresh pasta, followed by a melt-in-the-mouth chocolate truffle cake (*moderate*).

Le Chistera, 42 Rue Port-Neuf, **t** 05 59 59 25 93. An unpretentious little fish bistro with an excellent range of fresh fish dishes – marinated anchovies, squid cooked in its own ink, or *morue à l'ail*.

Le Pavé, 8 Rue des Gouverneurs, **t** 05 59 59 51 74. A popular little restaurant serving classic regional dishes, set in a stone cellar just by the Cathedral de Sainte-Marie (*moderate–cheap*).

The Bayonnais, 38 Quai des Corsaires, **t** 05 59 25 61 19. Traditional Basque restaurant in the old town, with décor dedicated to local sporting heroes. On the menu, you'll find roast Pyrenean lamb, a subtle Andalucían-style gazpacho, and a rich chocolate gâteau to finish up (*cheap*).

Le Petit Chahut, **t** 05 59 25 54 60. A hole-in-the-wall on Quai Galuperie. It offers fresh seafood: grilled fish or *thon à la basque* (*cheap*).

Entertainment and Nightlife

Theatre and Cabaret

Théâtre de Bayonne, Hôtel de Ville, Place de la Liberté, **t** 05 59 59 07 27. Classical music performances from the Orchestre Bayonne Côte Basque and all kinds of theatre. Tickets are sold Tues–Sat between 1pm and 7pm, and 1 hour before a performance.

Cabaret La Luna Negra, Rue des Augustins, **t** 05 59 25 78 05. Café-theatre with live

music – blues, jazz, Latin – and '*soirés dansants*', which feature all kinds of music from rock and swing to Sevillanas and Argentine tango. There are also puppet and mime shows for kids.

Cinema

L'Atalante, 7 Rue Denis Etcheverry, Quartier St Esprit, **t** 05 59 55 76 63. This is a very popular art cinema showing v.o. (undubbed) films with a buzzing but relaxed café-bar.

Bars and Clubs

Pick up a free copy of *Cultzine* (www.cultzine.com) from the tourist office for details of local clubs and visiting DJs in Bayonne.

Petit Bayonne is always very animated at weekends with plenty of lively bars. Rue des Cordeliers, Rue Pannecau and Rue des Tonneliers are good bets for friendly bars. Try the following:

L'Alambic, 17 Rue Pannecau, **t** 05 59 59 38 58. Bar-cum-club with live music and DJs.

Bodega Ibaia, 49 Quai Jauréguiberry. A neighbourhood fixture, this busy spot is full of locals of all ages gossiping, laughing and drinking.

La Txalupa, 26 Rue des Cordeliers. A cheerful young crowd gather here.

Zoco, 33 Rue des Cordeliers. For late-night drinking with a young, clubby crowd.

Chez Achille, 2 Rue d'Espagne. A favourite for rugby fans – and there's a pleasant terrace if you want to escape them.

La Tertulia, Quai Jauréguiberry. A tiny Spanish-style bar serving *tapas* and local cider.

François, 14 Rue Guilhamin, opposite the Halles, with an Art Deco décor, bustling from the crack of dawn on market days.

stained glass in the nave windows, heavily restored a century ago. Note the scene of Adam and Eve, where the serpent (with a female head) wears the bonnet of a medieval doctor of philosophy – just to show what a subtle argument she was capable of. In the left aisle, the **chapel of St Jerome** has one of the best windows (1531), a scene of the Canaanite woman (from Matthew, 15:22) crowned by a salamander, the symbol of King François I. The **sacristy** shelters the only original 13th-century sculptures that survived the Revolution: one tympanum of the Last Judgement, with the Devil boiling a king and a bishop in his cauldron, and another of the Virgin Mary, surrounded by angel musicians. This leads to a lovely **cloister**, also much damaged in the Revolution.

Château-Vieux

Just behind the cathedral, on Rue des Gouverneurs, the **Château-Vieux** was the city's stronghold and the seat of its governors: first the English (parts of what you see date from the 12th century; one of the governors was the Black Prince), and then the French (the outworks were added in the time of Louis XIV to guard against revolts by the Bayonnais).

Although the Château-Vieux is usually closed to visitors, the tours organized by the tourist office will take you through here, and also through the amazing expanses of underground chambers that underlie much of the city, some of them as properly vaulted as the cathedral's aisles. In medieval times they were used for storing wine waiting to be shipped to England.

Petit Bayonne

The smaller but livelier side of Bayonne, this is a *rive gauche* on the right bank of the Nive. The narrow back streets of Petit Bayonne are crowded with popular neighbourhood bars and restaurants – you won't see the likes of an old, unspoiled city neighbourhood like this in many places in southwest France.

Right in the middle, on the Quai des Corsaires, is the **Musée Basque**. This 16th-century building facing the Nive started out as a convent, and later did long service as a customs house. In 1922 the city of Bayonne took it over as a museum that gradually turned into the largest collection of objects on Basque culture and folk life anywhere. In June 2001, after being closed for restoration for 12 years, the museum reopened, and from all accounts it is something quite special.

The Musée Bonnat

5 Rue Jacques Laffitte, t 05 59 59 08 52; open Wed–Mon 10–12 and 2.30–6.30pm, Fri until 8.30, closed Tues and hols; adm (free first Sunday of the month).

Bayonne's own Léon Bonnat was one of the best-known salon painters of late-19th-century France, the sort of happy Philistine who got rich painting celebrity portraits, collected prizes and medals, and sneered at the Impressionists when he served as a judge in the Salon competitions. When he died in 1922, Bonnat left his own considerable collection of art to Bayonne, and it has become the nucleus of one of the finest museums in the southwest.

Some of Bonnat's work takes pride of place in a gallery devoted to his work on the first floor: portraits of shiny bankers and blooming society ladies in corsets – another world. There's a portrait of Puvis de Chavannes, by Bonnat, and one of Bonnat himself – done by Degas, of all people. There are some superb late medieval and early Renaissance works which the French, ignorantly and infuriatingly, still call 'primitives'. Besides works by *quattrocento* masters Domenico Veneziano and Maso di Banco, there are also some obscure delights: a 14th-century *Christ and Virgin* of the Toulouse school, better than most of their work you'll see in any churches, and a number of Catalan-Aragonese paintings from the same age, with the Catalan love of extreme stylization and rich gold backgrounds. As always with this art, the works range from the really excellent, such as the *Saint Martin* of the unknown 'master of the Musée Bonnat', to some that are almost *naïf* – a bit of precocious Diego Rivera with halos and gold leaf.

Since 1999, most of the rest of the art has been arranged thematically rather than chronologically. Occasionally it works (although usually it doesn't). Sections devoted to figure studies, animals, war scenes and allegories have paintings crammed together in a dizzying clash of styles and methods, with apparently no sense at all of how one piece might complement another. On the ground floor, however, some of the museum's best pictures are hung with a bit of breathing space. There is a fine *Madonna* by Botticelli, from the late period when the artist renounced his magical-mythological works and lapsed into extreme piety. It didn't always work; this one, despite the Christian trappings, is still plainly Botticelli's *Venus*. From the late Renaissance and Baroque there are some good Flemish tapestries, a couple of pieces by El Greco (including a grim portrait of Duc de Benarcat, who was said to have been an Inquisitor, and another of Don Pedro de Buja, a languid fop), and an entire section devoted to Rubens: a blatant *Leçon d'Amour*, a number of smaller paintings taken from Ovid and from the life of Henri IV, as well as a good number of the artist's sketches.

Almost all the great schools of 17th- and 18th-century painting are represented here. Standouts include a Murillo, *Daniel in the Lions' Den*; a bit of chilly militarism from the time of the Thirty Years' War in Jan Bronkhorst's portrait *General Octavio Piccolomini*; and an equally disturbing painting by Ribera, *Femme Désespérée*, with a distraught girl clutching her hair. This work, in its weird intensity, seems to prefigure Goya, and there are some Goyas here in the museum to compare it to, including a fascinating self-portrait.

There's no telling whose face is going to turn up on the walls of this museum. Among the English paintings, you will see Lawrence's portraits of the composer Karl Maria von Weber and Johann Heinrich Füssli – better known as Henry Fuseli, crazy painter and friend of William Blake. Ingres, one of the spiritual fathers of salon painting, was understandably a favourite of Bonnat's; among 10 of his works here is an unspeakable portrait of the unspeakable last Bourbon, King Charles X.

An important part of Bonnat's collection was the 36 works by his friend Antoine Barye, the most popular sculptor of his day. Nearby, not always open (write in advance for permission to visit), is the *cabinet des dessins*, a wonderful collection of almost 2,000 drawings and prints from the Renaissance up to the 20th century. And down in the basement is the museum's archaeological collection. Many of these works were Bonnat's, and he chose well: Greek pots and Roman glass, votive reliefs, and lovely statuettes of various goddesses that caught the painter's fancy. The Carré Bonnat holds temporary exhibitions of contemporary art.

The Château-Neuf and Ramparts

On the eastern edge of the walls, the Château-Neuf (*t 05 59 59 08 98; open Tues–Fri 2–6, Sat 9–1, closed Sun and Mon*) looms over the town, a stronghold begun in 1460 by the French to consolidate their control over the city. Some rooms are devoted to temporary exhibitions from the Museé Basque while it remains closed. The adjacent parts of Vauban's walls, however, were tidied up by the city and opened to the public a decade ago. On these **Remparts de Mousserolles** you can see what was going through Vauban's mind, and what war was like in the late 17th and 18th centuries. To defend a city properly, it was usually necessary to destroy at least half of it for the fortifications. Baroque fortifications are notable for the space they take up: one or two rings of low-slung, zigzagging ramparts, with a complex of earthen salients and trenches beyond them, all designed to counter artillery rather than repulse a direct attack, which with the improved firearms of the age would have been suicidal. Today the Mousserolles ramparts are an attractive city park, with a lagoon and open-air theatre.

Quartier St-Esprit

The third district of Bayonne, cowering under Vauban's haughty Citadelle and half-demolished 150 years ago for the train station, is the Quartier St-Esprit, reached by the long bridge across the Adour. Quartier St-Esprit was Bayonne's ghetto until the Revolution, but the Jews once forced to live here have left few traces. At the end of the bridge, the **St-Esprit** church was a gift to Bayonne from Louis XI, that most excellent monarch who wore old clothes and kept a troupe of dancing pigs to entertain him when he was blue. This 15th-century Gothic building retains from its original decoration a polychrome sculpture of the Flight into Egypt; Mary sits looking unconcerned on a donkey, and this has become a popular little shrine to Our Lady of Travellers.

Not far away, you can initiate yourself in Basque peculiarity with a tour of the **Izarra Distillery** (*9 Quai Bergeret; open summer Mon–Sat 9–6, winter Mon–Fri 10–11.15 and 2.30–5*). Izarra is the sweet, alarmingly chartreuse-coloured liqueur you see in every bar down here, made from Pyrenean herbs, spices and a little Armagnac.

On the other side of the Citadelle, the working end of Bayonne, an impressive stretch of docks and factories, follows the wide Adour down to the sea. At the northern edge of town, off Avenue Louis de Foix, is the **English cemetery** from Wellington's campaigns; Queen Victoria and other members of the royal family always came to visit when they were in Biarritz.

The Labourd Interior: Around La Rhune

The name of La Rhune, westernmost peak in the Pyrenean chain, comes from the Basque *larrun*, or pasture land. It's full of cows and sheep all right, just as it has been for the last few millennia. The tracks around its slopes have been one of the main Basque smugglers' routes for centuries. A Basque tale has it that La Rhune was once covered in gold. Some evil men came to take it away; they cut down the trees and burned them to get at it, but the gold all melted and flowed away. The mountain's summit also had a reputation for its *akelarre*, ritual orgies of witches; until the 18th century, the mayors of the villages around it paid a monk to live on top as a hermit for a term of four years, to keep the witches away and pray for good winds.

Ascain and La Rhune

Coming in from Hendaye or St-Jean, the first of the villages below La Rhune is **Ascain (Askaine)**, with its landmark three-arched medieval bridge over the Nivelle and a 16th-century church on its lovely square. From here a hiking trail leads up to the 2,925ft summit of La Rhune, or else you can take the D4 up to the Col de St-Ignace, where there is another trail and also an old, open tramway to the top, the **Petit Train de la Rhune** (*t 05 59 54 20 26; mid-March–mid-Nov daily every half-hour from 9am, in summer from 8.30am, plus night runs in July and Aug*).

Tourist Information

Ascain: *mairie*, t 05 59 54 00 84; out of season t 05 59 54 68 34.
Sare: Herriko Etxea, t 05 59 54 20 14, f 05 59 54 29 15, *pays-basque@calva.net*.
St-Pée-sur-Nivelle: Place de la Poste, t 05 59 54 11 69, f 05 59 54 17 81.
Espelette: Rue Karrika Nagusia, t 05 59 93 91 44, f 05 59 93 89 71.

Market Days

Espelette: Wednesday mornings, and Saturday in July and August.

Where to Stay and Eat

Prices for both rooms and meals in the Labourd will be a relief after the coast. And you'll never be disappointed with the quality of either – in fact the modest joys of an old Basque country inn may be one of the major reasons for coming here.

Ascain ✉ 64310

**Du Pont, Route de St-Jean-de-Luz, t 05 59 54 00 40 (*inexpensive*). With rooms overlooking the Nivelle and its bridge, and a delightful restaurant with a garden terrace, where *feuilleté de langoustines* and other delicate dishes are served. *Open March–Oct.*
*Achafla Baïta, Route d'Olhette, t 05 59 54 00 30 (*cheap*). Out in the peaceful countryside. There is also a good restaurant with lots of fish in a variety of sauces, from *cèpes* to *beurre blanc* (*moderate*).
Maison Arrayoa, t 05 59 54 06 18 (*cheap*). Bed and breakfast on a farm.

Sare ✉ 64310

In the Labourd, hotels tend to be sweet and simple, with immaculate rooms in white traditional buildings with red shutters and oak beams. Sare provides a bewildering choice of these, all wonderfully inviting.
***Arraya, Place du Village, t 05 59 54 20 46, f 05 59 54 27 04 (*moderate*). Quite expensive for the area, but with a memorable restaurant. There are menus, but you might want to surrender a few francs more for specialities such as the *mesclange*, veal stuffed with foie gras, artichoke and morels.

In Neolithic times, La Rhune was a holy mountain, as evidenced by the wealth of monuments around its slopes. Ancient Basque religious rites were usually celebrated on mountaintops, hence their reputation in Christian times as haunts of sorcerers. You'll need a *série bleue* map and a day's hiking (at least) to find the monuments; there are eight small stone circles around a place called the **Crête de Gorostiarria**, and several dolmens and circular tumuli on the northern and western slopes. On the slopes of La Rhune towards Sare, the easiest to find are the four dolmens at a farm called **Xominen**, just off the Col de St-Ignace; further away at the **Aniotzbehere** farm are two more. The northern side of the **Pic d'Ibanteli** has four of them.

Sare

Just beyond the Col de St-Ignace lies **Sare**, one of the true capitals of the Basque soul. Because of its isolation and its traditionally independent ways, people jokingly call it the 'Republic of Sare'. Since the 15th century, the 'republic' was one of the main centres for what the Basques call *gabazkolana*, or 'night work' – smuggling. Folk on both sides of the border never really saw the logic of paying duties for moving their flocks around to French and Spanish foreigners. Smuggling sheep and cows gradually led to other things too. The French authorities usually treated all this with commendable humanity. The story is still told of a zealous customs man, just arrived from

---

*De la Poste, in the centre, t 05 59 54 20 06 (*inexpensive*). Old-fashioned classic. *Open summer only.*

Pikasseria, just outside Sare at Lehenbizkai, t 05 59 54 21 51, f 05 59 54 27 40 (*inexpensive*). Also has a good restaurant (*moderate*).

*Col de St-Ignace, at the pass on the D4 near the Rhune train, t 05 59 54 20 11 (*inexpensive*). Has a simple restaurant (*cheap*).

Les Trois Fontaines, Col de St-Ignace, t 05 59 54 20 80 (*moderate–cheap*). A country *auberge* near the cable car. There's a charming terrace and garden, serving Basque specialities.

St-Pée-sur-Nivelle ✉ 64310

Ferme Uxondoa, Quartier Elbarron, t 05 59 54 46 27, t 06 85 87 84 75 (*inexpensive*). *Chambre d'hôte* rooms on a farm, with facilities for catching your own trout.

Ainhoa ✉ 64790

Itthurria, Place du Fronton, t 05 59 29 92 11, f 05 59 29 81 28 (*moderate*). A large Basque house with a celebrated restaurant, featuring dishes such as pigeon with garlic and local foie gras (*expensive– moderate*).

**Oppoca, Place du Fronton, t 05 59 29 90 72, f 05 59 29 81 03 (*inexpensive*). On the main street of this pretty village, in a restored 17th-century post house. Despite lovely rooms, some furnished with antiques, it still seems a bit dear. There is also a fine restaurant with a terrace, serving seafood and *confits*.

**Ohantzea, t 05 59 29 90 50 (*inexpensive*). Cosy rooms in another 17th-century Basque house, with tables on the terrace made of slices of tree trunk.

Espelette ✉ 64250

**Euzkadi, Rue Principle, t 05 59 93 91 88, f 05 59 93 90 19. Worth travelling out of your way for, even in an area rich in good restaurants. There are nice rooms with a small pool and tennis, and a remarkable restaurant where the chef is passionate about traditional Basque recipes. Some of the house specialities are things you won't see elsewhere, such as *axoa*, a stew of veal and peppers, and *tripoxa*, a black pudding in a pepper and tomato sauce (*moderate*).

Alsace in the 1920s, who shot a local man in the leg while he was taking some cows over the slopes of La Rhune. His superiors went to the mayor of Sare and to the man's family to explain the situation and express their regrets, and then sent their officer over to the hospital to make his apologies. In 1938 and 39, Sare's night workers found a more rewarding if less lucrative business – helping their countrymen from the Spanish side escape Franco's troops; a few years later, they were doing great work smuggling Allied pilots and spies and Jews back the other way. If they were caught, the pilots and spies were usually sent to a big prison camp at Miranda de Ebro, but the Basques often as not would be shot or never seen again.

Sare's **church** is a wonderful example of the traditional Basque style, with its three levels of wooden balconies; memorials inside include the tombs of one of the early figures of Basque literature, the 18th-century Pierre Axular (*see pp.49–50*). More than most villages, Sare has retained a number of fine **town houses** with carved lintels, both in the village and in the *quartier* of Lehenbizkai to the south – in the Basque country, outlying hamlets are considered as 'quarters', or neighbourhoods of the main village.

South of town, a side road off the D306 takes you to the **Grottes de Sare** (*open 2 Jan–Shrove Tuesday Mon–Fri 2–4, Sat–Sun 11–4; Shrove Tuesday–Easter and 11 Nov–Christmas Mon–Fri 2–5, Sat–Sun 11–5; Easter–June and Sept Mon–Fri 10–6, Sat–Sun 10–7; July–Aug daily 10–8; Oct–11 Nov Mon–Fri 11–5, Sat–Sun 11–6; adm; guided tours and sound-and-light show*), with Palaeolithic drawings largely destroyed by vandals in 1918; it's said that you can go in here and find your way out at the Cuevas de Zugarramurdi, across the border in Spain; no one has tried it lately, but the overland *route des contrabandiers* to the same is a popular walk. The D306 continues on to the Col de Lizarrieta and the Spanish border on its way to Pamplona.

Saint-Pée-sur-Nivelle, Ainhoa and Espelette

In the late 16th century, many Gypsies and converted Muslims fleeing from Spanish persecution took refuge in the Labourd. In that most credulous of ages, all manner of stories about sorcerers and heathen rituals started circulating. The trouble began in 1609, started not by the Inquisition, but by the Parlement de Bordeaux. A lawyer named Pierre de Lancre was sent, and like most professional witch-hunters this one revealed himself as a murderous psychotic. De Lancre installed himself in **Saint-Pée**'s château, and soon accused the baroness herself of forcing him to participate in a black Mass where the Devil himself was present. With authority from the king, de Lancre started a reign of terror that lasted three years. Relying largely on the testimony of children and tortured women, he had several hundred people condemned to the stake. When he started barbecuing parish priests too, the bishop of Bayonne finally put an end to it.

Today St-Pée looks like your typical sleepy Basque village, built around its *fronton* court. This *fronton* holds a special place in Basque lore: here in 1857 a certain Gantixiki Harotcha had the idea of catching and throwing the *pelote* ball with a basket, the same one he had used to scoop up potatoes in the harvest, giving birth to *cesta punta*, or *jaï-alaï* as Americans call it, the fastest game of all.

Hot Stuff

Espelette is synonymous with *Capsicum annuum L*, or *piments d'Espelette* (*Ezpeletako Biperra*), and it's a great source of local pride that these hot red peppers were made AOC in 2000. Brought back from America by Columbus' Basque pilot, the peppers are grown in Espelette and nine surrounding *comunes*; they are planted in February and produce until the first frost. You can see them in the late summer hanging everywhere, drying on houses, on walls, on roofs; and you can buy a string of them, or reduced to a powder like paprika, or you can buy them mushed up in a paste in a jar. According to the locals, a pinch improves just about every dish, while gracing it with its hidden virtues – as a stimulant, an aphrodisiac, and cure for hangovers.

The Espelette *mairie* sells a book entirely devoted to them, with a selection of recipes; and the last Sunday in October is given over to a gastronomic hootenanny, in which the peppers appear where you might not expect them, even in chocolate. One highlight of the festival is the election of Madame or Monsieur Piment, a local who wins their weight in local food products.

In Europe, the hot pepper was one of the very few items brought back from America that didn't catch on, and in both Spain and France the only regional cuisine that you'll find that packs any heat is Basque – a bit surprising for people living in a rainy and generally cool climate, but by now you should realize that Basques are exceptions to the rule. In fact, perhaps the ultimate test of one's Basquehood is not the ability to play *pelota*, run with boulders, or speak Euskera, but the capacity for eating a mess of *piments d'Espelette* without flinching.

Ainhoa, one of the southernmost of all *bastides*, or medieval new towns, was founded in the days when the English were fighting with the Navarrese for control of the region. A 13th-century Navarrese baron started it, not only to keep the English out, but with the intention of charging tolls and otherwise making money off pilgrims to Compostela. Despite the straight streets, Ainhoa is another lovely Labourd village with many old houses – note the lintel over the door of the Maison Gorritia on the main street, telling how a mother built it in 1662 with money sent home by her son in the West Indies. For a pleasant if steep walk, take the path up to the pilgrimage chapel of Notre-Dame-de-Aranzazu, with panoramic views over the valley.

From either St-Pée or Ainhoa, the next step is **Espelette** (**Ezpeleta**). Here, too, are many attractive old houses, a church with a Baroque altarpiece, and an interesting cemetery full of discoidal stones; you might note an odd modernistic one, marking the tomb of a local girl who became the very first Miss World.

The Valley of the Nive

The little river that comes to such a handsome end among the quays and half-timbered houses of Bayonne has a long way to go before it gets there. Starting in the Spanish Pyrenees, it opens out into a narrow valley that cuts a diagonal swath across the Basque country. The D932/D918 that follows it is the high street of the Labourd and Basse-Navarre; a train follows it from Bayonne as far as St-Jean-Pied-de-Port.

Hasparren to St-Etienne

From Bayonne, an alternative route to the D932 into the heart of the Basque country is the D22, the **Route Impériale des Cimes**, a beautiful road over the hilltops that was built in the time of Napoleon. It will take you to **Hasparren**, a grey, hard-working town where there is an unusual Roman altar behind the church. Close by, **Urcuray** comes into its own in August when it hosts a famous *irrintzina*, or Basque yodelling contest, not to be missed if you're in the area (contact the Hasparren tourist office for precise dates). Nearby, **La Bastide-Clairence** was founded by the king of Navarre in 1314; settled by Gascons, it long remained a non-Basque enclave among the Basques, although the pretty houses lining its streets are pure Basque. Just outside the village is a Jewish cemetery, from the community of Spanish refugees that formed here in the 17th century. Today many of the houses in the centre are occupied by craftspeople.

Southeast of Hasparren, near the village of St-Esteben, the **Grottes d'Istaritz et d'Oxocelhaya** (*t 05 59 29 64 72; open mid-March–mid-Nov, daily exc Mon and Tues morning, 10–12 and 2–6; July and Aug 10–6; adm; guided tours*) are one of the most important prehistoric sites in Europe, especially for the quality of their 'furnishings' or *art mobilier*. In the 19th century, folks all across this area were poking around in caves in search of guano deposits, the best fertilizer in the world. The guano hunters here

Tourist Information

Hasparren: 2 Place St Jean, **t** 05 59 29 62 02, **f** 05 59 29 13 80, *hasparren.tourisme@wanadoo.fr*.

Ustaritz: Centre Lapurdi, **t** 05 59 93 20 81, **f** 05 59 70 32 80.

Cambo-les-Bains: Parc Publique, **t** 05 59 29 70 25, **f** 05 59 29 90 77.

St-Etienne-de-Baïgorry: Place de l'Eglise, **t/f** 05 59 37 47 28, *baigorry.tourisme@wanadoo.fr*.

Market Days

Hasparren: Every other Tuesday, and Saturday for farm produce.

Ossès: Saturday mornings (*summer only*).

Where to Stay and Eat

Hasparren ✉ 64240

★★★**Les Tilleuls**, 1 Place Verdun, **t** 05 59 29 62 20, **f** 05 59 29 13 58 (*moderate*). In the heart of the village, a renovated Basque house with trendy trimmings and restaurant, serving tasting *cuisine de terroir* with a special touch; try the *terrine de foie gras*.

La Bastide-Clairence ✉ 64240

Chez les Foix, **t** 05 59 29 18 27, **f** 05 59 29 14 97 (*inexpensive*). Beautiful *chambre d'hôte* in a 16th-century house, run by an enthusiastic Basque–Irish couple.

Des Arceaux, **t** 05 59 29 66 70. Bar-restaurant serving hearty cheap meals in a home-like setting with a picture of granny on the wall; the centre of life in La Bastide.

Cambo-les-Bains ✉ 64250

★★★**Relais de la Poste**, Place de la Mairie, **t** 05 59 29 73 03 (*inexpensive*). Offers 10 pretty rooms in the lower part of town, a little garden and a restaurant that turns out some truly refined dishes: roast pigeon with *cèpes* and salmon *roulés* with foie gras (*expensive–moderate*). There is outside dining in summer.

★★**Bellevue**, Rue des Terrasses, **t** 05 59 93 75 75, **f** 05 59 93 75 85 (*inexpensive*). An old, pleasant establishment with a view, near the top of town, with a restaurant.

★★**St-Laurent**, Rue des Terrasses, **t** 05 59 29 71 10 (*inexpensive*). Similar to the Bellevue in style and price.

★★**Chez Tante Ursule**, Bas Cambo, **t** 05 59 29 78 23, **f** 05 59 29 28 57 (*inexpensive*). Small,

were surprised to find a massive pile of prehistoric cave-bear bones that crumbled into dust at the touch and some peculiar carvings, and only reluctantly did they let the palaeontologists in to investigate. Tools, paintings, reliefs and other relics were found here going back some 40,000 years, including the oldest musical instrument ever discovered, a flute that very closely resembles a three-holed Basque *txistu*. The sculptures were also extraordinary: the head of bear carved in flint, elaborate sticks carved with spirals and other symbols, a mysterious bone engraved with two naked women and two bison, and a feline carved from a reindeer antler, purposely made headless and pierced with strange holes, often cited as evidence of Palaeolithic hunter magic; it certainly bears a resemblance to the supernatural animals of Basque folklore. Most of the artefacts have been spirited off to museums, and visitors will have to content themselves with a look at the underground stretch of the river Arbéroue, and some exceptional cave formations – delicate stalactites that have grown down to the floor to become columns. The ruined tower on the hill of Castelu above the cave was long rumoured to hold the golden treasure of the *laminak*, although old (and empty) Roman pots is all anyone ever found.

On the main road, the D932 up the Nivelle valley, the first big village is **Ustaritz**, once the meeting place of the *biltzar*, the local assembly, and famous in Basque lore as the

---

rustic hotel with a modern annexe. There is also an excellent restaurant (*moderate*). Try the pimentos stuffed with *morue* or salads with foie gras or *boudin noir*.

Domaine de Xixtaberri, Quartier Hegala, t 05 59 29 85 36 (*moderate*). A *ferme-auberge* up in the hills with superb panoramas. There is a restaurant (*moderate*) with menus full of duck and foie gras, all raised *in situ*. The hotel is open year-round, but the restaurant opens May–Sept only; be sure to book.

Itxassou ✉ 64250

★★Fronton, Place du Fronton, t 05 59 29 75 10, f 05 59 29 23 50 (*moderate–inexpensive*). The hotel of choice in the village. The restaurant has a room with a view, and the artichoke hearts with foie gras followed by a fillet of sole St-Jacques or a *confit* make a satisfying dinner (*moderate*).

★★Du Chêne, t 05 59 29 75 01, f 05 59 29 27 39 (*inexpensive*). Quiet little hotel by the church.

★★Etcheparre Sallaberia, Place de la Mairie, t 05 59 25 75 14, f 05 59 29 80 59 (*inexpensive*). The least expensive accommodation in the village. Try their *maigret de canard* with cherries.

Bidarray ✉ 64780

★★Pont d'Enfer, t 05 59 37 70 88, f 05 59 37 76 60 (*inexpensive*). Faces Bidarray's medieval bridge and has red-shuttered, pleasant rooms. There is a restaurant with a terrace where you can get a *ttoro* from the sea or a trout from the Nive (*moderate–cheap*).

★★Barberenea, Place de l'Eglise, t 05 59 37 74 86, f 05 59 37 77 55 (*inexpensive*). Peaceful and simple, with welcoming owners.

St-Etienne-de-Baïgorry 64330

★★★L'Auberge du Pont d'Arcé, Route du Col d'Ispéguy, t 05 59 37 40 14, f 05 59 37 40 27 (*moderate*). A former smugglers' inn overlooking the Nive. Traditional Basque kitchen, and a lovely terrace overlooking the river.

Château d'Etxauz, t 05 59 37 48 58, f 05 59 59 01 90 (*expensive*). Romantic *chambres d'hôte* in the town castle, which dates back to the 11th century, surrounded by a park of century old trees.

Izarra, t 05 59 37 43 96 (*moderate–inexpensive*). When you have a hankering for foie gras and *maigrets* and other ducky dishes. Try the local Basque sauce, *Sakari*.

The *Pottok*

Although it stands only 4ft high, it has a face that would make you suspect there was a camel somewhere in the family tree – but a sweet face just the same, with big soft eyes and a wild shaggy mane. It is quite shy, hiding out on the remotest slopes of the western Pyrenees, but it's not afraid of you; come too close and you'll get a bite to remember. The *pottok* is the wild native pony of the Basque country. They've been around for a while; drawings of *pottoks* have been found in the prehistoric caves up in the Dordogne.

Though they're hard to catch, people have been molesting the poor *pottoks* for centuries. A century ago, they were shipping them to Italy to make salami, or to Britain to pull mine cars, a dismal task for which their strength and small size made them perfectly adapted. Annual horse fairs took place in the villages of Espelette and Hélette. Business was so good that the *pottoks* were on the road to extinction a few decades ago. A famous mayor of Sare, the late Paul Dutournier, stepped in and got the government to set up a reserve for them on the slopes of La Rhune. A second, private *pottok* reserve can be visited in Bidarray (*see* below).

first place where corn was planted, brought back by yet another Basque sailor who had accompanied Colombus. Near the entrance of the communual forest, just off the road to Saint-Pée, stands a tall schist monolith known as the Croix des Anglais. The English in question may have been the Black Prince, who raided in the area, but the big stone itself was only 'converted' from a menhir in 1713 with the addition of a cross.

Next comes **Larressore**, known for the manufacture of *makilas*, and then the biggest village of the interior, **Cambo-les-Bains**. The name of this placid and genteel spa seems to come from a Roman army camp; locals called the site 'Caesar's camp' long ago. The spa grew up in the 16th century, and became briefly fashionable when Napoleon III and Eugénie visited from Biarritz. The Prince of Wales (Edward VII) also liked to drop in during his Biarritz holidays to watch a legendary *pelote* star named Chiquito de Cambo. Cambo's main attraction is the Villa Arnaga (*open Feb school hols–March Sat–Sun 2.30–6.30, April–Sept daily 10–12.30 and 2.30–6.30, Oct daily 2.30–6.30*), the home of dramatist Edmund Rostand, who, after the success of *Cyrano de Bergerac*, came here in the 1900s to treat his pleurisy at the baths. The house contains mementos from his life and the Paris of the turn of the 20th century; the real attraction, however, is the splendid 18th-century-style French garden, venue of the Chanteclerc theatre festival in August.

After Cambo, the foothills begin rising steadily. Nearby, off the D918, is the sweet, tiny village of **Itxassou**, famous for its orchards that produce the dark cherries which go into a jam used to fill the classic *gâteau basque* or are served – deliciously – next to a slice of *pur brebis* cheese. Its pretty church has a fancy interior of woodwork and paintings, including a *St Francis of Assisi*, attributed by some to Murillo. Ask to see the treasure, donated by a local who made good in America. It was hidden during the Revolution, which had a policy of expropriating the wealth of the Church for 'the people', and the secret of its whereabouts was confided to three local men, one of whom was tortured with fire by the Revolution's henchmen, but still refused to tell.

In the 1960s, a sapling from the Gernika oak was planted in Itxassou, a symbol of the reawakening of patriotic feeling in the Pays Basque.

From here, through the hamlet of Laxia, a steep and difficult road can take you to the summit of 3,010ft **Artxamendi** on the Spanish border, another ancient holy place. Besides a number of natural wonders, including waterfalls, small herds of *pottok* and rock needles, this 'mountain of the bear' has human remains ranging from long-abandoned iron mines and shepherds' huts to Neolithic dolmens and cromlechs.

From here, you cross the ancient boundary from the Labourd into Basse-Navarre. The next villages down the valley are **Bidarray** and **Ossès**, centres of a rich, rolling country known for its *pur brebis*. Their prosperity 300 years ago has given both a number of fine houses, many with 17th-century inscriptions. Bidarray has a graceful medieval bridge, the Pont d'Enfer, and a rare 12th-century church, once the chapel of a hospice for Compostela pilgrims. If you have yet to see a *pottok*, you can visit them at the Maison du Pottok (*t 05 59 52 21 14, pottok@aol.com*).

If medieval churches are rare in these parts, it is only because of Basque tidiness; just as families rebuild their houses every few centuries on the same site, so they cannot stand to see an old church or any other building looking frowzy. Ossès' church, St-Julien, was entirely rebuilt by the villagers in the 16th century, with a built-in *fronton*, a later Baroque façade and a rich interior decoration similar to the churches of Spanish Navarre. The hills around the nearby modern village of **St-Martin-d'Arossa** offer three examples of another peculiarity of the Basque country, the *gaztelu*. This is an earth- and rock-built hilltop fortress dating from the Iron Age; no one knows if the native populations or invading Celts built them.

St-Etienne-de-Baïgorry, the principal centre for the production of Irouléguy wine, is really a collection of villages around the Nive and its branch, the Nive des Aldudes. St-Etienne, the centre, has another lovely humpbacked medieval bridge, and the château of the feudal *seigneurs*, the Etxauz.

Irouléguy

From the sunny Palaeozoic Basque highlands come the red, rosé and white wines of Irouléguy, the wine that 'makes girls laugh'. Tucked in sheltered pockets in the mountains, and trained on vertical *espaliers* to protect the vines from frost, the first vineyards were planted in the 11th century by the monks at Roncesvalles, 'to comfort wayfaring pilgrims'. Although it is one of the smallest wine regions in France, the once-vast number of grape varieties has been limited since 1952, when Irouléguy was given its AOC status: cabernet (or *acheria*, 'fox' in Basque) and tannat for reds, and courbu and menseng for whites. 2000 was an exceptional year. Try the generous, sombre red Domaine de Mignaberry, the leading label produced by the co-operative **Maîtres Vignerons du Pays Basque** in St-Etienne-de-Baïgorry (*t 05 59 37 41 33; open daily 9–12 and 2–6.30; closed Sun April–Oct*), or the co-operative's fine fresh rosé, Les Terrasses de L'Arradoy. Of the independent growers, **Domaine Brana** (*3 bis Av du Jaï Alaï, St-Jean-Pied-de-Port, t 05 59 37 00 44; open July–Aug daily 10–12 and 2.30–6.30*) has bottled some excellent, peppery reds and also produces a whole gamut of eaux-de-vie. **Domaine Ilarria** in Irouléguy (*t 05 59 37 23 38*) produces a lovely rosy rosé.

St-Jean-Pied-de-Port

Bethi Gazte eoïteko
Secretu bat bada hemen
Bizi on bat pasatzeko
Gauden Donibanen

(To remain ever young/the secret is kept here./To always live happily/
Stay at St-Jean-Pied-de-Port)
Basque song

This town's real name, in Basque, is Donibane Garazi, and they have spelled it out in flowers at the entrance to remind us. The French name is even more curious, but *port* is an old mountain word for a pass, and St-Jean, or Donihane, stands at the foot of the pass of Roncesvalles (Roncevaux), the 'Gate of Spain' of medieval French legend and poetry. The location has made it a busy place. From the 8th century, Arab armies must have passed this way many times on their way to raid France; Charlemagne and Roland came back the other way to raid Spain, and pass into legend along the way (*see* pp.230–1). Pilgrims from all over Europe came through on their way to Compostela, and another famous visitor, Richard the Lionheart, put the original town – now nearby St-Jean-le-Vieux – to siege in 1177. When he took it, that most pitiless and destructive of warriors razed it to the ground; the kings of Navarre refounded St-Jean on its present site soon after.

Though it still holds four big fairs each year, just as in medieval times, St-Jean today makes more of its living from visitors; it's the main centre for mountain tourism in the Basque lands, and in summer it can be quite a crowded place. Bars, restaurants and souvenir shops pack the centre, along the D933, and the picturesque streets around the **Vieux Pont** over the Nive. Old houses with wooden balconies hang over the little river, and facing the bridge stands the **church of Notre-Dame**, originally built by Sancho the Strong of Navarre in commemoration of the Battle of Navas de Tolosa (1212), where the Christians finally put an end to Muslim dominance of the Iberian peninsula. The current building is Gothic, rare in these parts, though it has been much reworked since. Along Rue de l'Eglise, have a look at the lintels of the houses at Nos.45, 30 and 28, and try to figure out the original owners' professions.

The old streets climb up from here to the house which the St-Jeanais have called the **Prison des Evêques** (*41 Rue de la Citadelle, t 05 59 37 00 92; open 22 April–21 Oct daily 10–12.15 and 3–4.15*), and turned into a tourist attraction. The house in fact seems to have belonged to a merchant, and the unusual vaulted underground chamber may have been for storing his wares, like the similar cellars in Bayonne. The chains and shackles in the cellar wall were probably used by local authorities in the 18th century to lock up poor peasants who didn't pay their salt tax. The bishops who lived in the mansion above *c.*1400 weren't exactly kosher – supporters of the Antipope at Avignon during the Great Schism. If you climb to the top of the town for the view, you'll find the **citadel**, a castle last remodelled in the 17th century by Vauban.

Getting There and Around

St-Jean is the terminus of the pokey but picturesque Nive valley railway line out of Bayonne. You can also get above it all in a hot-air balloon, a Montgolfière, from the **Maison Mariotenia**, La Madeleine, at St-Jean-le-Vieux, t 05 59 37 24 18, f 05 59 37 24 42.

Tourist Information

Tourist office: Place Charles-de-Gaulle, t 05 59 37 03 57, f 05 59 37 34 91; they offer free guided tours of the town on Mon and Fri mornings in summer. A little tourist train, *Zézette*, makes a similar tour. Ask here about the Iraty–Ossau *Route de Fromage*.

Market Day

Monday; its the biggest in the Pays Basque.

Where to Stay and Eat

St-Jean-Pied-de-Port ✉ 64220

Being a popular tourist base, St-Jean's hotel prices are substantially higher than the other villages in the area.

★★★★Les Pyrénées, Place Général de Gaulle, t 05 59 73 01 01, f 05 59 37 18 97 (*expensive*). A prestigious Relais et Châteaux member, with spacious modern rooms and a delightful garden terrace by the pool, where breakfast is served in the summer. The restaurant is one of the most esteemed culinary temples in all the Basque country, run by master chef Firmin Arrambide. People come from miles around for cooking that, while not notably innovative, brings the typical Basque-Gascon repertoire of duck, foie gras and game dishes to perfection; they're especially noted for their desserts. A gratifying 250F/€38 menu (*except Sun*) puts Les Pyrénées within the reach of most (*other menus 300–550F/ €45.5–84*).

Hôtel Central, Place Charles de Gaulle, t 05 59 37 00 22, f 05 59 37 27 79 (*moderate*). Old family hotel and restaurant with views over the river Nive, which according to the fishing season yields such delights as salmon and eels for the table.

★★Ramuntcho, 1 Rue France, t 05 59 37 03 91, f 05 59 37 35 17 (*inexpensive*). One of the nicest places to stay in the old town, just inside the Porte de France. Rooms have balconies and a view. The restaurant serves good simple dishes (*cheap*).

★★Hôtel des Remparts, Place Floquet, t 05 59 37 13 79, f 05 59 37 33 44 (*inexpensive*). The cheapest hotel option.

Suzanne and Raymond Landaburu, t/f 05 59 37 08 05 (*inexpensive*). Bed and breakfast with a mighty mountain view.

Pecoïtz, Aincille, just south of St-Jean-le-Vieux on the D118, t 05 59 37 11 88 (*cheap*). Rooms here are cheaper than anything in the town; in a quiet and lovely setting, and with a very good restaurant that does game dishes in season, trout and *confits* (*moderate–cheap*).

Chez Arrambide, t 05 59 37 01 01 (*moderate*). Hearty traditional dishes with an exotic touch.

Ciderie Aldakurria, in nearby Lasse, t 05 59 37 04 94. Local cider from the barrel and traditional cuisine served in a former pilgrims' inn; in summer you can dine out on the terrace overlooking the apple orchards (*moderate*).

Chez Dédé, 3 Porte de France, t 05 59 37 16 40. The best (and only) place for *pintxos*.

Pâtisserie Artizarra, 17 Rue d'Espagne, t 05 59 37 03 34. The place to stop for a *gâteau basque* or a creamy *chaumontais*.

Uhart-Cize ✉ 64220

Arrostegia, Route d'Arnéguy, t/f 05 59 37 06 22 (*inexpensive*) Delightful, cosy and peaceful *chambres d'hôte* packed full of antiques; roaring fire in the winter, a tinkling piano and delicious dinners.

Estérençuby ✉ 64220

★★Sources de la Nive, 11km south of St-Jean, t 05 59 37 10 57 (*inexpensive*). Set among the mountain forests, next to the river, it offers all the calm you can stand, as well as a restaurant that serves *salmis de palombe* (don't ask where the dove came from) and other rural treats (*moderate–cheap*).

★★Aztzain-Etchea, at the top of Route d'Iraty, t 05 59 37 11 55. f 05 59 37 20 16 (*inexpensive*) Little hotel-restaurant that is a good base for mountain walks.

Just east on the D933 stands St-Jean's original, **St-Jean-le-Vieux**. The town destroyed by the Lionheart has only the Romanesque tympanum of its church to remind it of its former importance. It was the scene of a miracle in the *Codex Calixtinus* (*see* p.59): a pilgrim died during a vigil here and, as his companion mourned, St James himself galloped up on his white horse, scooped up the dead and living pilgrims and took them to Compostela, all in single night. Even older than the ruined church here are scanty remains of a large Roman camp, including baths. North of St-Jean-le-Vieux, on a height above the D933, a venerable stone pillar with a cross on top is locally known as the **Croix de Ganelon**, supposedly the spot where Roland's treacherous stepfather was pulled apart by wild horses on Charlemagne's command.

South of St-Jean, the D933 leads down to the Spanish border and, 16km beyond that, the cold, misty pass of Roncesvalles itself. For an alternative, if you want to get really lost, take the D301 from St-Jean down to the pretty village of **Estérençuby**, hub of a wild maze of steep narrow roads and hiking trails around the border. With a good map, you can find your way to the abandoned **Château Pignon**, a battered old castle last rebuilt by Ferdinand of Aragón that saw trouble in every conflict up to the Napoleonic Wars. Even better, take the D428 up to the **Col d'Arnostéguy**, passing the primeval beeches of the **Forêt d'Orion** in one of the remotest parts of the region; exactly on the border stands the mysterious **Tour d'Urkulu**, a circular platform of huge, well-cut stone blocks some 65ft in diameter. Some historians, for lack of a better explanation, suppose it to be the remains of a Roman victory monument, like the ones set up on the Mediterranean at La Turbie and Perthuis. It is just as likely, though, that it is far older; the surrounding slopes are littered with dolmens, crom-lechs and other Neolithic remains, and arrowheads dated from the Bronze Age have been found on the site. Some have speculated that the name Urkulu, which has no meaning in Basque, might have something to do with Hercules.

The Haute-Soule

By now, the mountains are getting taller and so are the roofs: steep slate ones become more common than the Roman tiles of the coast. From St-Jean-le-Vieux, the D18 will take you deeper into the remotest corner of the French Basque country, the beautiful, seldom-visited Haute-Soule, a 50km stretch of Pyrenees with scarcely more than 1,000 inhabitants. From the village of Mendive, an alternative route is the D117, narrow but marvellously scenic, passing near several peaks of over 3,000ft. The only settlement it passes is **Ahusquy**, a former spa; from here trails lead into one of the largest of Pyrenean forests, the **Forêt des Arbailles**.

The D18/D19 is just as good, though more difficult, crossing three mountain passes before it arrives at **Larrau**, the closest thing to a village the Haute-Soule can offer. The GR10, the hiking trail that runs the length of the Pyrenees, passes nearby, among many other trails, and if you have some time to spare there are a number of attractions: west of Larrau is a small ski station called **Les Chalets d'Iraty**, set amidst another lovely beech forest, the **Forêt d'Iraty**. This area is a major transit point for

Tourist Information

Mauléon: 10 Rue J. B. Heugos, t 05 59 28 02 37, f 05 59 28 02 21, *officetourisme.Soule@ wanadoo.fr*. Ask here about the possibilities of taking in a *pastorale* (a traditional Basque mystery play, put on by villagers around the Soule between from May to August).

St-Palais: Place Charles de Gaulle, t 05 59 65 71 78, f 05 59 65 69 15, *office.tourisme.stpalais @wanadoo.fr*. For the latest on *force Basque* sports, check out *www.force-basque.org*.

Market days

Mauléon: Tuesday and Saturday mornings.
St-Palais: Friday.
Tardets: Every other Monday, and every Monday in July and August.

Where to Stay and Eat

Mauléon ✉ 64130

**Bidegain, Rue de la Navarre, t 05 59 28 16 05, f 05 59 19 10 26 (*inexpensive*). This friendly, immaculate hotel across from the château is highly praised in a guidebook from the 1920s we found at an old book sale. The praise is still deserved, and what's more the place doesn't seem to have changed all that much in 80 years. The restaurant is a winner, with tables in a sweet covered terrace looking out on to the gardens (*moderate–cheap*).

Barcus ✉ 64130

**Chilo, t 05 59 28 90 79, f 05 59 28 93 10 (*moderate*). Way out in the middle of nowhere, 15km east of Mauléon, and it's worth the detour. Some rooms are fancy and furnished with antiques. There's a fine restaurant, with a garden terrace, which is especially good for fish, along with starters like a salmon terrine and a wide range of tempting desserts (*expensive– moderate*).

St-Palais ✉ 64120

Hôtel de Trinquet, t 05 59 65 73 13, f 05 59 65 83 84 (*inexpensive*). Traditional hotel in the central square of this market town, with a classic wood-beamed restaurant (*moderate–cheap*).

Larrau ✉ 64560

Hotel Restaurant Etchémaïté, 30km south of Mauléon, t 05 59 28 61 45, f 05 59 28 72 71. Reputed for its lamb dishes (such as artichoke bottoms stuffed with a purée of lamb and white beans), trout and game dishes in season, well-prepared desserts and its excellent wine cellar (*expensive*). *Closed Sun eve, and Mon from 11 Nov to May*.

many kinds of migrating birds; serious bird-watchers come from all over to see them in autumn. Hunters come too, and some of them still follow the practice of trapping doves by the thousands in great nets – remarkably this is still legal in France, although considerable hostility surfaces each year between hunters, birders, environmentalists and the local authorities.

East of Larrau, the GR10 leads you to the wild and spectacular **Gorges d'Holcarte**, a series of canyons explored for the first time only in 1908; now a trail runs along the top, with a cable footbridge across the gorge. Further east the GR10 meets another, similar sight, the **Gorges de Kakouetta**, also accessible by car on the D113 (*tours from mid-March–mid-Nov daily 8am–dark*). Here, too, a trail has been laid out; there's a lovely waterfall at the end. The D113 continues to a dead end in the mountains, passing tiny **Ste-Engrâce**. This is one of the most isolated and tradition-bound of all Basque villages; the twisting road up to it was only built a decade ago. It is also the unlikely setting for one of the most fascinating medieval churches in the Pyrenees. Built in the 12th century, this cockeyed church sits on a slope, tilted and asymmetric; pilasters added a century ago keep it from sliding away. The Romanesque tympanum shows the Chi-Rho symbol (the Christogram, or monogram of Christ), in a circle supported by two flying angels – a remarkable example of the persistence of symbolism. Replace the Christogram with a laurel crown and you have the emblem of the Roman Imperium from the time of Augustus. The carved capitals inside are painted in detail, as Romanesque sculpture was meant to be. One shows a pair of lovers; for lack of a better explanation they are said to represent Solomon and Sheba, accompanied by a medieval European's idea of what an elephant might look like. Others seem to show Salome's dance and the three Magi. Behind the church is an old cemetery with some strange discoidal tombstones.

Heading north from the Haute-Soule, the D26/D918 follows the valley of the Saison (or Gave de Mauléon, depending to whom you're talking), a stream popular with canoeists. The valley is a rich land, thick with tiny villages of which the largest is **Tardets. Ordiarp** has an interesting Romanesque church and cemetery in a pretty setting. There are caves with prehistoric paintings around **Ossas** and **Camou**, but they are currently closed to the public. The peculiarity of this area is its large number of *gaztelu*, or prehistoric fortifications; good examples can be found near the villages of Aussurucq, Idaux-Mendy, Etchebar (an especially impressive one with three circuits of fortifications), Alçay and Ordiarp; this must have been as hot a border region in the Bronze Age as it was in the time of Louis XIII.

East of Tardets, the D918 takes you to the villages of **Aramits** and **Arette**. The former is the home of Dumas' musketeer Aramis; there have always been some people here who won't admit he's a fictional character. The latter is largely new, rebuilt after a surprise earthquake in 1967.

The Inner Reaches of the Soule: Mauléon

At first glance, the temptation to leave this grey industrial town immediately might be irresistible. But hang around a while; Mauléon, the town of the evil lion (*mauvais lion*), has character. They make furniture, sheep cheese's and fabrics here, too, but everyone knows Mauléon as the world capital of the espadrille. And even though most pairs of the Basques' classic hemp-soled footwear may be produced in Asia these days (what isn't?), Mauléon's little factories still do their best to keep competitive. The capital of the Soule is a proper Basque village with its working clothes on, that's all.

To prove its Basqueness, there is the busy and famous *fronton* right in the centre, on the park called Les Allées. Mauléon's château faces it, the **Château d'Andurain du Maytie** (*1 Rue Jeu de Paume, t 05 59 28 04 18; open Tues–Sun 10–12 and 2–5.30; adm*), also known as the Hôtel du Maytie. This stern yet graceful building was erected in the early 17th century by a local boy who became bishop of Oloron-Ste-Marie in nearby Béarn. It is still in the original family; highlights are the Renaissance fireplaces and the grand oaken carpentry that holds up the steep roof, designed by a shipwright. Old Mauléon climbs precipitously up to the town's other castle, the **Château Fort** (*open May–mid-June and mid–end Sept Mon–Fri 11–1.30 and 3–7; mid-June–mid-Sept daily 11–1.30 and 3–7; adm*). There has probably been a castle on this site for at least 3,000 years; this latest version dates from the 14th century, rebuilt after Richard the

Lionheart chased out the French viscount and wrecked the place in 1261. Mauléon and the castle remained English until 1449, when the viscount of Béarn seized it. In 1642, Richelieu ordered it destroyed, but before the work was done he changed his mind and ordered it rebuilt, and sent a bill for 130,000 *livres* to the Mauléonais, causing a fierce but short-lived fracas called the Revolt of Matalas. A tour of the castle may be wonderfully evocative, but watch your step – parts of it could collapse any minute.

St-Palais (San Pelayo)

The northeastern corner of the Basque lands is a humble country, where you'll see plenty of livestock and farming paraphernalia and little else. Its only centre is an equally humble though quite pleasant village with a memorable Friday morning market, St-Palais. Once St-Palais had a viscount and a mint, and the village disputed with St-Jean-Pied-de-Port the honour of capital of Basse-Navarre; today it's best known as host to the annual **Festival de Force Basque** each August (and a lot of the farmers you'll see walking around on market day look as if they could be competitors). A famous horse fair takes place on 26 December; another, on 21 July in nearby Garris, dates from the 12th century and is the oldest in this corner of France.

From the old days all that survives is the mansion called the **Maison des Têtes**, across from the chapel of St-Paul on Rue du Palais-de-Justice. A 17th-century house of a noble family, its façade is decorated with odd 'heads' making funny faces, including those of Henri IV and Jeanne d'Albret. Nearby, in the courtyard of the *mairie*, you can mull over St-Palais' history in the small **Musée de Basse Navarre** (*Place Charles de Gaulle, t 05 59 65 71 78; open Mon–Sat 9.30–12.30 and 2.30–6.30, plus Sun 10–12.30 in July and Aug*).

Chronology

Denbora badoa eta gu harekin. (Time goes by, and we go with it.)

old Basque proverb

58 BC Caesar's lieutenant Crassus takes over Aquitainia, including Vasconia, which subsequently becomes Novempopulani.

AD 448 Visigoths control most of Iberia and try to subdue Basque resistance.

711–13 Moors sweep across Iberia and over the Pyrenees.

778 Charlemagne attempts to take Zaragoza from the Moors and destroys Pamplona. His rear guard is ambushed by the Basques near Roncesvalles.

824 Birth of the Basque kingdom in Pamplona under Inigo de Aritza.

892 St Leon, attempting to convert the heathens, is decapitated in Bayonne under Norman occupation. The Normans are finally pushed back by the duke of Vasconia.

950 The French bishop of Le Puy blazes the pilgrimage route to Santiago.

1004 The Basque king of Navarra, Sancho the Great, reigns over the Basque regions as well as Gascony, Aragón, Castile and the County of Toulouse.

1023 Sancho the Great creates the title of viscount of Labourd for his cousin Loup Sanche in Bayonne, and gives the Soule to the Viscount Guillaume Fort.

1179 The French Church calls for excommunication of Basques and Navarrese, based on the horror stories in the *Codex Calixtus*, a guide to the Compostela pilgrimage.

1193 Henry Plantagenet, king of England and duke of Aquitaine, takes the French Basque country.

1200 Alava is taken by Castile. Basques recognize the king of Castile on the condition that he recognizes their *fueros* (municipal charters/laws).

1234 The Basque dynasty of Navarra dies with Sancho the Strong and the crown falls into the hands of Thibault, a Franco-Basque relative of the French royal family.

1332 Alava is forced to recognize the king of Castile as its lord.

1379 Juan de Haro, the lord of Vizcaya, becomes king of Castile.

1450 Treaty of Ayherre: Labourd acquiesces to the king of France's authority in exchange for its independence.

1471 After riding roughshod over Basque *fueros*, Henry IV of Castile is disqualified by the *junta general* and replaced by his sister Isabella. He sends an army to crush Viscaya; instead the Basques thrash him soundly at Mungia.

1483 Catherine d'Albret of the Béarn inherits the kingdom of Navarra.

1492 Ferdinand and Isabella complete the Reconquista and expel all Jews from Spain; Basques accompany Columbus to the New World.

1512 The armies of Ferdinand and Isabella take Pamplona and occupy all of Navarra.

1522 Sebastián Elcano (Magellan's lieutenant) from Getaria, tours around the world.

1534 Ignatius of Loyola founds the Company of Jesus (Jesuits).

1589 Henri III of Navarre becomes king of France under the name of Henri IV.

1609 Pierre de Lancre leads witch trials in Labourd.

1659 The Treaty of the Pyrenees sets the international frontier throughthe Basque country; Louis XIV renounces his rights to southern Navarra.

1713 The Treaty of Utrecht ends War of the Spanish Succession and bars Basque cod fleets from the Grand Bank.

1765 The Treaty of Elizondo officially splits Navarre between France and Spain, but the treaty is not applied because of protests from the citizens of Navarre.

1789 The French Revolutionary government overrules the autonomy of Soule, Labourd and Basse-Navarre.

1790 Creation of the French *département* of Pyrénées-Atlantiques.

1813 Peninsular War; Wellington decisively defeats the French at Vitoria, then burns down San Sebastián.

1833–9 First Carlist War.

1835 Church properties across Spain are confiscated by Madrid and auctioned off.

1841 The Spanish customs office is transferred from the Ebro to the French frontier. Alava, Vizcaya and Guipúzcoa lose most of their *fueros.*

1845 Basques emigrate en masse to South America.

1856 The Franco-Spanish Convention splits Navarre once and for all.

1872–6 Second Carlist War.

1877 Vizcaya and Guipúzcoa are the poorest provinces in Spain.

1887 Vizcaya and Guipúzcoa are the richest provinces in Spain.

1890 Workers in Bilbao lead the first general strike in Spanish history.

1895 Sabino Arana founds the Basque Nationalist Party (PNV).

1898 Spanish-American War; Spain loses last remnants of its overseas empire.

1913 Founding of the Basque Academy to create a Standard Basque language.

1936–9 Spanish Civil War.

1936 José Antonio de Aguirre forms the first government of Euskadi.

1937 The Nazis bomb Gernika for Franco, 26 April.

1959 ETA (Euskadi eta Askatasuna – Basque Country and Freedom) is founded.

1970 Trial in Burgos of alleged ETA-ists.

1973 ETA blows up the Spanish prime minister Carrero Blanco in Madrid.

1975 EHAS (Basque Socialist Party) is founded. Franco dies.

1980 Creation of the Autonomous Government of Euskadi in Vitoria for Alava, Vizcaya and Guipúzcoa, and the Autonomous Government of Navarra in Pamplona.

1981 President Mitterand begins regionalization in France.

1986 The Herri Batasuna party is legalized.

1997 Opening of the Guggenheim Museum Bilbao.

2000 ETA assassinates the propular ex-minister Ernest Lluch in Barcelona; this is followed by a street protest with over 900,000 participants.

Language

For a brief guide to the Basque language, *see* **Culture**, pp.48–51.

French

Even if your French is brilliant, the soupy southern twang may throw you. Any word with a nasal *in* or *en* becomes something like *aing* (*vaing* for *vin*). The last vowel on many words that are silent in the north get to express themselves in the south (*encore* sounds something like *engcora*).

What remains the same as anywhere else in France is the level of politeness expected: use *monsieur, madame* or *mademoiselle* when speaking to everyone (and never *garçon* in restaurants!), from your first *bonjour* to your last *au revoir*.

Pronunciation

Vowels
a/à/â between *a* in 'bat' and 'part'
é/er/ez at end of word as *a* in 'plate' but a
 bit shorter
e/è/ê as *e* in 'bet'
e at end of word not pronounced
e at end of syllable or in one-syllable word
 pronounced weakly, like *er* in 'mother'
i as *ee* in 'bee'
o as *o* in 'pot'
ô as *o* in 'go'
u/û between *oo* in 'boot' and *ee* in 'bee'

Vowel Combinations
ai as *a* in 'plate'
aî as *e* in 'bet'
ail as *i* in 'kite'
au/eau as *o* in 'go'
ei as *e* in 'bet'
eu/œu as *er* in 'mother'
oi between *wa* in 'swam' and *wu* in 'swum'

oy as 'why'
ui as *wee* in 'twee'

Nasal Vowels
Vowels followed by an **n** or **m** have a nasal sound.
an/en as *o* in 'pot' + nasal sound
ain/ein/in as *a* in 'bat' + nasal sound
on as *aw* in 'paw' + nasal sound
un as *u* in 'nut' + nasal sound

Consonants
Many French consonants are pronounced as in English, but there are some exceptions:
c followed by *e, i* or *y*, and *ç* as *s* in 'sit'
c followed by *a, o, u* as *c* in 'cat'
g followed by *e, i* or *y* as *s* in 'pleasure'
g followed by *a, o, u* as *g* in 'good'
gn as *ni* in 'opinion'
j as *s* in 'pleasure'
ll as *y* in 'yes'
qu as *k* in 'kite'
s between vowels as *z* in 'zebra'
s otherwise as *s* in 'sit'
w except in English words as *v* in 'vest'
x at end of word as *s* in 'sit'
x otherwise as *x* in 'six'

Stress
The stress usually falls on the last syllable except when the word ends with an unaccented **e**.

Spanish

Castellano, as Spanish is properly called, was the first modern language to have a grammar written for it. When a copy was presented to Queen Isabel in 1492, she understandably asked what it was for. 'Your majesty,' replied a perceptive bishop, 'language is the perfect instrument of empire.' In the centuries to come, this concise, flexible and expressive language would prove just that: an instrument that would contribute more to Spanish unity than any laws or institutions, while spreading itself effortlessly over much of the New World.

Among other European languages, Spanish is closest to Portuguese and Italian – and of course, Catalan and Gallego. Spanish, however, may have the simplest grammar of any Romance language, and if you know a little of any one of these, you will find much of the vocabulary looks familiar. It's quite easy to pick up a working knowledge of Spanish, but Spaniards speak colloquially and fast (and although the Spanish spoken in the Basque country is very close to standard Castilian, the intonation is Basque, making it sound sing-song to other Spanish speakers); expressing yourself may prove a little easier than under-standing the replies. Spaniards will appreciate your efforts, and when they correct you, they aren't being snooty; they simply feel it's their duty to help you learn. There are dozens of language books and tapes on the market; one particularly good one is *Teach Yourself Spanish*, by Juan Kattán-Ibarra (Hodder & Stoughton, 1984). If you already speak Spanish, note that the Spaniards increasingly use the familiar tú instead of usted when addressing even complete strangers.

Pronunciation

Pronunciation is phonetic but somewhat difficult for English speakers.

Vowels

a short *a* as in 'pat'
e short *e* as in 'set'
i as *e* in 'be'
o between long *o* of 'note' and short *o* of 'hot'
u silent after *q* and *gue-* and *gui-*; otherwise long *u* as in 'flute'
ü w sound, as in 'dwell'
y at end of word, or meaning *and*, as **i**

Diphthongs

ai/ay as *i* in 'side'
ei/ey as *ey* in 'they'
au as *ou* in 'sound'
oi/oy as *oy* in 'boy'

Consonants

c before the vowels *i* and *e*, it's a *castellano* tradition to pronounce it as *th*; many Spaniards and all Latin Americans, however, pronounce it as an *s*
ch as *ch* in 'church'
d often becomes *th*, or is almost silent, at end of word
g before *i* or *e*, pronounced as *j* (*see* below)
h silent
j ch in 'loch' – a guttural, throat-clearing *h*
ll y or *ly* as in 'million'
ñ ny as in 'canyon' (the ~ is called a tilde)
q k
r usually rolled, which takes practice
v often pronounced as *b*
z th, but *s* in parts of Andalucía

Stress

If the word ends in a vowel, an *n* or an *s*, then the stress falls on the penultimate syllable; if the word ends in any other consonant, the last syllable is stressed. Exceptions are marked with an accent.

If all this seems difficult, consider that English pronunciation is even worse for Spaniards. Young people in Spain all seem to be madly learning English these days; if your Spanish friends giggle at your pronunciation, get them to try to say 'squirrel'.

English	French	Spanish
General		
hello	*bonjour*	*hola*
good evening	*bonsoir*	*buenas tardes*
good night	*bonne nuit*	*buenas noches*
goodbye	*au revoir*	*adiós*
please	*s'il vous plaît*	*por favor*
thank you (very much)	*merci (beaucoup)*	*gracias (muchas)*
yes	*oui*	*sí*
no	*non*	*no*
good	*bon (bonne)*	*bueno (buena)*
bad	*mauvais*	*malo (mala)*
excuse me	*pardon, excusez-moi*	*disculpe*
Can you help me?	*Pourriez-vous m'aider?*	*¿Me puede ayudar?*
My name is...	*Je m'appelle...*	*Yo me llamo...*
What is your name?	*Comment t'appelles-tu?* (informal), *Comment vous appelez-vous?* (formal)	*¿Cómo te llamas?* (informal), *¿Cómo se llama Usted?* (formal)
How are you?	*Comment allez-vous?*	*¿Cómo estás?* (informal), *¿Cómo está Usted?* (formal)
Fine	*Ça va bien*	*Bien*
I don't understand	*Je ne comprend pas*	*No entiendo*
I don't know	*Je ne sais pas*	*No sé*
Speak more slowly	*Pourriez-vous parler plus lentement?*	*¿Podría hablar más despacio?*
How do you say ... in French/Spanish?	*Comment dit-on ... en français?*	*¿Cómo se dice ... en español?*
Help!	*Au secours!*	*¡Socorro!*
WC	*les toilettes*	*los servicios/aseos*
men	*hommes*	*señores/hombres/caballeros*
ladies	*dames* or *femmes*	*señoras/damas*
doctor	*le médecin*	*el doctor*
hospital	*un hôpital*	*el hospital*
emergency room	*la salle des urgences*	*la sala de emergencias*
police station	*le commissariat de police*	*la comisaría de policía*
tourist information office	*l'office de tourisme*	*la oficina de turismo*
No Smoking	*Défense de fumer*	*Prohibido fumar*
Shopping & Sightseeing		
Do you have...?	*Est-ce que vous avez...?*	*¿Tiene Usted...?*
I would like...	*J'aimerais...*	*Quisiera...*
Where is/are...?	*Où est/sont...*	*¿Dónde está/están...?*
How much is it?	*C'est combien?*	*¿Cuánto vale eso?*
It's too expensive	*C'est trop cher*	*Es demasiado caro*
entrance	*l'entrée*	*la entrada*
exit	*la sortie*	*la salida*

English	French	Spanish
open	*ouvert*	*abierto*
closed	*fermé*	*cerrado*
push	*poussez*	*empujar*
pull	*tirez*	*tirar*
bank	*une banque*	*el banco*
money	*l'argent*	*el dinero*
traveller's cheque	*un chèque de voyage*	*los travelers*
post office	*la poste*	*correos*
stamp	*un timbre*	*un sello*
phone card	*la télécarte*	*una tarjeta de teléfono*
postcard	*une carte postale*	*una tarjeta postal*
public phone	*une cabine téléphonique*	*el teléfono público*
Do you have any change?	*Avez-vous de la monnaie?*	*¿Tiene cambio?*
shop	*un magasin*	*la tienda*
central food market	*les halles*	*el mercado*
tobacconist	*un tabac*	*el estanco*
pharmacy	*la pharmacie*	*la farmacía*
aspirin	*l'aspirine*	*la aspirina*
condoms	*les préservatifs*	*los preservativos*
insect repellent	*l'anti-insecte*	*el repelente de insectos*
sun cream	*la crème solaire*	*la crema solar*
tampons	*les tampons hygiéniques*	*los tampones*
beach	*la plage*	*la playa*
booking/box office	*le bureau de location*	*la taquilla*
church	*l'église*	*la iglesia*
museum	*le musée*	*el museo*
sea	*la mer*	*el mar*
theatre	*le théâtre*	*el teatro*

Accommodation

Do you have a room?	*Avez-vous une chambre?*	*¿Tiene usted una habitación?*
Can I look at the room?	*Puis-je voir la chambre?*	*¿Podría ver la habitación?*
How much is the room per day/week?	*C'est combien la chambre par jour/semaine?*	*¿Cuánto cuesta la habitación por día/semana?*
single room	*une chambre pour une personne*	*una habitación para una persona*
twin room	*une chambre à deux lits*	*una habitación con dos camas*
double room	*une chambre pour deux personnes*	*una habitación doble*
... with a shower/bath	*... avec douche/salle de bains*	*...con ducha/baño*
... for one night/one week	*... pour une nuit/une semaine*	*...por una noche/una semana*
bed	*un lit*	*una cama*
blanket	*une couverture*	*una manta*
cot (child's bed)	*un lit d'enfant*	*una cuna*
pillow	*un oreiller*	*una almohada*
soap	*du savon*	*el jabón*
towel	*une serviette*	*la toalla*

English	French	Spanish
Directions		
Where is...?	*Où se trouve...?*	*¿Dónde está... ?*
left	*à gauche*	*a la izquierda*
right	*à droite*	*a la derecha*
straight on	*tout droit*	*todo recto*
here	*ici*	*aquí*
there	*là*	*allí*
close	*proche*	*cerca*
far	*loin*	*lejos*
forwards	*en avant*	*adelante*
backwards	*en arrière*	*hacia atrás*
up	*en haut*	*arriba*
down	*en bas*	*abajo*
corner	*le coin*	*la esquina*
square	*la place*	*la plaza*
street	*la rue*	*la calle*
Transport		
I want to go to...	*Je voudrais aller à...*	*Quisiera ir a...*
How can I get to... ?	*Comment puis-je aller à... ?*	*¿Cómo puedo llegar a... ?*
When is the next... ?	*Quel est le prochain... ?*	*¿Cuándo sale el próximo... ?*
What time does it leave (arrive)?	*A quelle heure part-il (arrive-t-il)?*	*¿A qué hora sale (llega)?*
From where does it leave?	*D'où part-il?*	*¿De dónde sale?*
Do you stop at... ?	*Passez-vous par... ?*	*¿Para en... ?*
How long does the trip take?	*Combien de temps dure le voyage?*	*¿Cuánto tiempo dura el viaje?*
A (single/return) ticket to...	*un aller or aller simple/aller et retour) pour...*	*Un billete (/de ida y vuelta) a...*
How much is the fare?	*Combien coûte le billet?*	*Cuánto cuesta el billete?*
Have a good trip!	*Bon voyage!*	*¡Buen viaje!*
airport	*l'aéroport*	*el aeropuerto*
aeroplane	*l'avion*	*el avión*
berth	*la couchette*	*la litera*
bicycle	*la bicyclette/le vélo*	*bicicleta*
mountain bike	*le vélo tout terrain, VTT*	*una bicicleta de montaña*
bus	*l'autobus*	*el autobús*
bus stop	*l'arrêt d'autobus*	*la parada*
car	*la voiture*	*el coche*
coach	*l'autocar*	*el autocar*
coach station	*la gare routière*	*la estación de autobuses*
flight	*le vol*	*el vuelo*
on foot	*à pied*	*a pié*
port	*le port*	*el puerto*
railway station	*la gare*	*la estación de tren*
ship	*le bateau*	*el buque/barco/embarcadero*
subway	*le métro*	*el metro*

English	French	Spanish
taxi	*le taxi*	*el taxi*
train	*le train*	*el tren*
delayed	*en retard*	*con retraso*
on time	*à l'heure*	*puntual*
platform	*le quai*	*el andén*
date-stamp machine	*le composteur*	*la fichadora*
timetable	*l'horaire*	*el horario*
left-luggage locker	*la consigne automatique*	*la consigna automática*
ticket office	*le guichet*	*la taquilla*
ticket	*le billet*	*el billete*
customs	*la douane*	*la aduana*
seat	*la place*	*el asiento*

Driving

English	French	Spanish
breakdown	*la panne*	*la avería*
car	*la voiture*	*el coche*
danger	*le danger*	*el peligro*
driver	*le chauffeur*	*el conductor/chófer*
entrance	*l'entrée*	*la entrada*
exit	*la sortie*	*la salida*
give way/yield	*céder le passage*	*ceda el paso*
hire	*louer*	*alquiler*
(international) driving licence	*un permis de conduire (international)*	*carnet de conducir (internacional)*
motorbike/moped	*la moto/le vélomoteur*	*la moto/ciclomotor*
no parking	*stationnement interdit*	*estacionamento prohibido*
petrol (unleaded)	*l'essence (sans plomb)*	*la gasolina*
road	*la route*	*la carretera*
road works	*les travaux*	*las obras*
This doesn't work	*Ça ne marche pas*	*Este no funciona*
Is the road good?	*Est-ce que la route est bonne?*	*¿Es buena la carretera?*

Months

English	French	Spanish
January	*janvier*	*Enero*
February	*février*	*Febrero*
March	*mars*	*Marzo*
April	*avril*	*Abril*
May	*mai*	*Mayo*
June	*juin*	*Junio*
July	*juillet*	*Julio*
August	*août*	*Agosto*
September	*septembre*	*Septiembre*
October	*octobre*	*Octubre*
November	*novembre*	*Noviembre*
December	*décembre*	*Diciembre*

English	French	Spanish
Days		
Monday	*lundi*	*lunes*
Tuesday	*mardi*	*martes*
Wednesday	*mercredi*	*miércoles*
Thursday	*jeudi*	*jueves*
Friday	*vendredi*	*viernes*
Saturday	*samedi*	*sábado*
Sunday	*dimanche*	*domingo*
Numbers		
one	*un*	*uno*
two	*deux*	*dos*
three	*trois*	*tres*
four	*quatre*	*cuatro*
five	*cinq*	*cinco*
six	*six*	*seis*
seven	*sept*	*siete*
eight	*huit*	*ocho*
nine	*neuf*	*nueve*
ten	*dix*	*diez*
eleven	*onze*	*once*
twelve	*douze*	*doce*
thirteen	*treize*	*trece*
fourteen	*quatorze*	*catorce*
fifteen	*quinze*	*quince*
sixteen	*seize*	*dieciséis*
seventeen	*dix-sept*	*diecisiete*
eighteen	*dix-huit*	*dieciocho*
nineteen	*dix-neuf*	*diecinueve*
twenty	*vingt*	*veinte*
twenty-one	*vingt et un*	*veintiuno*
twenty-two	*vingt-deux*	*veintidós*
thirty	*trente*	*treinta*
forty	*quarante*	*cuarenta*
fifty	*cinquante*	*cincuenta*
sixty	*soixante*	*sesenta*
seventy	*soixante-dix*	*setenta*
seventy-one	*soixante et onze*	*setenta y uno*
eighty	*quatre-vingts*	*ochenta*
eighty-one	*quatre-vingt-un*	*ochenta y uno*
ninety	*quatre-vingt-dix*	*noventa*
one hundred	*cent*	*cien*
two hundred	*deux cents*	*doscientos*
one thousand	*mille*	*mil*

English	French	Spanish
Time		
What time is it?	*Quelle heure est-il?*	*¿Qué hora es?*
It's 2 o'clock (am/pm)	*Il est deux heures (du matin/de l'après-midi)*	*Son las dos*
... half past 2	*...deux heures et demie*	*... las dos y media*
... a quarter past 2	*...deux heures et quart*	*... las dos y cuarto*
... a quarter to 3	*...trois heures moins le quart*	*... las tres menos cuarto*
it is early	*il est tôt*	*es temprano*
it is late	*il est tard*	*es tarde*
month	*un mois*	*un mes*
week	*une semaine*	*una semana*
day	*un jour/une journée*	*un día*
morning	*le matin*	*la mañana*
afternoon	*l'après-midi*	*la tarde*
evening	*le soir*	*el anochecer*
night	*la nuit*	*la noche*
today	*aujourd'hui*	*hoy*
yesterday	*hier*	*ayer*
tomorrow	*demain*	*mañana*
day before yesterday	*avant-hier*	*antes de ayer*
day after tomorrow	*après-demain*	*pasado manaña*
soon	*bientôt*	*pronto*

Menu Reader

Spanish

Fish (*Pescados*)
acedías small plaice
adobo fish marinated in white wine
almejas clams
anchoas anchovies
anguilas eels
angulas elvers
ástaco crayfish
bacalao codfish (usually salted)
bogavante lobster
calamares squid
cangrejo crab
chanquetes whitebait
chipirones cuttlefish
   ...en su tinta ...in its own ink
cocochas hake cheeks
dorado, lubina sea bass
escabeche pickled or marinated fish
gambas prawns
langosta lobster
langostinos giant prawns
mariscos shellfish
mejillones mussels
merluza hake
mero grouper
navajas razor-shell clams
ostras oysters
percebes barnacles
pescadilla whiting
pez espada swordfish
platija plaice
pulpo octopus
rape anglerfish
trucha trout
veneras scallops
ttora fish stew
centolo spider crab

Meat and Fowl (Carnes y Aves)
albóndigas meatballs
asado roast
buey ox

callos tripe
cerdo pork
chorizo spiced sausage
chuletas chops
cochinillo sucking pig
conejo rabbit
corazón heart
cordero lamb
faisán pheasant
fiambres cold meats
hígado liver
jabalí wild boar
jamón de York raw cured ham
jamón serrano baked ham
liebre hare
lomo pork loin
morcilla blood sausage
pato duck
pavo turkey
perdiz partridge
pinchitos spicy mini kebabs
pollo chicken
rabo/cola de toro bull's tail with onions
   and tomatoes
salchicha sausage
salchichón salami
sesos brains
solomillo sirloin steak
ternera veal
Note: *potajes, cocidos, guisados, estofados,*
   fabadas and *cazuelas* are various kinds of
   pulse stew.

Vegetables (*Verduras y Legumbres*)
alcachofas artichokes
alubias beans
apio celery
arroz rice
berenjena aubergine (eggplant)
cebolla onion
champiñones mushrooms
col, repollo cabbage

coliflor cauliflower
endibias endives
espárragos asparagus
espinacas spinach
garbanzos chickpeas
habas broad beans
judías (verdes) French beans
lechuga lettuce
lentejas lentils
patatas potatoes
   (*fritas/salteadas*) (fried/sautéed)
   (*al horno*) (baked)
puerros leeks
remolachas beetroots (beets)
setas Spanish mushrooms
zanahorias carrots

Fruit and Nuts
albaricoque apricot
almendras almonds
avellana hazelnut
banana banana
cacahuetes peanuts
castañas chestnuts
cerezas cherry
ciruela plum
ciruelas pasas prunes
coco coconut
dátiles dates
durazno nectarine
frambuesas raspberries
fresas strawberries
fruta de la pasión passion fruit
granada pomegranate
grosella redcurrants
grosella o casis blackcurrant
higos figs
lima lime
limón lemon
mandarina tangerine
mango mango
manzanas apple
melocotón peach
membrillo quince
moras blackberry
nueces walnuts
pera pear
picotas black cherries
piña pineapple
piñones pinenuts
pistachos pistachio
pomelo grapefruit

sandía watermelon
uvas (pasas) grapes (raisins)

Desserts (*Postres*)
arroz con leche rice pudding
bizcocho/pastel/torta cake
blanco y negro ice cream and coffee float
canutillos rolls of flaky pastry filled
   with custard
flan crème caramel
galletas biscuits (cookies)
helados ice creams
pantxineta an almondy *gâteau basque* filled
   with cream or cherry jam
pasteles pastries
queso cheese
requesón cottage cheese
tarta de frutas fruit pie
turrón nougat

Miscellaneous
bread *pan*
butter *mantequilla*
eggs *huevos*
omelette *tortilla*
rice *arroz*
sugar *azucar*
oil *aceite*
vinegar *vinagre*
salt *sal*
pepper *pimienta*
salad *ensalada*

Restaurant Vocabulary
breakfast *desayuno*
lunch *almuerzo/comida*
dinner *cena*
menu *carta/menú*
bill/check *cuenta*
change *cambio*
set meal *menú del día*
waiter/waitress *camarero/a*
Do you have a table? *¿Tiene una mesa?*
   for one/two? *¿...para uno/dos?*
Can I see the menu, please? *Me daría el menú,*
   por favor
Do you have a wine list? *¿Tiene una lista*
   de vinos?
Can I have the bill (check), please? *La cuenta,*
   por favor
Can I pay by credit card? *¿Puedo pagar con*
   tarjeta de crédito?

Drinks

agua (mineral) water (mineral)
  con gas sparkling
  sin gas still
agua potable drinking water
botella (media) bottle (half)
brandy brandy
café coffee
café americano filter coffee
café con leche white coffee
caña draught (beer)
cerveza beer
chocolate caliente hot chocolate
dulce sweet (wine)
expreso espresso coffee
hielo ice
leche milk
seco dry
semi-seco semi-dry
spumoso sparkling (wine)
té tea
té de hierbas herbal tea
vaso glass
vino (tinto, blanco) wine (red, white)
zumo juice

French

Starters and Soups
(*Hors-d'œuvre et Soupes*)

amuse-gueule appetizers
assiette assortie plate of mixed cold
  hors d'œuvre
bisque shellfish soup
bouillon broth
charcuterie mixed cold meats, salami,
  ham, etc.
consommé clear soup
potage thick vegetable soup
tourrain garlic and bread soup
velouté thick smooth soup, often fish or
  chicken

Fish and Shellfish
(*Poissons et Coquillages*)

aiglefin little haddock
alose shad
anchois anchovies
anguille eel
bar sea bass

barbue brill
baudroie anglerfish
belons flat oysters
bigorneau winkle
blanchailles whitebait
brème bream
brochet pike
bulot whelk
cabillaud cod
calmar squid
carrelet plaice
colin hake
congre conger eel
coques cockles
coquillages shellfish
coquilles St-Jacques scallops
crabe crab
crevettes grises shrimp
crevettes roses prawns
cuisses de grenouilles frogs' legs
darne slice or steak of fish
daurade sea bream
ecrevisse freshwater crayfish
eperlan smelt
escabèche fish fried, marinated and
  served cold
escargots snails
espadon swordfish
esturgeon sturgeon
flétan halibut
friture deep-fried fish
fruits de mer seafood
gambas giant prawns
gigot de mer a large fish cooked whole
grondin red gurnard
hareng herring
homard Atlantic (Norway) lobster
huîtres oysters
lamproie lamprey
langouste spiny Mediterranean lobster
langoustines Norway lobster (often called
  Dublin Bay prawns or scampi)
limande lemon sole
lotte monkfish
loup (de mer) sea bass
maquereau mackerel
merlan whiting
morue salt cod
moules mussels
oursin sea urchin
pagel sea bream

palourdes clams
petit gris little grey snail
piballes elvers
poulpe octopus
praires small clams
raie skate
rouget red mullet
saumon salmon
St-Pierre John Dory
sole (meunière) sole (with butter, lemon and parsley)
telline tiny clam
thon tuna
truite trout
truite saumonée salmon trout

Meat and Poultry (*Viandes et Volailles*)

agneau (de pré-salé) lamb (grazed in fields by the sea)
andouillette chitterling (tripe) sausage
autruche ostrich
biftek beefsteak
blanc breast or white meat
bœuf beef
boudin blanc sausage of white meat
boudin noir black pudding
brochette meat (or fish) on a skewer
caille quail
canard, caneton duck, duckling
carré the best end of a cutlet or chop
cassoulet haricot bean stew with sausage, duck, goose, etc.
cervelle brains
chapon capon
châteaubriand porterhouse steak
cheval horsemeat
chevreau kid
chorizo spicy Spanish sausage
civet meat (usually game) stew, in wine and blood sauce
cœur heart
confit meat cooked and preserved in its own fat
côte, côtelette chop, cutlet
cou d'oie farci goose neck stuffed with pork, foie gras, truffles
crépinette small sausage
cuisse thigh or leg
dinde, dindon turkey
entrecôte ribsteak
epaule shoulder

estouffade a meat stew marinated, fried and then braised
faisan pheasant
faux-filet sirloin
foie liver
frais de veau veal testicles
fricadelle meatball
gésier gizzard
gibier game
gigot leg of lamb
graisse, gras fat
grillade grilled meat, often a mixed grill
grive thrush
jambon ham
jarret knuckle
langue tongue
lapereau young rabbit
lapin rabbit
lard (lardons) bacon (diced bacon)
lièvre hare
maigret/magret (de canard) breast (of duck)
manchons duck or goose wings
marcassin young wild boar
merguez spicy red sausage
mouton mutton
museau muzzle
noix de veau (agneau) topside of veal (lamb)
oie goose
os bone
perdreau, perdrix partridge
petit salé salt pork
pieds trotters
pintade guinea fowl
plat-de-côtes short ribs or rib chops
porc pork
pot au feu meat and vegetables cooked in stock
poulet chicken
poussin baby chicken
quenelle poached dumplings made of fish, fowl or meat
queue de bœuf oxtail
ris (de veau) sweetbreads (veal)
rognons kidneys
rosbif roast beef
rôti roast
sanglier wild boar
saucisses sausages
saucisson sausage, like salami
selle (d'agneau) saddle (of lamb)
taureau bull's meat

tournedos thick round slices of beef fillet
travers de porc spare ribs
tripes tripe
veau veal
venaison venison

Vegetables, Herbs, etc. (*Légumes, Herbes, etc.*)

ail garlic
aneth dill
anis anis
artichaut artichoke
asperges asparagus
aubergine aubergine (eggplant)
avocat avocado
basilic basil
betterave beetroot
blette Swiss chard
cannelle cinnamon
céleri (-rave) celery (celeriac)
cèpes ceps, wild boletus
  mushrooms
champignons mushrooms
chanterelles wild yellow mushrooms
chicorée curly endive
chou cabbage
chou-fleur cauliflower
choucroute sauerkraut
choux de bruxelles Brussels sprouts
ciboulette chives
citrouille pumpkin
clou de girofle clove
cœur de palmier heart of palm
concombre cucumber
cornichons gherkins
courgettes courgettes (zucchini)
cresson watercress
echalote shallot
endive chicory (endive)
epinards spinach
estragon tarragon
fenouil fennel
fèves broad (fava) beans
flageolets white beans
fleurs de courgette courgette blossoms
frites chips (French fries)
genièvre juniper
gingembre ginger
haricots beans
  (rouges, blancs) (kidney, white)
haricot verts green (French) beans
jardinière with diced vegetables

laitue lettuce
laurier bay leaf
lentilles lentils
maïs (épis de) sweetcorn (on the cob)
marjolaine marjoram
menthe mint
mesclun salad of various leaves
morilles morel mushrooms
navet turnip
oignons onions
oseille sorrel
panais parsnip
persil parsley
petits pois peas
piment pimento
pissenlits dandelion greens
poireaux leeks
pois chiches chickpeas
pois mange-tout sugar peas, mangetout
poivron sweet pepper (capsicum)
pomme de terre potato
potiron pumpkin
primeurs young vegetables
radis radishes
riz rice
romarin rosemary
roquette rocket
safran saffron
salade verte green salad
salsifis salsify
sarriette savory
sarrasin buckwheat
sauge sage
seigle rye
serpolet wild thyme
thym thyme
truffes truffles

Fruit and Nuts (*Fruits et Noix*)

abricot apricot
amandes almonds
ananas pineapple
banane banana
bigarreau black cherries
brugnon nectarine
cacahouètes peanuts
cassis blackcurrant
cerise cherry
citron lemon
citron vert lime
coco (noix de) coconut
coing quince

dattes dates
figues (de Barbarie) figs (prickly pear)
fraises (des bois) strawberries (wild)
framboises raspberries
fruit de la passion passion fruit
grenade pomegranate
groseilles redcurrants
lavande lavender
mandarine tangerine
mangue mango
marrons chestnuts
mirabelles mirabelle plums
mûre (sauvage) mulberry, blackberry
myrtilles bilberries
noisette hazelnut
noix walnuts
noix de cajou cashews
pamplemousse grapefruit
pastèque watermelon
pêche (blanche) peach (white)
pignons pinenuts
pistache pistachio
poire pear
pomme apple
prune plum
pruneau prune
raisins (secs) grapes (raisins)
reine-claude greengage plums

Desserts
Bavarois mousse or custard in a mould
biscuit biscuit, cracker, cake
bombe ice-cream dessert in a round mould
bonbons sweets, candy
brioche light sweet yeast bread
charlotte sponge fingers and custard
  cream dessert
chausson turnover
clafoutis batter fruit cake
compote stewed fruit
corbeille de fruits basket of fruit
coulis thick fruit sauce
coupe ice cream: a scoop or in cup
crème anglaise egg custard
crème caramel vanilla custard with
  caramel sauce
crème Chantilly sweet whipped cream
crème fraîche slightly sour cream
crème pâtissière thick pastry cream filling
  made with eggs
gâteau cake
gaufre waffle

génoise rich sponge cake
glace ice cream
macarons macaroons
madeleine small sponge cake
miel honey
mignardise same as petits fours
mousse 'foam': frothy dessert
œufs à la neige floating island/meringue
  on a bed of custard
pain d'épice gingerbread
parfait frozen mousse
petits fours sweetmeats; tiny cakes and
  pastries
profiteroles choux pastry balls, often filled
  with chocolate or ice cream
sablé shortbread
savarin a filled cake, shaped like a ring
tarte, tartelette tart, little tart
truffes chocolate truffles
yaourt yoghurt

Cheese (*Fromage*)
brebis (fromage de) sheep's cheese
chèvre goat's cheese
doux mild
fromage (plateau de) cheese (board)
fromage blanc yoghurty cream cheese
fromage frais a bit like sour cream
fromage sec general name for solid cheeses
fort strong

Cooking Terms and Sauces
à point medium steak
bien cuit well-done steak
bleu very rare steak
aigre-doux sweet and sour
aiguillette thin slice
à l'anglaise boiled
au feu de bois cooked over a wood fire
au four baked
barquette pastry boat
beignets fritters
béarnaise sauce of egg yolks, shallots and
  white wine
bordelaise red wine, bone marrow and
  shallot sauce
broche roasted on a spit
chaud hot
cru raw
cuit cooked
eminče thinly sliced
en croûte cooked in a pastry crust

en papillote baked in buttered paper
epices spices
farci stuffed
feuilleté flaky pastry
flambé set aflame with alcohol
fourré stuffed
frais, fraîche resh
frappé with crushed ice
frit fried
froid cold
fumé smoked
galantine cooked food served in cold jelly
galette flaky pastry case, pancake
garni with vegetables
(au) gratin topped with browned cheese and
  breadcrumbs
grillé grilled
haché minced
marmite casserole
médaillon round piece
mijoté simmered
pané breaded
pâte pastry, pasta
pâte brisée shortcrust pastry
pâte à chou choux pastry
pâte feuilletée flaky or puff pastry
paupiette rolled and filled thin slices of fish
  or meat
pavé slab
piquant spicy hot
poché poached
sanglant rare steak
salé salted, spicy
sucré sweet
timbale pie cooked in a dome-shaped mould
tranche slice
vapeur steamed
vinaigrette oil and vinegar dressing

Miscellaneous
addition bill (check)
baguette long loaf of bread
beurre butter
carte non-set menu
confiture jam
couteau knife
crème cream
cuillère spoon
formule/menu set menu
fourchette fork
fromage cheese
huile (d'olive) oil (olive)

lait milk
moutarde mustard
nouilles noodles
pain bread
œufs eggs
poivre pepper
sel salt
service compris/non compris service included/
  not included
sucre sugar
vinaigre vinegar

Drinks (*Boissons*)
bière (pression) beer (draught)
bouteille (demi) bottle (half)
brut very dry
chocolat chaud hot chocolate
café coffee
café au lait white coffee
café express espresso coffee
café filtre filter coffee
demi a third of a litre
doux sweet (wine)
eau water
  minérale mineral
  plate still
  gazeuse sparkling
eau-de-vie brandy
eau potable drinking water
glaçons ice cubes
infusion/tisane herbal tea
  verveine verbena
  tilleul lime flower
  menthe mint
jus juice
lait milk
moelleux semi-dry
mousseux sparkling (wine)
pichet pitcher
citron/orange
  pressée fresh lemon/orange juice
pression draught
ratafia home-made liqueur made by steeping
  fruit or green walnuts in alcohol
sec dry
thé tea
verre glass
vin wine
  blanc white
  rosé rosé
  rouge red

Glossary

Abbaye: abbey
Arenes: bullring
Auberge: inn
Ayuntamiento: city/town hall
Baserri/Borda: Basque farmhouse
Bastide: a medieval new town, usually rectangular, with a grid of streets and an arcaded central square
Batua: Standard Basque language
Bodega: winery
Cave: cellar
Cesta punta: *pelota* played with long wicker baskets; also known as *jaï-alaï*
Château: mansion, manor house or castle
Chemin: path
Churrigueresque: florid Baroque style of the late 17th and early 18th centuries
Cloître: cloister
Col: mountain pass
Cortes: Spanish parliament
Couvent: convent or monastery
Dolmen: Neolithic funerary monument shaped like a table
Eglise: church
Encierro: running of the bulls
Estación: train station (Renfe)
Euskal Herria: the Basque country
Euskera: the Basque language
Extea: Basque house
Fronton: *pelota* court
Fueros: exemptions or privileges of a region under medieval Spanish law
Gare: train station (SNCF)

Grange: farm
Halles: covered market
Hôtel: originally the town residence of the nobility; by the 18th century used for any large, private residence
Iglesia: church
Lauburu: the 'Basque cross'
Mairie: town hall
Mercato/Marché: market
Mirador: a scenic view point or belvedere
Modernista: Art Nouveau
Mudéjar: Moorish-influenced architecture; Spain's 'National style' in the 12th to the 16th centuries.
Oppidum: pre-Roman town
Pais/Pays: region or village
Parlement: a French juridical body, with members appointed by the king; by the late *ancien régime*, *parlements* exercized a great deal of influence over political affairs
Plateresque: 16th-century style; heavily ornamented Gothic.
Playa/Plage: beach
Plaza de Toros: bullring
Port: mountain pass
Pronunciamiento: military coup
Quartier: a division of land in a *comune*; each *comune* had six to 12 *quartiers*
Retablo: carved or painted altarpiece, often consisting of a number of scenes or sculptural ensembles
Tour: tower
Trinquet: indoor *pelota* court

Further Reading

Astrain, Luis Nuñez, *The Basques: Their Struggle for Independence* (Welsh Academic Press, 1997). Concise and well-balanced argument from the non-violent nationalist point of view.

Atxaga, Bernardo, *Obabakoak* (Vintage, 1989). Collection of stories by best-known living Basque author, the first to be translated into English.

Collins, Roger, *The Basques* (Blackwell, 1987). A good general introduction to the Basques.

Conversi, Daniele, *The Basques, The Catalans, and Spain* (Hurst and Co, 1997). An interesting comparison of two nations and their search for legitimacy in the New Spain.

Epton, Nina, *Navarre: the Flea between Two Monkeys* (1993). A good read but out of print, available only in libraries.

Forster, Kurt W., Arnold Hadley Soutter and Francesco Dal Co, *Frank O. Gehry : The Complete Works* (Monacelli Press, 1998). Great overview of the career of the architect of El Goog.

Foster, Nelson, and Linda S. Cordell (ed), *Chilies to Chocolate: Food the Americas Gave the World* (University of Arizon Press, 1996).

Gallop, Rodney, *A Book of the Basques* (published in 1930 and reissued in 1998). During his boyhood, Gallo, an Englishman, spent his summers in St-Jean-de-Luz, and his book has a great feel for the history and often-peculiar customs of the Basques.

Hemingway, Ernest, *The Sun Also Rises*, (Fiesta in the UK). The book that put Pamplona on the map.

Hooper, John, *The Spaniards* (Viking, 1993). A comprehensive account of contemporary Spanish life and politics.

King, Alan, *The Basque Language* (University of Nevada Press, 1994). Probably the most comprehensive learn-Basque book, with lots of grammar.

King, Alan and Begotxu Olaizola Elordi *Colloquial Basque* (Routledge, 1996). Shorter learn-Basque book, complete with cassettes.

Kurlansky, Mark, *The Basque History of the World* (Jonathan Cape/Vintage 1999). Wonderful, wide-ranging and simpatico account of the Basques; history, cuisine and much more.

Lojendio, Louis, *Navarre Romaine* (Zodiaque, 1967). One of the excellent illustrated volumes in the French Zodiaque series on medieval art.

Minta, Stephen, *Aguirre* (Henry Holt and Company, 1994). The adventures of Lope de Aguirre, the mad Basque conquistador, with lots about the Amazon and Basques, too .

Richardson, Paul, *Our Lady of the Sewers* (Abacus, 1999). An engaging collection of stories about almost forgotten corners and customs of Spain, including a description of Lekeitio's gruesome goose rodeo.

Thomas, Hugh, *The Spanish Civil War* (Penguin, 1977). The best general work.

Trask, Robert L., *The History of Basque* (Routledge, 1997). The authority on an intriguing subject.

Zulaika, Joseba, and William Douglas, *Terror and Taboo: the Follies, fabes and Faces of Terrorism* (Routledge, 1996). In-depth study on ETA.

Index

Main page references are in **bold**. Page references to maps are in *italics*.

Also available from Cadogan Guides in our European series...

The Italy Series

Italy
Italy: The Bay of Naples and Southern Italy
Italy: Lombardy and the Italian Lakes
Italy: Tuscany, Umbria and the Marches
Italy: Tuscany
Italy: Umbria
Italy: Northeast Italy
Italy: Italian Riviera
Italy: Bologna and Emilia Romagna
Italy: Rome and the Heart of Italy
Sardinia
Sicily
Rome, Florence, Venice
Florence, Siena, Pisa & Lucca
Rome
Venice

The France Series

France
France: Dordogne & the Lot
France: Gascony & the Pyrenees
France: Brittany
France: The Loire
France: The South of France
France: Provence
France: Corsica
France: Côte d'Azur
Corsica
Paris
Short Breaks in Northern France

The Spain Series

Spain
Spain: Andalucía
Spain: Northern Spain
Spain: Bilbao and the Basque Lands
Granada, Seville, Cordoba
Madrid, Barcelona, Seville
Madrid
Barcelona

The Greece Series

Greece: The Peloponnese
Greek Islands
Greek Islands By Air
Corfu & the Ionian Islands
Mykonos, Santorini & the Cyclades
Rhodes & the Dodecanese
Crete

The UK and Ireland Series

London
London–Amsterdam
London–Edinburgh
London–Paris
London–Brussels

Scotland
Scotland: Highlands and Islands
Edinburgh

Ireland
Ireland: Southwest Ireland
Ireland: Northern Ireland

Other Europe Titles

Portugal
Portugal: The Algarve
Madeira & Porto Santo

Malta

Germany: Bavaria

Holland
Holland: Amsterdam & the Randstad
Amsterdam

Brussels, Bruges, Ghent & Antwerp
Bruges

Cadogan Guides are available from good bookshops, or via **Grantham Book Services,** Isaac Newton Way, Alma Park Industrial Estate, Grantham NG31 9SD, **t** (01476) 541 080, **f** (01476) 541 061; and **The Globe Pequot Press,** 246 Goose Lane, PO Box 480, Guilford, Connecticut 06437–0480, **t** (800) 458 4500/**f** (203) 458 4500, **t** (203) 458 4603.

Acknowledgements

Dana Facaros and Michael Pauls

The authors would especially like to thank Mary-Ann Gallagher, the best and cleverest dogsbody in the world, for her enormous contribution to this book, and Christine Stroyan for her tireless editing and for uncomplainingly tackling all the nasty and boring bits.

Mary-Ann Gallagher

A big Basque thank you to Josune Garcia-Yanguas and family, who spent hours enthusiastically checking out the finer points of Basque cuisine, arts and language. Thank you, too, to Teresa and Juan in San Sebastián for looking after me so well.

Cadogan Guides

The publishers would like to thank the Fundación del Museo Guggenheim Bilbao for permission to use the floor plan and images of the Guggenheim Museum, and John McLeod, Blas Uberuaga and *Hizketa* (NABO newsletter), Winter 1992, for supplying the rules and terminology of *mus*.

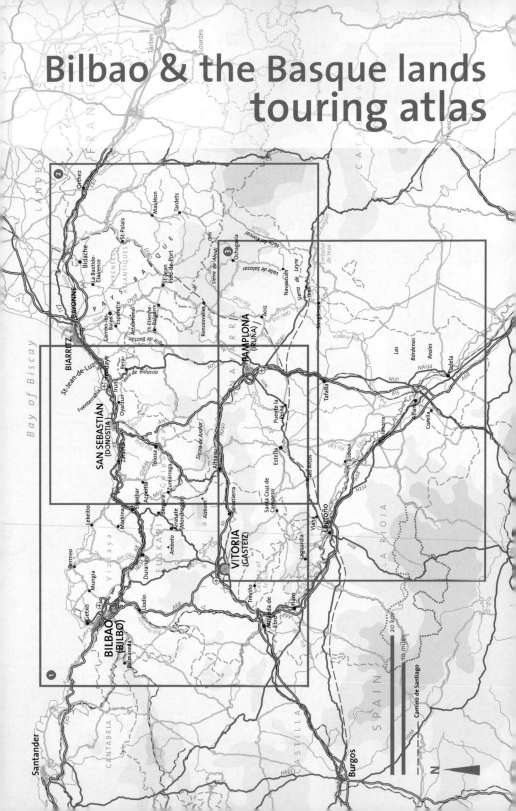

Bilbao & the Basque lands
touring atlas

20 km
10 miles
Camino de Santiago

N

CANTABRIA

San Juan de
Gaztelugatxa

Plentzia   Lemoiz   Bakio
Isla de   Playa de Laga
Izaro
Bermeo   Playa de Laida
Mundaka   Elantxobe

Algorta
Santurtzi   Getxo   Butrón
Mungia

Portugalete   Gernika   Ispaster   Lekeitio

Cueva de   Playa de
Santimamiñe   Cerraspio

BILBAO
(BILBO)
Basauri   V i z c a y a

Markina

Balmaseda   Bolívar

Río Oka

Llodio   A8   Bérriz   Ermua
N634   Eibar
Durango

Río Nervión   E U S K A D I

Elorrio

Amurrio   Urkiola   Arrasate
(Mondragón)
A68   Amboto
Otxandio

Uribarri

Bóveda   Embalse de
Urrunaga   Embalse de
Ullivarri

A l a v a

Mendoza   N1
Espejo   Iruña   Argómaniz   Gaceo
Trespuentes
VITORIA
(GASTEIZ)   Alaiza

Armiñon   Treviño

CASTILLA   C o u n t y   o f
Miranda de Ebro   T r e v i ñ o

Peñacerrada   Antoñana
(Urizaharra)   Urturi
Toloño
Briñas   Sierra de Cantabria   Bernedo
A68   Labastida   Balcón de la Rioja
Río   Abalos
Haro   Ebro   Samaniego   Elvillar
San Vicente   Leza   Lanciego
de la Sonsierra   Villabuena
Río Tirón   Briones   Laguardia (Biasteri)

3

Scale:
20 km
10 miles
‑ ‑ ‑ Camino de Santiago

N

Bay of Biscay

BIARRITZ
Anglet

Côte Basque

Costa Vasca

St-Jean-de-Luz
Bidart
Guéthary
Arcangues
Arbonne
Ahetze

Cabo
Higuer

Fuenterrabía
Jáizkibel
Pasajes
Errenteria
Irun
Hendaye
Urrugne
Ciboure
St-Pée-sur-Nivelle
Ascain

SAN SEBASTIÁN
(DONOSTIA)
Monte Igueldo ▲

Deba
Zumaya
Getaria
Zarautz
Oikia
Orio
A8
N1
Oyarzun
San Marcial
Col de St-Ignace
La Rhune ▲
Bera
Sare

Corniche
Basque

Hernani

Grottes de Sare
Zugarramurdi
Urdazubi

Dantxarinea

Cueva de
Ekain

EUSKADI

Rio Urola
Rio Oria
Rio Urumea

Lesaka
Etxalar

Valle de Bidasoa
Valle de Baztán

Azkoitia
Azpeitia
Loyola
Régil

Gl2634

Tolosa

Parque Natural
del Señorío de
Bértiz

Guipúzcoa
Zumárraga

N631

A15

Ituren
Zubieta

Elizondo

Ordizia
Beasain

Leitza

Segura
Zegama

Betelu
Errazquin
Azpirotz
Lekunberri
Beruete

Lanz

Sierra de Aralar

N21

Aizkorri ▲

NA751
Santuario de
San Miguel in Excelsis
Huarte Arakil

Altsasu
Eguilaz
N1
N240
A15

Berrioplano

PAMPLONA
(IRUÑA)

Zudaire
Baquedano

Monasterio
de Iranzu

N111

Noain

Urroz
Artaiz

NAVARRA

N240

Estella
Monasterio
de Irache
Ayegui
Cirauqui
Puente la
Reina
Obanos

Santa María
de Eunate

Sorlada
Basílica de
San Gregorio

Los Arcos

Rio Ega

Artajona

Torres
del Río

3

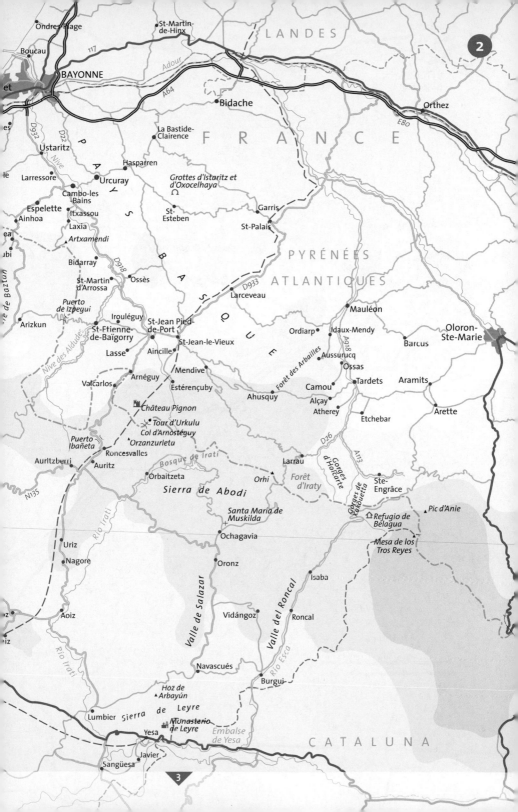

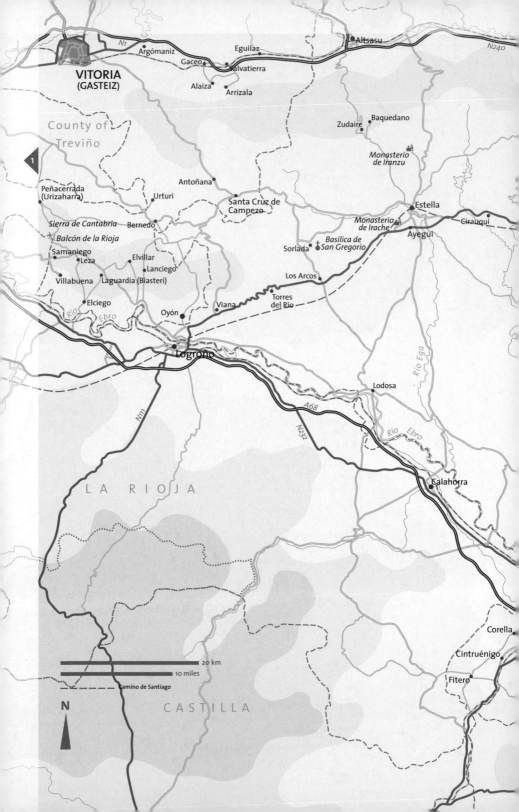

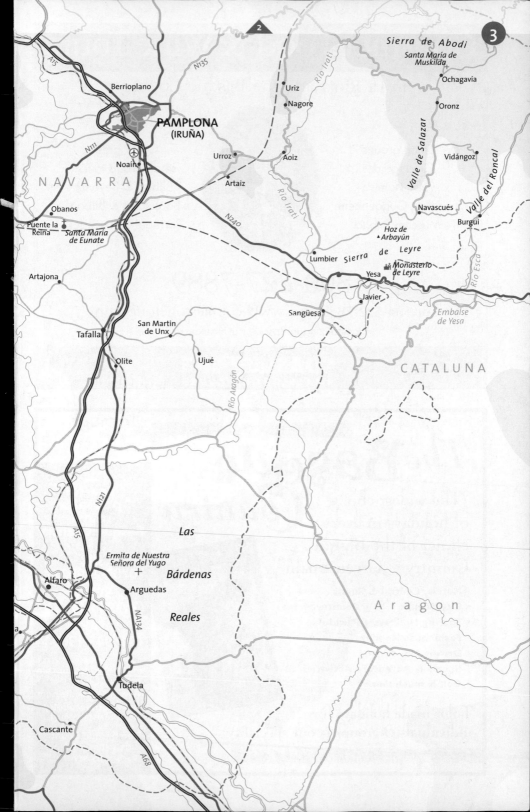